MARK CORNWALL

The Devil's Wall

*The Nationalist Youth
Mission of Heinz Rutha*

HARVARD UNIVERSITY PRESS

Cambridge, Massachusetts
London, England
2012

Library of Congress Cataloging-in-Publication Data

Cornwall, Mark.
    The devil's wall : the nationalist youth mission of Heinz Rutha / Mark Cornwall.
      p. cm.
    Includes bibliographical references and index.
    ISBN 978-0-674-04616-0
    1. Rutha, Heinrich, 1897–1937.   2. Sudetenland (Czech Republic)—Politics
    and government—20th century.   3. Czechoslovakia—History—1918–1938.
    4. Youth movements—Czech Republic—Sudetenland—History—20th century.
    5. Nationalism—Czech Republic—Sudentenland—History—20th century.
    6. Sudetendeutsche Partei. 7. Germans—Czech Republic—Sudetenland—Biography.
    8. Gays—Czech Republic—Sudetenland—Biography.   9. Henlein, Konrad,
    1898–1945.   I. Title.

  DB2500.S94C67 2012
  943.71—dc23   2011045268
  [B]

For Dan

Contents

Abbreviations

For archive abbreviations see bibliography

ANV   Amt für Nationalitäten- und Völkerbundfragen
BdD   Bund der Deutschen
BH   *Burschen heraus! Fahrtenblatt der Deutschböhmen*
Blätter   *Blätter vom frischen Leben*
CLS   Česká Lípa: Krajský soud (trestní spisy)
DGFP   *Documents on German Foreign Policy, 1918–1945*
DjD   *Der junge Deutsche*
DNP   Deutschnationale Partei
DNSAP   Deutsche Nationalsozialistische Arbeiterpartei
DPA   Deutschpolitisches Arbeitsamt
ENC   European Nationalities Congress
FAD   Freiwillige Arbeitsdienst
FO   Foreign Office
JCH   *Journal of Contemporary History*
KB   Kameradschaftsbund
Liga   Deutsche Völkerbundliga
MJT   *Mitteilungen des Jeschken-Iser-Turngau*
NPA   Neue Politisches Akten
PG   Pädagogische Gemeinschaft
SdP   Sudetendeutsche Partei
SEER   *The Slavonic and East European Review*
SHF   Sudetendeutsche Heimatfront
SVH   Sudetendeutsche Volkshilfe
TBA   Turnbauamt
TZ   *Turnzeitung des Deutschen Turnverbandes*
VdTO   *Verhandlungsschrift deutscher Turnverein für Oschitz*
VDV   Verband der deutschen Volksgruppen in Europa
VuF   *Volk und Führung*
WÖF   *Wandervogel. Österreichisches Fahrtenblatt*

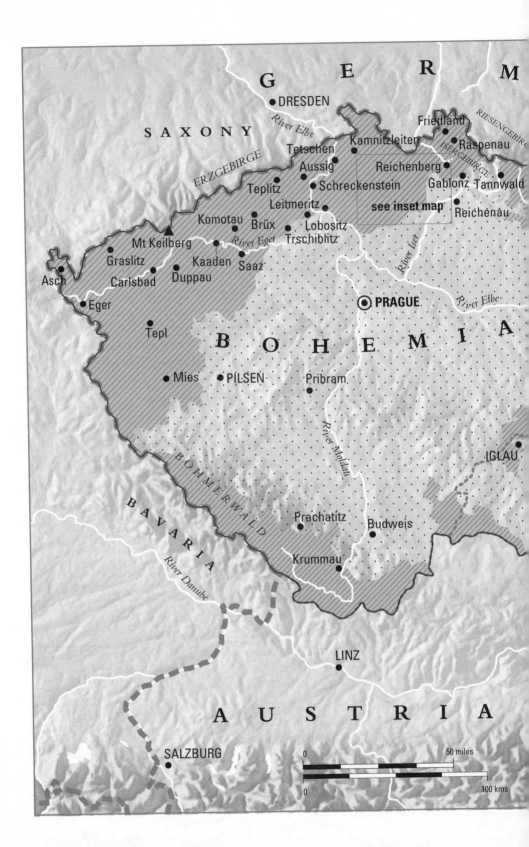

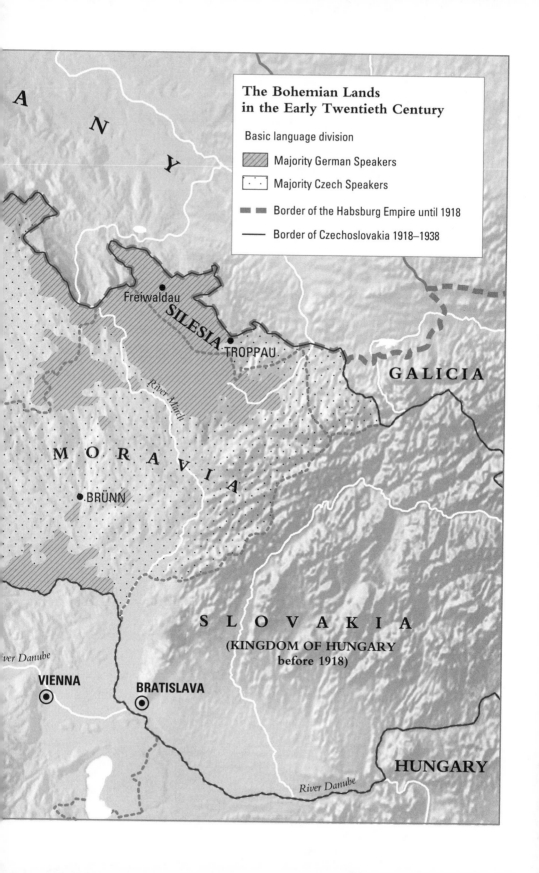

The Bohemian Lands
in the Early Twentieth Century

Basic language division

▨ Majority German Speakers

⬚ Majority Czech Speakers

▬ ▬ Border of the Habsburg Empire until 1918

▬▬ Border of Czechoslovakia 1918–1938

A N Y

Freiwaldau

SILESIA

TROPPAU

GALICIA

River March

M O R A V I A

•BRÜNN

S L O V A K I A

(KINGDOM OF HUNGARY
before 1918)

ver Danube

VIENNA
◉

BRATISLAVA
◉

HUNGARY

River Danube

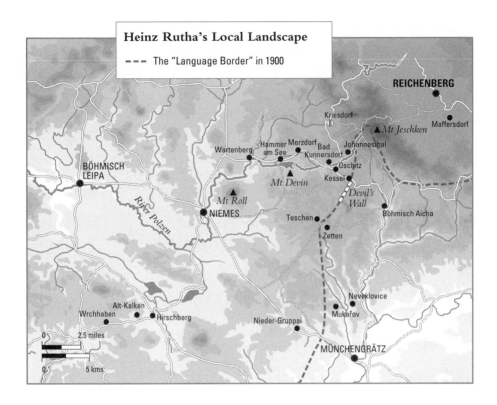

Heinz Rutha's Local Landscape

--- The "Language Border" in 1900

REICHENBERG

Kriesdorf
▲ Mt Jeschken   Maffersdorf
Johannesthal
Wartenberg   Hammer   Merzdorf   Bad
am See   Kunnersdorf
BÖHMISCH   Oschitz
LEIPA   ▲   Kessel
                          Mt Devin
                    ▲   Devil's
                   Mt Roll   Wall
              ● NIEMES   Teschen ●   Böhmisch Aicha
    River Polzen   Zetten

                                                Neveklovice
    Alt-Kalken   ●
Wrchhaben ● Hirschberg   Nieder-Gruppai   Mukařov
0
  2.5 miles
                                        MÜNCHENGRÄTZ
0
  5 kms

The Devil's Wall

Introduction

A Forgotten Life

To the prison guard everything seemed quite normal that night. Peering through the cell peephole every half hour he could see the captive sleeping peacefully in bed, his feet protruding slightly from the blankets. At six thirty in the morning the prisoner had not stirred, and the guard entered the cell with breakfast. He discovered that the figure was made only of bedclothes, its "feet" a pair of shoes. In a corner of the room hung the naked body of Heinrich Rutha. He was suspended from the door bolt of the cell closet by a cord taken from his underpants. His mouth was stuffed with a handkerchief, his feet bound with a tie, and he had carefully placed his pajamas on the ground beneath him. The prison doctor was immediately summoned and the body was cut down, falling heavily to the floor. The doctor diagnosed suicide, sometime around midnight. It was clear it had been meticulously planned to succeed.[1]

Rutha's death in the prison courthouse of Böhmisch Leipa was a shock to all.[2] None of those who had visited the previous day, 4 November 1937, had sensed anything untoward, for Rutha had readily been discussing his plans. Yet the many letters and notes written in his last week of life had signaled an ambiguous message: pondering his legacy while preparing for a future where he might be absent. On the jacket of the last book he was reading, a biography of Michelangelo, he had scribbled down some personal instructions that hinted at posterity. If his face was undamaged he wished a death mask to be sculpted; his body should be cremated and the urn displayed in the Oschitz primary school. A final note confirmed his intentions on the fatal night, if not the precise motive: "He who loves life cannot fear death."[3]

In the ritual of the funeral five days later, the diverse threads of Heinrich Rutha's life were drawn together. The ritual was enacted across his north Bohemian landscape, stretching the twenty-five miles from Böhmisch Leipa to the city of Reichenberg. His body, when laid out in the Leipa mortuary, was, in keeping with his long-term wishes, watched over by some handsome young men who were members of a local work camp. As the traditional song "Good Comrade" was softly intoned, the plain black coffin was carried out to the waiting hearse. "The crowd stood still as silently the procession embarked on its journey from the site of death and final struggle, through the German homeland which the deceased with his strong personality had fought for and loved so much."[4]

Skirting a war memorial, the cortège slipped easily out of the town and moved eastwards, along a route reinforced with Czech gendarmerie.[5] Women threw flowers in its path as it passed through the crowded market-place of Niemes, round Mount Roll into Wartenberg, and on through hamlets where the death knell could be heard sounding faintly. At the Rutha mill in Bad Kunnersdorf, the coffin was borne briefly into the deceased's house for employees to pay their respects; then outside, uniformed men of the work camp raised their spades in formation before it continued on its way (fig.1).

A photographer captured the scene as the cortège crossed the market square of the neighboring village of Oschitz. While the "spade men" now guarded the vehicle, Rutha's sisters were in mourning behind it and a snake of hundreds in their train; local residents appeared in their Sunday best and children ran alongside in curiosity (fig.2). Nervous about potential disorder and the procession's slow speed, the authorities finally put their security car at its head to quicken the pace. On the outskirts of Oschitz they divided it up, for the main road to Reichenberg would pass through a sparsely inhabited Czech-language area. Rutha's coffin continued alone on this official route, the road twisting through woodland up and over Mount Jeschken, then following a police diversion down through the Reichenberg suburbs to reach its destination. The mourners and their vehicles had to take a detour, avoiding Czech villages, to meet the hearse at the crematorium.[6]

The Reichenberg crematorium, the first of its kind in this part of Europe, still today resembles a classical temple, with larger-than-life medieval warriors defending its portal. By midafternoon on 10 November thousands had gathered outside. Once again the "spade men" were conspicuous, marching up in military formation to flank the steps for a line of official mourners. As the organ struck up the grail music from Richard Wagner's opera *Parsifal,* the chivalry of the deceased was deliberately evoked, his ceaseless quest to rescue the German spirit of the Bohemian lands.

The final ceremony began. Members of a Prague student guild sang "Holy Fatherland in Peril, Your Sons Gather around You," one of Rutha's requests and guaranteed to stir emotions. Then Wilhelm Sebekowsky stepped forward to give the main oration. Rutha's death was enveloped in mystery and misery, but this paled into insignificance when compared with his achievements. Extolling the various phases of Rutha's career—especially his pioneering role in youth education—Sebekowsky termed him a "leader-personality" with a "chivalrous demeanor, illuminated by kindness." "Heinz Rutha was a great and good man with bright and dark sides like any other. We are eternally conscious though of one thing: he who climbs to the heights approaches the grave of danger. He who never climbs mountains can never fall." Turning to address the coffin directly, Sebekowsky concluded: "Heinz Rutha—you fell as a victim and as a man. You trained and led thousands of young men, revealing to them the concept of a wonderful life of self-sacrifice. At this moment they are all united with you . . . Your work has entered into the history of the Sudeten Germans. We honor your selfless labor for our people and homeland. It rests as a foundation-stone for our future and your lasting memorial!"[7]

As the coffin disappeared, strains of "True Friendship Should Not Waver" echoed out of the crematorium and were taken up by the crowd in the bitter wind outside.

The plot of the Rutha family lies in a cemetery on the outskirts of Oschitz. Here for the dead as for the living the landscape competes, with Mount Jeschken dominating all from the distant horizon. The statue of a white angel protrudes over the graves, proclaiming eternal peace, but the laurel bushes have grown vigorously, obscuring the black metal plaques bolted to a stone wall. One of these plaques commemorates Heinrich Rutha and bears a biblical inscription in gold lettering: "Greater love hath no man than this, that he lay down his life for his friends" (John 15:13). Those who knew of Rutha's activity with young men over a generation would have understood its cryptic homoerotic significance.

*   *   *

This book has begun and will end in a bleak prison cell. The intervening chapters follow the rise and sudden fall of one of the most influential German nationalists to flourish in the Czech-German borderland of central Europe in the early twentieth century. Heinz Rutha's short life (1897–1937) began in rural northern Bohemia, now in the Czech Republic but then a province of the multinational Habsburg Empire. As a child in the years before the First World War, he experienced at first hand the tense nationalist discourse that was saturating the Bohemia of Czech- and German-speakers. Both Czech and German agitators were stirring their constituents, instigating periodic riots, and regularly paralyzing the Bohemian provincial assembly in Prague or the central Austrian parliament in Vienna.

Rutha, growing up on the so-called language border that theoretically separated Czechs from Germans, could not remain deaf to this rhetoric. Even so, as an adolescent he self-identified as both German Bohemian and German Austrian, since for many German Bohemians the embrace of German-speakers to the south in Austria proper gave reassurance in numbers against the Bohemian Czech-speaking majority. However, when the Habsburg Empire lost the war and disintegrated in 1918, a new Czech nationalist state of Czechoslovakia sprang up on its ruins in the Bohemian lands. Many German nationalists of Rutha's generation reacted to this blatant Czech dominance by refashioning their identity. They labeled themselves "Sudeten Germans," a term first used around 1900 but popularized in the 1920s, as a way of trying to assert a new German regional unity against the "Czech masters" of Czechoslovakia.

To study Heinz Rutha's career means exploring this revolutionary transition from empire to nation-state in the period circa 1910–1925, probing both the German Bohemian and Sudeten German mindsets. Striking is not just the traumatic experience of the Great War for the "1900 generation" in Habsburg central Europe, but its cataclysmic aftermath for young nationalists like Rutha. Their Bohemian world seemed shattered, or as one contemporary put it, they felt shipwrecked, struggling in a turbulent ocean to find some safe dry land.[8] In the new Czech nationalizing framework of interwar Czechoslovakia, they pursued their own complementary nationalist obsession: to build a new Sudeten German national community out of a spatially scattered and politically disunited German population.

Only in the 1930s was a new political movement launched that finally seemed to achieve this Sudeten nationalist dream of challenging the Czech nation *Volk* to *Volk*.[9] As Czechoslovakia suffered economic depression, as Adolf Hitler's Germany in contrast looked dynamic and confident, so in 1935 a new Sudeten German party led by Konrad Henlein triumphed at the Czechoslovak parliamentary elections. The way was set for an immense trial of strength between the Czechoslovak regime and frustrated Henleinists, the latter increasingly gravitating toward Hitler's Third Reich for a solution. Infamously, the dénouement arrived at Munich in September 1938 when in the classic example of appeasement, Britain and France allowed Hitler to annex the Sudetenland, surrendering the Czechs and their state to a full pan-German solution.

Few now, even in central Europe, will know the name of Heinz Rutha. Yet until late 1937 he was at the heart of this Sudeten nationalist mission and had become notorious, nationally in Czechoslovakia and even internationally across Europe.[10] For years across Sudeten German communities, he had been the pioneer of a nationalist youth program, systematically training a vanguard of male youths from the postwar generation who would lead the Sudeten nation toward utopia. From the mid–1920s he was also a key mentor to Konrad Henlein, and from 1935, as his foreign minister or ambassador-at-large, was well known in the European corridors of power, flirting with diplomats in London and Geneva, while courting immense controversy at home.

When Rutha died in November 1937, in shady circumstances and engulfed in a major but now forgotten homosexual scandal, many were eager to recognize his legacy and historical significance. According to one eulogy, "his pioneering work, awakening the Sudeten Germans and furthering their inner national revival, remains a foundation-stone in the proud structure of the new national community. History will be the final judge of his life and work."[11] In fact it was a hollow prediction. By 1938, as Nazi Germany loomed over Czechoslovakia, Rutha was fast becoming a taboo topic, one omitted from the public discourse and excised from the history books. In March 1940, Henlein himself, in one of his more unsavory acts, proceeded publicly to disown his former mentor and make a prophecy of his own: that in a few years the name of Rutha would be totally forgotten.[12]

*   *   *

The idea of analyzing Rutha's life, using him to rethink the Czech-German nationalist disaster in central Europe, came to me incrementally. It first began seriously in the summer of 1999 when I visited Rutha's home village of Lázně Kundratice (Bad Kunnersdorf in German), some fifty miles north of Prague. Set in a gently rolling and forested landscape under the eternal gaze of Mount Jeschken, the tranquil settlement retained little evidence of its German-speaking history, for the whole border region had been repopulated by Czechs after 1945. As Henlein had predicted, Rutha—at least here—seemed forgotten. However, the red mill of the Rutha family survived intact (fig.3), and so did their well-tended plot in the local cemetery. After showing too much interest in the latter, I was questioned by a suspicious villager who directed me to "the only remaining German in the village," an eighty-three-year-old who for half a century had cared for the Rutha gravestones.

In her interviews with me, Marie Isaides opened up about the Rutha family of the 1930s, describing Heinz Rutha as "a homosexual" who always had "handsome lads" around his mill.[13] Most importantly, she introduced me to a close Rutha relative in Germany, a Sudeten German in his nineties (but as lucid as a nineteen-year-old student), whom I have since visited regularly. His witness to everyday life in interwar Kunnersdorf and the atmosphere of the Rutha household has been invaluable. The many conversations fleshed out Rutha's personality, revealing his bourgeois respectability and the precision he expected in business and professional transactions. It matched the self-discipline he maintained in his own life, where until the end he was a workaholic, constantly active and sleeping little.[14]

That a Rutha project might illuminate both national and sexual allegiances in the Czech-German region was further suggested by untapped archival sources. Since millions of Sudeten Germans after 1945 were expelled from their homeland and dispersed across Germany, the documents of their past lives were widely scattered too. Rutha's case was typical. Most significant was my discovery of the trial papers linked to his homosexual scandal. These survived the war, for he was dead and the Sudeten German cause defeated. Their location in the Czech regional archives at Litoměřice and Liberec helped ensure that they were preserved but largely inaccessible to western scholars until the fall of Czechoslovak communism in 1989. Crucially, these police and court records supply a wealth of confidential material, including Rutha's private diary and many intimate letters from the 1930s. They offer unique insight into the secret world of a public figure and betray a homosexual dimension rarely accessible to historians. Through them, we can piece together the jigsaw of Rutha's private life retrospectively from the standpoint of 1937. His public activity in turn offered the challenge of locating its many complex threads. Through youth archives in southern Germany I secured a set of the youth magazine that he edited in the 1920s, *Blätter vom frischen Leben;* through research in Prague, Vienna, Berlin, and Geneva, a picture of his frenetic activity as Sudeten German foreign minister could be constructed for the first time.

It soon became clear that many standard histories of the "Sudeten problem" needed revision. In the last half century there has never been a shortage of historical works scrutinizing how Czechs and Germans clashed in the Bohemian lands during central Europe's most radical decades (the 1930s and 1940s).[15] For many years the historiographical spotlight was on the Germans of interwar Czechoslovakia, how they behaved and were treated. While Sudeten campaigners in postwar Germany blamed Czech nationalism, there was a predominant East-West historical discourse that challenged them. Until the 1990s, Czech and Anglo-American historians generally agreed that the German minority, having succumbed to Nazism, was responsible for betraying democratic Czechoslovakia to Adolf Hitler; after the amputation of the Sudetenland, Czech territory in March 1939 was swallowed up by the Reich and abandoned to six years of Nazi terror. This interpretation remains very forceful in the public imagination, especially to Czechs, because of the easy moral associations conjured up by "Nazi" or "Munich." The touchstone for assessment, moreover, is a Czech one, for the parameters are usually set at 1918 and 1938, the birth and death of the first Czechoslovak republic.[16]

In the past decade historians have begun to stray from this predictable path, writing innovative studies about the Czech-German social or economic relationship. Most attention has focused on the 1940s, on Nazi-occupied Bohemia-Moravia and the supposed moral equivalent of the German betrayal of 1938: the Czechs' mass expulsion of Sudeten Germans after 1945.[17] Yet despite or because of this new research, the Sudeten question remains one of the most sensitive topics in modern Czech history. It continues, according to one expert analysis, to be a "mental problem" that troubles both German and Czech societies, especially afflicting the Czech historical consciousness.[18] It resonates during Czech parliamentary elections when a nationalist card is played, and it was a factor in 2009 when the Czech president Václav Klaus, citing the danger of Sudeten German property claims, hesitated to sign the European Union's Lisbon Treaty. In other words, thanks to the impact of midcentury violence, the Sudeten problem, like the Holocaust, remains a living issue, one often interpreted in stereotypical fashion in public memory.

The book before you not only opens up the history of youth and homosexuality in central Europe, but overturns some deep-seated assumptions about the Czech-German relationship. A biographical approach is useful in itself for making a complicated topic more accessible.[19] It allows close scrutiny of the nationalist mentality, in contrast to those in the Bohemian lands who might be nationally apathetic. Rutha's life supplies a case study of someone typically obsessed with promoting national unity at all costs, but it reveals in the Czech-German context the inherent contradictions that constantly surfaced about what that unity really meant and whether it ever really existed beyond the nationalist mindset.[20]

This is also a dramatic life of singular interest. As Professor Ferdinand Seibt told me in 2000, Heinz Rutha is a forgotten or even taboo figure. In Anglo-American works he usually secures only a passing reference.[21] In German and Czech historiography his role has been ignored or distorted. On the Sudeten German side, despite all the plaudits after his death, there was deep reluctance after the war to probe further because of the homosexual scandal that besmirched his reputation. Typical in 1949 was a personal study about the "Sudeten German tragedy" that covered many fields where Rutha was influential but omitted him altogether.[22] Eventually from the late 1960s, he appeared in histories of the Bohemian or German youth movements; and one meticulous study, by Andreas Luh, indicated his leading role in the national gymnastics association.[23]

Yet all these works focused on the national-political and ignored the homoerotic framework for Rutha's mission. Surviving contemporaries were equally circumspect, at least in print. Walter Becher, who knew Rutha in the 1930s, praised him as "a key figure of the Sudeten German youth movement and the nation's spiritual-political development in the interwar years," but refuted the homosexual allegations. Only at the end of his life did Becher write more candidly about Rutha's "homosexual disposition."[24]

Czech historians in turn usually described Rutha as a Sudeten Nazi. They simply assumed his homosexuality—he was "widely known" as a homosexual who had corrupted male adolescents—and, like their German counterparts, they were prudish in tackling the sexual material.[25] The authors of a 1983 biography of Henlein labeled a photograph of Rutha with a young man as "sick," and commented on one letter: "It is a shocking document. We are prevented from quoting it not only by law but, above all, by our conception of the sense and purpose of literature."[26] While the archival material exists for interpreting Rutha's sexuality, Czech historians have been reluctant to unveil his homosocial world; at best, they have started to explore his pedagogic work.[27]

Any life of Heinz Rutha therefore supplies controversial subject matter. First, there is homoeroticism and male homosexuality in the Bohemian lands, a taboo subject and still embryonic in Czech research, which we can explore in the context of Rutha's grand youth mission.[28] In the wake of the Great War, he combined his own (homo)sexual and nationalist insecurities when he launched a pedagogic crusade among male adolescents. This crusade had in fact emerged from his personal devotion to "pedagogic Eros," which he translated from classical Greece and honed to the demands of a Sudeten German nation in crisis.

This was not wholly original. Across the border in Germany, there were others who privileged homoerotic male bonding as an agent of national renewal, or were fervently committed to pedagogic Eros. Yet Rutha was a pioneer in applying this homoerotic theory practically and single-mindedly to shape a militant nationalist program. Many German nationalists in the new threatening Czechoslovak framework naturally welcomed his obsession with male discipline, leadership, and unity. His concept of training an elite male organization or *Männerbund* also sat easily amid the enhanced male camaraderie that had emerged from the wartime trenches. Even so, and even if Rutha always kept his Eros vision as sublimated as his own sexuality, there was always potential tension in the early twentieth century between tight male bonding and homosexuality. In Nazi Germany, it periodically erupted in scandal, especially if youth seemed to be endangered.[29] Similarly, Rutha walked a homosocial tightrope, for his mission powered by Eros was particularly focused on male adolescents. In 1930s Czechoslovakia, both his sexual and nationalist "deviances" increasingly left him exposed to enemies who wanted to assert "normality."

A second contentious theme of this book is the character of Konrad Henlein's Sudeten German Party. It is a well-worn path, but needs retreading in Rutha's steps to understand Sudeten German nationalism on its own terms. The subject usually breaks down into two alternative interpretations. Was the Henlein movement always a wolf in sheep's clothing, Nazi in its essence and bent on the irredentist goal of joining the Third Reich and destroying Czechoslovakia? Or were some Henleinists "moderate" non-Nazis, aiming at Sudeten German territorial autonomy in a federal Czechoslovak state? Those who adopt the former stance often see the Sudeten problem teleologically through the "Munich prism" of 1938, reading back into 1933 the proofs of that traumatic year. It is a view propagated by the social democrat historian J. W. Bruegel, by much Czech historiography, and by those who perceive few ideological differences between Henlein's movement and National Socialism.[30]

Those who have questioned a simple labeling of Henleinists as Nazis might easily be associated with Sudeten German apologists. However, they include historians who seek a more nuanced approach to the heterogeneity of Henlein's movement, whether in terms of its unusual Czech-German context; its actual goals in central Europe, including its relationship to Germany; or the way that it altered its shape in the 1930s. Ronald Smelser, in *The Sudeten Problem,* portrayed a contest among the Henleinists between what he termed "radicals" (Nazis) and "traditionalists" (supposed Sudeten conservatives like Rutha). While his work was praised by some survivors of the latter persuasion,[31] critics have rightly questioned the term "traditionalist" for implying moderation and obscuring that camp's own destructive agenda vis-à-vis Czechoslovakia. Yet the same historians tend to concur that "traditionalists"—or what we might better call "Sudeten loyalists"—had a set of non-Nazi priorities for the region. They might be fascists of an interesting Sudeten breed, eminently *völkisch* in their radical national awareness, but they were not defined by a virulent anti-Semitic agenda—the essence of German National Socialism. Nor were they simply irredentists taking orders from Nazi Germany.[32]

In following the career of an archloyalist like Rutha we can test these theories in a fresh framework. His death in 1937 ensures our inquiry avoids the anachronistic Munich prism and allows us to focus instead on the opportunities or restrictions facing the Henlein movement in the 1930s. What emerges is the singular mindset of many Sudeten German nationalists. Born first in the context of Habsburg-Bohemia, it evolved after 1918 into a utopian quest to build a special national community vis-à-vis the Czech neighbor and to impose a distinctly Sudeten pan-German solution on central Europe. That remained the priority of many Sudeten nationalists, not irredentism and *Anschluss* to the Third Reich. Although most by 1938 would be opportunistically drawn into Nazi Germany's orbit as the best solution for Sudeten Germans, their long-term national crusade had often been at a tangent to its ideological priorities. That ambivalence was shown later in the war years when many Sudeten Germans felt disappointed by the realities of Nazi rule.

A third controversial theme is how the Sudeten problem developed internationally in the 1930s. To many, "Sudeten" is a byword for western appeasement of Hitler, yet there exists no thorough analysis of how the Czechoslovak crisis was shaped abroad by the Sudeten German leadership: in short, a study of Sudeten German foreign policy. Most studies of Sudeten internationalization focus either on Henlein's dependency on Nazi Germany or take a moralizing Czech perspective, one that assumes Sudeten treachery abroad in cahoots with Hitler and therefore derides, in particular, British stupidity at being hoodwinked by the "Nazi Henlein."[33] A detailed analysis of Rutha as Henlein's foreign minister reveals most clearly the Sudeten nationalist mission in its European framework. The diplomatic avenues he pursued show his Sudeten priorities, his pragmatism despite radical goals, and how his foreign policy from the start was determined by an international system in flux. Not least, we see why the Sudeten German nationalists were welcomed in London. There, their grievances were taken seriously while the future viability of Czechoslovakia, a creation of the Versailles settlement of 1919, was justifiably questioned as an unstable element at the heart of Europe.

Heinz Rutha's life thus encompasses international, regional, and local angles, and provides a challenging breadth of disciplinary approaches. Since his local world of northern Bohemia was the permanent backdrop to his career, there is the potential for a holistic study with the local constantly intruding upon national or international dimensions.[34] As for those who eulogized him, it was his modern youth crusade that seemed most striking and destined to have the finest legacy. For years he focused on a pedagogic mission powered by Eros: a generation of charismatic Sudeten German young men would be molded to lead a national revolution across what they saw as Czech-dominated space. How this materialized, and how it ultimately caused Rutha's downfall and national excommunication, is the main subject of *The Devil's Wall*.

The Devil's Wall

The devil has often featured in the legends of northern Bohemia. Just south of Mount Jeschken, dark volcanic rock breaks through the surrounding sandstone and runs for about twenty miles in a southwesterly direction. Through weathering, this natural phenomenon of basalt has come to resemble a wall. In places it is thirty feet high and, but for local quarrying, would be even more extensive. For those raised in the neighborhood the wall could only be explained through a series of myths, as the work of the devil.

By the late nineteenth century, an extra legend had materialized, portraying the Devil's Wall as a national barrier. In this region, so the story ran, Czechs and Germans had long been seeking ways to harm each other. A simple German farmer living in Kessel, the village next to Oschitz, decided one day that the only way to stop this was to build a wall to separate the Czechs and the Germans once and for all. Since he could not do so himself, he made a pact with the devil; in return for the farmer's soul, the devil agreed to build a wall one night before the cock crew for the first time. By midnight the wall was fast nearing completion and the farmer began to regret his stupidity: he was only saved by his mother, who cleverly stirred up the local cockerels, at which the devil panicked and fled. He left behind his handiwork, which thereafter marked as a physical barrier the local language border between Czechs and Germans.[1]

This legend imposed a nationalist construction on the landscape, and decades later would be retold with a Czech peasant in the Doctor Faustus role.[2] It implied that the language border and the Czech-German struggle were physical realities as age-old as the Devil's Wall, as eternal as nature itself. In fact only the wall was ancient: the rest was as recent and humanly constructed as the myth. Although Czech- and German-speakers had lived next to each other in the Jeschken locality for centuries, it was only from the 1850s that a language border had been carefully delimited, its course thereby transformed from a vague local understanding to something official, set out in words and maps. Such work was a direct result of state modernization in the Habsburg Empire, an increasing desire by the imperial authorities to sort and calibrate the state's resources. In this spirit the head of the Austrian statistical office, Karl Freiherr von Czoernig, in 1855 had produced an ethnographic map of the Austrian monarchy. It was the first of its kind to use grassroots inquiries and statistics to plot cartographically a precise division between the Czechs and Germans of Bohemia.[3]

Czoernig's map, vividly colored in red for German and yellow-green for Czech, showed how those living under the gaze of Mount Jeschken were "border folk." The boundary, when described in words, seemed to be quite precise, so that villages could be categorized as "German" or "Czech." Hardly any settlements were mixed, except the small textile center of Böhmisch Aicha with its German minority.[4] Half a century later, this ethnic pattern of settlement did not seem to have altered. From 1880 the Habsburg monarchy's decennial census had begun inquiring about an individual's "language of everyday use" (*Umgangssprache* in German, *obcovací řeč* in Czech); the authorities used this single linguistic criterion, as opposed to Czoernig's broader ethnographic inquiry, as the gauge by which to plot the nationality proportions throughout the empire.[5] In 1900 the divide south of Jeschken appeared much as it had in the 1850s. What had changed was an intensified public perception of the language border as a national barrier, one that, for some Germans at least, had to be maintained at all costs. The legend about the Devil's Wall chimed with this mentality. Its very invention suggested that, on this section of the language border, some tension had evolved between the two national communities.

Where such tension might be nebulous, there it was still eagerly propagated by external activists who were always alarmed at "national indifference."[6] A study published in Germany in 1902 was typical, detailing how a "little war" was being waged along the language border in Bohemia, with German-speaking communities on the defensive against aggressive Czech invaders. According to Johannes Zemmrich, the barrier south of Mount Jeschken was particularly at risk. In villages on the German side of the

Devil's Wall like Teschen there had been an influx of Czechs, enabling even Czech representation on some formerly German parish councils.[7]

The reasons, however, that Zemmrich gave for this national shift undermined his own argument about national antagonism, for he could not deny that the number of Czechs had jumped partly because of German farmers marrying Czech women . He also admitted that the 1890 census had shown a Czech increase because bilingual individuals had been changing their *Umgangssprache* from German to Czech. Such behavior might well cause irritation, particularly in those parishes lying right across the language border where a demographic shift could mean the election of a Czech council leader.[8] But the evidence equally suggests that, for many in this border zone, national allegiance was not always the priority the Devil's Wall legend implied. Zemmrich's account was one of many that imposed a rigid nationalist construction upon a landscape still witnessing a far more fluid social interaction.

Heinz Rutha was born into this environment where ethnic antagonism and intimacy coexisted, and his childhood was immediately shaped by it. At the end of his life, enemies would suggest that something sinister could be inferred from his sharing a birthday, 20 April, with Adolf Hitler.[9] More intelligibly, we might examine the state of the Czech-German nationalpolitical relationship in Bohemia when Rutha and his generation were born. For precisely in April 1897 the relationship entered a crisis phase, a watershed after which both sides were nationally radicalized as never before.

A GERMAN OR CZECH BOHEMIA?

A demographic base underlay the idea by the late nineteenth century that there existed a tense Czech-German relationship, but upon this was imposed a strict nationalist construction. In the crownland of Bohemia, Czechspeakers, or more accurately those who felt themselves to be Czech (and would give that as their *Umgangssprache* in the census) were in the majority; in 1900 they represented about 62 percent of Bohemia's population. The rise of a modern Czech national consciousness over the previous century had complex roots but was directly related to the Habsburg authorities' provision of education in the Czech language. Beginning with universal schooling at a primary level in 1775 and some limited instruction at Prague University, an expansion over successive generations had enabled Czech-speaking men to climb the social ladder and move into positions of cultural, economic, and even political importance. In doing so they encountered the reality of a predominantly German cultural world in the Bohemian lands.[10]

The German language, which had been fostered from the 1780s by Emperor Joseph II as a practical means of centralizing his realms, had become the prevailing language of administration, culture, and politics; its social status was affiliated to a German-speaking elite of aristocratic landowners and businessmen. In the early nineteenth century, the notion of a Bohemian identity, even a Bohemian patriotism, still seems to have prevailed among many Czech- and German-speakers in the province. But those like the academic Bernard Bolzano, who in 1816 hoped that a Bohemian outlook might fuse Czechs and Germans together, subsuming any ethnic-based identity within a territorial nationhood, were idealistic.

By the 1840s the amorphous Bohemian identity was becoming nationalized. The burgeoning groups of educated Czech-speakers with their own culture in Prague were fast interpreting their German surroundings in terms of either domination or discrimination. The German Bohemian social elite, long encouraged to think of Czech as an inferior peasant language, was in turn stimulated in its own German identity by a national-liberal movement in the non-Habsburg German world to the north. It is hard to judge how far or fast this split in Bohemia between a specific German and Czech national consciousness developed under the Metternich regime in Austria; the authorities certainly permitted a Czech cultural expansion in the 1830s but repressed anything political. What might be bubbling under was largely hidden and only erupted with the fall of the Metternich regime in 1848.

The 1848 revolutions in central Europe set out for the first time the three territorial frameworks within which the Czech-German relationship evolved over the next seventy years: pan-German, Austrian, and Bohemian (or Bohemian-Moravian). Out of these three, it was the pan-German and Bohemian frameworks that most stimulated German and Czech national aspirations, respectively. It was the Austrian framework that offered the relationship the most room to maneuver (a framework eliminated with the collapse of the Habsburg Empire in 1918, creating the tighter Czech-German space of interwar Czechoslovakia). In early 1848, just as the empire's future was in doubt, so any Austrian framework was eclipsed until the summer, when the Habsburgs began to restore their authority. Until then the pan-German and Bohemian frameworks for the Czech-German relationship were sharply juxtaposed against one another. Most German Bohemian liberals, viewing Bohemia as a natural part of the German cultural world to the north, enthused about Bohemia entering a new pan-German national state. Czech liberals, under the historian František Palacký, rejected this revolutionary shift, as it would place Czechs in a minority in a German national sea much vaster than the Bohemian cultural lake of recent decades.

The Bohemian framework that Czech liberals embraced in 1848 envisaged the beleaguered Habsburgs giving self-government to Bohemia and restoring the historic powers of its assembly in Prague. This quickly became anathema to many local Germans, since thanks to the sharpening national demographics, it presaged their own eventual drowning in a sea of Czechs: a theoretical "pan-Czech" solution. The mounting clash, however, was postponed as the Habsburg regime recovered its power. Both the German (pan-German) and the Czech (Bohemian) solutions lost momentum, surrendering again in late 1848 to an Austrian framework within which Czech and German leaders pragmatically had to discuss their relationship in an Austrian parliament. Within a few months the Habsburgs felt confident enough to abolish this forum. But after a decade of Habsburg absolutism and the return of constitutional rule (1861), the Czech-German question reappeared as well—as did the three frameworks of the revolutionary year.

For the rest of the century Austria became the overriding context within which the Bohemian problem was pulled back and forward.[11] Since the Austrian constitutional government in Vienna needed a compliant parliament [*Reichsrat*] in order to function efficiently, it was in the interest of Austrian prime ministers to try periodically to resolve Czech-German grievances, or at least to win over one side through concessions. For German Bohemian liberals, a centralized regime in Vienna offered the best security, especially as hopes of any wider German framework were soon dashed: Otto von Bismarck's creation of a united Germany in 1866–1871, and Austria's exclusion from it, meant that German Bohemian nationalists sought ever more safety in numbers with fellow Germans in Austria proper. They at least were the dominant force in the Austrian governments of the 1860s and 1870s, and could gain extra solace in 1879 from the empire's alliance with Germany. Pan-Germanism might increasingly seem a chimera, but for most German Bohemians the broader German homeland and culture remained embedded in their mentality. One small expression of it was the monuments raised in northern Bohemia in later decades, not just to Bismarck but to Prussian soldiers who had invaded in 1866 and died on Bohemian soil. Thus a fluid German allegiance persisted even if by 1870 it was the Austrian imperial context that was gaining primacy.[12]

The Czech leadership could not indefinitely ignore the reconfigured Habsburg context either. For a new generation, Palacký's son-in-law František Rieger portrayed Czechs as the "primary owners" of Bohemia, entitled by "natural right" to have equality with Germans in their language, education, and administration.[13] There were soon promising signs in this direction, for in 1859 the imperial authorities allowed Czech as the language of instruction in secondary schools in predominantly Czech districts. For practical purposes, Rieger would acknowledge German as the overriding administrative language across Austria, but pressed for the Czech-German relationship to be firmly adjusted in its Bohemian context: in other words, Bohemia must gain home rule. While the Czechs portrayed this as a matter of natural right in the face of German social dominance, it was of course perceived menacingly by many educated Germans who increasingly feared being swamped by a Czech majority who were socially-inferior. When Vienna refused home rule, the Czech politicians boycotted the Reichsrat for fifteen years, leaving the Germans in effective control.

Only in 1879, when the government of Count Taaffe persuaded the Czechs to return, did they change tactics and adopt a long-term course of "activism," cooperating in the Austrian framework in order to secure equality in Bohemia. This swiftly brought rewards from Vienna and threw the German Bohemians onto the defensive. The Stremayr language decrees of 1880 for the first time told local authorities throughout Bohemia, whether in German or Czech areas, to use the Czech language if dealing with Czech petitions or public correspondence. Even if German remained the common administrative language across Bohemia as a whole, the ruling implied some linguistic equality, emphasizing that Czech was equal to German in mixed-language communities. Many town councils in the German-speaking borderlands saw it as the thin end of the wedge and refused to abide by the decrees.[14] Indeed, in the 1880s Bohemia's German leaders campaigned vigorously for German to be officially recognized as the Austrian state language. They also pushed for Bohemia's administrative districts to be delimited precisely into Czech and German zones, so that the "pure German" regions—claimed to be a third of Bohemia—would be protected from any future pan-Czech solution.

This second demand spoke volumes about the slow revolution that both sides perceived in these decades. Formerly it had been Czech leaders who hoped for "national delimitation" and Germans who opposed it, on the grounds that all of Bohemia was a German domain. By the 1880s the stance was reversed, since economic and social advances made many Czechs more confident in insisting on a Czech character for all Bohemia. It fitted their mythical notion of historic "state right," according to which Bohemia in the past had been governed as an entity by its "own people." But it also matched a growing national-demographic trend. From the 1860s, Czech-speaking agricultural workers had been migrating to German mining or urban areas, offering cheap labor, and often resisting attempts to assimilate with the local communities. In doing so, these Czech national minorities upset the very notion that Bohemia could be neatly split into two national regions as ethnographic maps had suggested since the time of Czoernig.[15]

Despite this, the older Czech liberal generation was prepared to compromise. When Taaffe mediated Czech-German talks in 1890, Rieger finally conceded a national divide in administrative districts in return for some local electoral reform and a lifeline thrown to Czech minority schools in German areas. But this real glimmer of hope was now sabotaged by "Young Czech" politicians, a younger radical generation who protested loudly and swept the board in the Reichsrat elections of 1891. Thus the national struggle was ratcheted up another notch. Well might Franz Schmeykal, the German liberal leader who had banked on a breakthrough, sigh that "things in Bohemia are becoming more and more complicated." In the final decades of the nineteenth century, a new virulent nationalism was crystallizing. The German national liberalism of those like Schmeykal was being challenged by what can be termed a *völkisch* phenomenon: socially inclusive in its populist appeal, but nationally exclusive in its interpretation of a Germanness based on blood to the exclusion of any Czechs or Jews.[16]

The 1880s had witnessed the start of a "little war" in many regions of Bohemia, a penetration of Czech-German nationalist agitation into grassroots communities. Partly it resulted from a public increasingly educated to think nationally, many of whom were gaining the vote (thanks to Taaffe's franchise reform of 1882) and were being wooed by nationalist politicians campaigning over the Stremayr language decrees. The 1880 census intensified local perceptions of two separate national identities, for all had to nail their colors to the mast by opting for either Czech or German linguistic affiliation (this included Jews and anybody who might self-identify as bilingual or even Bohemian). Since the tabulated results were used to justify local linguistic policy, a virulent competition ensued over each side's "national assets" *[Nationalbesitzstand]*. These might be measured in terms of land, wealth, or souls (people) and were inevitably scrutinized most closely by agitators on the language border or where outsiders had "invaded" the ethnic space. The cry was particularly strident in key nationalist strongholds like Reichenberg where, with a *völkisch* clique taking over the town hall, the German council refused any concessions whatsoever to Czech-speakers.[17]

Alongside these enthusiastic local campaigners, the key engines behind the grassroots struggle were a series of new propaganda societies founded in 1880. The German and Czech School Associations—the *Deutscher Schulverein* and the *Ústřední matice školská*—saw it as their mission to save children for their nationality by financing private schools in sensitive minority areas. Within a few years each association had established a mass network with schoolteachers as some of the key local activists.[18] By the 1890s the obsessive mindset had penetrated further, producing new "defense societies" such as the *Národní jednoty severočeská* (North Bohemian National Union) or the *Bund der Deutschen in Böhmen* (Union of Bohemian Germans) which by 1900 had sixty thousand members.[19] Each aimed to uphold all facets of what they viewed as national property against the outsider. And as Pieter Judson has shown, their propaganda began to impinge on villages formerly bypassed by the nationalist struggle.

In July 1897 torrential storms lashed through northern Bohemia, causing unprecedented flooding across the Jeschken landscape as the rivers burst their banks.[20] It was a natural calamity, and it paralleled the nationalist storm that had burst three months earlier across all Czech and German communities. On 5 April, the Austrian prime minister, Count Kasimir Badeni, a self-assured but idealistic individual, had published new language ordinances for Bohemia. They decreed what Czech nationalists had long coveted and Germans long dreaded: full linguistic equality in the province and the demotion of German from its unofficial status as the common administrative language. Since by 1901 the Czech language would be on a par with German across Bohemia's administration, all state officials, whether on the railways or in the police, would have to become bilingual within four years. In view of the national-demographic balance, the decrees therefore seemed to forecast and accept a Czech-dominated Bohemia for the future. Badeni, eager for Czech political support for his Austrian government, was oblivious to those who warned against any further undermining of the Germans' position.

The result was predictable, though perhaps not its combustible quality. German politicians exploded in rage and their constituents gathered in their thousands for national days of protest and solemn oaths against the decrees.[21] As the chaos mounted, Czechs and Germans brawled not only in the streets of Prague and Vienna but in the Reichsrat itself, where pipes and drums were smuggled in to sabotage parliamentary business, forcing the government to have unruly members ejected by the police. Badeni in his wild optimism still hoped to salvage something. But after surviving a pistol duel with one German radical politician, he did not survive in the monarch's good books and was forced to resign. As Emperor Franz Joseph observed, "Count, you are creating a revolution for me."[22]

The crisis had raised to fever pitch the German Bohemians' group paranoia and the Czech Bohemians' group aspirations. In parliament thereafter, Czech and German obstruction became the norm, so the Austrian government increasingly turned to rule by decree. In Bohemia, as Badeni's ordinances were quietly dropped, a fierce nationalist perspective became preeminent, vocal Germans clamoring for a clear national division while vocal Czechs held out for compulsory bilingualism. For many on both sides, the "little war" had escalated, and, if nationalist rhetoric was to be believed, it could only be won at the expense of the other. It was in these years that a new strain of virulent nationalism was evident along sections of the language border or in "language islands" like Iglau in Moravia. Emerging political groups like the German Workers' Party (1904) spoke provocatively about "defending living space" against the menace of Czech migrants and directly challenged the older liberal-national generation.[23]

The village of Oschitz in northern Bohemia could not remain immune from the Badeni crisis and its aftermath. As petitions demanding repeal of the ordinances had streamed into the Reichsrat from Reichenberg and other German bastions, so Oschitz parish council had added its own small request to that number. In a meeting at the end of November 1897, the council duly expressed "joy" at Badeni's dismissal, and fully backed the rumpus that German deputies had brought into Parliament, urging them to press on with the "sharpest obstruction" until the language decrees were withdrawn. Their own loyalty was to their German nation and to its rightful privileged position within imperial Austria. A year later, the councilors expressed their full devotion to the emperor on his golden jubilee and dispatched a personal greeting to Vienna; they then retired to Oschitz church for a Catholic mass of thanksgiving.[24]

THE RUTHAS AND THE STORCHS

In interwar Czechoslovakia, Oschitz and the adjacent village of Bad Kunnersdorf gained their notoriety as the home base of the Sudeten German nationalist, Heinz Rutha.[25] For most Czechs now, however, the local region is famous either as the setting for the "village novels" of Karolina Světlá or because of an age-old natural phenomenon: the spa at Kunnersdorf, which from 1901 served to put the "Bad" into "Bad Kunnersdorf." Already in the early nineteenth century a shack with two tubs had been set up in the bog land so that mud baths could be taken.[26] But it was Josef Schwan, a tradesman based in Oschitz, who first noticed the potential of the local hot ponds. After buying up the land in 1879, his vision of creating a mud spa was fully realized by his son (also Josef) who opened a complex of buildings at the turn of the century. Immediately a flood of wealthy customers began to arrive, making their way down the birch-lined avenue and injecting a stir into the sleepy locality. When Schwan died suddenly, his widow in 1908 sold the spa to the parish of Bad Kunnersdorf. For the next decade it was administered industriously by two brothers who were both local mill owners, Adolf and Franz Rutha.[27]

Since 1661 Kunnersdorf had been a parish separate from Oschitz, its few hundred inhabitants living chiefly off the land, engaged in forestry, or employed in a small domestic industry in slippers [*Tuchschuhe*]. But the two communities were effectively seamless. In their common historical experience was benevolent rule in the sixteenth century by Karl von Biberstein, who founded and was buried in Oschitz church; turbulence in the 1600s when the parishes were briefly owned by Albrecht von Wallenstein, witnessing re-Catholicization and almost total destruction by an invading Swedish army; and periodic military billeting and requisitioning during the Napoleonic wars. The parish chronicles over the centuries had recorded many epidemics, droughts, storms, and fires, not least the damage wrought to the church in a conflagration of 1825. For eighty years Oschitz could not repair it due to sheer impoverishment. Even at the turn of the century photographs from the market square reveal the village poverty, the children raggedly dressed and posing against the faded aftermath of the Counter-Reformation: a gilded Marian statue with Bohemian acolytes, Saints Vitus and John of Nepomuk (fig.4).[28]

Eulogies from the 1930s would claim that the Ruthas had lived here for centuries, remembered usually as mill owners or irrigation builders, as "very distinctive, confident and gifted individuals."[29] Heinz Rutha's grandfather, Josef Rutha, had been born in 1822 in the nearby village of Merzdorf, the son and grandson of millers who had only recently escaped from feudal obligations. In 1844 Josef proceeded to build his own mill on the River Polzen in Kunnersdorf and carved that date on the lintel of the main entrance.[30] Three years later he married a local girl, Karolina Ullrich, whose family had long been active in the administration of Oschitz; Josef Schwan the elder was a witness.[31] In the 1850s the couple began to create a family, Karolina giving birth ten times over twenty years; four of the children survived, living in the Rutha mill and attending the elementary school in Oschitz.[32] At the same time a series of proper roads was built through the district, ensuring that its future would be ever more closely entwined with developments in the rest of Bohemia.

The midcentury inhabitants of Oschitz-Kunnersdorf were certainly German-speaking. But in their rural isolation, their identity or consciousness of who they were remained tied up with their livelihood and status in the local community, only mildly affected by the Czech-speaking "outsiders" encountered at Oschitz's weekly or annual markets. Identity in other words had not yet been nationalized: it required outside intervention.

One might suggest that the parishes received a more defined German Bohemian orientation from 1869 when they were allotted, for administrative and judicial purposes, to the predominantly German political district of Böhmisch Leipa and thereby officially separated from Czech-speaking communities to the east.[33] Over the next twenty years, as migration and communications expanded, so the national-political frictions of Bohemia permeated into Oschitz-Kunnersdorf. Villagers were asked for their *Umgangssprache* in the 1880 census and encouraged to join a local branch of the German School Association (1884). But besides this tightening of national identity, often via enthusiasts with a political agenda, there was always the reality of a German community living in proximity to Czech-speakers, whose interaction regularly breached the bureaucratically or nationally defined frontiers. The Ruthas were just one family whose development in the late nineteenth century proves the amorphous reality of the emerging language border.

Adolf Rutha, Josef's eldest son, was born in July 1851, and at the age of thirty married Marie Storch, the daughter of an innkeeper from Nieder-Gruppai. Nieder-Gruppai was a hamlet lying about ten miles south of Oschitz, in deep woodland used by the Wallenstein family as a hunting estate; most villagers there lived off the estate or tried to work the poor sandstone soil.[34] It was chiefly a German-speaking settlement, with 418 Germans and 32 Czechs according to the 1880 census, but its location gave it a bilingual coloring. The blended Bohemian history was only too evident in the ancient church, dedicated to the tenth-century martyr Saint Václav (Wenzel) with a reredos depicting how he was murdered by his brother Boleslav. This Bohemian patron saint, known to English-speakers as Good King Wenceslas, was by the late nineteenth century adopted by Czech nationalists as their special guardian (lending his name to Prague's main square where an equestrian statue would be a focal point of twentieth-century Czech identity and independence).[35] Like Wenzel-Václav, Gruppai's families too usually had a blended linguistic identity, fused together from contact with Czech-speaking villages a few miles away.

In the 1930s, accounts of Heinz Rutha's lineage would mention how on his mother's side the family tree could be traced back to the fifteenth century, as a family of farmers and village justices originating from the west (from Leitmeritz and Hirschberg).[36] These ancestors were named Storch. They had arrived in Nieder-Gruppai in the early 1830s when a Johann Wenzel Storch had married Elisabeth Gröger in the parish church. Storch hailed from a family of peasant farmers in Alt-Kalken, a hamlet in the Hirschberg region. For him it was undoubtedly an advantageous match. While his family seems to have been tightly bound into a feudal relationship with local landowners, the Grögers had possessed land and status in Nieder-Gruppai for generations and owned an inn on the main road.[37] Three children resulted from the union, including one son, Wenzel, who would be Heinz Rutha's maternal grandfather.[38]

What would later be ignored or obscured in the scraps of information that leaked out about Rutha's ancestry was its Czech dimension. It paralleled the background of the Sudeten German leader Konrad Henlein, whose mother was later discovered to have been of Czech-speaking descent.[39] If this was unsurprising for families from the "border" region, in the Rutha case it has remained unnoticed until now. In 1859, Wenzel Storch had taken as his wife Barbara Holasová, a peasant farmer's daughter from over the hill in the purely Czech-speaking village of Neveklovice. Nor was this a singular event, confined to an era before the mental cementing of the language border: future generations of the Storchs would maintain an emotional traffic between Neveklovice and Nieder-Gruppai, largely oblivious to the Devil's Wall.[40] We cannot know whether German or Czech prevailed in the inn in

Gruppai where Wenzel and Barbara Storch brought up their family from the 1860s. But it seems highly likely that their four children—Marie, Josef, Wenzel, and Anastasie—were raised in a bilingual environment where interaction with their Czech grandmother Elisabeth (widowed since 1859 and living with them) was supplemented with visits to Czech relations in Neveklovice.

It was to this mixed culture that Adolf Rutha became attached when he married Wenzel Storch's eldest daughter, Marie, perhaps having met her by chance at the wayside inn when out on business for his father's mill. Back in Kunnersdorf, Marie Storch bore him three children, a son (Richard) and two daughters (Marie and Friederike or Friedel), but she died aged twenty-five in March 1888, a week after giving birth to Friedel. Adolf was overwhelmingly devoted to his first wife, always retaining a picture of her in a prominent position on his desk, and it was six years before he married again. When he did so, his choice reflected his children's need for a stepmother and the emotional connections he retained with Nieder-Gruppai. It also appears to have been pragmatic, a way of maintaining a financial input into his milling business from the comfortably well-off Storch family.[41] Adolf's second wife was therefore Marie's younger sister, Anastasie. She was in her mid-twenties when she arrived in Kunnersdorf, eighteen years younger than her new husband, and the children followed in leisurely fashion: Heinrich, or Heinz as he was usually called, in April 1897, and Margarete or Gretel in March 1903. Both were incorporated into a tight family structure where no distinction was made between the siblings from Adolf Rutha's two marriages, but where Marie Storch's children would effectively act as role models for Anastasie's.

In keeping with the separate spheres into which he divided his adult life, Heinz Rutha never spoke publicly about his childhood. But something can be glimpsed from family mementoes and the surviving parish records of Oschitz, which unlike those of Kunnersdorf were salvaged by chance at the end of the Second World War. By the turn of the century, Adolf Rutha's position in the community extended far beyond his mill—to which he had added a sawmill[42]—or the parish affairs of Kunnersdorf. He was running the new savings bank in Oschitz, and after a period as guardian of Josef Schwan's children, he would become director of the mud spa itself. He injected substantial capital to modernize it so that, by the 1930s after his death, the birch-lined avenue to the health resort would temporarily bear his name.[43]

For Heinz, the Rutha family was always an extended and extensive one, rooted in all corners of the community but bearing a propertied lower-middle-class stamp, which raised it above the village's laboring class. Heinz's first appearance in a family photograph is testament to this (fig.5). The scene appears to be the eightieth birthday of his grandfather Josef Rutha in October 1904, with one of the leading local bourgeois families gathering in the snow for a group portrait. Josef presides rather grimly. Heinz nestles at the front, close to the infant Gretel, his expression as disconcerted as that of his mother, Anastasie. Behind stand his (step)sisters, Marie and Friedel; his grey-mustachioed father; and a cluster of Rutha aunts and uncles. There is Uncle Franz, sometime mayor of Kunnersdorf, with his buxom sunken-eyed wife, Klara; Ferdinand, the bachelor brother who had set up as a lithographer in Reichenberg; and the balding elderly Emanuel Max, "organ-builder" by profession, who was married to Adolf's sister.[44] The adult males are stiff, matching their starched collars. The women have donned their decorated frocks for the occasion. Only the children, disciplined and proper, suggest a hint of mischievousness; but Heinz himself seems already to share the serious world of the adults.

By this time aged seven, Heinz had attended his first year at Oschitz primary school, which had a pure German-speaking catchment area including Kunnersdorf and Kessel. If the class sizes over a period of five years were large, numbering about fifty pupils each, the evidence suggests that the teachers were very diligent. They were spurred on by the headmaster, Eduard Grunge, to be creative with their children and less authoritarian, in line with the pedagogical reform movement of the era.[45] Not only did the small teaching corps hold monthly meetings to exchange pedagogic ideas; their example to the children persisted outside the classroom through their full involvement in the German cultural life of Kunnersdorf-Oschitz. For Heinz there was immediately a personal dimension to this model, for two of his teachers, Franz Effert and Franz Polifka, were romantically attached to his sisters Marie and Friedel. They appear hazily in the Rutha photograph of late 1904, linked together already by blood and profession— just as they would be linked together in the manner of their death.

Franz Effert, who came from Niemes, had gained his teacher-training certificate in Reichenberg (and some experience in western Bohemia) before joining the Oschitz staff in 1903.[46] In February 1905 at one of Grunge's monthly meetings, Effert enthused his fellow teachers with a talk about "schools of the future," based on a treatise by the progressive Swedish pedagogue Ellen Key. He noted how at elementary school the priority was for children to read well, to write with both hands, to draw simple things, and to learn the decimal system, some basic geography, and perhaps even some English; but he added that "further general education has to be adapted to the needs of each individual, governed especially by the pupils' own experiences and observations."[47]

If these maxims were tested on the young Heinz when Effert taught him in the boy's third year, Effert's wider social interests probably shaped Rutha's early curiosity about his German cultural roots. He was a proactive teacher who was prominent and respected in local associational life—the type of man that Tara Zahra has identified as promoting *Heimat* education for the German national cause in the border regions.[48] Besides his membership in the local choral society, he was a leading figure in the Oschitz branch of the Turner movement, the German nationalist gymnastics association that had a thick grassroots network across the Bohemian lands (and had its parallel in the Czech Sokol organization).

But Effert also threw himself into a new conservation society that evinced a slow dispersal of civic values into the countryside, beautifying and controlling the local landscape while stamping a nationalist imprint upon it.[49] Its first project was to erect a memorial to Schiller, marking both the centenary of the poet's death and the twenty-fifth anniversary of the German School Association. In May 1905 the local elite gathered in their top hats, with the Turners and firemen in their uniforms, to witness the unveiling of a "Schiller stone" on the outskirts of Oschitz. As secretary of the society, Effert was certainly among them. Whether we should quite term him a "nationalist activist" is questionable, but certainly he personified a generation that was sharply conscious of its national identity, one that brought a nationalist mindset to the fore in the locality.[50]

It was surely not fortuitous that, when Effert left the school in 1907 and moved with his new wife Marie to take up a teaching post in Böhmisch Leipa, his replacement at Oschitz was his own future brother-in-law, Franz Polifka. In order to be together with Friedel Rutha in Kunnersdorf, Polifka seems to have engineered a straight exchange of posts with Effert, for he had been employed in the same Leipa school since 1904. Polifka himself was a Leipa man who had attended the Realschule there and (as with Heinz's later experience) had undoubtedly absorbed the town's fervent German nationalism. When Heinz entered his fifth and final year at the Oschitz school in 1907, Polifka became his class teacher. A talk on children's literature that

Polifka gave to his peers in March 1908 hints at least at his German reformist outlook, circumscribed by respectable bourgeois values but not overly stuffy. After humorously satirizing some of the "grotesque" books on the market for boys and girls, including Catholic and Social Democratic examples, he "offered a brief overview of so-called 'trash literature' and damned it."[51]

For Heinz the significance of his imaginative, reformist Oschitz schooling is revealed in his desire, thirty years later, to have the urn with his ashes displayed in the school. The *Heimat* values imbibed there from Effert or Polifka were simply an extension of those he observed in the local culture, values that impinged steadily on the Rutha household in Kunnersdorf. All the indications are of a secure and happy childhood in a lower-middle-class Catholic family, conscious of its relative wealth and respectability in the community. (The social status of the Rutha name is clear in the family's adoption of its own precious stone, the amethyst, for use in marriage rings.) It was a unit whose broad composition allowed the boy an extra degree of independence but also a specific niche in the familial hierarchy since, surrounded by adults, he might act as Gretel's protector (fig.6).

But how far did the Devil's Wall intrude into Heinz's childhood consciousness? At the end of the First World War he would write a piece, portraying the edifice itself as the frontline barrier that had protected German soil in a centuries-old struggle against the Slav flood.[52] In 1908, the German culture of Kunnersdorf-Oschitz, a settlement "hard on the language border" as it was often described in nationalist literature, was ubiquitous; it was clear in the nationalization of recreation and the behavior of parish councilors who regularly felt obliged to register their German national or imperial allegiance. In Kunnersdorf-Oschitz there was little evidence of the bilingualism or even national apathy that some historians have suggested is a key characteristic of so-called border settlements.[53] Rather, by the twentieth century, most villagers from their education at school or in the wider community had a sense of German national belonging and usually defined "Czech" as something "other." Occasionally too, some might be whipped up to take a stand if they saw their community directly targeted by a local Czech nationalist offensive. In 1900, according to Zemmrich, this had occurred when a Czech chaplain in Oschitz was discovered spreading leaflets calling on villagers to self-identify as Czech in the census.[54]

However, juxtaposed to this potential German defensiveness, and a useful case study, was the reality of the Rutha household. Heinz Rutha was faced here with perhaps the first internal struggle of his life, since figuratively the

Devil's Wall ran through his own family. His father seems to have been a German of a *völkisch* or at least nationalist persuasion and the household language was only German.[55] Yet if Anastasie Storch fully embraced the Germanness of her adopted environment, she certainly kept her contacts to Czech-German Nieder-Gruppai, and indirectly to Czech Neveklovice, linking her new family to them. Visits to the Gruppai inn, run by Uncle Wenzel from 1902 after Anastasie's parents had died, were for Heinz perhaps his main early expeditions outside Kunnersdorf. Trips further afield to Niemes or Reichenberg would have been rare, for only in 1910 did a motorized bus service make these urban centers more accessible.

For Anastasie too it was important—perhaps a sign of her own "national indifference"—that her children should learn some Czech, her mother's language. Across the Czech-German language border for many decades there had been a well-established practice of families exchanging their Czech and German children so that they could benefit from a year's schooling in the other linguistic environment. It was an example of customary Czech-German fluid interaction at a grassroots level, cutting across the increasingly strident nationalist rhetoric from turn-of-the-century German or Czech activists.

Yet at the Rutha mill there may have been some keen discussion on this point between the two parents, with Adolf perhaps finally conceding to his wife that Heinz in late 1908 should follow a customary path. From Oschitz primary school he went for a year to the top class of an equivalent school in the Czech town of Mnichovo Hradiště (Münchengrätz), five miles east of Nieder-Gruppai. The Rutha family's relative prosperity ensured that, unlike poorer families, no exchange with a Czech child was necessary: they simply paid for his education. Nor was Heinz required to live in the midst of a Czech-speaking household. Instead, through Storch connections, he was able to lodge with the administrator of the town's most notable edifice, the Wallenstein château.[56]

Looking back a decade later, Heinz would identify the first weeks in Mnichovo Hradiště as the worst of his life. As an eleven-year-old boy accustomed to the securities of Kunnersdorf, he was suddenly thrown into a small-town Czech environment that felt cold and alien.[57] The street names now celebrated Czech heroes such as Jan Hus and František Rieger, and a marble plaque commemorated the birthplace of the mid-nineteenth-century Czech radical politician Emanuel Arnold. At his Czech school he may even have rubbed shoulders briefly with a local lawyer's son, the later communist martyr Jan Šverma (born 1901). On the other hand, his domicile, presumably on the Wallenstein estate itself, must have reinforced a socioethnic and elitist separation from his fellow pupils at the school. The Wallenstein château—with its mixture of Renaissance and Baroque styles, its rich picture gallery, its "English" park and terraces—dominated the local Czech community and evinced the ancient social hierarchy of the region. It was there in 1833 that the monarchs of Austria, Russia, and Prussia had gathered in a show of conservative solidarity of their "Holy Alliance." Aside from the diplomacy that produced the Treaty of Münchengrätz, they had also attended a play in the château theatre entitled *Czech and German,* which, to the delight of Tsar Nicholas I, had been performed in the Czech language.[58]

Eighty years later, Heinz Rutha too experienced the linguistic divide in Bohemia from the vantage point of the château, and for him, even if interspersed with visits to Gruppai relatives, it was a lonely existence. Unlike other Czech or German children who might well look back on such schooling with nostalgia, he was an example of one who did not.[59] Rather, it reinforced his independent streak and probably served to give him a better sense of a distinct national division running through the Bohemian lands. Instead of the nebulous cultural identity of Gruppai with its confusing implications for his own family, the Czech-German divide might begin to appear as simple and concrete as the Devil's Wall itself. Possibly his love for his mother helped always to temper his national intolerance, but otherwise a *völkisch* mindset was evolving and destined to be shaped by further schooling: first among the German minority of Prague, the Czech capital, and then in the German stronghold of Böhmisch Leipa.

TWO

A German Bohemian Education

When Heinz Rutha arrived in Prague to start his secondary education in the baking summer of 1909, he entered a metropolis of half a million people that for fifty years had been shaped as a Czech cultural and political center. Since 1861, when Czech-speaking liberals had taken control, the city council had worked consciously to fashion what one mayor on his inauguration proudly proclaimed as "Golden Slav Prague."[1] It meant the creation of a Czech national capital to rival that of imperial Vienna or the dynamic Hungarian capital of Budapest. Not only would it be an urban focus for Czech dominance over Germans in the Bohemian lands; it substantiated Czech nationalist claims for political autonomy in the Habsburg monarchy on a par with that which Emperor Franz Joseph had accorded Hungary in 1867.

As Prague's inner city—its ancient four towns—was slowly molded together with bridges, parks, and new thoroughfares, so a cultural space was created to meet the needs of an expanding Czech middle-class population. A Prague that was both "golden" and "Slav" began to dominate the skyline through new golden-roofed buildings such as the National Theater and the National Museum, designed by leading Czech artists of the day. The Czechs' primordial roots were suggested in the creation of a cemetery for Czech patriots within the ancient fortress of Vyšehrad, while the nation's enviable future was displayed in a stock exchange and a network of banking houses led by the Živnostenská Banka. By 1909 statues of "Czech" heroes—Wenceslas, Palacký, and Hus—were appearing in the main squares or were under construction, and artists such as Alfons Mucha were decorating a Municipal House *[Obecní dům]* in a Secessionist style expressive of rising

Czech confidence and wealth. It was a modern noisy city with expanding suburbs, linked together by a network of electric trams, which, as one famous insomniac observed, passed through quiet neighborhoods "with a roaring rude as the wind's . . . like spoiled clocks."[2]

GOLDEN SLAV PRAGUE

According to the census, the number of Prague's inhabitants who gave German as their first language declined from 15.3 percent in 1880 to 7 percent in 1910. The drop was caused chiefly by a mass migration into the city of rural Czech-speakers, but as the full German figures hint, thirty-nine thousand falling to thirty-three thousand, it was also due to new generations of Germans, and especially German Jews, deciding to adopt Czech loyalties.[3]

Since the 1860s the remaining German minority, led by a propertied and professional elite, had felt forced to delimit its own national identity in the face of an increasingly demonstrative Czech Prague. Excluded wholly from the city administration after 1882, the German liberals under Franz Schmeykal, with their own special cultural center (the German Casino), proceeded to carve out a public national apartheid. Through a mass of political and social associations, their own schools, university, and German theater (a counter to the Czech National Theater), they fought to defend their ostensibly superior national-cultural values against what they viewed as the Czech intruders. But from the 1880s they faced a different challenge, from the lower-middle-class and *völkisch* strain of German nationalism that was gaining a hold in northern Bohemia. This more radical nationalism, fueled in part by frustration at liberal values, also made inroads into Prague's suburbs and among university students. For the German liberals, both of these battles, against the Czech and the German *völkisch* threats, were elitist; and as the franchise expanded at the end of the nineteenth century, both were doomed to be lost.[4]

Despite this public German exclusivity, the private reality was that Prague's Germans consistently rubbed shoulders with Czech-speakers in their everyday lives. In apartment blocks, on trams and in the street, in shops, businesses, or social outlets that were not explicitly national, the majority and minority mingled together—for there were no exclusively German neighborhoods. Germans at most never represented more than 30 percent of local inhabitants and were not ghettoized.[5]

Heinz Rutha, during his two years of schooling in the city, had most experience of the districts where the Germans congregated most thickly: Královské Vinohrady and the Lower New Town. Vinohrady, lying southeast of Wenceslas Square, was the suburb with the highest number of recorded Germans: seven thousand or 9 percent of inhabitants in the 1910 census. It was also one of the fastest-growing parts of the metropolis, expanding its population by almost 50 percent in the first decade of the twentieth century. Primarily it was a residential area, home to professionals and businessmen who could walk from here to the inner city. And it was partly this prestigious reputation, the self-esteem of its propertied classes, that spurred Vinohrady's Czech council consistently to reject the suburb's incorporation into the city of Prague. Instead, it remained officially the third-largest town in Bohemia, benefiting from proximity to the city center but asserting its autonomous character with modern high-rise houses and even its own theater as a rival to the Czech and German national edifices.[6]

This fashionable quarter was Heinz's home for two years, for we know that he lodged there in the apartment of his half brother Richard. In his twenties, Richard had made the move from Kunnersdorf to work as a bank clerk in the city, and he now served as Heinz's parental guardian.[7] It was one example of lower-middle-class upward mobility, and it cannot have been lost on the younger Rutha in shaping his aspirations.

Heinz's all-male school, one of three German Realschulen in Prague, was located on Jindřišská (Heinrichsgasse), just off Wenceslas Square in the Lower New Town. The area contained many banks, some of the city's best shops and apartments, and one of the highest concentrations of Germans: it sustained some German group identity to offset the imposing Czech surroundings. It also directly introduced Heinz to a people who did not seem to fit neatly into either a Czech or German national category: the Jews. According to one calculation, wealthy Jews were a substantial proportion (68 percent) of the German residents here and in two neighboring parishes.[8] In the previous half century, as the city's Czech character had been asserted, Prague Jewry had felt forced—not least by a census omitting any Jewish *Umgangssprache*—to declare either a Czech or German national allegiance. Some had shifted to a Czech loyalty, forsaking the German identity that had been a key secularizing route for them since their emancipation began in the 1780s.

This shift had fomented anti-Semitism among those lower-middle-class Germans who had a *völkisch* outlook, many of whom had homes in suburbs like Vinohrady (where five thousand Jews resided). During the Badeni crisis and after, it also evoked hostility among Czech nationalists who remained suspicious about the Jews' residual German allegiance, for it was a fact that over 80 percent of Jews continued to send their children to German secondary schools, viewing them as culturally superior. Heinz Rutha's new school was no exception. Almost half of the 290 pupils were Jewish. The same was true in his own class, where each week a rabbi would single out the twenty-four Jewish boys for separate religious instruction, thereby identifying them as different.[9]

Why did Heinz begin his secondary schooling in Prague? Probably his parents wanted to broaden his horizons, perhaps on the advice of the family pedagogues, Franz Effert and Franz Polifka. Richard's residence in Vinohrady undoubtedly played a role too. The III Deutsche Staatsrealschule was the nearest Realschule to Vinohrady with almost half of Heinz's class living in that suburb. Yet the boy was certainly an outsider; most of his fellow pupils, even if born outside the metropolis, lived with their parents in the city. The fact that Heinz attended a Realschule is easier to interpret. It was a sign that his parents expected him, with some extra qualifications, to assume the family business in Kunnersdorf. Since the educational reforms of the mid-nineteenth century, Austria's secondary school network had been divided into Gymnasien and Realschulen. While the Gymnasium supplied a classical education for boys destined for the professions or civil service, the Realschule was educating the empire's future technicians and businessmen. From the 1860s, the Realschule curriculum was less vocational, with pupils studying for seven years and taking a final examination to enter higher education. The perception, however, remained among Austria's social elite that the Realschulen were training a slightly different cohort. With the economic boom around 1900, the expectations of lower-middle-class families had expanded, not least in industrializing Bohemia-Moravia, and over twenty years the number of Realschulen there doubled.

The Ruthas' aspirations for Heinz therefore had clear vocational parameters, but their thinking matched the raised horizons of their generation and the next. Their son would have the opportunity to join that 3 percent of teenagers across Austria who attended secondary school.[10] Whether at Realschule or Gymnasium, this experience immediately fashioned a group with a sense of its own social status, one being molded to become leaders. The national outlook of the cohort was also highly likely to be enhanced, especially if, as in Prague, many pupils could sense every day their German minority status in a Czech nationalist environment.

The New Town Realschule's annual reports suggest that Heinz's education was typical for German pupils in the Bohemian Realschulen.[11] Alongside a weekly curriculum of German, mathematics, geography, natural history, religion, and other staples, it privileged the German cultural heritage of Bohemia while placing it in a framework that focused on the Habsburg dynasty and its achievements. Thus in Heinz's second year, his prescribed history textbook for the medieval period emphasized the higher culture that German colonists had brought to Bohemia in the thirteenth century. Emperor Charles IV had allegedly affirmed it by founding Prague's first "German university" as an academic center for the region and for Germany as a whole.[12] In their free time pupils were encouraged to explore the school library, letting their imaginations develop through immersion in the myths and stories of Austria or German Bohemia; for Heinz it was a significant continuation of "reform pedagogy."[13] And, in keeping with a governmental ruling of 1875, the physical side to Germanness was emphasized twice a week when pupils were compulsorily drilled in Turner gymnastics.

Imperial allegiance was then asserted in commemorative days that punctuated the academic calendar. In 1910–1911, for instance, not only was the emperor's eightieth birthday celebrated at the start of the academic year, but the school, in common with others across Austria, organized a special "patriotic commemorative day" to recall once again his golden jubilee of 1908. A celebratory mass was followed by choral singing, a speech by the teacher of Catholicism, and a rousing rendition of the imperial anthem.[14]

Within the boys' thirty-hour week of formal curriculum there seems to have been little attention paid to the Czech culture that surrounded them, even though seven Czech children were present in Heinz's class (and fifty in the school as a whole). The priority was clear when it came to language teaching. Compulsorily, he had to take five or six hours of French per week, and it became his main foreign language thereafter, but there was no automatic instruction in Bohemia's other provincial language. Through the infamous Article 19 of the Austrian Constitution of 1867, Bohemia's German leadership had sabotaged any chance of formal bilingualism in the schools by outlawing any forced learning of a second language.[15] German-speaking pupils would only learn Czech if their parents allowed them to opt for the subject. In fact, the school records show that Heinz, despite his earlier Czech experience, was one of the vast majority of his class who "voluntarily" chose two hours of weekly instruction in Czech.[16] But the secondary status of the language was self-evident, and although Heinz excelled in it, it was his last attempt at the subject. His generation had inherited a bitter linguistic legacy, one enshrined in law, that helped to distort its perception of Czech-speakers and rationalize them as a distinct breed of people.

Heinz's first experience of Prague is hard to reconstruct because in later years he barely recalled it.[17] Clearly in his own mind it paled in comparison to the five years of education and maturing he would acquire in Böhmisch Leipa, where he would next continue his studies. We can speculate that, even if he did not witness the violent Czech-German clashes that had beset Prague in 1908, he probably experienced the rising German *völkisch* sentiment in Vinohrady and may have balked at Czech and Jewish cultural differences, that cosmopolitan peculiarity that permeated his own classroom. His transfer to the Leipa Realschule may simply reflect a desire to be nearer Kunnersdorf or may have been long foreseen. For it was common for pupils to divide their secondary schooling; the first school was treated as a preliminary step before entry into what by the twentieth century was viewed as the distinctive life-stage of adolescence or "youth."

Certainly, his move was not caused by academic or financial weakness. In both years in Prague, he was one of a handful of pupils who passed with distinction, with no weakness in any subject, even Turner gymnastics. That itself would have qualified him for exemption from tuition fees, as would sheer poverty.[18] But the Rutha family's resources were not meager anyway. When in 1910 the New Town school had held a biannual collection among its pupils to raise funds for extra school equipment, Heinz's contribution of 1.50 crowns was one of the most generous in the class.[19] In the summer of 1911 he proceeded to his new Realschule with a glowing academic record, but also perhaps with a clearer grasp of a disturbing non-German world, one that was a direct contrast to the proud German stronghold of Böhmisch Leipa.

A GERMAN BASTION

Since 1998, the space outside Rutha's Leipa school, now known as Liberation Square, has contained a monument in red granite commemorating the military exploits of the Czechoslovak Legion in the twentieth century. Its purpose, the inscription reads, is to serve as a "symbol of patriotism for our future generations." There is a striking disjunction between this memorial, with its implications of a dominant Czech historical memory in Leipa, and the realities of the town before 1945. Prior to the expulsion of Germans and the influx of Czechs into what became Česká Lípa, Leipa had been a German-dominated bastion with only a small Czech-speaking minority.

As *böhmisch* was the usual German term for "Czech," the name "Böhmisch Leipa" had always hinted at a Slav origin for the settlement. Not surprisingly, local German nationalists around 1900 had tried to proclaim German possession by changing the town's name to "Deutsch Leipa" or at least "Leipa in Böhmen."[20] They did not succeed. But Leipa's German and dynastic loyalties were already notorious across the Bohemian lands. They were encapsulated in the space outside the Realschule, then known as Joseph Square and containing a bronze bust of Emperor Joseph II that weighed 600 kilograms. As with the current Czech legionary memorial, this sculpture from 1882 was a collective memory selected from the past and used for didactic purposes. Like so many German communities across northern Bohemia, the anxious Leipa Germans in the 1880s were venerating Joseph II for trying to centralize Austria and impose German uniformity a century earlier. The bust, its richness commensurate with local allegiances, symbolized Leipa's dynastic loyalty. But even more, it underlined the security that German Bohemians obtained through their links with German Austrians to the south, and their collective north-Bohemian stand against rising Czech demands for a federal empire.[21]

Leipa's own civic pride was fostered in the late nineteenth century, partly through some energetic mayors who took full advantage of Austria's wide-ranging local council autonomy. In a liberal spirit of regulating the urban environment progressively, they laid out an impressive town park and channeled the River Polzen in order to create, in extravagant local parlance, a "Böhmisch Leipa Venice."[22] Their aspirations were evident in the town hall, which, as in Reichenberg, was renovated in neo-Gothic style (1884) to match that on the Ringstrasse in Vienna. By the turn of the century, a new hospital, theater, courthouse, and abattoir (in Secessionist style) bolstered Leipa's confidence as a self-sufficient community. The evolution was accelerated because this was a key railway junction where six lines converged across northern Bohemia, making it a hub of social and commercial traffic. Moreover, one of the town's most illustrious sons was Franz Schmeykal, the German liberal leader in Prague. Even if by the 1880s Schmeykal's defense of German interests was already deemed inadequate by Leipa's clamoring *völkisch* elements, the town was still bathing in his reflected glory as it asserted its nationalist credentials. With his slogan, "Germans of Bohemia be united and strong," Schmeykal retained a presence long after his death in 1896, commemorated in street name and sculpture: the council erected a statue, twice life-size, on the edge of the town park.

And by 1900 Leipa had an extra reason to boast: it was now a famous town of schools. Since the local elite in the 1860s, after a decade of Habsburg absolutism, typically backed a liberal drive for wider secondary education across the Bohemian lands, the council in 1863 founded a full Realschule to cater for demands that its long-established Gymnasium was failing to meet. The Realschule lay at the heart of the German community both geographically and politically, viewed as an integral part of Leipa's civic achievement and funded by the council for thirty years (fig.7). Even after the state assumed control in 1892, the council's input was retained, for the headmaster was always an elected councilor and the town hall continued to pump in 200,000 crowns in the years up to 1914.[23]

The celebrations for the Realschule's golden jubilee in July 1913 are vividly revealing. They show a school fully on par with the more prestigious Gymnasium in its self-perception, bearing quality traditions and a mission of molding Leipa youth in the service of both the German *Volk* and the Austrian emperor: in short, a holistic *Heimat* education. On the festive day, much of the town was decked in flags as a witness to the school's community role. The teachers and their guests, who included alumni, delegates from neighboring schools, and the whole of the Leipa council, first attended a performance of Mozart's coronation mass, then processed to the town's gymnastics hall for a series of eulogies.[24] These unanimously sounded a local nationalist note in recalling the school's past achievements and its future direction. To thunderous applause, one councilor pressed the school to remain "a cultivator of German character, German beliefs and German feelings." The head of the Gymnasium urged the Leipa schools to carry on producing true German men for the benefit of the German people. And on behalf of the students, a precocious pupil spoke up for youth as embodying the promise of both nation and fatherland: "If youth is corrupted, then the *Volk* perishes . . . Contemporary youth is Austria's future."[25]

It would be misleading to interpret this event as unadulterated national chauvinism. In his laudatory historical review, the headmaster, Anton Pechmann, scored few nationalist points and even expressed regret that the Czech language had for so long not been compulsory in German secondary schools. But he too ended the proceedings with the assurance that youth would be educated as Germans with a "burning love for our German people."[26]

As spelled out here, the role of the Leipa Realschule, in common with thousands of other secondary schools, was to mold adolescents, guiding them from boyhood into the adult world. Since the mid-nineteenth century, as secondary education had expanded across Europe, a new life-stage of youth *(Jugend)* had been created due to middle-class aspirations. It meant that the onset of adulthood was now being delayed for an elite group of adolescents who were trained in a spirit of strict conformity within the confines of the secondary school.[27] As a day school, the Leipa Realschule's control over its pupils, in loco parentis, might not be as absolute as that of an English public school, but it still dictated most of the adolescents' daily timetable and presumed to instruct parents or guardians on how best to reinforce the school's supervisory lead. The institutional framework, with its rules and traditions, naturally honed a conservative social outlook, shaping pupils' self-perception as a privileged male cohort. And blended with this in Leipa was a national exclusivity: a school with few non-Germans, a town with a strong *völkisch* stamp where Czechs or Jews were less than 5 percent of the population.[28]

This environment ensured that Heinz Rutha would be drilled in both social and national conformity. Not surprisingly, others prominent in the interwar Sudeten German nationalist movement were passing through the same prism at this time: Otto Kletzl, a year ahead at the Realschule, and Ernst Kundt at the Gymnasium. Like theirs, Rutha's formal schooling was to be only one element in the *Heimat* training that Leipa supplied; more significant, as we will see, was the romantic world opened up by the local youth movement. It was a dual education, but its two wings were complementary.

Rutha's five years at the Realschule shaped his evolution as an independent-minded individual with a thirst for learning. Once again he entered an all-male school as an outsider, as one of only three boys in a class of forty-four who had transferred from another Realschule.[29] Once again his personal circumstances encouraged self-reliance. While he must have visited Kunnersdorf regularly, his parents had arranged for him to board in the town, not with his sister Marie and her husband Franz Effert but with a wealthy Aunt Berta, a relation of Polifka.[30] It was a reflection of the boy's diligence and his early ability to compartmentalize his affairs that this arrangement did not detract from his studies. In each of his years at the Realschule he was one of a small group who secured a distinction.

Since Rutha joined the school in September 1911 and completed his final oral examination in July 1916, the Great War cut right across his education. His professors were gradually enlisted and replaced with supply teachers. His class, for the same reason, had dwindled to only six pupils in his final year. And from April 1915, when a garrison was quartered in Leipa and requisitioned the Realschule building, the school was forced to share accommodation with the Gymnasium and restrict its teaching to half days only.[31] The town, as portrayed later in a novel by Karel Poláček, who was briefly stationed there, became a training camp for the reserve of an infantry regiment recruited from the Czech-speaking region of eastern Bohemia. Yet despite its billeting among eleven thousand German inhabitants, evidence of any nationalist tension was minimal. The local authorities, while eager to display their German allegiance and brotherhood with the German Reich, were never less than enthusiastic in their loyalty to the Habsburg monarchy; they seem to have viewed the Czech regiment as a partner in the patriotic struggle and even celebrated its exploits at the front.[32]

In the same way, although the war clearly disrupted the Realschule's daily existence, it accelerated that prewar national-patriotic philosophy that had been just as evident in Rutha's Prague schooling. While usually the academic calendar was studded with dynastic anniversaries and patriotic reminders (as in October 1913 when the centenary of Austria's victory over Napoleon was specially recalled in history lessons),[33] from September 1914 the school hierarchy was speedily attuned to the contemporary crisis and understood its duty to prepare students for imminent imperial service. The teachers led by example, subscribing to government war bonds and contributing a percentage of their salary to the war effort. Some teachers enlisted and the pupils would learn they had won medals for bravery on the battlefield. Others became martyrs for the school, like Rutha's energetic class teacher of 1912–1913 who was reported to have died a hero's death in the Balkans.[34]

As the hostilities continued, the curriculum was duly adjusted. Shooting practice, which a few pupils in the upper grades had volunteered for in peacetime, gave way by 1916 to compulsory military training, held once a month under the supervision of the Czech regiment.[35] Written work too began to assume a martial-patriotic vein. In his last year at the school, Rutha was writing free essay compositions on subjects like "How true love of the

fatherland is expressed" and "Dying for the fatherland is sweet and glorious." For the final written examination in German in June 1916, the candidates had a choice of patriotic themes to prepare in advance. Between
them they opted for either "The former glorious conduct of our current campaign," or "War is terrible like the plagues of heaven, but it is good and like
them it is fateful." Implicit in these topics was a confidence about Austria's
future, a belief that life was a moral struggle and sacrifice inevitable on
behalf of some higher cause—ideals that the wartime school was doggedly
inculcating in its pupils.[36]

Offering us a personal microstudy of a young German Bohemian, there is
no doubt that Heinz Rutha subscribed to these values and acquired something of the Austrian patriotism that the Habsburg state had long tried to
promote in its secondary schools. But equally, his patriotism was strongly
infused with German Bohemian loyalties nurtured inside and outside the
classroom. For over three years, partly on his own initiative, his was a dual
education, the life at school increasingly playing second fiddle to enthusiastic involvement in the regional youth movement. It was that which formed
the real base upon which he would develop his singular brand of national
idealism. Not least, by the middle of the war he would rise meteorically to
become one of German Bohemia's main youth leaders.

THE WANDERVOGEL VISION

For many German nationalist leaders in interwar Czechoslovakia, taking
part in the Wandervogel youth movement in Bohemia had been a formative
experience. It created a framework of bonding for a generation of young men,
tying them into a fraternal union that, if at first escapist and aloof from the
world, was jolted in a more practical direction when they experienced the
sacrifice of the Great War. Theirs was a *völkisch* mission explicitly tied to
the Bohemian landscape, its past and future. It was one that proclaimed a
regeneration of German society through youth, seeking to shape a traditional "national community" *[Volksgemeinschaft]* alongside the Czechs, and
specifically eschewing the road of bourgeois party politics to achieve that
aim. Refocused by the war, the vision was entrusted to the first Wandervogel generation in postwar Czechoslovak politics and culture, its permuta-
tions clear in many branches of interwar Sudeten German development.

Despite this, the Bohemian Wandervogel phenomenon has received little attention from historians. Apart from one recent Czech study, the focus has either been documentary or a simple chronicle of the Wandervogel's evolution; or, as in the case of Johannes Stauda's classic account, the author was closely affiliated to the movement and lacked critical detachment.[37] Since Wandervogel activists often argued that only former members could really empathize with the youth movement, the result has been a failure to submit it to rigorous analysis.

In the Bohemian lands the Wandervogel acquired special native traits due to the Czech surroundings and the wider Austrian context. But its origins lay in Germany, where in 1901 on the outskirts of Berlin, a society was established to organize excursions into the countryside for middle-class secondary school boys. The adopted name "Wandervogel"—"wandering bird"—underlined both its mission to commune with nature and its didactic agenda, conjuring up an image of the wandering scholar of the Middle Ages. In essence, the Wandervogel might be viewed as just one element in a cyclical revolt by youth against the values of the preceding generation, but specifically, they were middle-class urban youths who were supposedly rejecting one dimension of modern Germany: their parents' bourgeois lifestyle with its stuffy conventions and regulations, its focus on economic progress and modernity.

The Wandervögel perceived this nineteenth century value system—liberal and rational—as in crisis anyway, unable to offer solutions to the burgeoning social and political tensions besetting capitalist Wilhelmine Germany. They themselves, although in a sense rebelling, offered a conservative direction in response to contemporary insecurities and in keeping with a neoromantic nationalist outlook. In 1887, one German sociologist, Ferdinand Tönnies, had set out a stark polarity between modern industrial society *[Gesellschaft]*—cold, rational, and self-centered—and traditional rural society *[Gemeinschaft]* which, allegedly, "signified a social community regulated by inner feelings, spontaneity, friendship, warmth and emotion."[38] Through a youth network, the Wandervogel aimed to reaffirm this traditional national community across Germany. It was extremely idealistic in terms of the past and the future, building on a mythical image of past society, then using this as the basis for future regeneration.

In this romantic vision the Wandervogel's main vehicle was the regular "expedition" into the countryside. There the youth group would educate itself by communing with nature, while in its home base it established a den *[Nest]* where members bonded together at the weekend, exchanging ideas and singing folk songs. A small literature quickly emerged to support their personal and group development. Books of maxims dwelled on the importance of the spiritual journey against the superficiality of the world, and set out the virtues expected of Wandervogel leaders, since moral leadership in each group was essential.[39]

Inevitably perhaps, as the organization expanded across Germany (twenty-five thousand members by 1914), it splintered into sects because of disagreements. One enduring issue, never really resolved, was how far youths should educate themselves independently or whether they required guidance from sympathetic adults. From the start, the theory that Wandervogel groups were autonomous was debatable, for the "youth protest" was usually encouraged and steered by youthful adults.[40] Local branches were often founded by an enthusiastic *völkisch* teacher, who continued to act as an adviser or at least mediator with the local school; and for most groups, a local "council of parents and friends" *[Eltern- und Freundenrat] (Eufrat)* kept an eye on activities. And although the movement certainly generated charismatic youth leaders from within, the actual limits of social rebellion were clear. It retained autonomy, distinguishing it from other socially integrated youth groups like the Scouts, something famously reaffirmed in October 1913 at a meeting of independent youth groups on Hoher Meissner near Kassel. But its activities were always more about constructing an alternative edifice, parallel to existing society, than about direct subversion.

The spread of the Wandervogel into Austria came via several routes, penetrating slowly across the border and finding fertile soil among local pedagogues.[41] Particularly it was in north Bohemia that some *völkisch* secondary school teachers, enthused by the reform pedagogy of the early twentieth century, moved to encourage extracurricular activities and streamline their pupils in a healthy nationalist lifestyle. Most striking was Karl Metzner, a mathematics teacher in Leitmeritz, whose own school education in the 1890s had encompassed years in *völkisch* Leipa and in the German villages of southern Bohemia; on his own admission he was inspired by notorious nationalist demagogues like Georg von Schönerer. In 1907 he created a school rowing club at Leitmeritz (equating it to the founding of Eton, the English public school) and in the winter of 1908–1909 took his boys to a ski camp in the mountains.[42]

Meanwhile, a second Wandervogel godfather appeared in Hans Mautschka, an ascetic language student at Prague's German university. Inspired by many teetotal "wandering birds" from Germany, Mautschka in April 1911, together with fellow students like Johannes Stauda, founded a Prague group and took it on its first trip into the countryside. The sense of a mission on behalf of youth and *Heimat* could only increase when, after long hikes through simple villages and cornfields, the band returned to the "stony sea of houses" that was Prague, full of its "dandies and flirts with their high-heels and uplifted breasts." Then, as Mautschka observed, "one realized precisely how far the 'culture' of humanity was embedded in a lack of culture."[43]

To challenge this trend, he dispatched hundreds of letters to the provinces in order to stimulate an Austrian Wandervogel movement, and after a healthy response (including eager support from pioneers like Metzner) convened a first regional meeting or *Gautag*. From Prague, Leitmeritz, Reichenberg, and even Vienna, small groups of teenagers and their mentors converged in June 1911 on the rural idyll of Hirschberg (near Leipa) to brainstorm the way forward. They agreed to create an independent, loosely organized Austrian Wandervogel. Undoubtedly at this time they had only a basic notion of how it all might develop; in Bohemia, its structure and purpose would really materialize as it expanded across German-speaking communities in the next two years. From May 1912 Metzner began to issue a common journal for Wandervogel groups in Bohemia called *Burschen heraus! (Lads Get Out!)*. It was a pugnacious, stirring title, and early on he felt the need to defend it against critics: "We are really dealing here with great upheavals! But not in the field of social organization—rather, in the field of self-education and the individual's philosophy of life . . . Our culture has become an urban culture. The pale-cheeked, narrow-chested and *blasé* individual is its representative. Just take a look at the weaklings who fill our schools! . . . Beer and tobacco, flirting and nights of roaming form the ideal of so many young people today; this should be changed."[44]

The transformation would be through a Wandervogel network, groups of secondary school boys aged ten to eighteen, who would explore the natural world of their Bohemian *Heimat* and shun the false culture that had crept into everyday bourgeois life. To the aid of a public who allegedly were slaves to decadence, a phalanx of young men would arise, healthy in body and spirit, who from their own experiences and tight comradeship would reassert "true" German practices in society.[45] Both Mautschka and Metzner were inclined from their background to favor a physical toughening of boys and, from the start, to employ military metaphors: "In Bohemia there sits a high-ranking general, commanding all Bohemian Wandervogel battalions which on his signal can be mobilized," wrote Metzner in June 1913.[46] In line with this, cultivating leadership in each Wandervogel group was essential, as was voluntary obedience to the youth hierarchy that emerged.

As in Germany, this naturally provoked questions about where power lay in the movement and how far adults should participate. Metzner for one always insisted on youth being autonomous, their local groups only loosely linked in a regional organization. Despite his own adult mentoring, he expected the "birds" to be in control, and initiatives, like leadership, to arise from their own ranks rather than descend from above. However, according to Austrian law, schoolchildren were forbidden from joining official associations, so each Wandervogel branch was bound to be linked to a school and a *Eufrat*.[47] Metzner typically viewed the *Eufrat* as superfluous and obstructive unless the local Wandervögel needed special protection. Thus, inevitably, tensions could arise between the autonomy of youth and the role of adult pedagogues, all the more so when older adolescents matured into adults yet still wished to continue advising their protégés.

With a *Heimat* focus that was Bohemian and Austrian, it was not surprising that the enthusiasts at Hirschberg decided to launch a movement independent of Germany. While always retaining some links to Reich brethren, the Bohemian Wandervogel from the start was stamped with its own German Bohemian *völkisch* agenda because of its specific Czech-German environment. As one Wandervogel magazine noted, "On this classic battleground where the Czechs are greedily striving to rip off whole scraps of German flesh, any spiritual movement without a *völkisch* basis is unthinkable."[48] Those who took the lead, like Metzner or Stauda, were what we might term typical nationalist missionaries from the decade before the Great War, strong evidence that it was secondary school teachers (even more than primary school) who were crucial to this new mobilization on behalf of the *Heimat*.[49] Indeed, precisely these teachers could tap into the natural adolescent spirit, adventurous and idealistic, and twist it in a nationalist direction.

In the decade before 1914, the wider context for this new mission was continued deadlock in Czech-German party politics in Prague and Vienna, and a common nationalist illusion that a united Czech crusade was steadily conquering the Bohemian lands. These factors had produced many local nationalist initiatives to protect German interests. Most significant was the German National Council *[Deutscher Volksrat]*, established near Leitmeritz in 1903 by a charismatic doctor, Wenzel Titta, as an organization that would transcend political parties in order to galvanize German unity. Although it had limited success, the *Volksrat* made a lot of noise and set a clear example for nationalist German Bohemians in later decades. Above all, Titta strove to sabotage any Czech-German compromise, and vociferously called for a radical division of Bohemia into two national sectors with their own administrations.[50] In March 1911, hoping to boost publicity and unity among *völkisch* groups, he convened a "cultural assembly" in Prague. There one illustrious university professor, August Sauer, made an impassioned speech against the Czech advance in Bohemia. It was vital, he said, to ensure, on the (supposedly) efficient Czech model, a much tighter link between German national culture and its people.[51]

Both Metzner and Mautschka were present to hear this siren. It spurred them on to Hirschberg three months later, and it informed their picture of the Wandervogel's mission in Bohemia. Alongside the campaign against bourgeois decadence, the Wandervogel youths were to be the vanguard of true Bohemian Germanness in its nationalist struggle. In the columns of *Burschen heraus,* elders who retained close links to *völkisch* defense societies duly warned about the struggle raging around the "hard-pressed national community," the absence of "true Germanness" in society, and the Wandervogel's sacred duty to lead people along the correct road.[52] Through fortifying themselves physically and spiritually in nature, German youth would be ready to meet the Czech challenge. For in an era "when the national element has come more strongly to the fore than in any other period, so that in Austria to be German means to fight," it was the Wandervogel who would supply a "more powerful, healthy-thinking male blow *[Männerschlag]*."[53]

Admittedly, despite this public rhetoric, the angry anti-Czech dimension of the Bohemian Wandervogel before 1914 was not always apparent. There was a discrepancy between the nationalism of teachers like Metzner and their less fervent adolescent pupils for whom hiking was often a simple adventure. Some Wandervogel groups even reported back from their rural expeditions that the Czechs they encountered were kind, hospitable, and wholly lacking in hostility. Yet the public message propagated via *Burschen heraus* often spoke differently about a defensive anti-Czech mission, for that was the outlook of the elders. After one expedition when Mautschka's Wandervögel had marched through a Czech village and been greeted merrily by its inhabitants, he himself likened the experience to that of a garrison marching through enemy territory.[54]

Fashioned by its peculiar environment, the Bohemians' loose position within a federal Austrian Wandervogel movement quickly became untenable. While tensions arose partly because many Bohemian Wandervögel felt they had interests distinct from their "Alpine" comrades to the south, there were also fundamental differences over organization. The leaders of the federation *[Bund]* in Vienna believed in a tightly centralized body where they would cooperate closely with a network of *Eufräte* in monitoring local branches, confirming group leaders and even having a veto over all Wandervogel expeditions. It was a view naturally anathema to those like Metzner who championed "autonomous youth," and it led, as in Germany, to a rapid splintering of the Austrian organization.

When the Bohemians held their annual Gautag in May 1913, they officially announced autonomy (a *Gau Deutschböhmen*) within the Austrian federation, electing as their first leader or *Gauwart* the head of the Prague Wandervogel, Karl Günther, with Metzner as treasurer. The move led to a showdown at a *Bundestag* in Krems near Vienna, where Wandervogel leaders from Moravia and the Alpine lands effectively ostracized the autonomists.[55] Although a few Bohemian groups stayed loyal to the Bund, and the split caused some splintering on loyalist lines in Prague, the chief result of the watershed was to assert a more nationalist agenda for Bohemian Wandervögel in their own interests. It was at this time that Metzner moved closer to Titta's National Council, agreeing to head a youth branch of the council from a base at Leitmeritz. For many Bohemian leaders, the priority was to sharpen the vision of German Bohemian youth; some might regret the split from the Bund and periodically appeal for reconciliation, but that had to wait until wartime.

Meanwhile, on the eve of war, the Bohemian Wandervogel was becoming more cohesive. A highpoint was reached in May 1914 when it met for its fourth Gautag in the small mountain town of Duppau. The presence of delegates from Germany was testament to how, since the standoff with Austria, Karl Günther and other leaders had drawn closer to the Reich and promoted the notion of a *Wandervogeldeutschland*.[56] Moreover, the number of Bohemian groups had dramatically mushroomed (to sixteen) since 1913, so over three hundred members assembled for the first time. With their leaders keen to reinforce the movement's identity through joint activities, the teenagers seem to have successfully bonded together, camping, singing, and competing in sports. The new editor of *Burschen heraus*, Johannes Stauda, captured the spirit, describing youths singing "on the market place until the moon's crescent appeared over the roofs and steeples and the little town lay in deep soft evening shadows, for no shameless street lighting disturbed the evening slumber there." His verdict was that a new sense of Bohemian identity was forged: "We have moved forward and the next Gautag will find us even more internally solid and mature."[57]

It is quite likely that Heinz Rutha took part in the Duppau experience as a delegate from the Wandervogel group at Böhmisch Leipa. The Leipa branch had been created in 1912, the fourth in Bohemia. It was initially the work of Karl Grund, who like so many early activists had passed through the German university in Prague, completed military service, and advocated toughening up adolescents through sport.[58] Typically, when Grund left Leipa in January 1913, his place as overall mentor was taken by a teacher from the local Realschule, Karl Markus. Markus had joined Rutha's school the previous September to teach German, French, and physical education. Although the official Wandervogel leader was Erich Pelikan, a pupil two years senior to Rutha, it was Markus who acted as the group's real advisor, establishing a *Eufrat,* supervising expeditions and war games, and stimulating recruitment through the school.

Markus's role highlights for us again the ambiguity over adult participation. The Leipa Realschule, unlike some of its contemporaries, fully condoned the local Wandervogel as a "new type of sporting activity," particularly as it had adult supervision; indeed, in July 1913 Markus was the main delegate on behalf of the Leipa *Eufrat* at the Austrian Bundestag in Krems.[59] Yet with the Bohemians' expulsion from the Bund, their leadership was far more critical of unnecessary adult interference. In late 1913, with one eye on Markus's Leipa group, Gauwart Günther advised elders not to go too far, not to remove the initiative from what was essentially a movement of youth.[60]

Despite this, the reports from Leipa that reached *Burschen heraus* from early 1913 suggest that the group under "Leader" Pelikan was usually left to its own devices to ramble in the countryside. In February the boys made their first independent expedition, walking northwards across the German border into Saxony; in July they were more ambitious, hiking for a whole month in western Bohemia and covering five hundred miles on foot.[61] While Rutha seems to have joined the group by that summer, one of a school influx that raised its number to thirty, we do not know what motivated him. We can only speculate that after his Prague sojourn he was attracted by the antiurban and *völkisch* agenda, but also by the male camaraderie and probably the charisma of somebody like Otto Kletzl. Kletzl was a few months

younger than Rutha but a year above him in the Realschule; his brother
Erich was in Rutha's class. The outlook of the Kletzl brothers, who hailed
from Leipa, is evinced by their willing participation in school activities
(where Erich sang a solo during the school's golden jubilee) and, more
importantly, by their close familial tie to Wenzel Titta, the pioneer of the
German National Council. By late 1913, Otto Kletzl was writing the Leipa
report for *Burschen heraus,* enumerating trips and the weekends spent creating their own den.[62] Some way off from the town, it was meticulously
constructed as a base for Wandervogel bonding: "Now we've finally finished
setting up our den after some strenuous efforts in the last few weeks. A long
table, a couple of benches and chairs, a big cupboard, several pictures and a
huge kitchen stove, the pride of our den—these form the somewhat meager
furniture. So on 14 December we held the first meeting here. E. Pelikan and
Professor Markus spoke a few words to the assembled Wandervögel, then
we sang many beautiful songs and our 'orchestra' consisting of two fiddles,
one mandolin, one cello and three guitars, played for us many beautiful
pieces."[63]

By 1914 Rutha was fully enveloped in this Wandervogel lifestyle. Since at
school Markus was now in charge of his class, teaching him German, the
Wandervogel mission was pedagogically integrated, not just a weekend
hobby. While the Leipa den was the local base for group unity, for discussing German Bohemian culture or the ideas of *Burschen heraus,* the major
bonding experience remained the adventures in the rural wild. There, for
instance in a winter camp in the Riesengebirge at New Year 1914, the chance
could be seized for bonding with dozens of teenagers from branches across
northern Bohemia. After an evening spent exchanging stories and songs,
the youths set off on 1 January for the Plattenberg peak, struggling through
a bleak landscape. As one participant recalled, "There unfolded before us on
the snow caps a magnificent panorama of the whole Riesengebirge that
seemed like a fairy-tale mirage. On all sides stretched the ever beautiful,
ever majestic mountainous world in infinite ranges, crest behind crest, ridge
behind ridge, all glittering in a regal bejeweled sky."[64] This communing with
an eternal landscape was enhanced by a personal bond to like-minded adolescents; a sense of common ownership grew as they jointly walked the
"national" mountains and valleys.

Memories of acting out a youth mission deeply affected the hundreds who
by 1914 made up the Bohemian Wandervogel. But theirs was never a lone
voice. Precisely in the last years of peace other youth groups had emerged as

competitors, most strikingly the socialist and Catholic movements with idealistic goals of their own. In prewar Austria, Bohemia became a key center for socialist youth, with strong recruitment in the borderland German towns where local branches by 1913 numbered 222; if like the Wandervogel they hiked and expected abstinence from alcohol and other bourgeois vices, their fight otherwise was geared toward working-class adolescents and carefully controlled by the party machinery.[65] Similarly, an independent Catholic youth organization grew up after 1907 and numbered seventy-six groups in Bohemia on the eve of war. While principally challenging socialism, it had the potential to compete with the Wandervogel, for it too scorned the depravity of modern society and offered adolescents a (Christian) rebirth as the solution.[66]

Where the Wandervogel was distinctive was not so much in its outdoor expeditions and the moral maxims expounded in *Burschen heraus*—for by 1913 a new organization, the Scouts *[Pfadfinder]*, would take up that baton too in Bohemia. Rather, it excelled through its nationalist focus—not international like the socialists, Catholics, and Scouts—and particularly its obsession with regenerating German Bohemia in the face of the Czech antagonist. Thus Rudolf Feldberger, one of Rutha's later idols, explained, "from this young generation a new nation will arise and . . . for our descendants it will be better in the future when this purifying stream has rushed through society."[67]

Rutha had entered the Leipa Wandervogel when it was confidently expanding and already contained energetic role models. His branch was fully committed to a German Bohemian agenda, for in early 1914 its *Eufrat* under Markus approved secession from the Austrian Bund. Since the grooming of new leaders was a precept of the Wandervogel, it was natural that Rutha as a precocious seventeen-year-old came quickly to the forefront of his group, moving into a senior role as Pelikan and others departed. The result by June 1914, in the aftermath of Duppau, was Rutha's first published statement, a report for *Burschen heraus*. Written in a formulaic "youth style," it nevertheless captures his own idealism:

> We've been leading a lively, merry life and have only good to report. Returning from the excellent Whitsun trip [to Duppau], our strapping little ones through their enthusiastic stories have recruited a cluster of new capable lads who, I hope, will grow into true Wandervögel. . . . Because of the adverse weather we have postponed our already planned parents' excursion

until the end of June. First the parents' council wants to hold its foundation meeting. At the solstice we will all gather round the glowing flames of a simple fire outside in a forest glade; we already expect it to be very nice. In the holidays we will of course go off on expeditions, most on short trips, and a few of the elders for three to four weeks.[68]

It was when Rutha and other senior Leipa members were camping in the mountains of Upper Austria near Salzburg that a European war broke out and shattered their boyhood world.[69] Until then, the Bohemian Wander-vogel with almost a thousand adherents was still largely an escapist activity, divorced from reality, of little social or cultural importance. However, pushed on by some fervently nationalist teachers, its underlying anti-Czech and *völkisch* agenda was sowing seeds in youthful minds, encouraging a mass of German boys to view themselves as a select cohort with their own mission of defending "true culture" against alien encroachments. Rutha was one among many who was acquiring this mindset. At school, whether in Prague or Leipa, he had been drilled in Austrian patriotism and absorbed it to a degree. Yet louder than that supranational message was the German *völkisch* clamor of a holistic *Heimat* education; it was present in Oschitz, but he mainly learned it at the Leipa Realschule and had it reinforced in the congenial setting of the Wandervogel den. The youth movement sketched out an adventurous male crusade and provided a terrain for its fulfillment in the nationalist rural landscape. Its antithesis was everything alien—urban, "non-German," and morally suspect: exactly what he had glimpsed and shunned before he found security in the German bastion of Leipa.

That the future would be some kind of national battle already seemed to be implied in 1913–1914 in the rhetoric and war games sponsored by the Bohemian Wandervogel. But as Stauda suggested in the final prewar edition of *Burschen heraus,* for all its healthy numbers, the movement still had to prove its strength.[70] The war years of 1914–1918 would do this by chal-lenging its purpose during a military struggle and testing its actual levels of unity. New leaders like Rutha were pushed forward and forced, in the midst of male sacrifice, to reassess the character and aims of German Bohemian youth.

THREE

The Sacrifice

On 8 August 1914, a few days after the war erupted, Heinz Rutha's sister Friedel finally married her schoolteacher fiancé Franz Polifka.[1] Immediately afterward, Polifka and his brother-in-law Franz Effert, both of whom were reservists and among the first to be mobilized, departed for their regiments and different battle zones.

Their separate destinations mirrored the uncertainty that initially reigned over the Habsburg Empire's main military target—whether it was Serbia, which the army command envisaged crushing quickly, or Russia, clearly the greater threat and viewed as the priority by Germany. Reflecting this confusion, most of Austria-Hungary's Second Army was sent first against Serbia, only to be transferred weeks later to the eastern front. But its 9th Corps (recruited from northern Bohemia, and to which Polifka and Effert belonged) was split from the beginning, some brigades heading to the Balkans while others traveled east to face the Russians in Galicia. Polifka's unit arrived at the Serbian border and concentrated around the town of Šabac; there in mid-September, during a major battle with the Serbians, he was wounded and sent back to convalesce in Bohemia. Effert's unit had traveled straight to eastern Galicia, where it took part with heavy losses in the so-called "victory" of Komarów in late August; very soon he too was invalided out with dysentery and sent home for a brief respite.[2]

Between them, the brothers-in-law had experienced the sharp shock to Austrian military prestige on two fronts. Together, a few months later, they rejoined their units on the battlefield in Galicia with the goal of ejecting the Russians from the province. As the enemy retreated in mid-December, both were taken prisoner, just two out of two million Austro-Hungarians who would eventually languish in Russian captivity.[3] There began an interminable thirty-six-day transport deep into the Russian interior. First a long march on foot, then a train ride to an assembly station near Kiev to be registered as prisoners and categorized as Germans, then a rail journey to their end destination. The prison camp of Kattakurgan near Samarkand in central Asia was squalid, overcrowded, and an incubator for epidemics. There on 22 August, Polifka died of typhoid. The next day in Bad Kunnersdorf his wife gave birth to a son, Friedrich Heinrich. On 24 August, Effert too succumbed to typhoid in the camp hospital. On hearing the news, Marie, his wife, decided to sell up in Böhmisch Leipa and move with her two small children to Prague to be nearer her brother Richard.[4]

DEATH AND SELECTION

Heinz Rutha fully shared in this typical family tragedy. In later years he would take a special interest in the well-being of his nephew Friedrich (Fritz), who had lost a father. To gauge Rutha's own initial view of the war, we can only interpret his seemingly negative remark that hostilities had suddenly banished him and his Wandervögel from the mountains.[5] Alongside those who rushed to the colors or cheered the troops—what Hew Strachan has termed the "conspicuous froth" of war-enthusiasm in August 1914—there were many Germans of the Habsburg Empire who reacted, like their Czech compatriots, with passive acceptance or a sense of reluctant duty.[6] And despite the prewar martial tinge to its mission, ambiguous sentiments were present even in the Bohemian Wandervogel. In the words of one youth leader, "I curse the war because it brings discord into my calm beautiful world, irritates my peaceful heart. However I must bless it as the cleansing storm which may launch a fresher era. I hope we will live splendidly after the war."[7]

As the Wandervogel elders departed for the front and the first deaths were announced—Hans Mautschka in Serbia, Karl Grund in Galicia—those left behind had to make sense of the mounting sacrifice and how the new environment would change their youth mission. Thus Rudolf Feldberger, another elder, could not bring himself to "curse this terrible war" even though, early on at Šabac, it had claimed the life of his brother. For the all-embracing conflict seemed to offer the Wandervogel a practical focus and fresh opportunities; in view of the speed of events, where years were condensed into months, it might act as a catalyst on the nationalist mission.[8]

Not least, war accelerated as much as it disrupted the flow of members through the Bohemian Wandervogel ranks. Since over the first year of hostilities about a hundred senior members were called up, in line with conscription for those aged eighteen to forty-two, their juniors suddenly became "leaders," with all the significance that this title already conferred. When Karl Günther and Karl Metzner left for the front, Johannes Stauda, the editor of *Burschen heraus,* became acting Gauwart, hoping with the aid of the journal to build on the German Bohemian bonding he had witnessed at Duppau. The adjustments that occurred in Rutha's Böhmisch Leipa group were now typical. Into the shoes of the conscripted teacher Karl Markus there stepped the charismatic Rudolf Feldberger, who had entered the Wandervogel as a Prague student but was also a native of the Leipa region. At a meeting in December, attended by Stauda, Feldberger helped reorganize the Leipa *Eufrat* before departing to take up military duties. Over the next two years would exemplify a new type of "wandering bird" that constantly hovered between front and hinterland. In March 1915 two other Leipa leaders, Otto Kletzl and Willi Riewald, were also called up. As their comrades gathered in the moonlight near the Leipa den to serenade them with romantic songs, it was Heinz Rutha who was thrust forward to lead the group.[9]

Despite the depletions due to conscription, the organization had enough enthusiasts and grassroots initiatives to sustain some continuity during the war. In May 1915, Stauda could summon a respectable number of over two hundred to a Gautag on the Czech-German language border. Branch activity also owed much to devolution around the network (uninhibited by the adult control that always characterized Catholic and socialist youth groups).[10]

Rutha's Leipa branch serves as an example. In the winter of 1914 it went skiing; in the spring it began to make regular visits to Wrchhaben, a country den nearby owned by one of the Prague Wandervogel groups. Rutha assured *Burschen heraus* that the "lads," far from being idle, were roving across "our dear north Bohemia" more diligently than ever before.[11] And the escapist trips were increasingly interpreted patriotically, the mission refocused by the wartime sacrifice. Before his call-up, Kletzl, whose elder brother had already been killed, announced that the countryside must be explored whatever the weather: "It is doubly vital now that you are strong Wandervogel, now at this difficult time when every man is precious to the fatherland; we too want to contribute and help to strengthen our nation."[12]

The adult world of war unavoidably and steadily impinged on the adolescents, expanding the horizons of their youth mission. The evolution is one useful example of how the home front became closely tied to frontline sacrifice in wartime Austria-Hungary, something that historians are only now turning to study.[13] It was not just that the movement's early mentors were drafted—five hundred from across Austria by the end of 1915—but that many senior members like Feldberger continued to keep close contact with their local groups. Younger "birds" knew that the call-up to follow their elders would eventually come. They learned about the front at first hand from those on leave, as when Willi Riewald returned and was fêted in Leipa in March 1916.

Through letters and reports from elders in the field, *Burschen heraus* also constantly set evidence of frontline sacrifice before the younger members. They were encouraged to interpret a Wandervogel's role on the battlefield as an intense extension of the struggle at home. In April 1916 in one article, Rutha reminded the movement not to forget those at the front but to contact them with books and photographs. A Wandervogel's special virtues of gratitude and friendship ought now to embrace those leaders who, having donned the emperor's uniform, had entered a totally different life, one full of hours of bitter strife: "Th[eir] mental struggle for pure youth and its ideals is certainly the harder one."[14] This remark, as we will see, concealed a personal yearning on his own part. It also indicated how the war was a vehicle for accelerating the Wandervogel's prewar mission of regenerating the youth of the *Heimat*.

But how far this national mission was synonymous with the Habsburg Empire's war effort, how far it had a separate idealistic agenda to pursue, was more contentious. Before the war, of course, the Wandervogel creed had never been wholly esoteric and was sometimes given a very practical focus. In the summer of 1913, for example, Metzner had begun to organize a "land service" through the youth branch of Wenzel Titta's National Council; Wandervögel were encouraged to commune with workers of the soil by gathering in the German harvest. Such voluntary aid was repeated during the call-up of August 1914 (and thereafter), when a third of Wandervögel were involved, something matched in the Czech countryside by Czech Scouts. The work had a *völkisch* dimension, wholly in harmony with the

Wandervogel's core belief in landscape and soil as the essence of the nation, or—as Metzner once observed—that the fields of the countryside were the real source of the "people's strength."[15]

But the question soon arose of how youth should be integrated into state wartime mobilization. At stake, firstly, seemed to be the Wandervogel's highly prized "youth independence." In June 1915, in line with the empire's increasing mobilization of children, the Austrian authorities pronounced that all boys aged sixteen to eighteen should have premilitary training in order to prepare for imminent enlistment; youth groups and secondary schools were asked to cooperate. Some youth bodies, including Catholics and Social Democrats, initially agreed, and (as we have seen) some patriotic schools like Rutha's in Leipa duly began military training with the aid of the local Czech garrison. But there was also considerable opposition from teachers, youth leaders, and parents across Austria who saw it as an encroachment on the normal patterns of education. Many schools, notably in Bohemia, simply ignored the ordinance.[16]

On behalf of his organization, Stauda publicly rejected the training as an infringement of Wandervogel autonomy and a needless "playing at soldiers"; many military experts and serving soldiers also viewed it skeptically. Stauda, like Metzner, was anxious to isolate his recruits from such adult pursuits, but his stance toward military engagement was also ambiguous, rather on the lines of the movement's unspoken accommodation with local school authorities. For while accepting that members over eighteen like Feldberger had to undergo conventional military training, he claimed that the Wandervogel with its physical exercise and single-mindedness was already the best military schooling. Stauda here trod a fine line, trying to preserve Wandervogel exclusivity while acknowledging that it was playing a full part in the wartime struggle.[17]

It was an unresolved subject, and one that exposed something even more fundamental: for which *Heimat* was the Wandervogel really campaigning? From the front, Metzner warned Stauda against "Austrian" premilitary training because it would subsume the Wandervogel's Bohemian education under an Austrian umbrella: "Our state is a nationality state and the nations will rebel against any pure Austrian education."[18] As this suggested, the whole question of which fatherland the Wandervogel defended was fluid, testimony to the overlapping loyalties of those who hailed from German Bohemia. Although the Europe-wide struggle sometimes evoked vague pan-German identification in the pages of *Burschen heraus,* as a war against "the enemies of German existence," this rarely went much further than a fraternal standing shoulder to shoulder with Germany.[19] Usually the patriotic focus for Bohemian Wandervögel was a specific commitment to the German Bohemian *Heimat* in a primordial struggle with its Czech neighbor that was understated and implicit—as with the deliberate staging of the 1915 Gautag on the Czech-German language border.[20]

This was normally accompanied by feelings of allegiance to the German-led Austrian Empire. According to Stauda (who significantly had been born in Linz in Upper Austria and brought up in Germany), those meeting at the Gautag had sung the Austrian anthem with tears in their eyes.[21] But for many like Metzner (a "full Bohemian"), the Austrian sentiment had its limits. The context of German Bohemia was their immediate horizon and priority; the German-Austrian Empire was a secondary framework for allegiance, one in which adolescents like Rutha had formally been schooled. Both frameworks therefore constituted the fatherland, and those who made the ultimate sacrifice were doing so for both.

For German Bohemian teenagers the idea that a patriotic death was worthwhile, even welcome, was part of their school education. In the hands of Wandervogel elders it had an added potency. The boys were told of the supreme sacrifice of senior members like Mautschka who were dying at the front as patriots and youth-martyrs. Implicit was the idea that the Wandervogel prewar crusade of regeneration had now been extended from homeland to a foreign field. There, young men were demonstrating their true manly virtues of steadfastness and loyalty, dying for the nation, and by their very sacrifice were celebrating the eternity of youth over those left alive to grow old. Through the trenches, as George Mosse has observed, "youth was securely enthroned in life and in death."[22]

The message that death was something beautiful was most clearly set out by Feldberger, who himself by 1918 would personify the Wandervogel myth of youth sacrifice. In a short piece entitled "Death," published in April 1916, he challenged the frightening image of a grim reaper, urging Wandervögel instead to think of death as a world that might readily be embraced; similarly, life, for those who were at ease with their existence, could easily be shaken off. As the soil of the *Heimat* was endangered and the funeral bell was tolling, so it was time to think about dying: "So at sunset let us go and die for the homeland, let us fall, friend next to friend, for the fatherland."[23]

By 1916, larger Wandervogel meetings usually concluded with a vigil where all clustered round an outdoor fire to remember the ultimate sacrifice of older comrades. Most dramatic was the Bundestag in Linz in August 1916, which both Rutha and Feldberger attended. Around the evening fire a solemn oration was made by the Linz leader, Wilhelm Flatz, recalling those who now lay in distant graves. As sparks shot into the night sky and the flames illuminated the bright-red youthful faces, the orator imagined that an array of blue-uniformed spirits was conjured up behind the boys: "We see in spirit a blond-bearded warrior figure in our midst, upright before us, his hand pressed to a bright-red blood clot on his chest; we see a tall figure with a weathered pale face, a dark-red bullet hole in the middle of his forehead; we see a German boyish figure, his lips tightened in pain, with a blood-red gaping wound in his wheat-colored hair . . . We feel that you are with us, you dear dead brothers who fell before the enemy." The dead had gathered to participate with the living. Flatz spoke for those who remained at home, who could only ask the spirits to have patience with "wandering birds" who were left alive. Then the latter threw wreaths into the flames, one for each of the deceased.[24]

This constant impinging of front on hinterland deeply affected Rutha and does much to explain his wartime behavior. For while many of his mentors, whether from family, school, or Wandervogel, were conscripted to sacrifice themselves, he was forced to stay at home. Like Kletzl, who was the same age, Rutha should have been able to enlist as a one-year volunteer. But in March 1915 he was diagnosed with a heart defect and judged unfit for duty. As a result, when not at school in a class that had dwindled to six by 1916, he poured his energy and frustrations into Wandervogel activities. With many of his peers absent, his own scope for activity was wider; as an older adolescent—at eighteen passing into adulthood—he could cultivate among juniors a leadership role that seemed to exceed the usual model of youth autonomy.

Indeed, partly in order to make an impact on the home front, Rutha was one of a small number of older Wandervögel who moved in a racist direction, demanding much tighter criteria for youth recruitment. This requires explanation. At a time when the youth ranks were being shattered anyway, it may seem surprising that thoughts should suddenly turn to producing an elite German Aryan cohort. Yet the Wandervogel, with its secondary school focus, had always been selective; before the war Stauda had reminded leaders carefully to select only the best German adolescents from the masses available for membership.[25] Alongside this general maxim, the war emergency heightened many members' sense that they were an exclusive national cohort embarked on a moral mission against "outsiders." Their alleged heroism and sacrifice for the nation (or empire) might be contrasted with rumors soon circulating about Czech soldiers' apathy or even desertion on the eastern front. Thus there slowly emerged that stereotyping of German as loyal and Czech as disloyal, something readily credible to a *völkisch* Wandervogel, even if most German and Czech nationalists vaunted the crude distinction openly only from 1917.[26]

The Aryan (anti-Semitic) direction is harder to unravel, both in the Bohemian framework and from Rutha's perspective, but it probably owed as much to Viennese influence as to regional wartime circumstances. From the 1880s racial anti-Semitism, which under Georg von Schönerer had blossomed in Vienna, had also gained footholds in the communities of northern Bohemia.[27] For although the number identifying there as Jews might be minimal (officially only 3 percent in Reichenberg or Gablonz in 1910), the notion that the elusive Jew was a danger could appear logical to those of a *völkisch* mindset who felt nationally and economically on the defensive. And for many Wandervogel leaders, steeped in a nationalist and antimodern outlook, the Jewish "stranger" was naturally suspect. Apart from his supranational identity, flitting disloyally between Czech and German nationality, his common urban base and capitalist credentials jarred with the youth movement's rural idealism.

In this spirit, at the Krems Bundestag in 1913, the Austrian Wandervogel had bluntly demanded "racial purity" and added an Aryan paragraph to its statutes. There seems to have been no dissent from the German Bohemians present whose major concern anyway was the clash over centralization.[28] But thereafter an anti-Semitic direction was not at all clear-cut in the Bohemian Wandervogel. For all those who readily subscribed to such "purity" (like Metzner, who had once joined an anti-Semitic society at the University of Vienna), others like Mautschka or Stauda remained largely indifferent, not bothering to challenge Jews who were loyal to the Wandervogel ideal. As a result, and especially with no Viennese enforcement of the ruling, the Bohemians' stance on the eve of war was cloudy, probably emulating their cousins in Germany, where in 1913 branches had been allowed to decide for themselves. The subject was rather academic anyway unless, as in Prague, Jewish boys could be recruited; there some groups became Aryan-only, while the Smichow branch was one where Jewish members were accepted because they fervently declared their "German blood and spirit."[29]

Rutha's own anti-Semitism was first publicly displayed in 1915 when he formed what became known as the "Wrchhaben circle." If his prejudices had been stirred through early contact with Prague Jewry, they were certainly honed during his Leipa education. There his *völkisch* mindset would rigidly categorize those who were "non-German"—besides Czechs and gypsies, the Leipa Jews, who were a thriving community of over four hundred with an impressive synagogue[30]—and we might even infer something from the fact that Karl Markus, his schoolteacher, had been a Bohemian delegate to the Krems Bundestag where Aryanism triumphed. Since 1914 it also seems highly likely that Rutha had encountered some of the sixty thousand Jewish refugees who, as Russian troops advanced into Galicia, had flooded westwards into Bohemia. While their distinctive "uncivilized" appearance and their drain on wartime resources quickly fueled anti-Semitism, Rutha's perspective is clear from his racist warning by 1918 about the "Jewish current sneaking in from the East."[31]

Even so, what really focused Rutha's attention in 1915 seems to have been his contact with others who favored tight selection, and particularly with Oskar Just, a local youth leader. Before the war Just, a physically imposing and charismatic individual, had unilaterally started his own Wandervogel branch in Gablonz near Reichenberg, independent of any school control and tied directly to the Austrian organization in Vienna.[32] Judged unfit to be drafted, the nineteen-year-old departed to study architecture at the *Kunstakademie* in Vienna, joining a local Wandervogel branch and (undoubtedly) coming into direct contact with racist students. When he returned to north Bohemia at Christmas 1914, he moved to create the model Wandervogel group, constituted from the best Aryan specimens, and he quickly ejected seventeen individuals because of their laziness. Erich Frühauf, one of his assistants, noted later that "there was a process of sieving and choosing, for the lads had to represent an elite which he [Just] would present to the others."[33] On the basis of racial aesthetics, only Nordic types were now selected, blond and pure.

One inspiration for this was a popular Aryan didactic work by an Austrian reform pedagogue, Ferdinand Büttner. In his book, *Ich und meine fünf Jungen (My Five Lads and I)*, Büttner had described in meticulous fashion how before the war in Germany he created a home to train five boys, carefully selecting them for their blond racial purity. He aimed to rise above the "racial chaos" threatening the German nation and educate "a phalanx of noblemen in the physical and spiritual sense." Büttner's work had homo-erotic undercurrents, hinted at by the naked boys on its cover(fig.8). And he even admitted that the pedagogic relationship with his pupils might be termed "homosexual" in the purest sense of the word, though he took impressive measures to repress their physical sexual urges.[34]

Frühauf's candid memoirs highlight how Oskar Just copied Büttner's example: "Just in his choices was aiming at a particular ideal type, which in the statutes was expressed by the broad term 'German Aryan,' but which essentially was determined by a leader's personal taste within this frame-work. With Just one could very easily follow his viewpoint that 'what is beautiful is also good.'" Indeed, Just was motivated not simply by racial purity but by his own same-sex desires. As Frühauf observed: "Just became increasingly convinced that he could only be emotionally fulfilled with a lad. At the start he had been a repressed type. However he leapt over the obsta-cles and expanded his viable and legitimate stance on sexual morality into a practical system, consciously established and practiced."[35] When not in the imperial capital, imbibing anti-Semitism, Just was to be found in Gablonz honing a cohort of male youths whose selection was racist with a homoerotic undercurrent. For the moment, it was the racial dimension that particularly enticed Rutha, but as we will see, Just and a reading of Büttner also offered a homoerotic path to explore.

The leaders of the Wrchhaben circle were forceful, opinionated characters who together could spark ideas but easily might antagonize each other. Together with Rutha and Just, a third protagonist was the irascible Ernst Leibl (born 1895 in the Egerland) who as a Prague student was moving around the Wandervogel branches; in February 1915 he broke with the Smichow group due to its Jewish tolerance and joined "Prague-Lützow" instead.[36] The latter had its country den at Wrchhaben only a few miles south of Leipa. While Rutha and the Leipa Wandervögel were visiting Wrchhaben from the spring, enthusing about its rural tranquility, Just's Gablonzers began to make regular trips from the summer both there and to Leipa. Through this chance interaction there was a meeting of Aryan view-points that was taken further.

The circle really crystallized on 1 November 1915, the traditional Teu-tonic festival of All Souls, when the Leipa, Gablonz, Lützow, and Alt-Prague Wandervögel assembled at Wrchhaben. Only cryptically were the intense discussions reported in *Burschen heraus*, for little was initially dis-closed, but clear enough was the divisive nature of what was proposed.

Rutha's short public report announced that despite some escapist activity, the meeting had drawn together four groups for "serious common work together": "Yes, now we want to redouble our efforts in the Wandervogel so that it remains for us what it has been and must be in the future: a selection of the best of our nation, a community of healthy-thinking and conscious German youths."[37]

This statement effectively equated with what became known as the "Tetschen declaration" on racial selection (so named after a Tetschen group that adhered to the Wrchhaben principles). In the following months, with Just back in Vienna and Leibl dispatched to the Italian front, it was mainly Rutha who reinforced the new solidarity, with a flurry of mutual branch visits. The declaration was also not just empty words—as Stauda had first hoped, for he soon received direct demands from Just. Although professing to want harmony, Just expected the Gauwart to vet and eject non-Aryan elements—especially from the Prague-Smichow group of which Stauda was nominal leader.[38]

The easy-going Stauda resisted this anti-Semitic pressure from one small clique. He felt correctly that the Bohemian Wandervogel lacked any tradition of racial selection, nor had it officially signed up to the Aryan paragraph at Krems. He therefore publicly criticized the Wrchhaben circle and its divisive tactics, claiming that "whether justified or not, the politicizing approach which has been expressed here as a demand, has not previously existed in our Wandervogel and will, we are certain, not be repeated."[39] It was a premature line in the sand, for a few months later Just produced an "Aryan-only" proposal to be voted at the annual Gautag. Since the Gautag of 1916 was held at Hammer am See near Kunnersdorf at the express invitation of the Gablonz group, attention was all the more focused on its racist motion. In June, over three hundred adolescents assembled in the pouring rain (but "with sun in their hearts") for games and singing competitions in the lakeside summer resort. The leaders meanwhile gathered anxiously in private to debate Just's proposal—and quickly rejected it.

If this seemed a sign of Just's actual isolation on the race issue (he duly appealed for his group's attitude to be publicized more widely), it also signaled covert friction among the Wrchhaben "young Turks" and a reluctance to endanger the movement's unity when face to face with their respected elders. While Stauda at Hammer typically pleaded for unity and trust, Feldberger, in a rosy account written for *Burschen heraus*, expressed pleasure that those in the circle wanted "to help create a fine, joyous life for youth that will lead on to serious German manhood." He himself was not deaf to Aryan selection (that summer he would read Büttner's book with admiration), but his own pleas for discipline sounded a warning to the Wrchhaben diversion, reminding them about their three hundred brothers who were sacrificing at the front.[40]

The elder's remarks seem decisively to have swayed Rutha. Unlike Just he had not labored the race issue and seems to have followed Feldberger's lead. Although the evidence is slight, ever since Feldberger had rejuvenated the Leipa group in 1914 he had been Rutha's model, albeit someone only intermittently in contact, for alongside military training he was a trainee schoolteacher in northwest Bohemia. Rutha deeply respected Feldberger's wider moral vision for adolescents, one that made sense of the frontline sacrifice and interpreted the mission at home in more than just romantic terms. The idolization is evident in Rutha's report of a *Eufrat* evening held in the Leipa den in early 1916 where Feldberger presided: "Actually it was held in the afternoon and I can divulge that it was splendid . . . Our Feldberger spoke about the Wandervogel, the room was as quiet as a mouse and only our eyes were shining. I wish you all could have heard him speak and picked up something of the joy with which he filled everyone. Then we sang our songs, old and new, and finally showed a series of [lantern] slides of our time on expeditions and at the rural den."[41]

At Hammer it was Feldberger who was elected to be the new Gauwart as Stauda was keen to retire, but it was Rutha who was named as successor should Feldberger be drafted. If this choice suggests Rutha as Feldberger's protégé, it also implies that at Hammer he had upheld his reputation as a reliable and charismatic leader—"our dear Heinz" to many groups—despite the divisive behavior of Wrchhaben.[42] Just as the loose Wrchhaben circle was now already dissolving, so the question of racial selection had been adjourned and would only return at the end of the war. Then too Rutha would take a stand for a short while, but for the moment he had broader sights and a year to prove himself on the wider Bohemian stage.

BOHEMIAN GAUWART

In the summer of 1916 the Habsburg Empire suffered a major defeat on the eastern front and a second wave of Jewish refugees flooded the Bohemian lands. As the empire tied its military fortunes ever closer to Germany, so

Austria's domestic scene was shifting toward a "German course" for the future. Since 1914 the Vienna parliament had been adjourned, public politics eliminated in favor of a bureaucratic dictatorship where emergency laws were used to stifle dissent. In this framework, German nationalist politicians, especially in Bohemia, moved to shore up their position against what they saw as the creeping Slav menace.

Fully in line with their policies since the 1880s, the German leaders in the Easter program of 1916 publicly advocated a "German solution" for Austria. By various maneuvers, a permanent German majority would be secured in parliament, while Bohemia's administration would finally be divided along strict national lines to ensure that Germans were never subject to the Czech-speaking majority. It was a radical solution trumpeted for the rest of the war, emboldening German nationalists as much as it alarmed Czech patriots. The "unpolitical" Wandervogel might look askance at these political machinations, but its own nationalist agenda was not dissimilar and was bound to be affected by the political discourse. From 1916, thoughts increasingly turned toward the aftermath of the war.

For Rutha too this period was a watershed. Just as he was about to become Bohemian Gauwart, he departed from his formal education at Leipa, his five years there at an end. Immediately after the Gautag he had taken his written examinations, followed on 3 July by an oral test chaired by the headmaster.[43] In all he passed with distinction, but the success was undoubtedly diminished through his isolation. Nineteen of his peers had been drafted during the year, and only six were left to take the final exams. Proceeding to the military was still not an option as he continued to be judged unfit. "Because of an 'intensified heart defect,'" he complained to Stauda, "I am still not a soldier and I fret stupidly—it is just a disgrace to have to sit behind like this but unfortunately I can't change anything."[44] Only indirectly could military life be experienced. In the summer of 1916 he made a three-week expedition south with other Wandervögel to Austrian Carinthia, looking up some soldier friends en route. As he stood on the Preber summit surveying the spectacular landscape, the tranquility was broken only by the distant boom of guns from the Italian front.[45]

For the moment Rutha's military aspirations were dashed, and he could only choose further education in Prague. Instead of the German university that beckoned for any pupil of distinction, he elected for the *Handelsakademie* or business school, based in a side street off the Old Town Square, which ran a one-year course in German and English for prospective businessmen.[46] Possibly the choice was caused by pressure from Adolf Rutha, who wanted his son soon to assume his affairs in Kunnersdorf. Despite his separate sphere in the youth movement, Heinz had always remained close to his roots; from Christmas 1916, when his father fell ill, he felt increasingly bound to spend time at home helping to run the Oschitz savings bank.[47]

Prague had altered since his prewar schooling, its mood dampened by wartime censorship and the rationing introduced by 1916 for all foodstuffs. In retrospect, Heinz would judge that year at the Handelsakademie as one of the best of his adolescence, yet the city also evoked disagreeable memories. Once again he stayed in Vinohrady in the apartment of brother Richard, who had now married an attractive French woman, Andrée (enabling Heinz to perfect his schoolboy French). Yet the evidence hints at tensions that soured the domestic atmosphere. Richard, who was no nationalist, was accustomed to inviting home a Czech banking colleague named Ivan Šámal with whom he played piano duets. Probably this was the "foreign guest" whom Heinz mentioned in his diary, noting that although he endured the visits, they were a "heavy strain on his German sensibility." Richard's marriage also was already deteriorating, not aided by a forceful French mother-in-law who wondered out loud why her vivacious daughter had married a "Bohemian farmer." Heinz's diary noted that Richard was uncommunicative, resented their lack of children, and tended to treat Andrée like a doll. She in turn was dissatisfied and strayed (later she would marry Šámal). In 1916–1917, therefore, the couple was still married but leading separate lives.[48]

The brothers' relationship remained distant, a clash of viewpoints not least over national allegiance. While an irritated Richard felt business education should have the priority, Heinz was naturally obsessed with the youth movement, "roaming around in the Prague neighborhood with like-minded young men."[49] In itself it earned him Wandervogel respect, for one of his major achievements in Prague was to reconcile the youth branches that had become so estranged over the Aryan question. Although he himself had directly caused those tensions through the Wrchhaben circle, since the Hammer Gautag he had felt that unity was paramount. He once summed up conditions in the capital as a real "bedlam": "Just like the Balkans for the Great Powers, so Prague for ages has been the problem child of the Gau, and on hearing the name one immediately thinks of brawls and conflict."[50]

From October 1916 he attached himself to "Prague-Lützow" because of its Wrchhaben connections, but then moved toward reconciling the various Prague groups, probably by downplaying the racial question. On 12 January he organized a common meeting for all Prague branches and publicly announced that "the ice had melted a bit." It was the prelude to many gatherings in alternate dens, joint expeditions through the winter snow, and something that he increasingly relished: weekly "reading evenings" where elders would gather to discuss significant texts. While he tentatively described it all as a way for lads to learn about self-discipline and their mutual virtues, his peers proceeded to hail his own catalytic role. "Rutha", wrote Kurt Oberdorffer, "has finally cleared away all the obstacles and given an impetus toward union. This was laudable work but he should never begrudge himself the efforts, for we Pragers will always remember our Gauwart with gratitude."[51]

Indeed, it was precisely as Wandervogel Gauwart in 1916–1917 that Rutha rose to this challenge of trying to impose unity on a movement dissipated by war and geographically diffuse anyway. In late August 1916, as expected, Feldberger had been drafted and Rutha had automatically become Gauwart. For all his outward confidence, at the start he had private misgivings. Feldberger informed Stauda that Rutha thought himself too young for the post and that many in the movement would agree. After verbal assurances from Feldberger, he wrote to Stauda on 5 September, agreeing to assume the role as long as Feldberger was in the army but hoping that he would soon return; he asked to be sent details since he had no clear idea of its remit. As winter approached, as his new studies began at the Handelsakademie, he set out to inspect a range of Wandervogel branches and announced a winter youth camp in the north Bohemian mountains.[52]

His was an unenviable task for a number of reasons. At a time of shifting wartime membership, the Gauwart might naturally slacken the reins and give only loose guidance to disparate groups of "autonomous youth." In the absence of Metzner, that had largely been Stauda's philosophy, and it had permitted unsavory phenomena like the Wrchhaben circle to appear. Rutha like Stauda not only had to confront the perennial headache of how to build German Bohemian national unity—always an aim but always elusive. He also encountered from the start a situation where the Bohemian Wandervogel's independence was once again at stake within an Austrian framework.

Specifically, some sensitive decisions had been taken at the first wartime Austrian Bundestag, held in Linz in August 1916 and attended by a delegation of Bohemian Wandervögel. Since the acrimonious split at Krems in 1913, the Bohemian-Austrian relationship had only slowly healed, not least because with the outbreak of war the Bund leadership had disintegrated.

While restoring the link had begun in mid–1915 when the Austrians created a war-work committee as a centralizing body, the idea of broader unity owed much to pressure from Bohemian students in Vienna and the sentiment that both sides were experiencing a common baptism of fire. In this spirit, greater cooperation had been mooted at the 1915 Gautag.

A group of fifty Bohemian Wandervögel therefore accepted the invitation to attend the Linz Bundestag, Rutha traveling there on a crowded train from Prague. Faced with the Linz leader Willi Flatz's warm reception and impressed by the colorful processions, the magical fireside eulogy, and the energy of more than a thousand adolescents, the Bohemian leadership agreed to reactivate an Austrian federal organism made up of regions *[Gaue]* run by Wandervogel leaders. Alongside this autonomy, Bohemian-Moravian influence seemed clear when Oskar Just was elected new Bund leader and Ignaz Göth from Iglau was made responsible for managing a network of Wandervogel soldiers. However, outweighing all this to many observers was Johannes Stauda's concession. Under pressure from Flatz, he agreed to relegate *Burschen heraus,* the key Bohemian coordinating tool, to a mere supplement of a common Austrian journal. If Stauda and Feldberger actually had misgivings from the start, these were only confirmed when Stauda received a barrage of hostile reactions from other Bohemian elders. Metzner not surprisingly felt that Stauda through his concession was helping to weaken Bohemian identity. Another respected elder protested that at Linz Stauda had been bamboozled, "endangering if not destroying the auspicious beginnings of a vigorous and united German-Bohemia for the future." To many the movement seemed to have passed a fatal watershed.[53]

In the face of this dispute the new Gauwart took office (fig.9). Although Rutha too had ostensibly approved the Linz decisions, he began to regret them when thrust into coordinating the Bohemian Gau. His reaction in his first months bears witness to his own controlling character traits. He expected much more branch obedience than under Stauda and felt frustrated when many adolescents did not demonstrate diligence toward the Wandervogel ideal. Many groups simply ignored his circulars or offered only intermittent reports on their activity: "We still," he observed, "constantly lack discipline so every task swallows up double the time."[54] The real gravity of the mission he described at the end of the year in one of his first public missives as Gauwart, advising group leaders of their duty to those lying in the trenches. The Wandervogel, he explained, was not just simple fun but a total approach to life, and the war its crucial test. Those left at home should write to "their lost soldiers" in the field, nurturing them with pictures, food, or even a good book about Bohemian culture. The soldiers in turn should wear the silver griffin (the Wandervogel emblem) on their caps, seek out fellow members, and report their locations to a new military office under Ignaz Göth, for their strength would be needed after the war.[55]

By February 1917, with the Prague discord seemingly resolved and any further Bund coordination postponed for the moment, Rutha sketched out publicly a new agenda for his "dear German Bohemians."[56] There he scolded them for arrogantly ignoring the new Bund journal that embodied Austrian youth unity, but admitted that downgrading *Burschen heraus*, formerly the Bohemians' "spiritual focus," had seriously weakened Gau unity: it could not continue if German Bohemia was to stay strong and emerge "full of fresh life from the war." His main solution, aside from restoring a monthly journal, was to restructure the Gau, carving it up into four main districts (North, West, Elbe, and Prague) to achieve tighter coherence and closer interaction among branches from the same locality. If the scheme had some echoes of the ill-fated Wrchhaben circle, this time he was pushing autonomy as a means to firmer overall Gau cohesion, expecting the districts to hold regular meetings and recruit more effectively in the secondary schools.

This firm initiative bore fruit and suggests that Rutha during a difficult year directly galvanized the nationalist youth movement. Earlier he had feared the Gau was disintegrating, but by late spring five new groups had sprung up, branches were more diligent in writing lively reports, and much more mindful of their brethren in uniform. Most satisfying was when at Easter 1917 the districts [*Kreise*] were formally inaugurated. Groups in western Bohemia trudged through the snow and assembled as a "West" district. Those in the region of the Elbe valley met at the Leitmeritz den and, to Rutha's delight, were joined there by Wandervogel soldiers from the local garrison. And particularly striking was the genesis of a "North" district on Maundy Thursday at the Leipa rural den. About sixty youths came together in the presence of Rutha and Just to indulge in traditional games and songs, agreeing to hold monthly meetings. Two war veterans, labeled by some as the "general staff," added gravitas: Willi Riewald, who even in the field had organized Wandervogel events, was appointed district leader, while Otto Kletzl gave a fireside eulogy that moved all to tears. To the rest of the movement Rutha praised this as a model of unity, wishing that everyone had witnessed "how keen the lads were to bury all the trouble and strife" of the past.[57] While there was no room for complacency in school recruitment, it all seemed a favorable omen for the forthcoming Bohemian Gautag.

The Wandervogel Gautag of May 1917 was one of the most impressive youth gatherings in the wartime Bohemian lands. The twenty-year-old Rutha was alone in planning it in the village of Trschiblitz near Brüx. The château there had once belonged to Goethe's great unrequited love, Ulrike von Levetzow, but by the twentieth century it was owned by the Brüx council, who converted it into a holiday home for German children and readily placed it at the Wandervogel's disposition. Set in spacious grounds, with a rose garden and canopy of chestnut trees that still exist today, it was a romantic venue. It was also suitably located near the headquarters of Titta's National Council and on the language border, something not coincidental, for it might mischievously be expected that proximity to Czechs—the château right in the village center—would underline the German nationalist mission. Although Trschiblitz was completely Czech-speaking, Rutha after meeting the local priest and other villagers felt that "nothing would occur if we ourselves do not provoke them." In late April he inspected everything with members of the Brüx Wandervogel and agreed on accommodation. For the first time—a hint that he was himself a reformist pedagogue—he suggested creating an exhibition to showcase Gau activities as well as a model library that the branches might emulate. The games, he hoped, would be as "national" [volkstümlich] as possible, with everything geared toward forging the disparate youth groups into a united German-Bohemian Gau.[58]

This meticulous coordination was evident during the four-day event, when the number who converged far exceeded those at Hammer. Present were 450 Wandervögel from thirty-seven branches of the German Bohemian borderlands; 30 percent were girls, since, as in Germany, wartime had caused a burgeoning of female recruitment. The consensus, as reported later, was overwhelmingly positive: that the Gautag was unforgettable. It had been a "paradise," wrote one leader; "we grew in self-awareness and inner cohesion," wrote another.[59] Some recalled the abundant food available, for despite wartime rationing that had caused some northern branches to limit their rural expeditions, Rutha had managed somehow to secure eight hundred eggs and one hundred liters of milk as basic sustenance.

The Gauwart himself later highlighted the spiritual bonding that the Trschiblitz environment had encouraged. Like a "dashing whirlwind," youth had come to the château, recalling the olden days when powdered gentlemen and ladies in rustling hoopskirts resided there. When the ebullient adolescents were not turning the venue into a beehive, or dancing and singing in the grounds, they were sitting contemplatively in the rose garden, discussing the branch activities on display in the château exhibition or bonding together despite the strange mixture of their German dialects from north and south Bohemia. While this perhaps suggested real barriers to any national unity, Rutha pronounced that the Gautag had dissolved the "chinese walls" between branches, producing "a strong, splendid confession of our sense of solidarity."[60]

The *völkisch* dimension to this was vividly captured one evening during the traditional ceremony at the fire. What took place was an assertion of German Bohemian space, spirit, and communality against a background of local Czech irritation. It was quite normal at Wandervogel gatherings simply to ignore or minimize the Czech neighbor while focusing on the German Bohemian world outlook, but at Trschiblitz this was far less possible. Some villagers felt the presence of German adolescents in their midst was provocative, stones were thrown over the château wall, and, in Rutha's words, Czech "scoundrels" managed to set fire to the wood pyre intended for the climactic fire ceremony. Incensed, he ordered another one built, this time on the German side of the language border on a hill overlooking the Czech plains. Soon the village resounded with a "dull, threatening step" as the Wandervögel proceeded north from the château to the hilltop; two youths with cudgels led the way, others followed in serried ranks waving pennants and occasionally breaking into song. It was, as Rutha proudly recalled, an obstinate display of militant youth, as if they were going into battle.[61]

As they all sat in a semicircle under whispering oak trees, the Czech panorama spread out beneath them, the fireside ceremony resembled a religious ritual. To conduct it, Rutha had invited a veteran Prague youth leader, Rudolf Kampe, who hailed from Leipa and had been wounded early on the Balkan battlefield. His powerful oration at the fire left a lasting impression on the youth movement.[62] While the equivalent ceremony at Linz in 1916 had conjured up the spirits of dead Wandervögel, Kampe conjured up something even more reverend: the "German national soul" itself. The youths around the fire were, he said, greeting the "powerful genius of the German people [that] dwells palpably in our midst." Just as the flames were roaring, so, Kampe intoned, might the spirit rage in Wandervögel hearts, opening them up to embrace with love everything connected with the homeland. They were tied together like a single garland of flowers, stretching from north to south across the space of the *Heimat;* and they saluted everything in the German natural and human worlds, including those who dead and alive had defended the besieged fortress of Austria-Germany. For the Wandervögel in their fire ceremony were simply reprising the heroism of those ancient German tribes who, having conquered the earth, had constructed a new edifice out of the rubble. So now it was the adolescents' duty to construct German Bohemia, for, he stressed, "German Bohemia is still not a living nationality *[Volkstum]:* it is still just a throng of people wandering along together, not a shining living being. Only in a few silent valleys there flickers real national life. So let us move to create a nation out of our glowing hearts!" Kampe's sermon was effectively a long prayer for "German Bohemia's radiant future."[63] It could not fail to stir the hundreds present, including Rutha himself, reinforcing the *völkisch* side to their crusade with a utopian expectation that a new German Jerusalem could rise up and challenge Czech-dominated Bohemia.

Aside from this romantic dream, the practical way forward was agreed upon at a special leaders' discussion where Rutha made his formal report as Gauwart.[64] Despite the presence of both Oskar Just and Ernst Leibl, the spirit of Wrchhaben seemed dead, with no public mention of the race question. Doubtless, Just was now too preoccupied as Austrian Bund leader, while Leibl's overbearing behavior was steadily making him enemies (including Rutha, whose pacifying work in Prague he begrudged).[65] Rutha anyway was keen to prioritize Gau unity and recruitment. He stressed how, in the wake of the new Bund relationship, the Gau had threatened to disintegrate: in short, the bird hatched at Linz had been deformed. The leaders all agreed, especially in view of what they witnessed at Trschiblitz, that an independent Gau journal (namely, *Burschen heraus*) must be restored as the main way to maintain what was termed the "special tribal kinship" of Germans in the Bohemian lands. Indeed, at Trschiblitz it was the primacy of a German Bohemian mission that was specifically reaffirmed, while subsuming it too far under an Austrian umbrella was rejected.

Rutha's comments at this time shed interesting light on his own flexible German horizons as well as his continued self-identification as both German Bohemian and Austrian. If Bohemian interests were always fully to the fore, better relations with German Moravians to the east were also an aspiration; but both German tribes in the Bohemian lands—he now used the term "Sudeten German" for them—still needed to set aside their prejudices and work with "Alpine Germans" to the south to forge a united Austrian Wandervogel.

That larger aspiration had not been abandoned at Trschiblitz. Against the backdrop of a rising Czech nationalist discourse in mid–1917, Rutha pointed out that the Germans must not look inadequate in the face of "the united Slavs": they should match it with their own unity. At the same time, the Austrian Wandervogel should delimit its position clearly vis-à-vis its cousins in Germany, maintaining a separate identity: "We German-Austrians must finally learn to create something for ourselves and desist from mindless mimicking."[66] In this language Rutha revealed his typical hierarchy of war-time loyalties: to German Bohemia, to German Austria, and then to Germandom as a whole. While for Rutha Germany would always be at a mental distance, Austria in 1917 still offered support in numbers for the sacred German Bohemian cause.

Yet the aspiration for Wandervogel unity across Austria was even more elusive than forging together the disparate Bohemian strands. When in July 1917, together with a mass of Bohemian groups, Rutha attended the next Austrian Bundestag in the "language island" of Iglau, a rather disappointing lack of unity was on display. There was no question that dozens of branches were industrious and imaginative, and no problem in having the Trschiblitz decision about *Burschen heraus* confirmed. But the Bohemians, Moravians, and Alpine Germans still seemed to be competing against each other, and any real "inner warmth" was missing. The common oath to the Habsburg emperor that all Wandervögel took on Iglau town square felt like a vague substitute for what the Bohemians really aspired to: tighter German youth unity across Austria.[67]

It was at Trschiblitz that Rutha had laid down his office as Gauwart. He was already revising for his examinations in German and English at the Handelsakademie and, after passing them with distinction, returned to Kunnersdorf to help with his father's business.[68] Given this persistent juggling of interests, and his initial misgivings about the role of Gauwart, his conscientious ten-month stint was impressive. Out of what seemed a disintegrating movement he had overseen the creation of eleven new Wandervogel branches and imposed a new district structure to facilitate regional interaction; dissent in Prague had been quelled and the numbers at the Gautag suggested that the youth mission had a future. Rutha already sensed well the need to harness adolescent exuberance, channeling it in a disciplined nationalist direction.

A rare photograph from Trschiblitz catches him laughing, but underneath the mustachioed elder there was always a puritanical seriousness. His main criticism of the Gautag had been the excessive amount of dancing. Not only had it been insufficiently *völkisch*, but the boys had been too eager to participate in this "girls' activity"; thereby they had compromised their masculinity and might as well wear frocks next time.[69] It was a flippant comment, but it underlines Rutha's rigid understanding of gender roles, foreshadowing his own overwhelming commitment to masculine youth.

CONFESSIONAL

By 1917 most elders had direct experience of life at the front, while those exempted as teachers, like Stauda, were exceptions. Some like Kletzl or Riewald had managed to intersperse their military duties with service to the youth movement when on leave. Others had given their lives for the fatherland, their sacrifice steadily noted in *Burschen heraus*. In September 1917 news arrived that Erich Kletzl, who had attended the Trschiblitz Gautag, had been killed. Having lost both brothers, Otto Kletzl was relieved of frontline duty and allowed to return home where he gave fuller attention to the Wandervogel.

For Rutha, the major blow was another death, announced just before Christmas. Rudolf Feldberger was killed by a grenade on 24 October on the Isonzo front at the very start of the Austro-German offensive that dramatically swept through north Italy and reconfigured that battlefield for the rest of the war. The final entries in Feldberger's diary show that before the attack, true to form, he had looked confidently into the realm "on the other side." In *Burschen heraus*, Kletzl praised Feldberger and pledged that he was not dead, "for the pure determination which spoke to us from his trusting eyes, will again radiate in the eyes of many many boys."[70] On a hillside north of Böhmisch Leipa, the Leipa Wandervogel duly held a memorial ceremony and threw wreathes into a fire. Rutha was among them (he was home at Christmas) and could now feel an extra responsibility, for he had secured his wish to participate in the real national sacrifice. During the summer he had finally been judged fit as a one-year volunteer and on 15 October departed enthusiastically to join his regiment in the southern Bohemian town of Budweis.

It was the start of five months of military training and a life away from the Bohemian environment. Assigned to Heavy Artillery Regiment 21, he soon traveled south to Linz and began training there at the reserve officer artillery school. He knew the city quite well from two previous visits. Our sources for this period of his life are particularly rich—like no other until the 1930s—for on 17 February 1918 he began a diary and continued it for six months; it has survived unnoticed in the Czech archives, albeit in a faulty typed transcription.[71] It gives us access to Rutha's inner world, his thoughts about youth and wartime, about personal relationships and sexual anxieties, and he did not intend them for outside scrutiny. A different, insecure Rutha emerges here, one far removed from the Gauwart who had written so confidently and practically in the page of *Burschen heraus*.

The impression from the diary aside, Rutha's time at the artillery school in Linz was crowned with success.[72] His theoretical education covered twelve fields of instruction, including "artillery training," "terrain description," "tactics and field work," and "horse-riding." In the final examinations he would gain top grades in every category; out of sixty-two other candidates, most of whom were German-Austrian (with a few Czechs who did particularly badly), he came first over all. The final report set him slightly apart from the rest, employing all the adjectives deemed appropriate: a "serious, determined character, very industrious and hardworking, ambitious, very suitable and reliable, very unassuming and correct, a good commander."

Yet if as usual he was committed academically, his preference was for the time he spent with fellow officers in outdoor fieldwork. In an early diary entry, he wrote about climbing Pöstlinberg on the outskirts of the city to reconnoiter battery positions: "I understand why our [Wandervogel] lads are so enthusiastically cheery to don the soldier's uniform. They just think of life in nature, permanently out of doors, which otherwise we only get during our trips out on Sundays. How happy I am, thinking that the battery and even more the front will bring me what I long for: to be outside under a sky, whether blue or full of clouds, and always to be close to our dear mother earth. So I shall go off gladly to the front, though not without concern for my loved ones at home." He was at his happiest as he sat on Pöstlinberg, daydreaming about his last big Wandervogel trip the previous summer to southern Bohemia. While the other recruits engaged in trigonometry, he began with numb fingers to sketch the landscape stretched out before him, densely wooded with sunlight catching the farmsteads. He imagined the pleasure of being a proud farmer in Upper Austria.[73]

Rutha's single-minded commitment to the youth movement did not cease in Linz: the movement seems to have engaged much of his free time away from military duties. The Wandervogel naturally impinged, for one of his fellow trainees, Fritz Hänke, had been a student at the Handelsakademie and a leader of the Lützow Wandervogel, and they were inevitably pushed together. However, Rutha gradually scorned his colleague's carefree attitude and concluded that, for all his military competence, he lacked the steadfastness of a true Wandervogel.[74] Instead he sought out the energetic leader of the Linz Wandervogel Willi Flatz. Rutha had observed Flatz presiding over the Linz Bundestag in 1916, sympathized with his efforts to generate a more cohesive Austrian youth movement, and knew from the Iglau Bundestag that the Linz group was setting other Wandervögel an imaginative example.

The two first got to know each other properly one evening at the end of 1917 when they mutually poured out their feelings. A result of this "confessional night"—as Flatz termed it—was that Flatz sent his "dear friend" a blank diary where he might inscribe his innermost impressions in order later to leaf back through the pages with satisfaction. The idea of keeping such a record had long been encouraged by Wandervogel leaders. On a personal level it paralleled the romantic chronicles that local groups often kept of their activities. Thus Kletzl, whom Flatz knew well, had urged youths to keep a diary, stressing that he always kept his in a special shirt pocket; it should be an instinctive record of uplifting experiences, a private mirror and a reliable memoir to rejoice in later. For many weeks Rutha did not find the time or inclination to begin his. His tendency, he noted, was usually to keep his innermost thoughts in his head, not to commit them to paper; and anyway, since Trschiblitz, he had ceased to be "scribbler" and was almost as bad a correspondent as had been the "dear dead Rutsch" (Feldberger). Only in mid-February after his morning trip up Pöstlinberg did he resolve to capture in words something of the "fresh life" he was experiencing before it faded away.[75]

When in late March 1918 he completed the artillery training and left for a week's leave at home, he regretted not having devoted more time in Linz to the Wandervogel. Not only had military duties precluded regular meetings with Flatz, but as his diary reveals, that relationship might have blossomed quicker but for his own insecurities when faced with the charismatic Linz leader. As it was, he still sensed he had learned much from "fine hours" spent in Flatz's company and convinced himself that they had drawn closer to one another as "honorable fellows." Most notably, Flatz shared Rutha's persistent commitment to Aryan selection, namely that Wandervogel leaders when recruiting ought to uphold racial purity; for as Rutha noted, "how could they feel German if they themselves are not German."[76]

Yet over the previous months he had stayed well-informed about Wandervogel tribulations. The momentum from Trschiblitz had been hard to sustain, for youth recruitment on the home front was constantly offset by those departing for the real front line. And there was also a perpetual question about the exact role of elders in the movement. As new Gauwart after Trschiblitz, an accomplished musician, Julius Janiczek, had been elected; Rutha knew him well in Prague, both as a German teacher at the Handelsakademie and as founder of the Lützow Wandervogel, and backed him as a potentially firm centralizing leader. Yet for those who promoted youth autonomy, like Stauda, this went too far (and Janiczek's obsession with folk culture was also suspect). In mid-October 1917, matters had come to a head at a meeting of the Gau leadership in Prague. Rutha was present to back Janiczek in the face of critics like Leibl and Kampe. Publicly, as usual, all appealed for unity, and Janiczek did secure his position for a few months. But the whole incident underlined the personal as well as tactical squabbles among the elders; at issue especially was whether those passing into adulthood should continue to control the movement.[77]

By New Year anyway, an overburdened Janiczek was already keen to resign and resume his pedagogic-cultural activities. After Rutha conceded this and suggested Otto Kletzl as the successor, the Gau branches voted in favor, and from February Kletzl was official Gauwart-in-waiting. Typically he himself had misgivings as he was about to assume a teaching post, but he also sensed a recent deterioration in the movement (with branch subscriptions lapsing) as well as a duty toward the *Heimat* for which his two brothers had perished. His election was not unopposed. Despite the public discourse that front and hinterland were interlinked as "Wandervogel sacrifice," some elders felt Kletzl had been a soldier for too long. Others were irritated that he, like Rutha, might be too pro-Austrian or too much of a northern Bohemian. The latter view was personified by the irascible Ernst Leibl, whose animosity toward Kletzl and Rutha was fueled by a gripe that a northern clique was taking over the movement. It was clear that when the Gau leadership convened in Leitmeritz at Easter 1918 to approve Kletzl's election, Leibl, supported by some western Bohemian elders, would try to sabotage it.[78]

On Flatz's recommendation, Rutha, though nervous about publicly denouncing Leibl, decided to attend the showdown. On 1 April, after a night with his relations in Prague, he took the train out to Leitmeritz to be met by a member of the local Wandervogel and accompanied by bicycle to the meeting. There under Stauda's chairmanship a pleasant surprise awaited him. As he noted in his diary: "Many dear old well-known faces, it is so warm in this little room, only Leibl is like an ice pack. How happy I am. But to him I am still the old Heinz. In spite of the long time away. German Bohemia—the homeland, and all you dear young men. Despite much bitterness, I thank you all my young friends, I certainly can't think of my life without the Wandervogel."[79]

Sandwiched between Kletzl and Janiczek, Rutha watched as an ill-prepared Leibl was outmaneuvered by his colleagues. Kletzl was elected Gauwart without difficulty, Leibl only managing to insert a few conditions including a rule that the Gau maintain its independence from Austria; and despite Leibl's protests, *Burschen heraus* was surrendered to Kletzl since Stauda wished to retire as editor. Rutha observed also with schadenfreude how Oskar Just turned against his former Wrchhaben colleague. He blocked Leibl's desperate attempt to head the movement's public relations office, confiding cryptically to Rutha that Leibl was neither reliable nor even a proper "German fellow." Delighted that Just had finally seen through "the intriguer," it spoke volumes for Rutha's own animosity that he resolved in his diary to gather evidence for use against Leibl. When the meeting broke up in late afternoon and he headed for Kunnersdorf, he could feel wholly uplifted by the outcome: Kletzl would be in command at home while he himself did his service at the front.[80]

SHIFTS AND DILEMMAS

Through four years of war, adolescent nationalism was an escalating phenomenon on the Austrian home front, and the Bohemian Wandervogel was just one example.[81] Although thousands of teenagers chose not to be part of this experience, hundreds were passing through one of its thirty-odd local groups, participating in escapist hiking and becoming steadily aware of like-minded youths scattered across the space of German Bohemia. The young adults who steered this activity were training them to believe they were an elite who could regenerate the *Heimat*. And for all those who indulged purely for amusement, there were many like Rutha, or Karl Hermann Frank of the Carlsbad branch, whose nationalist mindset was shaped by the more serious message.[82]

The war ensured that these youths often gained a taste of leadership; and, if unable to enlist, they strove to prove themselves as men on the home front.

There the Wandervogel cohort could represent an alternative family for teen-agers whose home life was shattered by wartime, but it also offered an alter-native reformist war pedagogy alongside the similarly disrupted school education. Alongside the secondary schools, most Wandervogel groups estab-lished a loose modus vivendi, not least because they had originated under a teacher's protection in the first place. Thus, when in early 1918 the Austrian Ministry of Education decreed that youth groups should be incorporated fully into a school framework, the Wandervogel leadership was temporarily alarmed that it might disturb the existing amorphous relationship.[83]

But if wartime offered the youth movement freedom from many restric-tions, it also threw up dilemmas and tensions that divided the leadership. The question of leadership was itself controversial and exacerbated by the rapid youth turnover. On the one hand, senior elders like Stauda continued to proclaim the Wandervogel as a loose youth body, independent of adults and quite capable of producing its leaders without much direction. On the other hand, some Wandervögel who were just reaching adulthood (Rutha, Just) were nationalist activists of a new breed, seeking on the home front to direct the movement toward tighter unity, and claiming in their own defense that they were still "older adolescents." Many tensions arising from this activism stemmed from their pursuit of national or racial unity, and most could not easily be resolved because the parameters of that unity were so nebulous. The activists could clearly prioritize and accelerate the German Bohemian nationalist crusade, trying to fuse the disparate Wandervogel groups behind it. But certainties began to crumble when that crusade also had to be tightly Aryan or to encompass broader Austrian loyalties. After 1918 these latter pursuits would gradually dissolve, leaving the major ques-tion of elusive German unity in the Bohemian lands to the fore.

The youth movement gave Rutha the main framework for his *völkisch* horizons and, as Gauwart, he fostered a strong network of personal relation-ships across Bohemia. Yet the pull of Bad Kunnersdorf and his familial roots remained strong, supplying a secondary emotional support. Here he felt spe-cial responsibility for his aging parents; his father's ill health had occasion-ally drawn him home, and his mother continued to bear too much of the house work. Over the Rutha mill there hung the pall produced by the early deaths of Effert and Polifka, with Friedel Polifka ever-present as chief mourner. In view of the pain brought to their loved ones it was almost as if the two brothers-in-law were the ones who had really survived.[84] Heinz was also worried about his teenage sister Gretel, who seemed lacking in confidence; only his nephew Fritz gave no cause for concern as he grew fast and ran wildly around the Rutha mill.

On returning to Kunnersdorf on 1 April 1918, for the first time in three months, Heinz confided to his diary the timeless, undemonstrative, yet slightly tense family environment:

> At home really everything is the same, father a little more stooped, mother a little more looked after. And Friedel as housekeeper ever active. The poor thing, how much I would like to be able to help her. She's really young but already cheerless and worn out. Also the old nervous tone remains everywhere. It will certainly never be different, and it has already robbed many many hours and many experiences of their gentle charm. And yet they are all such kind-hearted souls, my loved-ones. But the ideal that they will all open up to each other can never be realized, for everyone's character has its own edges and corners. In general, where people come together the result is not fusion but friction.

He had a few days before his leave was over. He spent them packing, visiting old acquaintances and nostalgically absorbing the village of his childhood, where "quiet as the grave . . . one could never imagine something so ghastly as war." Otto Kletzl arrived, but Heinz spent the last evening gratefully alone with his parents. On the morning of 4 April he went with his mother and Kletzl to the local railway station: "It all happens quite easily. Mother goes to Reichenberg [the opposite direction]. Alone with Ott in the chilly compartment. Outside the Devin, Jeschken and Roll mountains sink behind us. My home. Ott also departs [at Leipa]. One last handshake and I am alone. For how long away from my dear ones, or for ever?"[85]

FOUR

Rebirth

On 12 October 1937, Czech police searched Heinz Rutha's apartment in the mill in Bad Kunnersdorf and discovered his short wartime diary in the safe. For almost twenty years he had kept it secure as a vital testament; its survival was then assured because of what it signified to the Czech authorities. The police at Reichenberg felt it could be used to diagnose Rutha's "disorder and confusion" over his sexual life in 1918. As they explained, "In this period of his life too, one can sense his inclination toward loving friendships with young men and the pleasure he found in the beauty of a boy's body, tendencies which then in the course of time crystallized into an unalloyed love of male youths [efebofilství]."[1] In 1937 the document would be extra proof of Rutha's long-term homosexual nature, but as the police noted, it also revealed his sexual uncertainties at the age of twenty-one.

SEXUAL ANGST

This diary has never been studied by historians. Analyzing it from a number of aspects introduces us to a personal and political watershed in Rutha's life, from 1918 to 1919. At this time he witnessed a traumatic upheaval in German Bohemia, for at the end of the war the Habsburg Empire disintegrated into "national" states and a new entity of Czechoslovakia was proclaimed across Bohemia-Moravia. For national activists like Rutha, whose vision was a regenerated German Bohemia surmounting the Czech danger, the creation of a Czech nationalist state in their midst was wholly unexpected and devastating. With the severing of the Bohemian lands from Austria, moreover, that hazy Austrian element to German Bohemian identity was weakened and with it a certain national fluidity. From 1919 the regional nationalist Germans were forced into something of a Czech straitjacket—a Czech-dominated country with firm state frontiers—which necessitated a fundamental rethink of their identities. Rutha and his fellow Wandervögel found the relatively secure world on the home front replaced overnight by an insecure environment.

Rutha himself now began to shape a fresh regenerative crusade for the Germans of Czechoslovakia, grounded in both his Wandervogel and military experiences. If his activities were adjusted to the Sudeten German national predicament, they cannot be divorced from private insecurities in the postwar world. Like thousands of veterans he was forced to adapt to civilian life, refocusing on his family at Kunnersdorf after the wartime struggle. It also meant, for someone who had long persisted as a "mature youth," creating a precise role for himself as an adult youth leader. And this range of unavoidable adjustments coincided with mounting anxiety about his sexuality and personal relationships with both men and women. The diary of 1918 provides a tantalizing glimpse into his sexual dilemmas in a transitory period; it also broaches the subject of same-sex relations in the youth movement, something that in time was at the core of his regenerative mission.

Not surprisingly, the subject of sex had created tensions in the Wandervogel organism. On the one hand, the very essence of the movement was to reject a bourgeois lifestyle with its hypocritical morality that sanctioned prostitution and casual sex alongside the traditional family unit. The "wandering birds" instead were to stay chaste in mind and body, eschewing sexual contacts with girls just as they abstained from tobacco and alcohol. On the other hand, the Wandervogel catered precisely to middle-class boys who were passing anxiously through their sexual awakening. Since their time in the movement coincided with secondary schooling, they tended to spend longer in the youth life-stage and experienced an extended puberty, even past the age of twenty, before entering the adult world. This offered a persistent challenge to the movement's ideal of sexual abstinence. It was compounded because from before 1914, despite some elders' resistance, girls were allowed to form their own groups and socialize with boys. As a result the leadership strictly monitored gender interaction, often banning joint expeditions if they contained overnight stays. But sexuality was allowed to permeate the movement in a different guise: a distinct homosocial culture evolved, which was "explained" in a notorious theory.

In late 1912 there had appeared in Germany a book entitled *The German Wandervogel Movement as an Erotic Phenomenon*.[2] The twenty-four-year-old author, Hans Blüher, had already published a two-volume history of the early movement in which he emphasized the "moral power" of older male youths communing with their younger followers. In this third installment he was much more explicit. He set out a grand theory of same-sex erotic relations as the Wandervogel's fundamental characteristic, employing the term "inversion" to describe this expression of homosexuality.[3]

Stronger on theory than concrete evidence, Blüher nevertheless based his concept on a decade of grassroots observation. One of his own heroes was a Wandervogel leader, Wilhelm Jansen, who in 1908 was forced to resign his offices because of homosexual accusations; it caused a major split in the movement in Germany, with one half supporting Jansen, lauding the freest expression of nongenital love among friends. Blüher, endlessly fascinated by contemporary sexual theories, also drew inspiration from prominent sexologists of his day: Sigmund Freud in Vienna and the homosexual campaigner Magnus Hirschfeld in Berlin, both of whom initially welcomed his exposé. He soon, however, concluded that Freud's notion of homosexuality as a neurosis could only be true for latent homosexuals. And while Hirschfeld wrote the introduction to the *Erotic Phenomenon*'s first edition, he too soon parted company with Blüher. Hirschfeld's main theory of homosexuals as an intermediate or "third sex"—between men and women—seemed applicable only to effeminate types and did not match the kind of male heroes who according to Blüher populated the Wandervogel.[4]

Instead, the core of Blüher's theory owed much to Germany's main alternative society for homosexual emancipation, the *Gemeinschaft der Eigenen* (Community of Self-Owners). Under the control of Adolf Brand, this elite circle, which included Jansen, expressly rejected Hirschfeld's modern medical definition of the homosexual as a distinct biological animal. Their purpose was to extol male erotic friendships as something natural in society, beautiful, and possessing a long historic tradition.[5] They pointed to Germany's Romantic era (ca. 1750–1850), when in certain educated circles intimate male friendship was commonplace, an erotic love lauded by great literary figures such as Goethe and Hölderlin; it was often placed on a pedestal above the "mere" sexual relationship between man and woman.

The Romantics—and in turn Brand's *Gemeinschaft*—had drawn inspiration from Greek classical tradition. Many knew, usually from their own classical education, about same-sex "Eros"—targeted sexual desire—in the ancient Hellenic world. Then, same-sex erotic companionship seemed to be fully integrated into society and celebrated in pedagogic sexual relationships between an older man and a male youth.[6] It was a love that in its purely spiritual dimension was lauded by Socrates as the ideal, superior to any love between a man and his wife. A male adult or *erastes* selected an attractive young man to educate and sexually initiate; the male youth or *eromenos* was bound to his *erastes* by an erotic, pedagogic, and paternal bond of love that lasted into adulthood. The *Gemeinschaft* emulated classical Greece's appreciation of male youth as the pinnacle of beauty; Brand described his journal *Der Eigene* as intended for men who "thirst for a revival of Greek times and Hellenic standards of beauty."[7] It was a vision of male intimacy where the line between friendship and homoeroticism was as blurred as in classical Greece.

Blüher's theory, as set out in the *Erotic Phenomenon*, was a confused amalgam of different contemporary approaches to homosexuality but with *Der Eigene* and its historic allusions to the fore. In essence, he portrayed the Wandervogel as a model body of male friendships that had a conscious "erotic tone." Although this could produce physical homosexual desire, Blüher like Socrates estimated the spiritual dimension of each relationship as the finest form of Eros.[8] He repeatedly quoted the Greek example in support: "The Greeks, who had their own special understanding of sexual drives, rightly grasped this natural fact. They understood the erotic undertone of friendship and accorded this a place in their culture. The Greek problem is most intimately bound up with that of same-sex love."[9]

And just as in ancient Greece same-sex eroticism had emerged with particular traits, such as naked athletics, so it manifested itself in the German Wandervogel in ways best suited to Nordic German culture. According to Blüher, "inversion" in the Wandervogel appeared in two male types. First, he praised the "full invert," akin in fact to "the homosexual" as defined by Freud or Hirschfeld. This man, even beyond puberty, was indifferent to women; he was the ultimate "male hero" (like Jansen) who moved only in male society and attracted youths as disciples "like a piece of crystal in brine."[10] Second, the most common invert was the *erastes*, who followed the path of his namesake in classical Greece. Like the "full invert," the *erastes* developed strong erotic male relationships, but after the age of twenty turned toward women to satisfy his physical sexual urges; even then, the female relationship was usually inferior to life-long homoerotic spiritual friendships that remained the higher form of Eros. Whether "full invert" or *erastes*, the male heroes were the activists who made the Wandervogel what it was, educating and nurturing youth in a highly charged homoerotic environment. The spark came because they found their erotic leanings reciprocated among youth. For adolescents, the movement was a key part of an extended life-stage where their heroes were substitutes for bourgeois father figures and any heterosexual urge was delayed or sublimated through prolonged steeping in a homoerotic culture.[11]

In Germany, Blüher's *Erotic Phenomenon* caused an uproar.[12] Wander-vogel critics acerbically dismissed the notion that their movement was rid-dled with "homosexuality," ignoring Blüher's own avoidance of that modern term and his belief in a timeless same-sex phenomenon. Some, however, acknowledged that Blüher had held up something of a mirror of contempo-rary Eros.[13] As the book was widely read across Germany, youths at least could acquire a vague framework within which to explain their close male friendships, the "purity" of their male intimacies (emotional if not physical), and their understanding of women as outsiders with whom sexual contact was taboo until adulthood. For most, perhaps, this homoeroticism was never equated with "homosexuality," but for some, who were attracted physically to their own sex, Blüher's theory might offer reassurance when they expressed their sexual feelings. Overall, then, while the Wandervogel repressed both male-female and male-male sexual relationships, male-male emotional links were allowed to flourish.

It is in this context that many of Rutha's sexual anxieties are explicable. How far Blüher's ideas were circulating in the wartime Bohemian Wander-vogel is unclear. In Johannes Stauda's history, in a passage about Rutha's life, the editor Kurt Oberdorffer suggests rather cryptically that there was wide-spread discussion of Blüher's *Erotic Phenomenon* by the middle of 1917. Twenty years later Rutha himself would confess to reading Blüher around this time but "not agreeing" with his views.[14] The sex question, in a Bohe-mian Wandervogel that had a burgeoning number of female groups, peri-odically reared its head in public. Thus at the Linz Bundestag (1916), it was agreed to ban mixed hiking, causing leading female Wandervögel to protest that this introduced sinful thoughts where there was otherwise innocence.[15] It was a ban Rutha upheld as Gauwart, for his stance on gender roles was very traditional.

Yet alongside this tentative public discourse on gender relationships, it seems clear that in private, it was male intimate friendships that provided more food for discussion, stimulated perhaps by Blüher but also simply reflecting the male bonding that was encouraged. The case of Oskar Just is instructive, for it seems fully to match what Blüher had observed in Germany. For appearance's sake, Just went through the motions of founding a girl's group in Gablonz, but his chief interest lay in selecting blond, Aryan youths and constructing an intimate Wandervogel cohort. In Blüher's interpretation, Just was probably a "full invert" and may well have used that controversial theory to underpin and understand his own sexual identity.[16]

For Rutha, any such overarching explanation came later in the 1920s. In his six-month diary, spanning his training in Linz and most of his military service, he poured out the "great anxieties" caused by his "unsatisfactory sex life." He was conscious that this personal record, while imbued with the usual Wandervogel instinctive approach, was unusual: "Since in the diaries of my friends I've never found such unreserved frankness about their sexual development, I consider my diary the most honest. I've overcome, thank God, my initial aversion of putting pen to paper and I write down everything as I really feel it *[empfindungsgetreu]*. My little book won't be any stylistic or stock-taking basis for my 'later works.' Only the truth through and through!" Despite this, he advised caution on what his intimate record could reveal: "I can't wish that these lines should be read by anyone other than me. They are such torn-up scraps of my thoughts and feelings that to another's critical eye they cannot really be a mirror of myself. Rather I see my booklet with all its scribblings as a restless affair, full of light and shadow."[17]

The diary therefore is at once illuminating and elusive, supposedly "honest" but inviting analysis of what it may conceal. By 1918, what Rutha termed his "sexual inner conflict" had two main facets, both of which drew their charge from what was permitted in the Wandervogel mindset. Firstly, he had sexual urges *[Triebe]* that had not been physically satisfied but would be—upon meeting the "right woman." Secondly, he recorded his emotional and physical attraction to the company of men, even if these were never openly described as physical sexual objects. The picture is of someone struggling to live by the moral prescriptions of the Wandervogel, notably the rule on sexual abstinence, while feeling guilty about his preference for male intimacy.

On 7 April 1918, when in Budweis again on the way to the front, he noted down how four years earlier, as a "dumb lad," he had promised himself never to go with a woman out of simple physical lust. True to Wandervogel morality, he had kept that promise, remained chaste, and up to 1916 still believed it a crime to have sex before marriage. Thereafter, however, particularly when in Prague, the "urges" had steadily grown, seeking an outlet and leading to "emissions" that he found shameful and disgusting. Perhaps, he mused, it was better "to satisfy the urges naturally than to agonize and be unnatural."[18] But how could this be done? He was shocked on learning of one Wandervogel who sought out girls for sex (for "I want to be pure"); he would be disgusted at the vulgar talk he encountered in the army.[19] His own ideal was the wholesome girls who frequented the Wandervogel dens. Such creatures he had come across in the Linz youth movement in the winter of 1917–1918, enjoying their liveliness and attention; he had even felt a stirring toward some of them, but in retrospect saw it was not love, only a "warm attraction."[20]

Rutha's ideal seemed perplexing and unobtainable because his attraction was rarely sexual. Anathema to him was a flirtation in Budweis, when his landlady's teenage daughter brought flowers on his departure for the front: "I find nothing natural about her, she did it with such pathetic raised eyes and deliberate hesitation that she had the appearance of an actress or a fawning whore . . . I was really angry at myself for acknowledging the flowers with such friendly words when deep-down I felt her so unnatural." In contrast, what was wholly desirable was another girl at his lodgings, a homely serving maid who personified everything "rustically pure and natural." He became excited that for once he was sexually attracted to a woman, even if he then felt a coward for failing to act upon it.[21] Often he rationalized these encounters by clinging to Wandervogel morality, the ideal of "remaining pure" until he met his life partner, and thinking of a model like Goethe who despite his great passions was an idealist and "pure."[22] In fact, this personal moral struggle, mentioned so often in the diary, was part of a confused self-deception. It obscured the deeper struggle that revolved around his predominantly same-sex inclinations.

It might be argued that Rutha's craving for male intimacy was just a characteristic trait in the ranks of the youth movement (clear for instance in many Wandervogel diaries from Germany). Like others trained in that mentality, Rutha expected to find intimates with whom to share his emotions, and at the start of 1918 could identify four such men who fell into this category as "true friends": Otto Kletzl, Willi Flatz, "Hansl" Martin, and one "Förster." With Kletzl (fig.10) he had a shared youth history, and they often seem to have corresponded; but while admiring Kletzl's drive and delighting in his "manliness," it seems unlikely that he offered real emotional support.[23] In contrast, Flatz was the elder to whom on that recent "confessional night" he had poured out his intimate thoughts, who had then supplied the diary as a further outlet. If Rutha regretted not having developed a closer friendship with Flatz, the main reason was not homoerotic but was rather based on admiration for a model Wandervogel. Flatz had cultivated his friendship and, above all, acted as a confessor.

Flatz anyway could not become what Rutha sought emotionally in 1918. As he embarked on his short military career he was ever more conscious of longing for a "blood brother" *[Blutsfreund]*, a sole companion to accompany him through life and death. He thought with pleasure of the warmth of many Wandervögel since his time as Gauwart, but what he really craved what that single friend who could absorb his being, becoming "his companion over the chasms of life . . . the strong pillar to lean on and stand next to."[24]

According to the diary, two Wandervögel whom he had befriended much earlier fitted that image, but both by 1918 were far away when he needed them. One was "Hansl"or Hans Martin, whom he termed his "dearest lad" on learning of his death later in the year. He had bonded closely with Hansl, probably from the time of the Linz Bundestag, and recorded the intimacy they had shared: "Your bright appearance, your dear words and the silent hours when only our hearts spoke between us." Now with his passing to another world, he could never be the comrade-in-arms he might have been.[25]

More significant anyway was a second close friend, identified only as "Förster." When imagining a blood brother it was usually Förster who appeared as the ideal: "Friend, friend, if only I could experience once again your devoted moments, your hand held in mine as we sit and talk in the quiet twilight. All the hard struggles where we take the wrong or the right path, everything will be laid naked before you. We will go often together into the darkness and I know you will be able to excuse before me your lapses . . . For I am a piece of yourself: our experience, our feelings, our striving upwards will lie naked before us."

These lines nevertheless conjured up someone whom Rutha may not have seen for two years. When in June 1918, by chance and very briefly, he came upon him on a railway platform in Tyrol, he found his appearance had altered from the "tanned wiry lad" he had met in Linz. There was now something of the "smooth actor" about him—an "un-German" artificiality that made him unmanly—yet Rutha still sensed the old spirit in his eyes and handshake.[26] The one-time intimacy with both Förster and Hansl had left a deep impression, so that in searching for a "close friend" in 1918, Rutha often compared new encounters with these elusive models.

While these feelings might be commonplace among Wandervögel, in Rutha's case they were strongly tinged with homoeroticism, expressing the spark that Blüher had observed in Germany. In 1937 the Czech police would make no distinction between this sentiment and evidence of homosexuality. Nor should we search too hard for such a distinction, for on the evidence of the diary Rutha was not only sexually attracted to young men; he sensed that his feelings were "unnatural," exceeding the bounds of what many construed as "normal" Wandervogel emotions. Thus he noted, "I find it much easier to pour out my feelings to a boy than to a girl. This has sobered me up like a cold jet of water." Later—in a passage highlighted by the police—he divulged, "I've stayed pure, yes in the face of women, but have not done so naturally . . . I want to be pure but I also want to be normal."[27]

The definition of "normal" or "natural" [natürlich] was at the heart of the conflict, for in the homosocial world of the Wandervogel it could become very blurred. When thinking about Förster as a bosom companion Rutha observed: "Common, impure men who in their own filth see nothing as pure, would perhaps—no certainly—class my feelings for you [Förster] as unnatural."[28] At the same time he was finding young men physically attractive (even if he then rationalized that urge). Contemplating one fellow officer in Linz he wrote: "He sits opposite me and when I look at his boyish-manly face with shining eyes, then I have just one wish, that he too become a Wandervogel with whom I could happily go out and fight or take off on an expedition." On arriving in Leitmeritz on 1 April for the Gau meeting, he spied a "tall blond lad," a Wandervogel from the Lützow branch, whom he found attractive and wanted to talk to; a few days later in Prague he sought him out.[29] Later diary entries often recorded same-sex magnetism, his admiration for "slender, brawny men," and highlighted his concurrent ambivalence toward women. Amid these sexual battles he was conscious of where the drives might be leading. This is evident from a striking passage, written again after visiting Leitmeritz, where he had encountered Oskar Just: "Just greeted me more heartily than ever before. Soon I saw the reason. For his sweetheart Ernst [Schöler] is also there. The lad is so pale and looks haggard and bleary-eyed. I would really like to know whether he doesn't have intense sexual conflicts. I think he wanders and therefore feels depressed, for he recognizes the shame of what he does yet is a slave of passion."[30]

Here was an equation with Rutha's own sexual turmoil, but there was also present, in the person of Just, a man who seemed to have come to terms with his sexuality (and was openly displaying it to his peers). Rutha at the age of twenty-one had not done so, and to some extent he never would. His sexual awakening, to quote Hermann Hesse's youth novel *Demian,* had overcome him "like an enemy and terrorist, as something forbidden, tempting and sinful."[31] While embracing a homoerotic youth culture, he knew there were same-sex boundaries that he pressed against, which others like Just had exceeded. Besides the diary, he had very few confidants for this aspect of his sexual angst. One exception was an adolescent, Ernst Juppe, whom he accompanied in August 1918 to a Wandervogel festival and whose "wonderfully developed body" stirred him. As they took a walk together arm in arm, "Jup" announced to a skeptical Rutha that he had now given up masturbation. Rutha in turn felt able to divulge his own unresolved same-sex "battles."[32]

It was a rare confessional moment. Only a few days earlier, he had briefly touched upon suicide as an honorable way out, noting the example of others who took that route when they "could not produce new life." He also thought of finding a humane doctor to whom he might unburden his "emotional confusion." But these avenues all seemed tantamount to surrender, weakness, rather than solving the issue himself. So the angst had not finished when the diary ended. The only respite was army service, for it stopped him brooding at home on his sexual conflicts.[33]

"TINY WHEEL IN THE CLOCKWORK"

Rutha had long wanted to follow in the footsteps of his Wandervogel mentors and sacrifice for the fatherland. By the time he reached the war zone as a one-year volunteer, Austria-Hungary's war had entered a critical final phase. With both Serbia and Russia defeated, the main military focus lay on the Italian front. There in October 1917 the armies of the Central powers had broken through at Caporetto and driven the Italians right back onto the Venetian plains where they came to a standstill at the River Piave. This apparent miracle shortened the front, but the victory was short-lived; supply lines were treacherous, and the Habsburg forces by 1918 were gripped by a material crisis where the resources demanded on paper increasingly diverged from reality.[34] Even so, the High Command was determined to maintain the offensive and overcome Italy once and for all. The plans for this "final" attack were just being settled as Rutha journeyed into the war zone in April 1918.

Rutha's short military life can be divided into three phases, two of which are well-documented in his diary. The first saw him traveling to Venetia and the Piave hinterland to attend a shooting school at Spilimbergo. In the second, in June, he moved to the Alpine front to form one cog in the machinery of the Austro-Hungarian offensive; it was his true baptism of fire, resulting in seven weeks' sick leave in Bohemia. The third phase, covering September and October 1918, is largely blank. All that we know is that he returned to the Piave front and was promoted to corporal on 16 October. Much later he wrote of his last hours in the trenches on a starless night, when before him there was "uncertain emptiness," and behind "the chaos of a gigantic collapse." As the enemy broke through in late October, his battery provided cover fire for the retreating Habsburg troops. Somehow he too managed to escape captivity and flee back into the disintegrating empire.[35]

Rutha viewed this frontline service as a key life-stage—another reason for preserving the diary. It taught him the value of charismatic leadership for young men and dramatically confirmed his belief that life was a struggle for survival. At one point in the trenches, when surrounded by corpses and subject to the full horror, he felt as though he had passed through an apocalypse and been reborn.[36]

Yet despite the war pedagogy he had imbibed at home and his yearning to stand with comrades shoulder to shoulder, what he immediately encountered was disappointing. From the start on 8 April 1918, when he took an oath to the emperor at the barracks in Budweis, he was disgusted by the indifference of many other recruits, contrasting their irreverence with the enrollment of volunteers in 1813 (against Napoleon) or the loyalty of those rushing to the colors in 1914.[37] Often he would identify those lacking the correct disciplined mindset as Czechs, Jews, or "shallow Germans." He also quickly sensed major failings in the Habsburg military machine. In a refrain common by 1918 in loyalist circles, he felt that "corruption and cowardice" allowed many "cowardly pigs" or Bolsheviks to hide in the hinterland. At the same time, soldiers entering the war zone seemed to be treated with crass indifference, as expendable pawns to be pushed around and left to die. As he noted angrily after being abused by one Hungarian officer: "For a long time I have myself believed that the free man of the twentieth century is just a number but I have never had it expressed so bluntly."[38] In later encounters he was shocked by the disrespect that many Habsburg officers generated due to their tactless management or openly weak commitment to the military mission. The reality was that by mid-1918 the mythical patriotic crusade that he so idealized was fast evaporating in the Habsburg army. His diary, written so late in the war, reflects this widespread disillusionment but also highlights his own naïve chivalry.

As he traveled southwards to the war zone in April together with hundreds of others, cramped in stuffy railway carriages, his Wandervogel credentials were on display.[39] He marveled at the Alpine peaks, "ever inaccessible and hostile for they want to remain untouched by human dirt," and regaled his companions with details about the Dolomite landscape. Once on the edge of the plains on the River Tagliamento, they disembarked and their commander, to Rutha's disdain, forced them to lug their heavy rucksacks through scorching heat before settling their accommodation in an empty villa.

Rutha took delight in furnishing it like a Wandervogel den, and so began a calm apprenticeship in the war zone. At first there was ample time to sunbathe and swim, write postcards home, and explore the winding streets of Spilimbergo, where palazzos with fading frescos nestled behind serene gardens with fountains and fig trees. But far from the front line, the tranquility was deceptive. While to the east, the hill town of San Daniele loomed up in the morning mist like a "castle of the Holy Grail," to the west in the mountains, there was the faint sound of rumbling thunder. Like other Austrian visitors, he was shocked at the destruction that Austro-Hungarian troops had wrought on property as they advanced after Caporetto, and understood only too well the hatred of Italian civilians who would return to find a devastated homeland.[40]

From 23 April when his gun training began, he awoke at dawn to attend the rifle range or receive instruction in all types of field artillery. Soon he felt a baptism of fire, for casualties from friendly fire or the splinters of shells occurred regularly and immediately became personal. On 14 May he attended the funeral of one German comrade killed like this; with irritation he listened to a padre "prattling" over the shattered body, and returned home numbed and grieving for a young man who had recently stood so close to him.[41]

The only consolation seemed to be the friendship of a man named Strecker. Rutha had met him a fortnight earlier on a special occasion. On 2 May the gunners were called out to display their technique before the visiting Emperor Karl. They waited around for hours in the sun before the imperial entourage appeared and a barrage of artillery fire could be let loose. It was at that time that Rutha came across a "slim, blue-eyed lad, ready for action," who had a north Bohemian accent and a Wandervogel-type mindset. A few days later Rutha walked through the scorching heat to the billet of his new friend. There they talked about sexual purity and all aspects of life, Strecker stressing (to Rutha's admiration) that he wished to be a teacher who would educate boys and girls to be good Germans. "In every way," noted Rutha, "I felt beating next to me a cognate heart and I had to restrain myself lest in the short time of our acquaintance my warmth should appear too obtrusive." It was a brief encounter, for soon after the funeral Strecker left the region for training elsewhere, and Rutha could only recall him in a poem:

> I hoped by your side
> I would stride through muddy heavy days.
> But of yourself you have left me nothing
> But the cool breeze on the evening streets.
> There arm in arm I walked with you as we took leave.[42]

Strecker exemplified a youth who emotionally and in his "conscious Germanness" seemed a model, but as so often, he was to remain just a memory.

When Rutha assumed he had already undergone his military baptism on the plains he was mistaken, for on 31 May he was commandeered for service in the front line.[43] Back in the mountains, his train passed through Trento where on the drafty station platform he observed "transport after transport, all human numbers in the lottery of war." Down the arteries of the congested railway network, a slow buildup was under way toward a grand Austrian offensive from both the plains and the mountains. It was an operation where there was no unanimity at High Command over which front had priority; as a result, "the whole thing was rather a bungled affair even before it started."[44]

He was to join the heavy artillery allotted to the 18th Infantry Division (18ID) on the Asiago plateau, a sector where a key breakthrough was expected. On 5 June, as he alighted in Val Sugana and noted how "grey and nebulous looms the rock face," what was to come seemed ominous. Only a few days earlier, frontline commanders had complained about inadequate supply lines, how the buildup of equipment had repeatedly stalled: the 18ID expected 950 horses but only 150 had arrived. The division could only be reached one way, a precipitous winding path that passed through the desolate Campomulo valley.[45] In the freezing drizzle, carrying a heavy knapsack and out of breath, he climbed this path and marched for hours along a road strewn with horse cadavers to reach the reserve camp at Campomulo. There he met his new regimental commander, Major Meindl, who resembled a typical "hard-drinking and smoking Oschitz burgher"—good-natured, but tactless. When he inquired if he could eat with the men in the mess, Meindl concurred but expressed his mistrust of one-year volunteers who "did not know how to behave"; he reminded an astonished Rutha not to put a knife in his mouth at meals. The incident reveals as much about Rutha's bourgeois self-perception as it does about his egalitarian and sensitive Wandervogel approach to the "ranks." Later, when eating in the men's mess, he put a knife in his mouth for the first time.

Late on 9 June the move to the front line began. A new battalion commander, a Pole who needed an interpreter, arrived and gave Rutha a special role.[46] He was to be one of the gun leaders *[Geschützführer]* and responsible for supervising fifty men who would take munitions up to the frontline positions. The route was treacherous, passing along a "death road" so exposed to enemy fire that movement had to be at night. Into the darkness the column edged forward, crouching behind rocks, slipping zigzag up the path, breathless, cursing, dripping with sweat, expecting the enemy. Turning a corner the ghostly ruined village of Gallio rose before them and a shell whistled down. "I lay flat on the ground next to a dead horse and a pile of tin cans. Then the second, the third . . . Now I was really quite calm as the terrible tension had found release." Reaching their goal in the pouring rain, the eight gun carriages were uncovered, tied to trees, and two hundred hands hoisted them down a slope in one horrific mass of iron, mud, and flesh: "So it went on until nightfall under rain and enemy fire. The beast shoots right at us as if he knows that we have to work here. Thank God it's so cloudy for otherwise Heaven help us, we would have had the planes on our skulls in a quarter of an hour."

On the eve of the offensive the divisional position was miserable. As its commander complained, the troops were already exhausted after carrying munitions to the front line, food was scarce, and shelter from the elements extremely difficult; the most primitive comforts for maintaining morale were absent.[47] Rutha's diary reflected this. His own shelter was a damp cave that offered little protection if struck directly by enemy fire. The Italian artillery positions opposite were uphill and wholly concealed in a wooded zone, yet it was into that wood that a successful Austrian advance was expected after the artillery barrage. Not surprisingly many Austrian officers were themselves pessimistic. Rutha's own superior, Oberleutnant Gärtner (a congenial Viennese Wandervogel), seemed jumpy, his mood infectious. Rutha in turn, as a *Geschützführer* responsible for one battery gun, nervously sensed that his men lacked training, and he hardly knew them. As he listened to trees being felled to clear the line of fire, "crashing down like wounded men," he resolved to "be a real man" when the hour required it. Already he felt ill and wrote a few lines home.

In the early hours of 15 June he awoke. His crew—a "team of twelve ants"—crawled over the gun to prepare it, Gärtner anxiously supervising the whole battery. At 3:00 a.m., though they were still not ready, the order came. Rutha bellowed. The first shell was trained and fired. Stone and metal hailed down. They pressed themselves to the ground, then jumped up and loaded another shell. "Suddenly no more light, only a screeching hell around us. We have no time to heed death, only lie down, load, fire. Mind feverish, tongue sticks to palate, then a terrible feeling—gas." Scarcely was the mask on than he choked and coughed his lungs out. The air was rent with missiles and a new shock intruded: shells exhausted. He dispatched the whole crew to the rear to collect them. Only seven men returned; the rest he would find torn apart near the munitions dump, one with his whole face blown off. The nightmare had lasted seven hours, and as he rested later in the cave, his lungs burning, he brooded with others about the "horrible uncertainty" of the day's events. The battalion commander arrived to praise them, promising decorations for all the "gun leaders." But as the Pole almost wept at the loss of a quarter of the battery, Rutha was most struck by his superior's unabashed despondency, his frank admission that everyone was in despair. The divisional infantry had indeed reached their target, but most enemy positions in the rear had held firm, thwarting any further Austrian advance.

The hell of these days had a lasting impact on Rutha's health and began to shape his approach to military conflict. Before the attack he had suffered bronchitis and diarrhea; afterward he had gas poisoning, as did 80 percent of one regiment, and he was running a temperature of 104 degrees Fahrenheit (40 degrees Celsius), a victim of the influenza sweeping the whole division.[48] On 17 June he was ordered to the rear and had to endure again the "death road" run to Campomulo, dodging shells and sweating profusely as his companions raced ahead of him: "Up on the road everything is shot at, but the fire at the moment is aimed to the left in the valley. So we run. In spite of all the pain, my eyes peer at every stone, my heart trembles, cowering whenever one comes over. Munitions scattered everywhere. Chaos. There in a road trench lies a corpse. Compassionate hands have laid a dirty coat on him to protect him from view and flies; only the rain-washed hands lie exposed, grasping at something. What did this lonely soldier see as he fell?" Once at the camp, a doctor pronounced that he would be cured on site rather than sent on leave. He was put to bed in a bleak shack where the wind whistled through the cracks. "Terribly miserable," he longed for anything that signified home and thought of resting his head on his mother's lap.[49]

There began three weeks' wretched existence as he lay in the shack, soiling the bed, sweating, shivering, and hallucinating. Warm memories of Kunnersdorf were stirred by a postcard from his mother—hens clucking in the courtyard, swallows arriving, the smell of coffee and baking—but they were overshadowed by "deathly miserable thoughts," an alienation even worse than when he was a child in Münchengratz. For his superiors, the supposed leaders, seemed so indifferent to the ill, sacrilegious to the fallen, treating them simply as numbers. His idealism about Austria's noble mission was similarly disintegrating as he observed the undisciplined postoffensive mood. Fellow officers seemed only too pleased with wounds that allowed them to escape the front; even Major Meindl, the regiment commander, had erratically expressed shame at the army's performance and said he would do anything to get home. Only because of his debilitation was that Rutha's goal too, and ironically it was Meindl who finally overruled the doctor. He was granted seven weeks' sick leave, and on 7 July left the mountains.

The emotional and spiritual rebirth Rutha underwent in June 1918 made him radically reassess what was important in life. His own metaphysical and moral world had long been dominated by Wandervogel communing with nature, with little time for religion.[50] Although he would always remain nominally a Catholic, and believe in something spiritual, he could never be a devotee of organized religion (thus in the future, as we will see, the Catholicism of his own "Spannist" creed was bound to be thin). In 1918, the rigid church dogma seemed to offer no solace for the carnage he had witnessed. And he was equally skeptical about any afterlife, Heaven or Valhalla, not expecting to see his dead comrades again. Man in fact seemed no different from the rest of nature, simply a "tiny wheel in the clockwork of the world," which, after fulfilling its role, broke off and disappeared.[51]

On leaving the war zone, he acknowledged that his experiences there had made him cherish all aspects of life:

> Since the days when I felt death creeping past me so closely, I have a boundless reverence for life. Life. It is something so immense, the embodiment of so much pleasure and pain, but then something so negligible when I think of the thousands of young bodies that lie torn apart and dishonored in this stone wilderness. I hear not only the laments of wives and mothers, no, I

hear the whimpering of unborn children, whose seeds in these dead men curse the madness of peoples who tear each other limb from limb, just because a few despots want it. They always preach that "war is a great mentor"—well, it has made me a democrat of the clearest type, an anarchist and terrorist against the *belligerents* in both camps.[52]

For spiritual guidance as well as emotional support, he could only return to the Bohemian Wandervogel, for at the front that link to the *Heimat* had regularly comforted him with memories and postcards, supplying something beyond what was typical for the rural soldier.[53]

But as the quotation above hints, life in the war zone had also given him much pause for thought about deficiencies in leadership, and particularly the qualities required to secure the best from men and sustain their morale. His diary was peppered with examples of cynical and bullying Habsburg officers who were insensitive to subordinates and who received little respect in return; others like Meindl were kind but wholly lacking in authority.[54] From this Rutha concluded not just that the Habsburg war machine was seriously flawed but that these lessons from army life needed to be transposed to the youth struggle at home to ensure firmer direction and unity. When he next confronted the leaders of the Bohemian Wandervogel, he came with a conviction that youth leadership should be more precisely formulated. In short, only charismatic "leader-personalities" could spark the dynamic bonding the youth movement needed to give it new vigor.

LEADER-PERSONALITY

By the summer of 1918, sheer economic exhaustion suggested that Austria-Hungary's war must end very soon. In the Bohemian lands, Czech and German politicians had long been considering the postwar world and refining their respective radical agendas. For both national camps the programs were hardly new; it was uncertainty about the empire's future that sharpened minds, spurring nationalists to outstrip their rivals before it was too late.

On the one hand, Czech politicians in January 1918 had publicly asserted their nation's right to self-determination in any peace settlement. Their declaration implied that Austria-Hungary would not survive the war, leaving the Czechs to form an independent state within the historic borders of the

Bohemian lands. On the other, 1918 witnessed an intensification of a "German course" across Austria, spearheaded by the government in Vienna to shore up the German position. It was notable that in March the emperor himself made a tour of German Bohemia only. In May, Vienna duly decreed that Bohemia in the new year would be administratively restructured, divided up nationally into twelve districts; the solution would destroy overall Bohemian autonomy under a Czech majority, ensuring that Germans could govern themselves with no Czech interference.[55] As such, it fully alienated Czech national politicians from Austria as much as it threw a lifeline to German Bohemian leaders. But all depended on the survival of the Habsburg Empire.

It was against this background of intensified political struggle that the Bohemian Wandervögel reassessed their future. For veterans like Karl Metzner the minimum national goal was to preserve German Bohemia against the Czech aggressor. In early 1917 Metzner had echoed Austria's German course, urging the Wandervogel to think more carefully about consolidating *Deutschböhmen* (German Bohemia) and nurturing it as a model for all other German lands.[56] Rutha agreed that the *Heimat* was wholly on the defensive against Czech chauvinism. In April 1918 when in Budweis, he had soaked up the "German" culture and architecture of a town that was now sadly in the hands of "Czech braggarts"; Germans, he reflected, needed to be as chauvinist as the Czechs to survive.[57]

Rutha had returned to this theme at the front. There he had read *O Böhmen*, a light nationalist novel by the southern Bohemian writer Hans Watzlik, where the main male protagonist naïvely underestimates Czech (female) deviousness. It made him very agitated:

We [Germans] want to meet eternal hatred with understanding and generosity, we certainly speak sharply, but our actions are the opposite. We don't understand how to sacrifice ourselves for the people, whereas the Czechs, whether big or small, poor or rich, make a corresponding contribution once their great orators sound in their ears. I feel so often that I'm still far too tolerant, conciliatory and flexible, and tactful when others speak ill of Germans and Germany. It's now the case that I too must condemn the mistakes of "Prussians" and recognize German errors when they are explained credibly to me. That a Czech will never do, even if he himself realizes a mistake a hundred times over. That is just their pride and hatred. Heinz, you must also become hard, very hard and partisan.[58]

Military service sharpened this stance against national apathy in the face of a Slav flood that supposedly was spreading across "historic German space." Rutha already believed the widespread nationalist myth that Czechs were sacrificing much less than Germans and thereby undermining the armed forces. His commitment to Aryan selection had also not diminished since Wrchhaben even if he had calmed that dispute when Gauwart. His diary simply equated Jews with vice, an "un-German" element who deserved no place in the youth mission. Most tellingly, at the front he had initially warmed to one idealistic comrade as a "kindred spirit"; soon afterward he discovered the man was Jewish and realized he could never be a real friend.[59]

It was in late August, at a Wandervogel Bundestag held at Krummau in southern Bohemia, that Rutha began to fuse his ideas about selection and leadership into a clearer theory. Organized exhaustively by Kletzl, the Krummau celebration brought together 650 teenagers from across Austria but was very much a Bohemian affair in a Gau now numbering fifty branches and a thousand members. Amid the usual adolescent high spirits, a small group of Bohemian veterans met on 26 August for private discussions about the postwar challenges and their own future. Some like Stauda were adamant they needed to move on, leaving the Wandervogel to autonomous youth itself; since early 1917, Stauda had successfully encouraged some Wandervogel veterans to form special groups in their local communities as a network of postwar activists. Other elders like Kletzl and Rutha, whose adolescence had been abnormally stretched by the war, still expected to play some role in the postwar Wandervogel.[60]

Alongside this generational issue, it was Karl Metzner in his officer's uniform who mapped out a broader agenda in Krummau. Grimly he predicted the collapse of Austria-Hungary and warned of the threat to German Bohemia since it lacked both unity and leadership.[61] He convinced his peers that in peacetime a new, more inclusive venture would be needed to regenerate the *Heimat*, a mission stretching beyond the Wandervogel or the veterans' groups, permeating all corners of the *Volk* as a grassroots nonpolitical movement. This visionary program he called *Herzogtum Böhmen:* the Duchy of Bohemia. The title conjured up a chivalrous past utopia when Bohemia was ruled by a German aristocracy, yet the program was one for the immediate future. Its vanguard would be those veterans who had outgrown adolescence or "youth" and were ready to offer their talents to a nation in distress.[62]

Although Rutha attended this meeting and approved its program, his diary reveals his relative indifference to Metzner's romantic Duchy. He was mulling over a different set of priorities, especially about reinvigorating the youth movement with charismatic leadership.[63] Krummau fell during the last week of his convalescent leave, and the frontline trauma had not left him. Other Wandervögel might see him as the "old Heinz," but he judged himself a changed man: "So far from them in battle and death and I cannot supply them with any leadership." He felt strangely alone in their midst. Nor was he inclined to take much part in the elders' meetings, finding them boring and obsessed with regulations, insufficiently geared to revitalizing the youth agenda.

What lifted his despondency was the mass of vivacious adolescents who were mingling excitedly in the ancient Bohemian venue. One sultry evening, hundreds sat in the open air outside the Schwarzenburg castle, their faces illuminated by burning torches. The special guest was the local author Hans Watzlik, who when the singing had faded rose to read from the last pages of his novel *O Böhmen*. He spoke, Rutha noted, like a prophet, swearing to preserve the eternal and God-given Bohemia: "Soft and caressing sounded his voice as he told of the homeland . . . Sacrifice and struggle rang out from dead words and his oath was mingled with the jubilant cry of seven hundred youths." It was a truly galvanizing experience for those young "hot pulsating hearts" encircling the speaker in the twilight.

After it, a second event occurred that made an even deeper impression. A blond teenager, who had caught Rutha's eye earlier, stood up and declared that, after so much talk from the elders, it was time for the lads themselves to speak out. A large group gathered under the ash trees to hear the charismatic youth. There followed criticism of Bohemian unilateralism, and Rutha himself felt bound to intervene and remind them that Austrian unity was indeed a priority. But the major upshot of the discussion then surprised him. The adolescents demanded not complete youth autonomy but that the current Wandervogel elders continue as their leaders. As Rutha noted, "It was the first time that spiritual leadership was recognized." In short—and contrary to Stauda—there was still a key role for senior youth leaders like Rutha or Kletzl in providing overall "spiritual" guidance for the movement. Spontaneity and leadership would of course still emanate from the youths themselves, but they were requesting mentoring and direction.

Besides offering elders a role, the idea of a revised Wandervogel hierarchy could meet nationalist anxieties about the lack of firm leadership at this turbulent time. From what he had observed during his brief military service,

Rutha was also sure that leaders of men needed certain qualities. And probably from reading Ferdinand Büttner and Hans Blüher, he instinctively linked charismatic leadership to notions of Aryan selection and, subconsciously, to homoerotic bonding. Here there immediately came to mind Oskar Just's model of an Aryan cohort with a sexual charge. Admiring one blond youth at Krummau, Rutha noted: "I am overjoyed that in *me* Oskar's efforts are taking ever deeper roots, enabling me to perform leadership-work with at best five or six German men."[64] There beckoned the idea of training an elite group that was racially pure: this had to be a criterion for youth selection—alongside "willpower" and "spiritual health"—and it irritated him that the elders' meeting did not pay it more attention.[65]

But intertwined with this prioritizing of blond Aryans was Rutha's sexual attraction toward such young men. At Krummau he tried vainly to revive some female friendships, but his eye was most alert to blond lads who radiated charisma and had the aura of "leader-personalities." One was the youth who had emerged after the Watzlik reading. Another was Fritz Medikus, a bear-like blond with a childlike face, with whom he struck up a conversation when sheltering from the rain. He quickly felt Medikus resembled his old intimates, Hansl and Förster, for not only was he very receptive, he was looking for guidance from an older man and could be classified as a "personality."

The conclusion from this and other encounters at Krummau was both personal and professional in terms of the youth movement's future. Rutha was attracted to "personalities" like Medikus who opened up to him as confidants and seemed ideal as disciples. Equally, he noted, he had "come to realize that to be a leader means to be a personality."[66] During the weekend he was able to convince many other elders that the movement must urgently cultivate charismatic youths as future leaders. To his surprise, it was especially Metzner, whom Rutha considered rather too "political," who proved receptive. They managed some quiet time together with the result that at an elders' meeting Metzner singled Rutha out to explain the case for enhancing youth leadership. In this way Rutha had begun to formulate his own agenda for youth development and secured his peers' endorsement. He declined any formal office in Metzner's Duchy, already envisaging his future not as a veteran but as a "spiritual" youth leader.

Although he departed for the front soon after Krummau (and his diary ended), Rutha's initiative on selective leader-personalities immediately bore fruit, for Kletzl was keen to promote it. He too was about to return to the trenches but managed first to edit a special number of *Burschen heraus* devoted to leadership. This so-called *Führerspiegel* (Leader Mirror) trumpeted Rutha's message that "the pivot of our movement must be the cultivation of leader-personalities." In a key article, written from the front and composed in the form of a personal letter, Rutha recalled how at Krummau one adolescent had complained about the lack of leadership. Youth education must indeed be based "on the impact of a personality," a leader not simply dictating in a "school-masterly fashion" but educating by example, helping young lads who anxiously struggled with "smoldering urges." In this advice there was more than a hint of Rutha's own personal struggles: "If you have ever experienced the depth of a young man's soul, the lad who will only open up from his tight reserve to someone not tainted by being a high-handed idol or a dry schoolmaster, then you will know how lonely and helpless most of them are in their youthful doubts and struggles." They needed a selfless leader to aid them as both brother and "fellow-combatant." Ideally, the youth movement should consist of such charismatic leaders whose influence would be limited to a small, specially selected group of followers.[67] It was a call that probably already matched Rutha's own plans for the future: to recruit a small group of blond disciples whom he would train in mind and body for the national mission. If it only hinted at racial selection, the ideal disciple was clear, for in a simple drawing by Oskar Just the *Führerspiegel* depicted a blond Aryan youth (fig.11).[68]

In retrospect, late 1918 was the high point of Rutha's obsession with Aryan selection. His anti-Semitism would mellow when faced with other priorities and retreat into a latent form; in any case, despite intemperate language, he had never wished the Jews violence but simply considered them "un-German."[69] Like many other nationalists, even Jewish nationalists, his rigid criteria for youth membership had sharpened in the war years, especially as the nation needed to be more vigilant about "outsiders." His own origins on the Czech-German language border substantially reinforced this divisive mindset (which someone like Stauda could not quite understand). Thus it was that in the summer of 1918, when he returned to Kunnersdorf, he took time to visit and contemplate the significance of the local Devil's Wall. For fellow Wandervögel he described it as a living symbol of the German Bohemians' dilemma, an age-old physical barrier to the Slav flood that was washing into the sacred *Heimat*. It was the young, he claimed, who had a real duty to uphold this wall for all Germandom.[70]

AN OATH FOR GERMAN RENEWAL

In the coming years Rutha would build significantly upon his ideas from the *Führerspiegel*, but he did so in a radically altered political framework. In October 1918, as the journal circulated around Bohemia, neither he nor Kletzl were available to continue their initiative. It tells us much about their sense of duty and continued allegiance to the Bohemia-Austria *Heimat* that they left again for the front despite the dim likelihood that the war would end favorably. They were not among the thousands of Habsburg soldiers who were now absent without leave in the hinterland.

When both returned home in mid-November they found the *Heimat* in a state of confusion. The empire had disintegrated, splintering into component national parts; in the Czech-German region, both political camps were moving ahead with radical national programs wholly at odds with one another. On 28 October a national council in Prague had proclaimed a Czechoslovak state, encompassing all the historic Bohemian lands as well as Slovakia. In response, German politicians—true to the "German course"—announced the creation of four German provinces across Bohemia-Moravia, free of Czech control and claiming to be constituent parts of an independent German Austria already proclaimed in Vienna.

It was a bewildering situation and clearly temporary, for the Bohemian-Moravian borderlands were economically and politically isolated, largely dependent on Prague's goodwill for survival. By December 1918, troops of the new Czechoslovak state had easily overrun them, toppling the four short-lived regimes, including the most influential, *Deutschböhmen,* based at Reichenberg. The latter had briefly had time to put a garrison of thirty men on the summit of Mount Jeschken. But on 11 December, the villages below were surprised to hear a voice ringing out, announcing via loudspeaker that Czech soldiers had disarmed the guard and conquered the peak.[71]

For Wandervogel veterans like Metzner, who at Krummau had predicted Austria's collapse before winter, the speed of events was still overwhelming. The achievements at Krummau, which included improved relations with the Austrian Bund, had rapidly evaporated as the initiative passed to German Bohemian politicians.[72] Even so, while the *Deutschböhmen* government was in existence, some Wandervogel elders were working energetically to implement the *Herzogtum* vision. With the Austrian link ostensibly severed, the priority was to establish a *völkisch* network across Bohemia. Kletzl now devoted himself in this direction, beginning in Prague where he successfully reactivated a *völkisch* forum among German university students. By late November, he and Metzner had decided to create for the Duchy eight districts spanning northern Bohemia and three regional offices to cater for the needs of the German diaspora in Prague and southern Bohemia. They also agreed that selected veterans would be invited to the ruined castle of Schreckenstein near Aussig in order to finalize the movement's constitution.[73]

It was at Schreckenstein on 5 January 1919 that the utopian *Herzogtum* program revived its momentum. The dramatic location, the inspiration for Richard Wagner's opera *Tannhäuser* and many romantic paintings, fully complemented the national-spiritual venture. Perched high above the River Elbe with Bohemia's landscape laid out before them, thirty Wandervogel veterans assembled in the Knights' Hall of the castle. They included Metzner, Stauda, Kampe, Kletzl, and also Rutha. Like the knights in Wagner's *Parsifal* committed to preserving the Holy Grail, they swore an oath to work for the renewal of the German people in a new Bohemian Lands Movement *[Böhmerland-Bewegung]*.[74]

Their concrete objective was to create in all walks of life across German Bohemia-Moravia a grassroots network committed to self-defense against the threat caused by the Czech seizure of power. As the veterans drew on their Wandervogel creed, so it was to be a crusade avoiding party politics, which had supposedly caused military defeat and imperial collapse. Instead, and largely due to Rutha's influence, the oath spoke innovatively about a movement led by "personalities," who as part of their activity would consciously encourage "mature youths" to take part in the mission.[75]

The Schreckenstein program might indeed seem otherworldly—and has been described by some Czech historians as "childish" and ineffectual.[76] Yet it had a practical pedagogic role in the early 1920s that subtly affected many German Bohemian communities, inculcating a *völkisch* outlook and formulating long-term goals for national renewal. For most Wandervogel veterans, certainly, it provided a postwar purpose, a life of national-cultural activism beyond the youth movement. For Rutha, however, despite the welcome slogan at Schreckenstein of "personalities," the new crusade would quickly prove nebulous and unfulfilling. His priority remained the cause of adolescents with the Wandervogel at least as his starting point. In 1919, focusing on the concept of charismatic leadership, he set out in a fresh direction to reinvigorate the youth movement so that it could best meet the Czech challenge.

It was a rebirth in more ways than one, for after a decade he was returning to live permanently in the tranquility of Kunnersdorf-Oschitz. Not that he desired this. In his diary he had briefly mentioned uncertainty about his future career and strongly objected to any stay-at-home job that implied a bourgeois existence at odds with the Wandervogel lifestyle. The only consolation was that after initial adjustments he might be his own man.[77] Other ambitions after the war were in vain. Possibly he had pondered a military career, but that seemed blocked due to the new Czech masters who did not recognize his officer rank (thus he simply remained a reservist and was called up briefly during the mobilization against Hungary in late 1921).[78] More decisive anyway was probably the attitude of his father. Adolf Rutha's ill health was increasingly evident, and he expected his son to take charge of the mill. Here the prospects were inauspicious, not least financially. During the war the elder Rutha, as a good German-Austrian and Habsburg patriot, had invested his savings in Austrian war bonds, which in the new Czechoslovakia were suddenly irredeemable. There was no money to finance Gretel Rutha's ambition of studying medicine at university and probably little left to invest in the family business.[79]

While the family unit exited the war seriously impoverished, its personal traumas had not quite ended either. At the end of hostilities, the worldwide Spanish influenza epidemic had infiltrated Prague, killing 673 civilians in October 1918.[80] Richard Rutha was one of the victims. Heinz had always bemoaned his elder brother's curtness and reserve, his lack of *völkisch* thinking, and his bourgeois lifestyle. At their last meeting in the summer of 1918 he bitterly regretted their distance from each other, noting how Richard was "more foreign to me than many ordinary acquaintances."[81]

The death cast a long shadow over the Rutha mill, comparable to the demise of Effert and Polifka, and had a tragic aftermath. Anastasie, Heinz's mother, had gone to Prague to care for Richard in his last days and caught the infection. She never fully recovered, grew steadily weaker in the following year, and finally on 20 December 1919 expired from heart failure. At the funeral three days later, Richard's body was transported from Prague to be buried next to her in the family plot at Oschitz.[82] Heinz publicly described the loss as a "heart-wrenching experience" that affected his activity for several months.[83] By death the family unit at Bad Kunnersdorf had been dramatically altered. Rutha's base there would be one that he could and would increasingly shape to his own liking.

FIVE

The Militant Youth Mission

Czechoslovakia in the 1920s has often been viewed as a success story. Of the new states emerging from the Habsburg Empire, it was the first to stabilize economically and attract foreign capital. Its energetic foreign minister, Edvard Beneš, quickly gave the state international security with an elaborate alliance system and propagated its image as a loyal bastion of the West, eager to defend the peace settlement in central Europe. Not least in domestic politics, Czechoslovakia when compared to its neighbors—Austria, Hungary, or Poland—seemed a stable liberal democracy with regular parliamentary elections and all shades of political and national opinion represented in the Prague parliament.[1]

The German minority, or Sudeten Germans as many of them began to term themselves by the mid-1920s, appeared part of this stability. Constituting 23 percent of the state's inhabitants in the 1921 census, or 33 percent in Bohemia alone, they are usually portrayed as gradually moving from a position of "negativism"—hostility to the state—to "activism" or realistic cooperation with the Czechoslovak government in order to secure the best possible deal. As one historian has suggested, "many Germans were hopeful of activism and willing to give it a chance."[2] The proof seemed clear in the parliamentary elections of 1925 when the activist political parties won over 70 percent of the "German vote": in October 1926 two of them joined the coalition government. To many observers, then and since, it was the key sign that ethnic relations were steadily improving with most Germans accepting their new state environment. Confirmation came in the 1929 elections when the three main activist parties again secured a majority of the German vote.[3]

Yet this common interpretation of German behavior is problematic and needs to be unraveled if we are to set the mindset of Heinz Rutha in proper context. The interpretation firstly tends to assume that German activist politicians were full converts to harmonious cooperation with the Czechoslovak state; in fact, as shown in the 1930s, many were quite ready to retreat into their "national castles" when their constituents expected it.[4] The move toward political activism, particularly from 1922, was an inevitable tactic that resulted both because Czechoslovakia seemed increasingly stable and because Weimar Germany declined to lend any support to the German minority. Secondly, and crucially, an interpretation centering on activism is overwhelmingly party-political and Czech-centered. It privileges German behavior in the Czechoslovak parliamentary system as the only reliable barometer of German public opinion. It also assumes that the German electorate's own focus was the activist/negativist issue, rather than those social or economic concerns that might lead them toward Agrarian, Social Democrat, or other loyalties at election time.

In fact, vast numbers of Germans in the 1920s were disengaged from the party-political system, and their mentality cannot be reliably assessed through that Czech prism. They would vote in parliamentary elections since voting was compulsory. But otherwise, the civic activity of many centered around alternative organizations that continued to promote a vibrant nationalist agenda at a grassroots level, including a revitalized *Heimat* education. These encompassed the defense societies that had emerged in the late Habsburg period, like the *Bund der Deutschen*, which in 1923 numbered 240,000 adherents. Then there was the *Turnverband* (German gymnastics society) with a network of 150,000 men, or the mass of postwar youth movements that mushroomed across Bohemia-Moravia. For many Germans these nationalist groups were an inherent element of their local community, natural for them to join. For the more *völkisch*-minded, or those who wanted to prove their national credentials, the wider regional networks of these groups gave the illusion at least of embryonic unity and security in the Czechoslovak framework. They dominated the local German landscape, yet most foreign diplomatic observers ignored them, as have most historians, focusing instead on party politics and the workings of Czech political democracy. Uncovering what Tara Zahra has termed this "autonomous segregated universe" of the nationalists is crucial if we are to understand the mentality of those Germans who, after living through the first decade of Czechoslovakia, "suddenly" in the 1930s seemed to veer in a negativist direction.[5]

THE *TURNVEREIN*

Heinz Rutha in the 1920s lived almost entirely in this parallel world where the stirrings of Czechoslovak democracy, including the slogans of "activist" and "negativist," were certainly glimpsed and understood but largely ignored. His own priority in the postwar decade remained the cause of German Bohemian youth. He was determined to educate male adolescents according to new principles, and increasingly thought about their potential as the vanguard of a revitalized German mission in the Bohemian lands.

Soon he would question whether the Wandervogel could really act as the vehicle for this. As he noted later, "I was anxious to confront romanticism in the youth movement and steer the whole of youth education along straighter, practical lines." It was a notion, pioneering in many ways, that would lead him from his initial Wandervogel base toward organizing a youth mission through the German Turnverband.[6] Along the way he drew on philosophers and writers, ancient and contemporary, both to make sense of his emotional interaction with male youths and to ponder youth's central place in a restructured Sudeten German society. The sources for this path of discovery are far sparser than those that, for 1918 alone, allow such insight into his personal world. But enough exists to plot the rather tortuous route that led him eventually from "romantic" Wandervogel toward "practical" Turnverband and the person of Konrad Henlein.

Rutha's connection to the regional Turn movement had started soon after his return to Kunnersdorf-Oschitz.[7] When his mother was buried on 23 December 1919, a delegation from the village Turn branch *[Turnverein]* participated at the funeral. It was testimony to his sudden involvement in an organization that previously he would have avoided, for it catered predominantly for male adults aged eighteen to thirty-eight with minimal regard for "youth." The Oschitz Turnverein, founded in 1897 and counting both Effert and Polifka among its members, had wholly lapsed during the war but was relaunched in January 1919 by a group of former elders. During the year they went on a recruitment drive, securing forty new members and temporary accommodation in Oschitz town hall.

This society was just one cell in a Turn network that stretched across the German regions of Czechoslovakia. Like the Wandervogel, its origins lay in Germany, conceived during the Napoleonic wars as a mass gymnastics movement in order to discipline Germans to defend their nationality; it was both racially elitist and anti-Semitic, enforcing tight selection and social cohesion.

In the 1860s it had spread to Austria, creating in the Bohemian lands a strong network of German groups and a precise Czech equivalent in the shape of the Sokol movement. From the 1880s the Austrian Turners veered in a *völkisch* direction: it was their fierce commitment to Aryan selection that finally caused them in 1904 to abandon Germany and create their own independent Austrian organization. After the war, Turners of the Bohemian lands inevitably split off from Austria, but their *völkisch* values remained, supplemented by a more intense anti-Czech focus. In November 1919 they were formally reconstituted as a new German Turnverband, encompassing all Turners of Czechoslovakia with a network of fifteen regions *[Gaue]*.[8]

The Oschitz Turnverein belonged with 116 other local branches in northern Bohemia to the Jeschken-Iser Gau, which in the early 1920s was one of the largest, with over fourteen thousand fee-paying members.[9] Although Oschitz was at the very bottom of the Turn hierarchical pile, it serves well as a microcosm. It was dominated by its Turn council *[Turnrat]*, a clique of a dozen elders elected annually by all members over the age of twenty-one, who usually passed the offices between themselves; they met intermittently in each other's houses depending on the urgency of business. In May 1919 one of their new recruits was Heinz Rutha. When in August they invited him to one of their meetings, his priorities were clear, for he proposed a local "youth festival" with songs, lantern slides, and Wandervogel participation; they in turn clearly admired his energy, plain speaking, and recent army record. A few months later, when the society discussed building a special "Turn hall," Rutha agreed to organize publicity and serve on the preparatory committee. And at the annual general meeting on 3 January 1920, when an open ballot was held for Turnrat positions, he was elected to the new office of *Dietwart*. It placed him in charge of *völkisch* education, a position he would hold for five of the next six years.

If the elders' overwhelming concern was adult male gymnastics activity, financing it was problematic in the new Czechoslovakia. Unlike the Czech Sokol, the Turnverband received no state funding and had to rely on its membership's goodwill. Already by the end of 1920 the branch was in financial crisis, and its officials, including Rutha, were forced to make personal advances to cover the rising debt.[10] By 1924, nevertheless, the Turnrat was determined to relaunch its Turn hall project. An extraordinary meeting of the membership, convened at the town hall on the evening of 29 April, witnessed a lively debate and an agreement to elect a new building committee. Rutha was among those who stood for election, having expressed firm opinions; significantly, he wanted the Turn hall to be a "national house" for the whole community and proposed inviting representatives from outside the Turnverein onto the committee.

That Rutha had participated so assiduously since 1919 can partly be explained by the organization's central role in the Oschitz community and his own acceptance that he was a permanent resident. Besides competing in regional gymnastic competitions or inviting neighboring branches to visit Oschitz, the Turnverein was a significant force for postwar social cohesion in the village, one that few villagers could ignore. Every year, not least to fundraise, it ran Christmas and New Year's parties, a masked ball, and other "Turn evenings" of gymnastics, singing, and dancing. It was the main *völkisch* society of Oschitz, selective in its membership (expelling a Jew in 1919) and taking pride in its didactic mission. In many ways it served as a community venue where the wounds of war could be healed, or in Benjamin Ziemann's phrase, war memories could be "transfigured" into peacetime activities. The Turnrat elders for instance were keenly aware of the ultimate sacrifice that many members had made, and in September 1921 organized a special event to honor them—a "victors' party." Dressed in black, they headed a procession that began early at the Kunnersdorf spa and ended in the center of Oschitz with speeches and a wreath-laying on behalf of the war dead.[11]

Rutha fully adhered to these familiar postwar rituals that commemorated the national sacrifice both past and present. As Dietwart, his job was quasi-religious, to act as "apostle of the Volk," the local *völkisch* educator who communicated ancient German values and celebrated historical and mythical anniversaries. The office gained new importance in the postwar Turnverband, where there was ample opportunity for fresh interpretation of the German historic mission.[12] While the rest of the Oschitz Turnrat admired Rutha's energy, being the local Dietwart matched his own postwar understanding of a deeper purpose where he himself had a "spiritual" role. It also made the humdrum branch activities more tolerable. Indeed, in December 1921, he was elected as *Sprechwart* or branch leader. Serving for a year, he intensified branch activity with a record number of Turnrat meetings and new social events that included a profitable "harvest and *Heimat* festival." His personal stamp and discipline were also present in the Turnrat minute book, notably his irritation that some colleagues were very lax in their attendance record.[13]

What is less evident from these records is how his ideas were evolving on the subject of Turner youth. As we will see, the picture is clearer when we assess his continued Wandervogel activity. Certainly, the Oschitz Turnrat's stance toward adolescence was one prevalent across the Turnverband. Although conscious of cultivating the next generation, they saw young Turners (those aged fourteen to seventeen who were patronizingly termed *Zöglinge* or "pupils") chiefly as an appendage who should adapt to the ways of the adult movement. In February 1920, the Turnrat discussed the disrespectful behavior of youths at social events and asked the Dietwart (Rutha) to give the troublemakers a stern lecture. Only in late 1924 did they think of actively engaging adolescents in the Turn hall project.[14]

Between these dates, however, the youth question had regularly surfaced in the wider Turnverband and its journal, the *Turnzeitung*.[15] Spurred on by an influx of young recruits after 1919, a group of "progressives" had suggested creating a proper Turn youth movement, urging the network to adapt to the spirit of its young Turners and not alienate them unnecessarily. Leading Dietwarts pushed the idea further, so that in November 1923 the Turnverband leadership finally decided to appoint its first youth leader [*Jugendwart*] and offered the post to the new Dietwart of the Jeschken-Iser Gau, Konrad Henlein. Although Henlein declined due to his Gau duties, the event is highly significant. It not only implies his own interest in cultivating Turner youth but hints at his friendship with Rutha.

Rutha and Henlein had much in common. Born in 1898 near Reichenberg, Henlein too had a mother of Czech descent, and he too had been scarred through service on the Italian front. In August 1919 he had returned from Italian captivity a very serious individual.[16] Although his everyday job was as a bank clerk in Reichenau near Gablonz, his passionate commitment was to the local Turn movement, where his father remained very active. Unlike Rutha, he lacked adolescent experience of the youth movement, but one of his first postwar Turnverein duties was to organize the Reichenau boys. His own qualities as a modern Turner were never in dispute, for he was highly proficient in gymnastics. He also quickly sensed that the Turnverband should not be a social club but a vehicle for revitalizing a nationalist struggle in the new Czechoslovak framework, applying the original movement's discipline to the current crisis. Already in 1920, like Rutha in Oschitz, he had been elected as the first Dietwart of his local branch and began to supply physical training with a contemporary *völkisch* dimension.

The idea of fusing the physical and the spiritual in a national training program for young Germans was precisely what Rutha was contemplating in the early 1920s, albeit from a different perspective via the Wandervogel. Both men saw youthful males as the main target for this holistic education, confining women to traditional feminine roles. And they shared one further crucial quality: through their personality, their age, and their distinguished war record, they could bridge the gap that yawned between Turn elders and the postwar idealistic adolescents, for they showed a keen sensitivity in both directions.

How precisely they met is hazy. It seems to have occurred in mid–1923 at a gathering of Jeschken-Iser Gau officials when Henlein had just been elected *Gaudietwart*. Rutha, who was probably attending as a branch Dietwart, listened to Henlein's "fiery speech," and, apparently, the two bonded immediately. As one account effusively recalls, "they realized that in both of them there burned the same passion to serve nation and homeland unconditionally."[17] While Henlein was attracted by Rutha's youth vision and experience, Rutha could admire Henlein's serious personality, his firm *völkisch* outlook, and his commitment to training a disciplined male cohort.

The relationship quickly bore fruit. In the summer of 1923, Henlein launched in Reichenau the first Gau youth meeting, with Turn gymnastics, singing competitions, and solemn commemoration of the war dead; among the nine hundred who attended were many non-Turner youths whom Rutha had probably brought along.[18] Henlein reciprocated at Christmas by attending a winter camp that Rutha organized for his own personal youth group in the mountains of northwest Bohemia.[19] The intimacy was even clearer when, on 27 January 1924, Henlein was a guest of the Oschitz Turnverein itself. His Reichenau group, already known as one of the best in the Gau, put on a gymnastics display for an audience of over three hundred.[20]

In a short period after the first encounter with Henlein, Rutha therefore had noted fresh opportunities for putting a youth mission into practice. It was no coincidence that in July 1923 he first suggested publicly that the Wandervogel should join up with the Turnverband. It also seems clear, though the evidence is scant, that thanks to the new Gaudietwart, Rutha finally assumed his first office in the wider Turn movement. While Henlein declined the youth leadership in November, he understood Rutha's own enthusiasm, and there was a logical result. On 25 March 1924, the Oschitz Turnrat minutes recorded with pride: "Turner Heinz Rutha has been elected as Gaujugendwart in Gablonz and earned great applause for the speech that he made."[21]

For the Oschitz Turnrat, one of their number had been elevated in the movement, someone whom they viewed as cosmopolitan anyway due to his network of contacts. For Henlein, Rutha was an ideal choice as first youth coordinator for the Gau (a pioneering move as he was officially appointed even before the first Jugendwart of the whole Turnverband). These years, 1923–1924, were for Rutha a critical turning point. A potential new framework had materialized on which to construct his plans for male youth, ideas that were increasingly drifting away from the "romantic" Bohemian Wandervogel. But since in the past five years that youth movement had absorbed much more of his time than the Turnverein, we need to retrace our steps to the confusion of 1919.

FRESH LIFE

Heinz Rutha's postwar behavior was colored significantly by the surge in *Heimat* education across the (German) Bohemian lands. The grassroots initiatives that sprang up in response to the creation of a Czech national state were diverse. But they had a common passionate belief in education as the main medium for renewing a shattered homeland and promoting elusive German unity in a newly hostile framework. A key coordinating force was the Bohemian Lands Movement, that chivalrous vision created by Wandervogel veterans at Schreckenstein in January 1919.

From that castle, to quote Johannes Stauda, a "secret band of blood brothers" had spread across the German communities, penetrating cultural-national groups and educating all about the "reality" of German national unity. Over six years, until 1925 when it was forced to dissolve, the amorphous organization was loosely linked together by newsletters and journals and hosted annually a "Böhmerland week," a kind of *völkisch* training camp. The leaders, independently carving out their own spheres of operation, included both veteran pedagogues like Emil Lehmann (with his didactic organ, *Heimatbildung*) and newer enthusiasts like Rutha, himself clearly guided by his personal experience of reform pedagogy. Thus, under a broad umbrella many nationalist seeds could be scattered and successfully germinate; the movement, however loosely defined, was crucial in shaping a Sudeten German national consciousness.[22]

The educational trajectory of some "Schreckenstein knights" in the early 1920s is an instructive contrast to Rutha's. Otto Kletzl gradually moved away from Wandervogel youth work in a more cultural direction, becoming editor of the Böhmerland yearbooks.[23] Karl Metzner, who like Stauda felt his Wandervogel days were over, nevertheless resumed his prewar vocation as a youth pedagogue.[24] After first establishing a youth home in Leitmeritz, in 1928 he opened his own private reform school, selecting up to fifty boys and girls for an education that encouraged both physical and spiritual well-being. With its focus on instilling discipline and devotion to the homeland via proximity to nature, Metzner pursued in microcosm many of the old Wandervogel precepts. He shared much with Rutha, not least the values he inculcated to prepare adolescents creatively for service in the national community.

Rutha too was loyal to the Schreckenstein oath, and it perhaps explains why in 1919 he joined his local Turnverein. His pedagogic mission, however, always focused on a revitalized male youth movement. While at first he drew inspiration from Wandervogel values, those were increasingly supplemented by the dynamic qualities he had highlighted since August 1918. Much later, in 1935, he would acknowledge the contribution of the Bohemian Lands Movement, but would describe it as too cultural and insufficiently focused to meet the national crisis:

> We young soldiers recognized after our return from the front and the collapse that no front could be victorious without the most profound unity of the nation in the rear! . . . Pioneers of a new nation could be created only from those front-line men whose own self-discipline served as a model for the masculine discipline of the whole nation and all young men . . . Here it was a question of firmly organizing a new education out of the simple laws of masculinity. First out of that a new political will could grow. But not only from the front soldiers! It also required the glow of young men *[Jungmannschaft]* and for both of them—youths and soldiers—to have the deepest understanding of history, and the strengths and weaknesses of our people, in order to learn lessons and behave accordingly in the future.[25]

In the postwar confusion, Rutha surely lacked quite this clarity of purpose, but the militant words still ring true in articulating his frustration in 1919, his determination after Schreckenstein to galvanize national unity by educating young men. Naturally he took the Wandervogel as his youth framework, for with Kletzl still its leader, he was optimistic that it could formulate his tighter youth agenda: privileging men, selection, and "leader-personalities."[26]

Yet in pursuing a special mission for German youth he was never alone.[27] Just as *Heimat* education mushroomed across German space, so now there was an explosion of youth groups. These catered to the enthusiasm of that postwar generation of adolescents who had missed out on the war adventure, but also represented initiatives by nationalist teachers who saw youth as the embodiment of renewal, able to replenish the wartime losses and challenge the Czech "aggressor." Besides individual ventures like Metzner's, or the youth wing of the Turn movement, most postwar political parties reactivated a youth organization (the German Agrarians soon with sixteen thousand members, the Social Democrats with thirty-two thousand before the Communists split off). Among the youth bodies that purported to rise above party politics, most significant and best documented is the Catholic youth group *Staffelstein,* launched in March 1920. Its leaders, well-informed about the Wandervogel heritage and the Bohemian Lands Movement, wanted to shape Catholic secondary school pupils; like other youth bodies they espoused German renewal, but theirs was renewal of both "homeland and faith" in the face of the encroaching Czech nation and its Protestant majority.

For many of these new youth groups there was a common tendency to borrow—and therefore compete with—Wandervogel precepts about self-discipline, obedience to leadership, and hiking in the *Heimat.* But most importantly, many concurred that youth groups should turn in a new *bündisch* direction. This meant that postwar youth needed to be united together in "movements," and specifically trained to serve the practical needs of a national community in distress.[28]

In the postwar youth debate about this crucial *bündisch* direction, Rutha immediately made a strong contribution, for in May 1919 he began to issue his own youth journal (fig.12), called *Blätter vom frischen Leben (Pages from Fresh Life).* It demonstrated a striking self-assurance that in a period of confusion he claimed to know how best to guide the youth movement—to act as a spiritual leader. The paper's title proclaimed its visionary purpose, but it also seemed to recall *Blätter für die Kunst (Pages for Art),* the journal of the enigmatic, domineering German poet, Stefan George.

For three decades from 1892, Stefan George with a small circle of devoted disciples had sought to impose a cultural-political revolution on Germany, predicting that national renaissance would come only out of violent catastrophe and offering his own "spiritual realm" as the real solution. His poetry collection, *The Seventh Ring* (1907), had particularly celebrated the dawn after mass slaughter, emphasized male ascendency, and eulogized mythical German heroes.[29] While Rutha knew about George's work and recommended it in the final number of the journal, his own *Blätter* contained nothing of George's impenetrable poetry. It seems unlikely that it immediately provided a practical framework as some have suggested.[30] But there were certainly distinct parallels between the two men's journals, between their aims to educate with a regenerative purpose, to target a younger generation, and deliberately to restrict circulation to a tightly delimited circle. If Rutha by 1922 was only just discovering George, he would soon feel a close affinity with the latter's spiritual and homoerotic perspective. By the 1930s he consistently returned to the poetry, circulating it among his own disciples and praising George as "the spiritual leader" of the past half century.[31] George became one model for his personal development.

Sixteen editions of Rutha's *Blätter* were produced, the last in July 1922.[32] Issued in three series, they appeared sporadically every few months depending on his workload as well as the amount of material available to him (only one was issued after May 1921). Although he edited most of them himself, he was prepared to collaborate with younger Wandervogel leaders if they had the same vision; much of the third series from late 1920 was edited jointly with a young Austrian from Linz. Stauda in Eger usually acted as the publisher, and the Wandervogel office at Leitmeritz dealt with the small number of subscribers. These were mainly German Bohemians and a few Austrian youth leaders, but circulation expanded as the *Blätter* gained a reputation.

From the start Rutha announced that it was not a new Wandervogel journal, nor did it offer a new program. He was simply producing a synthesis of what was "most valuable" from other Wandervogel publications while making apt judgments and suggestions for action.[33] Diligently, he scoured a range of youth newspapers across German central Europe, selecting much from Wandervogel journals in Switzerland and Germany where the debates seemed akin to his own perspective.[34] By 1920, his horizons were expanding to incorporate items from youth publications outside the Wandervogel, including even Social Democratic and Jewish Zionist journals. It reflected his widening perception of the national youth mission, as well as the swell of postwar discourse on a subject that crossed ideological boundaries.

While quite ready to publish readers' contributions and contrary opinions, the *Blätter* had a very personal stamp, with the editor regularly supplying critical commentaries. Its essential purpose, he wrote, was to "bring fresh life" to the youth movement, to combat complacency and stimulate the right kind of thinking. He claimed it as an independent organ for "liberating youths from irksome and restrictive formality while at the same time directing attention to their real essence, . . . to nature and the model example provided by male leaders"; it was there to appeal to all who had "young stormy hearts," who "yearned for the eternal."[35] And specifically, it aimed to educate a select cohort of individuals—those leader-personalities who were arising spontaneously to direct a new generation of male youths across German Bohemia.

One of Rutha's favorite metaphors for the Wandervogel was a lake. Its surface was a mirror, reflecting the nation, and from its depths there spurted up jets of water, a dramatic fountain of restless youth that was constantly refreshing itself in harmony with nature.[36] The fountain now needed to be properly controlled and nurtured. Many pieces in the *Blätter* warned against a postwar movement already set in its ways and ossified. It was essential that Wandervögel were able to uncover the real spirit of youth, that intangible essence that was sparked when they communed with nature, bonded intimately with one other and adopted the right charismatic leader as their guide and confidant.

These ideas were best expressed through an imaginary conversation between two male youths, A and B. Both agreed that although the Wandervogel was vital for their adolescent development, they had lacked guidance as they struggled with personal urges, for "no-one was there to say that the changes in my body, when preserved from impurity and abnormality, were something infinitely fine and natural." When B asserted that this was still "the most intrepid community of struggling youth," where leaders gathered youths as their companions, A asked where he could find these groups. B replied that A himself was such a leader: he should open up his soul to attract disciples, and perhaps in his chosen group there would be a special friend for him.

Rutha commented that adolescents must confide in each other and seek out that one special friend. Love, friendship, and leadership were the vital maxims—what was more beautiful than cultivating them within a small group or community?[37] He also recalled heroic pioneers like Feldberger and Mautschka, the right kind of "born leaders" who should now either be emulated or followed. The end goal was to work for the *Volk*, eschewing superficial engagement or self-gratification in favor of a spiritual crusade. For just as Germanness was always recreated by every generation, so the current youth leadership had a major mission of renewal on their hands.[38]

An immediate chance to test these ideas came at the Bohemian Wandervogel's annual assembly, convened in June 1919 near Carlsbad (fig.13). As the first Gautag after the national upheavals, it could be expected under

Kletzl's management to build on the ideas publicized in *Burschen heraus* and steer a tighter direction for the movement. Belying Rutha's claim of ossification, Wandervogel membership had risen to 1,400 (sixty-one groups), a new intake that mingled at the Gautag with war veterans and students in the usual round of games and orations at the sacred hilltop fire. For many, the magical spirit of Krummau was recaptured. Hans Watzlik was present to proclaim that Bohemia's future depended on the Wandervogel, and there resounded a new "Bohemian lands hymn," praying that a hero would arise and lead German Bohemians into a new dawn.[39]

Rutha contributed to these sentiments in a key lecture in which he explained the tasks confronting the new generation for shaping a "national community" *[Volksgemeinschaft]*.[40] Although the speech has not survived, for him the words primarily meant German Bohemia. But, as usual, when pinpointing national allegiance, there were overlapping spatial identities that in the aftermath of Austria's collapse were beginning to shift.

His local allegiance is evident in the *Blätter,* where he consistently gave north Bohemia *[Nordböhmerland]* as his address. He never wavered in that devotion, describing its wild secretive landscape, for example the Iser mountains, as the very essence of the German soul.[41] Yet his horizons always extended further. He identified with a broader German cultural community when he chose *Blätter* material from journals in Germany; in one article he even announced that "we too are Germany."[42] And parallel to that cultural allegiance, there was another that slowly eclipsed Austrian loyalties. At the Gautag, the leadership decided it was in the interest of the Bohemian Wandervogel to reach out to other Germans of Czechoslovakia. It agreed to form with the Moravian-Silesian Wandervogel, hitherto fully separate but part of the Austrian Bund, a common organization: the *Bund sudetenländischer Wandervogel.* Delegates were dispatched to have this approved at a Moravian Gautag.

For those whose community centered on German Bohemia, the national horizons were inevitably shifting, paving the way in the 1920s toward the slow manufacture of a "Sudeten German" identity across Czechoslovakia. Rutha too soon subscribed to this revised identity, for it gave security in numbers against a common "Czech threat" (parallel to that imagined "Czechoslovak" identity that allied Czechs with their Slovak cousins in the east). Yet when producing the *Blätter,* the attention he paid the Czechs was minimal, the threat implicit and rarely expressed. It is excessive to describe him at this time as a "zealous spokesman for nationally chauvinistic views."[43]

Rather, he usually condemned those youth groups who unthinkingly sang bloody songs of revenge and were filled with hatred for Czechs or Jews. He drew a line between this mindset and an honorable ongoing struggle. After the horror of war, he reminded his readers, "our future can only be one of defense and calm spiritual work, so that on the day when freedom returns to us, we are worthy and mature enough to bear it."[44]

In June 1919 he doubtless approved the new "Sudeten Bund" as a way of strengthening the national community. But otherwise he was dissatisfied with the Gautag results, for his fellow elders' insufficient dynamism (including even Kletzl, just retiring as Gauwart) seemed to scupper his own imaginative proposals. Firstly, he seems to have argued in vain that, instead of *Burschen heraus*, his own journal should become the principal organ for a leadership elite. Secondly, there was the gender question, which he now saw as fundamental. One evening he organized a leadership discussion and bluntly pushed for complete separation of the sexes, drawing congratulations from many present for the bold suggestion. It did result in the creation of a female Gauwart for girl groups, but there was no overall commitment to a full gender split, so on this matter he was left to fulminate in his *Blätter*.[45]

In Bohemia, this postwar youth debate about gender separation simply reflected a wider Wandervogel discussion across Germany and Austria.[46] Many, especially war veterans, felt that the female Wandervögel in wartime had unnaturally encroached upon a male sphere and compromised it. Rutha was prepared to present both sides of the argument, but as with racial division, his uncompromising view about gender distinction was never in doubt. On the eve of the Gautag, the *Blätter* had published articles describing how Wandervogel girls, instead of following a natural feminine course, had often mimicked boys and become a caricature of femininity. The result was "hermaphrodites"—laddish girls—whom adolescent boys rejected with "natural loathing."[47]

Since these views generated a lively correspondence through the summer of 1919, Rutha in November could devote a whole edition to the subject. While allowing some defense of gender interaction, he privileged the opposite view. Thus, one female correspondent argued it was time for girls to be "total girls," carving out their own sphere and emulating Wagnerian heroines like Brünhilde. Another (boy) stressed that male youths were not seeking women and did not need to learn about them. They wanted a model leader, a youth like themselves who rejected girlfriends, someone "strong, pure and devoted" who embodied their highest values, who could guide them through the sheer strength of his personality: "He ploughs their hearts and sows in the compliant soil his most precious qualities, his whole leadership, his strength, his love." This was a special love, not the physical kind that linked man and woman and produced a child, but spiritual—the very essence of a youth movement eternally striving for beauty and creativity.[48]

Rutha here was starting to advocate the transformation of the youth movement into a compact body of young men, what later would popularly be termed a *Männerbund*. This concept of an elite male body, bound together in friendship at the core of the state, was a German nationalist ideal of the nineteenth century.[49] But it had been sharpened in 1902 on the basis of anthropological observation by a German sociologist, Heinrich Schurtz. In his key book on Männerbünde, Schurtz had argued that while women were motivated solely by sacrifice for their family (a bulwark in the fabric of society), men, even married men, were always driven beyond the family toward a higher social association with other men. From that intense male bonding there came the creative spirit that shaped the main institutions of public life and the state.[50]

Schurtz's theory, warmly welcomed by many academics at the time, had chiefly been propagated late in the war by Hans Blüher. Having provocatively suggested that homoeroticism bound the Wandervogel together, Blüher went a stage further in his work, *The Role of Eroticism in Male Society* (1917/1919), emphasizing that throughout history Männerbünde, bonded together by Eros, had been society's key anchor. Blüher therefore amplified not only Schurtz but also his own Wandervogel theory, for he presented Männerbünde, the real state-building force, as led by male heroes, often "full inverts," who usually had one male lover but also a wide circle of disciples, all bound together in erotic friendship. He even called this phenomenon the "harem of the *typus inversus*."[51]

Just as the Männerbund idea permeated the youth movement in postwar Germany, so among Sudeten German youth leaders it was a term that resonated, suggesting not least—apart from any erotic dimension—a body of loyal comrades who had a creative impulse for reviving their nation. Rutha might publicly reject Blüher, referring bluntly in 1922 to his "unchaste and cynical spirit."[52] Nevertheless, he appropriated a great deal of Blüher's confused theory, for, as we will see, Eros and the idea of building a Männerbund with a "state-creating" drive were at the very heart of his youth crusade during the decade. In the early postwar years, however, his philosophy was still semiformed and publicly focused on leader-personalities. He was telling the Wandervogel that a network of male groups must be allowed to develop, each led by a charismatic leader with carefully selected disciples. In the *Blätter* he advised prospective leaders on how to achieve this, the mutual bonding it entailed; just as the leader selected his boys and strove to arouse their trust, so the boys chose a hero as the symbol of their dreams, opening up to him their uninhibited hearts.[53]

DISRUPTING THE WANDERVOGEL

When he impatiently encouraged this development, Rutha identified himself with youthful minds and assumed the self-appointed role of their "spiritual adviser" who knew best. As such, after the disappointing 1919 Gautag, he began to clash head on with other Wandervogel leaders whom he portrayed as bureaucrats, blocking a natural gender division and supposedly damaging youth's creativity. Youth, he argued, should seize control of the movement in the spirit of the blond charismatic lad he had witnessed at Krummau. The elders, especially those who lacked dynamism and were so often the "miserable prattlers" at meetings, should depart and organize themselves as adults in the Bohemian Lands Movement. If they refused, the youths must fight![54]

It was a combative message. Rutha was not only openly suggesting a generational divide where only "youthful minds" should dominate, but challenging the very structure of the Bohemian Wandervogel by privileging small cohorts led by charismatic leaders; the old regional districts should be replaced by an "organic" network of youth groups headed by leader-personalities. It was with this provocative agenda that at Easter 1920, still recovering from his mother's death, he invited the Gau elders to another leadership meeting. The location chosen was (and is) extremely remote, the hamlet of Kamnitzleiten lying adjacent to the northwest state frontier. There on 3 April, in a thickly wooded landscape where communing with nature was immediate, 172 leaders gathered for a heated discussion. Since disagreements were always soft-pedaled in Wandervogel publicity, the details are obscure, but many speakers shouted each other down as Rutha and his allies tried to force through their program.[55]

This produced a wholly unsatisfactory compromise. Although the majority was prepared to pay lip service to the concept of leader-personalities, Rutha viewed it all as tinkering around the edges. He wanted the "old guard" to retire and refused now to allow his *Blätter*, intended for a "youth aristocracy," to be used as the official leadership journal. The outcome was inevitable.

Despite all promises made at Kamnitzleiten, most elders simply ignored Rutha and continued to run the Wandervogel on the old lines.[56]

It was two years later, at Easter 1922, when Rutha again made his way to Kamnitzleiten, but he now took matters into his own hands. He summoned a cohort of charismatic youth leaders whom he had personally cultivated in the intervening period in order to shape his own network. Out of this second Kamnitzleiten was quickly forged what became known as the "Rutha circle" [*Ruthakreis*]. Its evolution is hazy, many of its leaders unknown. For not only did official youth publications still suggest a united movement, but Rutha had decided to end the *Blätter*, so his voice is lost to us at a critical juncture.[57] In the final edition in July 1922, he criticized the Wandervogel leadership's spiritual lack of purpose since 1919, and expressed disgust that his words had so often been misinterpreted, so little heeded. He then indicated a militant direction: "It was completely understandable that with the continuing spiritual splintering, alienation and softening of the Wandervogel, a few young men will struggle again for more natural and sturdier ties of operation and style, for a new more manly youth education than previously."[58]

In practical terms, this signified the consolidation of the Rutha circle, a personal network that cut across regional divisions as Rutha organized his own meetings and youth expeditions aside from the main body. At Christmas 1922, at Graslitz, in the far west of Bohemia, he discussed with some group leaders establishing a separate movement to meet the real requirements of younger male teenagers (a *Jungenschaft*). At the next Wandervogel Gautag in July 1923 at Mies near Pilsen, his circle of a dozen groups appeared for the first time as a united body and announced its full withdrawal from the conventional regional structure.[59]

Since Rutha was increasingly enticed by the potential of the Turn movement—at Mies he controversially suggested the Wandervogel merge into it—this influenced too the disciplined, masculine cohort on display. It was a model of tight but sensitive leadership that was steadily attracting disciples. One of his young leaders, Gustav Oberlik, had been part of Oskar Just's homosocial milieu and had started his own close-knit group in Gablonz.[60] Another recruit of 1923 explained why Rutha's model was so exciting: "He appeared like a leader of men, a fisher of men . . . Wherever he discovered a man he cared for him personally to a phenomenal degree, striving to integrate him into an important position in the community."[61]

While adhering to Wandervogel precepts of moral purity and communing with the *Heimat* landscape, this *bündisch* vision entailed educating a more disciplined male cohort to meet the contemporary national crisis. However, it also meant mobilizing youth from a wider swathe of German society. Potentially this was contradictory, for Rutha's model of course remained elitist with leader-personalities selecting only suitable disciples. Nevertheless, from early on the *Blätter* had pressed for a broader youth mission, a real symbiosis of youth and nation. In May 1920, Rutha devoted one edition to "we and others," urging Wandervogel leaders to recruit beyond secondary schools, to reach out to working-class adolescents rather than abandoning them to the beer halls of modern society; as he exclaimed, "We stupid Germans! Why can't it be 'we *and* them!'?" Rather than inventing class divisions, the whole youth community should be targeted, selecting those who would be specially trained as a vanguard. In their wake the masses would follow, and, he noted pointedly, "the tribe would then become ours."[62]

This approach to recruitment suggested itself because so many postwar youth bodies obviously shared a *völkisch* or at least *bündisch* vision. Alongside the Wandervogel, Rutha could highlight nationalist parallels and lessons in the Socialist, Catholic, and even Zionist youth movements; and at home, in the Oschitz Turnverein, he was only too ready to invite local Agrarian party youth to share in Turner festivals.[63] His message therefore was consistent: there was "one national youth" whose current divisions were artificial. It was a ubiquitous "human spring" that youth leaders should tap, shaping their own cohort of acolytes, then sending out ripples on the pond in order to draw other suitable adolescents into their fold.[64]

Yet such youth unity had to be on Rutha's own maverick terms, to produce a tight hierarchical, politicized organism. It explains why he shunned the *Sudetendeutsche Jugendgemeinschaft,* a loose body created in mid-1922 as an umbrella for uniting all Sudeten youth groups who had a *bündisch* mission; it seemed to be an archetypal manufactured construction and too focused anyway on mere cultural education.[65] In contrast, the *Heimat* pedagogy Rutha envisaged had a growing militant and political edge. In the *Blätter,* education had been mentioned only tangentially and from a Wandervogel perspective. But from 1923, not least through Turn influence, he was thinking more systematically about combining *völkisch* lessons with the physical toughening of expeditions and energetic exercise.

That summer this combination was on display when he led twenty-five of his circle on a hiking expedition to south Tyrol. To some extent he was retracing his own steps and exorcizing the trauma of 1918; he would write pensively about visiting a memorial to the fallen, high up in the desolate mountains.[66] But the trip had a politicized *völkisch* agenda too, for the group deliberately made contact with local youth leaders and educated themselves about the plight of other German minorities across Europe.

And it was this unilateral expedition that finally brought tensions to a boiling point in the Wandervogel.[67] In September 1923, when its leadership reassembled at Kamnitzleiten, Rutha's vision of a dynamic Männerbund was finally rejected by the majority. The result was a crack in the movement from which it never recovered, for after fraught discussions about twenty local groups announced they were indeed part of the autonomous Rutha circle.[68] Even if the latter remained within the Wandervogel, it became a cuckoo in the nest, organizing its own camps and festivals and undermining the authority of its host. At a special camp in June 1924 at Tepl, attended by two hundred boys, the circle officially constituted itself as a *Sudetendeutsche Jungenschaft*. The title revealed its aspiring national credentials and its remit of training younger male adolescents. A month later in southern Bohemia, the Jungenschaft attended its last Gautag, making a striking impression with its special uniforms and strict discipline. It was absent from the major Wandervogel gathering of 1925, and it was only a matter of time before it would abandon the movement altogether.

In retrospect, the Wandervogel elders would identify the confusion of the mid-1920s as years of crisis and single out Heinz Rutha as playing the most destructive role.[69] Typically he had held obstinately to his own principles, judging them to be in the real interest of youth, something that won him many converts but ensured many long-term enemies. What was really at stake only became clearer as he shifted ever more in a national-political direction. By 1922 at the latest, he was convinced that a revitalized youth movement could not remain in the cultural sphere, that the old Wandervogel was simply inadequate. His solution was a politicized and militant orientation; a male vanguard would be assiduously coached to lead the Sudeten Germans in their struggle against Czech dominance.

In encouraging this process, he had acted very much as a facilitator, supplying "spiritual direction" for dynamic youth leaders. Having created the Jungenschaft as a model, he was quite prepared to surrender it to younger leader-personalities in line with the principle of youth autonomy. He continued to attend and guide many of its gatherings, but it was Gustav Oberlik who took charge from October 1924, for Rutha, as facilitator, was now turning to other tasks. He was pondering a systematic youth program and embracing a philosophy that could serve as a framework for Sudeten German regeneration.

SPANNISM AND THE *KAMERADSCHAFTSBUND*

In line with the confused flux of youth organization in postwar Czechoslovakia, it was only after 1923 that Rutha's concept of a practical, politicized youth mission gained real substance.[70] Having openly challenged Wandervogel "romanticism" and created his own network of leader-personalities, it was probably the energy he witnessed in Turn branches like Henlein's that honed his ideas about a disciplined Sudeten Männerbund. Yet a broader pedagogic framework was also now emerging. He drew on classical and modern philosophers to understand not just the training his male cohorts required but the kind of German society they should create in the Bohemian lands. Here the worlds of Plato and the Viennese sociologist Othmar Spann converged to illuminate his path. Both offered utopian structures for a new society (and he selected from them what was appropriate). They also made his own *bündisch* program distinctive, raising it above the cultural education privileged by so many *Heimat* activists of the 1920s.

The key way that both Spann and Plato penetrated the Sudeten youth movement was Rutha's friendship with a Viennese academic, Walter Heinrich. Born in 1902 in north Bohemia, Heinrich had moved a decade later to Böhmisch Leipa when his father became headmaster of a primary school. He excelled there at the Gymnasium and in 1921 departed for the University of Vienna to study law and political science under Professor Spann.[71] Rutha had first met Heinrich around 1920 when one Leipa Wandervogel leader was visiting Kunnersdorf and Heinrich accompanied him. They quickly bonded, drawn together perhaps by Stefan George's apocalyptic poetry as much as by Heinrich's curiosity about the youth movement; soon he too was espousing the primacy of "spiritual youth" led by great personalities.[72] Rutha's new friend was both a personal confidant and a philosophical guide, impressively erudite and classically educated—something Rutha lacked. It was due to Heinrich that in 1922 the *Blätter* recommended Plato's *Republic*, noting its model of synthesizing hard physical and intellectual training to produce the ideal leaders or "guardians" of the community.[73] From a spark both intimate and creative, therefore, new ideas were emerging to frame Rutha's youth mission; his friendship with Heinrich was "a critical event intellectually and politically for the Sudeten Germans."[74]

Just as Othmar Spann's postwar writings had lured Heinrich to Vienna, so under such charismatic tutelage Heinrich became Spann's most devoted disciple. Since 1914, Spann had been formulating a theory of "universalism," summarizing it in a series of lectures published in 1921 as *The True State*.

Here he explained the world metaphysically and described national "spiritual communities" as the real basis for human government. Rejecting the rational, liberal beliefs that had dominated Europe since the Enlightenment (spawning creeds like liberalism, socialism, and "individualistic" democracy), Spann set out the supposedly harmonious social structures of premodern times as models for the future. In this vision, the society gathered together in each state would function as a spiritual interactive "whole" *[Ganzheit]* with the individual, in contrast to any liberal model, having significance only as a member of the larger community.[75]

In practical terms, Spann proposed a restructured state working in harmony. Instead of confrontation and competition—the bedrock of Marxism and liberal capitalism—he drew on Platonic and medieval models to present the ideal state as one reorganized into estates or corporations *[Stände]*. While these, akin to preindustrial guilds, would group together key socioeconomic interest groups such as farmers, industrialists, or skilled workers, the state that they served would become a tight hierarchical pyramid. At the pinnacle were true "spiritual" leaders—the philosophers of Plato's *Republic*—but real power was to be vested in a special political estate, an elite stratum who would make all political decisions and expect absolute obedience from the estates beneath them. In practice it would be an authoritarian state, yet one where all would work "harmoniously" for the common good.

With the state authoritative in all things, its members would all belong to the spiritual community of their *Volkstum* or nation (which as in Czechoslovakia, Switzerland, or the old Habsburg Empire might not precisely overlap with state borders). All Germans, for instance, formed a common spiritual community even though divided into various tribes *[Stämme]*. Spann's national canvas was as hierarchical as his state structural model, based on his own personal experience of the prewar Czech-German nationalist clash in the city of Brünn.[76] Since he felt the German nation was one of the most creative, it was bound to subsume into its ruling sphere inferior peoples like the Czechs.

At the same time, crucially, he did not take race as a key criterion for defining or limiting the nation. In contrast to National Socialist ideology, race for Spannism was of secondary significance, so Jews, although certainly inferior like Czechs, were not wholly alien to the national community. This racial ambivalence does much to explain the Nazi-Spannist clash of the 1930s. However, for National Socialism the Spannist *Weltanschauung* or world view was dangerous in other ways too. Notably, Spannists always privileged a vague spiritual universalism over any (Nazi) party affiliation, and their creed often suggested a suspicious kinship with Catholicism (even if their new order was to be a theocracy with the political elite dominating spiritual life). Spannists also rejected the Nazi assumption that life was a crude Social Darwinist struggle, preaching instead a harmonious social elitism, not least in terms of the leaders who would naturally emerge to govern each state community. In all this there was certainly a *völkisch* and authoritarian overlap with National Socialism, but there were also basic distinctions that in time seemed very clear to many Spannists or Nazi ideologues.[77]

Spannism could naturally appeal to idealistic Sudeten nationalists like Rutha whose regional community seemed endangered in a Czech-nationalizing environment. If central European space could be radically reorganized on Spannist lines, the Sudeten "tribe" might gain its own state (perhaps even dominate Czech space) and still be able to commune with the broader German spiritual community to the north and south. There beckoned for Sudeten Germans that overlap of state and national loyalties that might solve their historic and geographical predicament.

In addition, the Spannist state structure mirrored well certain elements in Rutha's youth mission, for it emphasized a nation's spiritual ties, possibly even convincing him that he himself was a Platonic spiritual leader of the Sudeten tribe. Spannism confirmed too the maxim of elite selection, where spiritually gifted men would naturally come to the fore as state leaders. If to Rutha these were his chosen leader-personalities, it seems clear nevertheless that his former obsession with Aryan purity significantly weakened in the 1920s when he confronted Spannist ambivalence over race. His own anti-Semitism was tempered, and he ceased to mention racial selection altogether.

Slowly the Spannist creed penetrated north Bohemia. In April 1923, at a leadership meeting of the Rutha circle in Kamnitzleiten, Walter Heinrich with other Spannist students took part for the first time. That summer, Heinrich's influence was clear in Rutha's tour of south Tyrol, an early Spannist effort to reach out and understand other strands of the embattled "spiritual community."[78] That winter, Rutha invited him to lead pedagogically the first camp of the embryonic Jungenschaft (which Konrad Henlein also attended). As their project for the Sudeten tribe built further upon their friendship, so they probably met whenever Heinrich visited Czechoslovakia.

The Rutha circle was also now expanding as some youth leaders entered student life. In October 1924, at Prague's German university, a new student society, the Pedagogical Community *[Pädogigische Gemeinschaft]* (PG), was created. Its dozen founding members, including Oberlik as head of the Jungenschaft, were all elders of the Rutha circle, still bound together by his mentorship as they took his ideas forward into the student and adult world.[79] Rutha could see these disciples as his own personal Männerbund. Not only had they successfully inspired youth; they also understood well the national-spiritual struggle that Heinrich was interpreting in a broader European context.

In September 1925, it was at Rutha's suggestion that some of them made a second expedition abroad, to Switzerland.[80] Ever since 1919 when Edvard Beneš had claimed that Czechoslovakia would emulate Switzerland, many Sudeten German leaders had eyed the Swiss model with its three nationalities and complained about Czech treachery.[81] The expedition of 1925 was carefully planned by Heinrich as a "programmatic test," aiming to investigate all aspects of Swiss nationality conditions and then use the lessons at home. Rutha himself did not participate, but the group of twenty under Heinrich's leadership included PG members like Oberlik, a few Spann students, and also Konrad Henlein.

Traveling by train to Zurich, the party encountered some Swiss Germans led by a conservative youth leader, Hektor Amman. On his recommendation they split up and explored three different "national" routes through Switzerland, reconvening ten days later to summarize their findings. All were pleasantly surprised at the national harmony they observed and contrasted it with the Czech-German environment. When one Swiss questioned why the Germans had not resisted Czech occupation in 1918, it was Henlein who stepped forward to explain that the Czech army had faced little opposition because so many Germans failed to return from the front. It was a passionate speech, belying Henlein's calm exterior, and it impressed both the Swiss and his Sudeten colleagues.

Rutha could admire scenes from the Swiss trip when a "magic lantern" slideshow was staged at the Oschitz Turnverein that autumn, and from the expedition there were three major repercussions.[82] First, it served as a model for annual PG-Jungenschaft summer trips abroad, for self-education in other regions of the German diaspora like Transylvania and Alsace (1926–1928). Rutha as usual remained just a "spiritual adviser" behind these.[83]

Second, it caused Henlein to make a career move. One of those on the trip, a Turner from Asch in western Bohemia, sensed that Henlein was highly competent and recommended him for the full-time position of Turn instructor in Asch, the largest and most prestigious of Turn branches. Henlein hesitated to make this leap away from north Bohemia into a permanent Turn career, but according to one source, it was Rutha who convinced him, seeing him as the ideal leader-personality for training a national body of young men—a *Männerschaft*. After intense discussions at the Rutha mill in Kunnersdorf, Henlein finally agreed, and in late 1925 secured the Asch position.[84]

A few months later he was unanimously elected as head of a new Egerland-Jahnmal Gau. He began to introduce radical reforms, shifting the emphasis of Turn activity away from traditional gymnastics toward sporting competition and military toughness, building an army of volunteers who, in a combination of *völkisch* awareness and disciplined fitness, were eager to serve the nation. As early as July 1927, he felt strong enough to criticize other Turn regions, presenting his own as a model of male discipline. In this process he seems to have drawn steady guidance from Rutha in a friendship based on mutual respect: for in the summer of 1926, Rutha was the best man at his wedding.[85]

A third outcome from the Swiss expedition was a formalization of that loose think tank, centered upon the Rutha-Heinrich link, which was considering Spannist theory as the basis for a Sudeten sociopolitical revolution. Although the details are obscure, a key catalyst was probably Walter Hergl, a former Wandervogel leader and now law student in Prague. As a one-time Bohemian Lands Movement enthusiast who had attended the Schreckenstein meeting, he too wanted to advance the didactic mission in a politicized elitist form. In Rutha and Heinrich he found willing collaborators. At Christmas 1925 in Reichenberg, the triumvirate established a Study Group for Social Sciences *[Arbeitskreis für Gesellschaftwissenschaften]*, which over the next three years met either in Prague or Reichenberg to elaborate a Spannist agenda for galvanizing the Sudeten German community. From the start, they recognized as the key instrument a specially trained male organization, a Männerbund, and that the Turn movement, if reformed and politicized, might be the ideal framework. Henlein was duly invited to some of the discussions, including the first meeting, and the study group slowly expanded through personal contacts.[86]

As a core element for the group, Rutha immediately promoted his PG-Jungenschaft leaders, probably envisaging the whole enterprise as their natural vehicle. Indeed, perhaps as early as 1926, this was reflected in the group's more popular name of Comrades' Union *[Kameradschaftsbund]* (KB). Much later, Walter Hergl would pen a bitter attack on Rutha and Heinrich, accusing them of wild degeneracy, of promoting their favorites to the exclusion of others. The indictment is vindictive and contradictory, but certainly the materialization of the KB, a body so molded by personal bonding, recruited as many enemies as friends. Those opposed to the politicization of youth, excluded from Rutha's personal network, or still smoldering from his divisive behavior in the Wandervogel, gathered together in mid-1928 to form a rival organization called Preparedness *[Bereitschaft]*, dedicated to *Heimat* cultural education. Hergl meanwhile had already resigned from the KB, largely because, as a strong-minded personality, he found the combination of Rutha, Heinrich, and their friends too dominant.[87]

Not until November 1930 would the KB register itself with the Czech authorities as an official society for "national and sociopolitical training." Until then it was mainly a secret organization of some hundred young men who through ties of friendship met for occasional lectures or conferences. Its loose character always lent it a certain mystique, then and since, and makes it difficult to research.[88] Certainly it was building on the recently defunct Bohemian Lands Movement, with a new set of "chivalrous" leaders proselytizing in the Sudeten community. But they now proposed a Spannist political solution and, through Rutha's influence, emphasized young men as the core instruments of that transformation.

Their new political struggle was first publicized after a KB conference in October 1928 at the château of Heinrichsruh near Teplitz. There, both Heinrich and Rutha gave keynote lectures that were privately published in a pamphlet entitled *The First Position*.[89] Heinrich's lecture was just one of many in the coming years to a receptive KB audience. After lambasting contemporary individualism and party politics, he prophesied the creation of a series of corporate states within a federal reorganization of central Europe. These states would be a fusion of conservative and revolutionary forces, run by leaders who would dictate to estates of the national community.[90]

Although Heinrich hinted here at the Sudeten context—that a *bündisch* youth was emerging, that a KB elite was now active creating local cells—he was always working on a grander Spannist canvas and by no means concentrating on Czechoslovakia. While his lecture mentioned Mussolini's emerging corporate state in Italy, another key target was neighboring Austria, where Spannists saw the paramilitary Heimwehr movement as an ideal vehicle for that state revolution.[91] Indeed, in 1929–1930 Heinrich would become Heimwehr secretary-general, using that platform to propagate Spannism and draft the famous Korneuburg oath (May 1930), only to have his hopes dashed when the heterogeneous movement splintered and ejected him from office. We should note therefore Heinrich's constant diversion from the Sudeten KB (including his sojourn in 1933–1934 in Nazi Germany), for it contextualizes his rather limited work with Rutha from the late 1920s. Later, when judging Spann's overall impact, Heinrich himself would place the Sudeten Germans third after Austria and Germany.[92] His own focus never quite matched Rutha's, and it would ultimately loosen their collegiality.

Rutha's own Spannist commitment was first expressed publicly in 1928. His KB lecture of October was delivered five months after one given to PG disciples in Prague, and in both talks Spann's universalism supplied the framework.[93] Noting the Sudeten struggle as fully integrated with that of the wider German nation, he expected Sudeten young men to educate themselves diligently about the European environment. But his primary focus was the mission in Czechoslovakia where, in typical Spannist language, he described a disunited Sudeten tribe that must rally and challenge wily Czech dominance. Typically too, he scorned the Sudeten Germans' "fragmentation," contrasted it with the Czechs' (allegedly) exemplary unity, and dismissed those German political parties that in 1926 had naïvely entered the Czechoslovak coalition government; such party politics, privileging faction above the national "whole" *[Ganzes]*, could never produce Sudeten unity. The latter was the real and realistic priority, overriding any broader German mission in Europe. For as he stressed: "We have decided, at least for our Sudeten Germans, to conquer this position on the territory of the existing state."[94] In short, while sympathetic to "brothers" in Germany and Austria, the main goal was to win dominance within Czechoslovakia or at least gain control of Sudeten German "space" (however that was defined).

This would occur by awakening a united Sudeten national consciousness through a concerted program of male youth training. Most of Rutha's lectures concentrated on this subject. Not only did he push the old refrain of a common youth body; he now suggested a systematic *bündisch* education to prepare Sudeten adolescents for adulthood and tribal leadership. He hinted at a curriculum combining physical fitness with a national-political (perhaps Spannist) education, but the real novelty was to suggest training in three stages, each carefully matching the age and outlook of the adolescent. Through tight leadership and comradeship at each adolescent level a united youth body, the Jungenschaft, would emerge, maturing into a cohort of young men, or Jungmannschaft, whose best leaders would direct the Sudeten struggle. Careful adolescent training therefore was a preparatory stage, a bridge, for those who would run the nation as an adult Männerbund: "The state and the nation are born in the boy, tested in the youth, and realized in the man."[95]

To his audiences, Rutha proposed specific action in two directions. On the one hand the embryonic Männerbund, of which the PG was a part, should maintain the youth mission, ensuring that adolescents were systematically trained. On the other, they themselves needed now to be actively joining groups and parties of the old state structure, rousing and then conquering all parts of the national community. As agitators in these various cells, they would be a ready-made elite leadership who could come together as the executive council of the Sudeten tribe (the "political estate"). All of this shows that by 1928 Rutha had loosely embraced Spannism as a broad philosophical and political framework for Sudeten German nationalism.[96] Even so, his obsession was always the pedagogic dimension: a politicized youth education to create the future Sudeten Männerbund.

INTO THE TURN MOVEMENT

As we will see, the confidence exuded in these speeches belied Rutha's underlying anxieties. For how could a united youth movement really emerge when youth bodies like the Wandervogel refused to abandon their cultural and otherworldly stances? He had openly challenged and disrupted the "romantic" Wandervogel as it did not match his own male-based militant mission. Yet it was some years after forsaking these roots before he could be sure of a practical vehicle for the youth experiment. This proved to be the Turnverband with which he had flirted throughout the decade.

It was in April 1926 that Rutha's own Jungenschaft finally took the plunge and abandoned the Bohemian Wandervogel. In a circular, the Jungenschaft urged the organization to follow suit and transform itself by introducing proper youth training. Not surprisingly this split, which some Wandervogel branches emulated, caused lasting resentment. The incoming Gauwart, Rudolf Staffen, was extremely bitter and founded Preparedness in 1928 to counter the KB's nefarious and growing influence.[97] For although Rutha's Jungenschaft was still very small (perhaps a hundred boys), its distinctive style was starting to be widely imitated by other youth groups like the Catholic *Staffelstein*. Characterized by muscular uniformity, strict discipline, alertness to *völkisch* training, and imaginative exploratory trips abroad, the

Jungenschaft promoted an image of vitality that far exceeded its numbers. Its adopted flag, the Bohemian lion, also suggested Rutha's pretensions, an ambitious youth agenda stretching across "historic German Bohemian" space.[98]

As a youth body it was also not isolated for long, for in October 1926 in Reichenberg it joined the Federation of Sudeten German Scouts [*Verband der sudetendeutscher Pfadfinder*]. Possibly Rutha saw this as a marriage of convenience, providing security as part of an official organization while allowing his group to retain its own identity.[99] However, the affiliation had a deeper purpose. When producing the last of his *Blätter* in mid–1922, he had highlighted the example of the "New Scout" [*Neupfadfinder*] movement in Germany. He admired not only its typical Wandervogel values, but also its goal of "tribal education," which included a systematic framework for training each age group toward manhood.[100] Here was an obvious model to copy.

In Czechoslovakia the upholder of the New Scout message, the Federation, had been created in 1921 with the typical goal of serving the German community in its hour of need, training Sudeten scouts to become responsible men with a life-long mission ahead of them.[101] For its leader, Ernst Krause, the influx of new members in late 1926 was only too welcome. For Rutha, the scouting vision meshed well, not least its focus on training in three clear age-stages. Thus it was not just a formality that he soon assumed various offices: he was elected as Krause's deputy in October 1927 and deputy (honorary) president in late 1930. While his own ideas penetrated the movement through lectures and leadership discussions in Reichenberg, he embraced, for a time at least, an environment that his Jungenschaft had lacked in the Wandervogel.[102]

Even so, since the Federation was one of the smaller German youth bodies, it could only be a staging post. In contrast, the Turnverband increasingly seemed the most propitious base for organizing Sudeten youth education. This realization came slowly, largely dependent on whether the Turn movement could be comprehensively overhauled. Despite various reforms early in the decade, including Dietwart activity, it remained a gymnastics organization in the hands of an older generation and with sluggish recruitment of younger members. This was true in Rutha's own Oschitz branch, perhaps explaining his diminishing interest there from 1926 (even if in that year he was still Turn youth leader in the Jeschken-Iser Gau).[103] Above all, it seems clear that he kept his Jungenschaft independent for so long mainly because of the unreformed state of the Turnverband.

Any prospect of change was embodied in Konrad Henlein, who was industriously creating a model *Turngau* in western Bohemia, stimulated in part by the example of the Czech Sokol. Probably from the start he had shared the broader "national" vision set out by the KB study group.[104] But it was only in May 1928, undoubtedly on Rutha's advice, that he publicized a new pedagogic approach, explaining in the *Turnzeitung* that the Turnverband had a purpose beyond competitions and festivals, with education as the critical task. In his own Gau, male education was about shaping a "new type of man," disciplined and obedient as defender of the *Volk*. Female education, on the other hand, was carried out separately; it involved "free exercise" in nature (especially dancing) and the cultivation of *völkisch* sentiment as a training toward motherhood.[105]

Rutha immediately responded to this article, telling the old Turn leadership publicly that youth needed a holistic physical-intellectual training under charismatic leaders, and especially a precise goal: to work selflessly as a "compact body of men" toward uniting the national community. When in October he addressed the KB about molding the Sudeten tribe, he further highlighted the Turnverband as an organization that transcended party loyalties, and as such one that could be crucial for education; what it still lacked was a clear political objective.[106]

Over the next two years it was Henlein who pushed forward with this political agenda. From May 1928 he was a member of the Turnverband leadership, so his voice was increasingly heard, his dynamism in the Egerland Gau nervously admired. He spoke of Turners "carrying a flame into the gloom of the present," cutting through Sudeten political divisions, standing as the guardians of national unity on the Turn model of a bygone age.[107] They, he observed in 1930, were fully in tune with the new antidemocratic mood across Europe, for "disciplined Männerbünde rule the present: fascism, the Hitler movement, the Heimwehr, etc." In practical terms it meant military-style training with annual defense days for his "combat troops." Most crucially, he was restructuring his own Gau, eliminating grassroots control in favor of tight centralization with a leadership who expected absolute obedience.[108] By late 1930, after he had toured the regions, it was a revolution most other Gaue were ready to approve. By that time, as he predicted, the "awakening" was imminent, for in May 1931 he was elected as Turnverband leader and could implement his reforms across the whole movement.

It is unclear how far, before this crucial watershed, Rutha had advised Henlein on the key regional reforms. Possibly, as we will see, a serious personal crisis disrupted his focus in 1929. But if so, he showed renewed interest in the Turn movement a year later when once again he became chair of the Oschitz branch. Faced with local stagnation, he began to implement in microcosm Henlein's plans for reform, recommending fresh elections and even a physical toughening of the village membership.[109]

Meanwhile, on the broader canvas the linkage between Henlein's reforms and a (Spannist) political and pedagogic mission was materializing. In March 1931, when the Turnverband leadership authorized Henlein to run a three-day training course at Asch for forty Turn leaders, it was to Rutha and Walter Heinrich that he turned for intellectual input (supplying himself the physical training).[110] For Heinrich, wounded by the embarrassing foray with the Austrian Heimwehr, it was a first opportunity to expound Spann's universalist framework before the Turner elite. Rutha's lecture in turn provided historical context for his elitist pedagogic mission by explaining the fatal error of nineteenth-century rulers. Abandoning laws well established in the ancient world, they had idolized "progress" and "equality," indiscriminately advocating "education for all" as if everybody could be raised to the same level of achievement; it had taken a genius like Nietzsche to condemn the obsession, but the trend had continued to the present day.[111] Confronting the current national crisis, he noted, it was time to reverse this false doctrine of equal rights, to combine the best theories of antiquity and modernity in a new pedagogic ideal. It was the Turnverband that would train a Sudeten vanguard, a model to galvanize a sadly disunited nation.[112]

Here, three years after he had publicly advocated a systematic program of education, eight years after first meeting Henlein, Rutha's ideas were coming to fruition. In May 1931, he stepped forward as Henlein's key adviser on youth education and was publicly acknowledged as such (even if later accounts deliberately omitted his role).[113] To his Jungenschaft elders, he confided, he was composing a great pedagogic program with ancient Greece as his favored example.[114] With "total" physical and intellectual character building on a Platonic model, this meant enunciating further the age-stages he had experienced in the Scouts. At each level, for those aged eleven to fourteen, fifteen to seventeen, and eighteen to twenty, there would be a special curriculum carefully tailored to the youths' maturity, with model leaders acting as teachers and heroes, supposedly as in Spartan or ancient Germanic society. Those entering adolescence—again a nod to "ancient practices"— would be sworn in, and a dramatic annual ceremony would mark the departure of youths entering manhood.[115]

When Henlein publicized this framework in June 1932, he noted the previous neglect of Turner youth, and called all Sudeten German youth groups to join the Turnverband and engage in national youth training. Although it was the kind of cohesion Rutha had demanded for years, he was probably not optimistic about an immediate breakthrough. Indeed, when the first Turnverband youth camp under the new guidelines was held in July near Komotau, only his Jungenschaft and one district of the old Wandervogel appeared in answer to Henlein's summons. The camp might well exude a new vitality, with its Turn activities, competitions, and strict discipline, but it was only a start. As one of Rutha's disciples noted, the absence of so many youth groups, the lack of uniformity even among those present—all demonstrated that it would take years of intensive work to produce a truly *völkisch* youth education.[116]

*   *   *

If we survey Rutha's activity in the 1920s, it is clear that he was one of a minority of war veterans who entered peacetime wanting to continue the national struggle rather than retire into civilian life. Out of his experiences in 1918 he appointed himself a spiritual leader of the postwar Sudeten youth generation, and signaled publicly in his *Blätter* that a clear generational divide existed over how best to proceed.

In fact, rather than an adult-adolescent divide, it was one group of veterans or youth leaders challenging the strategy of another.[117] While so many *Heimat* activists privileged a cultural approach to youth education, Rutha steered a militant course, championing out of the frontline trenches the maxims of heroic leadership, obedience, and male bonding. From the mid-1920s, he was seeking to inculcate these in a tightly organized youth movement, envisaging a Sudeten German youth crusade within Czechoslovakia. Conservative by nature, he hoped the Wandervogel might change and become the mission's vehicle, but he was uncompromising in the transformation he expected and soon took risks like the creation of his own circle of leader-personalities. Many Wandervogel peers could only see this as disloyal and as being hypocritical in the actual disunity it fostered.

Indeed, Rutha's youth mission might seem awash with contradictions that reveal his blend of conservative pragmatism and radical idealism. First, as a nationalist, he was preaching Sudeten German unity amid scattered German-speaking communities of Czechoslovakia where the actual strength of common (Sudeten) identification was questionable. He himself often acknowledged the disunity, the actual Sudeten "tribal diversity," but his solution was to try to rouse the allegedly "slumbering nation" with youths as missionaries.[118] Second, these zealots were an elite group of leaders, carefully chosen for their charisma, and their goal of uniting the tribe was therefore potentially divisive; while class and social barriers might be roundly condemned, a new set of hierarchical divisions was very clear in the Spannist project.

Third, there is the question of the mission's utopian character. Rutha portrayed the Wandervogel as "romantic" and ill-suited to confront united Czech militancy, something the Germans should match with a politicized and united youth cohort. In such rhetoric by the late 1920s he was mirroring the kind of *bündisch* discourse prevalent in Germany, where some sharply criticized those youth organizations that maintained an otherworldly stance.[119] Rutha's solution was similarly political: youth must be engaged and meticulously trained for the adult struggle. Yet his mission too had many utopian streaks of its own, not least in embracing the Spannist ideology. If the latter might fire up adolescents who wanted a vision both practical and idealistic, its implementation required a huge leap of imagination and nationalist faith. Not least, inevitably, it was a long-term enterprise of educating the national community via the KB Männerbund and a galvanized Turn youth movement.

Rutha conceived all this as a deeply moral mission, and it presents a final paradox. Some outsiders saw him as fanatical, disrupting youths' innocence, seeking to turn them in a militant if not militaristic direction that would simply produce violent confrontation in Czechoslovakia. Rutha questioned this logic, for after the 1918 traumas he abhorred violence. When describing the new emerging nationalism in 1928, he noted that the years of war and revolution had taught Sudeten Germans that "national" did not mean fanaticism or strong-arm tactics; it meant "restrained dignity and genuine social regrouping."[120] The project set out at Schreckenstein and then reinvigorated by the KB elite was honorable and selfless: creating a Männerbund who would chivalrously serve the nation like knights defending and venerating the Holy Grail. In this "state-creating" project, Rutha was driven forward by solid German Bohemian loyalties and a paternalistic faith in male youth. But, as a fisher of men, he was also fueled by Eros.

SIX

Eros

One weekend in the summer of 1932, some blond teenage boys from Reichenberg made an excursion on foot, over Mount Jeschken to the sandstone region south of Oschitz. Heading the group was an eighteen-year-old, Adolf Wagner, leader of the Reichenberg branch of Rutha's Jungenschaft, and in his wake were younger members like Werner Weiss and Willi Hoffmann. On their way back they called at the red-colored mill in Bad Kunnersdorf. Rutha personally greeted them in the courtyard, and, after introductions, they sat with him in the garden, talking and enjoying refreshments provided by his sister Friedel before proceeding on their way. A few weeks later, Wagner and the fifteen-year-old Weiss once again walked to Kunnersdorf. They wanted to talk with Rutha about the summer expedition of the Jungenschaft to north Italy and Yugoslavia, particularly in view of Rutha's wartime knowledge of south Tyrol. After discussing the trip with their host, they were shown to an attic bedroom where they had to share a single bed. That night in the Rutha mill, the first sexual contact occurred between the two youths.[1]

THE RUTHA MILL

By the 1930s, the mill had become something of a youth center, for as Rutha later recorded, "through my activity in the Turnverband I got to know a great number of Turner youths and cultivated comradely relations with them."[2] These, as well as members of the Jungenschaft, regularly sought out their mentor or were personally invited to visit him at the weekend. Often he took them to his library on the first floor of the house (one of his two private rooms) and read to them romantic poetry by George, Hölderlin, or Schiller, or extracts from the classics, particularly Plato or Plutarch. There would follow a lively discussion, and the boys would spend the night in the attic. "It was," Rutha recalled in 1937, "a heartfelt and comradely circumstance that young men often used to come, mostly on their own, to our house where sincere hospitality is an old family tradition. I sought to educate young men in everything grand and beautiful."[3]

If the mill was the very center of Rutha's homosocial network, it was also his livelihood. Very reluctantly in 1919 he had taken over the family business from Adolf Rutha, assuming responsibilities both in the mill and sawmill, even completing a "milling examination" in 1924.[4] But since water-powered milling now faced major competition from regional electric-powered mills, it was the sawmill that increasingly dominated the business and consumed his time. From these early years a group family photograph (fig.14) hints at his unease or impatience in the confines of Kunnersdorf; his suit and stiff bearing set him apart from his impassive sisters, or the cheekiness of his nephew Fritz, suggesting a desire to be away with his Jungenschaft boys. Very soon this independent streak was expressed at the mill as in the youth movement, and in both cases an indirect stimulus was the ex-Wandervogel associate, Oskar Just, who had studied architecture and proved so influential in the war years. As early as 1923, Rutha had begun to act as Just's agent in bringing his designs for interior decoration to fruition. He supervised Just's designs, took orders from customers, and placed them with local furniture businesses.[5]

Two years later it was from this base that he branched out to found his own furniture firm.[6] If this partly reflected frustrated ambition, as well as the existing business's economic difficulties, it also developed logically from the sawmill where suitable wood for furniture was already being cut, dried, and treated. Rutha's aim, linked to a long-time interest in the applied arts, was to become an interior decorator, running a firm that specialized in high-quality furniture. From the Storch (Czech) relatives in Nieder-Gruppai, with whom he always retained ties, he managed to borrow 40,000 Czech crowns; he reconstructed the mill space as a workshop, hired a master joiner from Styria (Michael Schüpfer) and a furniture designer from Bavaria (Otto Franke). In their efficient hands, and with Rutha's wide social network at its disposal, the firm's orders soon multiplied, attracting wealthy clients including even some German-Jewish families.[7] Gradually it focused on heavy and expensive veneered furniture, the veneer usually imported from abroad (fig.15). And one tradition from the early "Just" years continued: many contracts, after Franke had finalized the design, were farmed out to other firms for completion, with Rutha making a clear profit.

By 1927 the workshop employed seven joiners and two apprentices, the workforce ebbing and flowing as contracts materialized or as workers departed to complete their national service. Some were recruited through newspaper advertisements, some from technical colleges, but many arrived through a personal connection. One apprentice, Paul Ikrath, was a local boy with an athletic elder brother on the Oschitz Turnrat, his father chief forester on an aristocratic estate already supplying wood to the sawmill. Another, the joiner Hans Heinl, met Rutha in the winter of 1926 when he was visiting a Jungenschaft group in western Bohemia; Heinl asked for work and subsequently thrived in the Turnverein under Rutha's leadership.[8] In this way, there was a tendency to favor employing young men who hailed from the youth or Turn movement or at least matched Rutha's exacting criteria in terms of "personality."

While the business became one facet of Rutha's homosocial world, second only to the youth movement, he soon used it to accord himself a loftier social status. Although having no qualifications, and to the scorn of later Czech commentators, he began to call himself "architect" and usually referred to the business as an "architectural bureau" that manufactured "artistic designs for furniture and living rooms."[9] It was language bound up with his pride as a creative self-made man. Yet full control of the environment developed only from 1930. On 20 December 1929, precisely a decade after his wife's death, Adolf Rutha, the "sawmill owner" according to his gravestone, died at the age of seventy-eight. Just before Christmas the family assembled at Oschitz cemetery. By this time Heinz's business was flourishing, but the eclipse of his strong-willed father was still a watershed, for only now was the old mill business fully abandoned. When in 1931 Schüpfer, the master joiner, left and was replaced by Josef Spudich (already a joiner), it was natural that Rutha would take greater control of his "bureau."[10]

He was now head of the family, assuming a paternalistic care and control over all. Friedel continued diligently to manage the household, providing his meals and prompting him to wish he could give her a holiday.[11] To her son Fritz who was at school in Reichenberg he acted as a proxy father. But it was his younger sister, Gretel, briefly employed in the bureau, to whom he felt a special responsibility and affection. This is revealed in letters from

1930, covering an incident that exposes his strict view of male honor and his readiness to sever a friendship if a comrade behaved "dishonorably."

In late 1929, Anton Langhans, a Comrades' Union (KB) member from Carlsbad who revered Rutha as his model leader, spent a few days in Kunnersdorf and was captivated by Gretel. They proceeded to date regularly and, despite Heinz's cautionary advice, rushed to become engaged. Soon afterward, Langhans, who had never had a girlfriend, had second thoughts, sensing that his feelings were largely stirred because Gretel was the sister of the Rutha he idolized. When he broke off the engagement she was distraught, but Rutha was apoplectic at such brutal, "unmanly" behavior, stating that if the decision was not reversed it was the end of their friendship. In vain, Langhans's friends interceded, condemning Rutha's abruptness and asserting that as a loyal member of the "Rutha Männerbund," Langhans deserved trust from his leader in return. Rutha was unmoved. He objected to outside interference in a family matter, and also remonstrated when Langhans resigned from the KB, for, as he wrote in January 1931, he expected him at least to be discrete and uphold the common (KB) mission for the national community. Here Rutha implied that public and private could be divorced, but the Langhans case seriously brought this viewpoint into question and showed the tensions that could develop in a Männerbund so strongly predicated on close friendship. The case also illuminates Rutha's deep commitment to his sister's welfare: significantly, he stored the correspondence in his safe.[12]

In the 1930s, Rutha's concern for his family and its reputation, together with his attention to detail and aesthetic appreciation, found its logical expression in the mill environment. While Friedel's kitchen was redesigned, the garden was skillfully landscaped by an architect and sometime KB chairman, Gustav Knöchel. Rutha could enthuse, "For weeks the garden has been blossoming. Constantly new displays—wonderful—especially magnificent the great mass of lilies and peonies. I am often outside, watering, weeding and distracting myself from worries about the business."[13] Plans were also afoot by 1933 to build a new workshop and extend the old mill building right up to the house. Finally agreed to by the local authorities in late 1936, it seems to have been constructed the following year.[14]

Nevertheless, a business producing luxury goods could not remain immune from the economic depression. In the early 1930s, Czechoslovakia's foreign trade, on which Sudeten German industries particularly depended, declined by two-thirds.[15] If all still seemed bright in late 1932, the orders were drying up a year later and Rutha was having to drop his prices. Writing to a friend in the summer of 1934, he complained about the lack of clients: he had just finished an office for Konrad Henlein in Prague ("very simple but tidy"), but his only other contracts were to decorate Henlein's regional offices in Eger and construct a walnut living room and a maple-wood bedroom for a friend. Since the turnover was so slow, he thought of turning toward some mass production—perhaps of wooden buttons for dresses—in order to balance the books. He wanted a summer suit, but it would consume two-fifths of his monthly income.[16]

This was especially unsettling as he began to assume new political responsibilities that absented him often from Kunnersdorf, and it did not improve. In the spring of 1935, when the firm closed for ten weeks for lack of contracts, he privately berated the public for thoughtlessly buying foreign goods. The next year proved even worse, with employees temporarily laid off and the business shut down for months.[17] Advertisements in the press urged readers to buy the firm's native solid furniture, but only in 1937 could it recover some clients and take on fresh employees.[18] Thus did Rutha personally experience the economic and employment crisis besetting so much of the German border regions. By the end of his life his business was worth 100,000 Czech crowns, but to preserve itself, it was now "a property burdened with debts."[19]

EROS: THEORY AND PRACTICE

When the Reichenberg police raided Rutha's safe in late 1937 they discovered, apart from his wartime diary, a long enigmatic letter he had written on 22 October 1928 and addressed to "Dear Walter."[20] "Walter," whom the police failed to identify (and Rutha refused to), was clearly Walter Heinrich. Although the letter was never sent, its confessional tone reveals their close friendship, though Rutha acknowledged that Heinrich—"dearest" as he termed him—would never write so nakedly even to his most trusted colleagues. For here Rutha reflected candidly on the youth program of the past decade, including its homoerotic dimension, and confessed his utter dejection about developments. Confronted with the letter in 1937, he would dismiss the contents as idealistic, composed when he was in a very emotional state. The police, however, felt it could be a key to Rutha's personality, proving not least his homosexual disposition, even if that was "projected on a philosophical background and enveloped in secret mysticism."[21]

If the letter's tone seemed quite at variance with Rutha's public confidence in 1928, it was no coincidence that he penned it in October. For just then a major embarrassment had erupted in the Pedagogical Community *[Pädogische Gemeinschaft]* (PG), the Prague student society composed of his "disciples." As its spiritual leader, Rutha naturally admired the PG's dynamism and influence as an embryonic Männerbund; its leader, Gustav Oberlik, was also chair of the federation *[Bund]* of *völkisch* students, responsible for its coordination at the university. In late October, however, Rutha suddenly turned on Oberlik and demanded that the PG expel him. The reason was not made public at the time, and only later are there hints that it was sexual. It seems highly probable that one *völkisch* student from Brünn had publicly accused Rutha of homosexuality, and Oberlik, as chair, had not responded sharply enough to the calumny.[22] It was an early example of Rutha's private sphere invading the public, with catastrophic results. When Oberlik was dismissed a group of his friends followed, leaving the PG as a rump of Rutha loyalists; in 1929, when the Bund decided to readmit Oberlik, the PG petulantly abandoned the federation altogether and constituted itself as a separate body. In this way, Rutha's hotheadedness and arbitrary action—what Walter Hergl suggestively termed his "explosive nervous breakdown"—did much to unravel the whole Bund by 1930.[23] It is true that many of those expelled, including Oberlik, would later make their peace with Rutha, but some of the fissures never healed, and the rumors lingered. The episode reveals the tensions that could easily surface between the homosocial (male bonding) and the homoerotic/homosexual, an overlap that some observers were uneasy about but that Rutha always refused to acknowledge.

The "Walter" letter of October 1928 helps clarify the Oberlik incident in showing Rutha's distressed state of mind. In it, he wrote that every man was sustained by a "world force" that gave his existence meaning, a procreative vitality, the loss of which was catastrophic for the individual. His own "world force" had been Eros. Just as August Rodin had sculpted awakening youth, so he, Rutha, understood that his fate was to cultivate the most beautiful youths of the rising generation, drawing them out of solitude and hedonism, alerting them to the heroic models of spiritual creativity. It had been an enormous venture, advancing the most receptive—the "most beautiful"—in this period of Sudeten German revival, and he acknowledged (as in his KB lecture) that the work had been partly successful. Via circles of radiant youths, the seeds of the future state were being planted, the project was expanding, and would be victorious.

Nevertheless, this was insufficient. Rutha emphasized that, while for Heinrich and KB comrades the final vision of the Sudeten Spannist state was the priority, his own, tied to the divine Eros, was that "inner heart" of the movement, its masculine essence, as expressed through vibrant young men. They, to him, were not just a symbolic element in the whole enterprise; they were his very destiny, which he could not escape. His overriding anxiety in the letter was that, despite years of searching, he had found no single youth who could act as his "son," continuing his pioneering spiritual activity and thereby securing the movement's future in the next half century. The Spannist state would certainly materialize, but its essential youth composition would vanish with the present generation, just as he would die. Indeed, he concluded, if the "silent God," who had so far nurtured the revival, failed now to dispatch a "thunderbolt of fulfillment" (a son), then he could not continue in the movement. The alternative, a life bereft of a moral mission or any idealism, seemed to be dismal emptiness.

The way that Rutha elaborated on this theme shows it was more than a simple quest for a like-minded successor. Like no source apart from his wartime diary, the letter illuminates how he had consciously channeled his same-sex desires into the youth movement, finding or constructing there a rational framework for their expression. As he noted, "For me the [Sudeten state] idea comes alive and grows only where a young man loves me." Yet still, a decade after writing his angst-ridden diary, he faced periodic self-doubt because of the male environment he encountered. Gone might be his search for a "pure woman" or much guilt in that regard (even though, if he could banish "disturbing emotions," life with a woman might be possible). In fact, he felt no passion for women and totally rebelled against their temptations. His frustration was that others in the Männerbund did not share his single-minded devotion to Eros; they were constantly enticed or confused by women, the "dark rivers of nature" as he termed them, so that the number qualifying as spiritual sons was always diminishing.[24] Since even Walter Heinrich had, according to the letter, been enticed by a woman and failed to return to the "youth cause," it all made him doubt the idealistic life mission he had chosen for himself.

This despair makes more sense if we consider the state of the mission at this juncture. Although the KB circle was expanding by late 1928, the youth movement seemed in a cul-de-sac, for Henlein's energetic program had yet to take off. But perhaps most significantly, the Oberlik incident struck directly at Rutha's theoretical framework for a youth mission. It forced him to scrutinize Eros and realize that, while Oberlik and others could abandon that male passion as they matured, his own same-sex commitment was far greater. It showed him starkly, perhaps for the first time, that the Männerbund was unreliable and liable to disintegrate, so the prospect of finding a son to continue his life work seemed ever bleaker. Alone, and with no obvious solution, he seemed in the letter to be hinting at suicide. It was not the first time: the diary of 1918 had also briefly suggested it. The crisis of 1928 resulted again from his unresolved sexual anxieties, exposed all the more because of the public charge of homosexuality.

In the intervening decade, the fragmentary evidence we possess suggests how Rutha had normalized same-sex desire in the homosocial environment of the youth movement. In the *Blätter vom frischen Leben* he had suggested some sexual reference points, recommending to youth leaders not just Stefan George, but the homoerotic poetry of the "fervent, all-loving" Walt Whitman.[25] In the postwar years he also clearly retained links with Oskar Just's homosocial milieu in Gablonz, cultivating some of Just's disciples like Oberlik and emulating Just in several ways. And most important, as expressed in the "Walter" letter, was the homoerotic framework he himself constructed around his youth mission. How far this derived from Hans Blüher is unclear, for Blüher's theories were allegedly just based on existing phenomena in the Wandervogel and male society. Certainly, despite Rutha's constant refutation, Blüher's ideas meshed neatly with his own, not least the grand concept of a Männerbund, a body bound together erotically and directed by male heroes with "state-creating impulses."

It is equally likely that Rutha's conversion to "pedagogic Eros" drew on the example of Germany's best-known reform pedagogue and youth leader, Gustav Wyneken. Ironically—in view of what would eventually befall Rutha—Wyneken in 1921 had been arrested, tried, and imprisoned for sexually abusing two adolescent boys at his school. In publicly defending himself, he had admitted to being motivated by "pedagogic Eros," but stressed that that concept had nothing to do with sexuality or homosexuality; rather it was a spiritual relationship between teacher and pupil on the model of ancient Greece.[26]

Whether or not Rutha followed these arguments closely at the time (for they were widely circulated in Germany's youth movements), he certainly shared Wyneken's spiritual interpretation of Eros. Yet his own path toward the "world force" probably owed most to a direct, personal reading of Plato. This seems to have come after 1920 with Heinrich's help and via Stefan

George's poetry.[27] Plato's precepts about love, placed in the mouth of Socrates in the *Symposium* and *Phaedrus*, stated that its finest expression was the spiritual, didactic relationship between an older man and his young male lover. That bond between *erastes* and *eromenos*, manifest in antiquity, was now transposed to the Sudeten youth movement where hero-leaders loved and cared for their disciples, where homoerotic bonding was as prevalent as in ancient Athens or Sparta. Before youths turned to any sexual procreation with women—as Rutha expected—they must experience spiritual intimacy with a charismatic male leader. He would procreate in his own way, "[giving] birth, through a boundless love of knowledge, to many beautiful and magnificent discourses and ideas."[28]

Rutha's enthusiasm for this maxim was clear in his *Blätter*, where already by 1921 he was praising *Phaedrus* as "a discussion about souls, beauty and the love of young men."[29] In this interpretation, Eros meant spiritual creativity rather than any "targeted sexual desire," but he did also incorporate a nonsexual target in the form of "an ambitious venture, a grand project."[30] Thus Eros in the 1920s became an integral part of his Sudeten youth mission, with Plato's precepts informing many of its dimensions. He drew on the *Republic* when planning systematic training; he fully endorsed Plato's maxim that "the object of education is to teach us what is beautiful."[31] The classical world supplied a reassuring homosocial and moral structure that meshed comfortably with the homoeroticism already permeating the youth movement. And not least it calmed his own same-sex anxieties, supplying his desires with a noble and protective framework.

The personal crisis or breakdown of 1928–1929 was only gradually surmounted, and the silence of the sources over the next year testifies to this. But in nurturing Rutha's ideal of educating a Sudeten youth vanguard, Henlein by late 1930 provided an exit from the cul-de-sac. From afar in Vienna, Heinrich too may have lent support. In August 1929, he sent Rutha a book on the Greek god Dionysus with the cryptic assurance that "even in this cold, male-work far from boys *[knabenfernen Männerwerk]*, I am nourished by the fervent image [that lives] in you and me." Another present, a study of Plato, arrived later "as a token of thanks that you were the first of us in the homeland to realize what today is essential to meet the requirements, so that it alone appears meaningful and worthwhile for the best men of our nation."[32]

If such reminders about the vital youth crusade steadied Rutha's resolve, his same-sex anxieties were gradually subsumed within the framework of the Jungenschaft, where various shades of homoeroticism were fully accepted. Walter Rohn, from 1931 a fervent disciple who lauded Rutha's "beautiful, clear and pure ideal of friendship," explained later that tight bonding was essential to produce the right education:

> It was the appropriate expression of adolescents' firm instincts during their years of growth. Out of this, their communal life was stamped with a natural impetuosity that was manifest in their personal relations with one another, in games and in other forms of life. I can remember that before going to sleep we would slip our arms around each other, kiss, and tease and wrestle a little. Easily excited in these years, it was very possible that suddenly, without intention, there was some sexual stimulation. In these years, however, our life was too pure and too natural for us to have done anything bad to one another. We never saw anything perverse or base in our warm friendship.[33]

While Rutha was always energized by the environment of hiking and camps, he began from about 1932 to invite youths who had attracted his attention to visit the mill and stay overnight. Regularly at weekends, and very much in the tradition of his idol Stefan George (a "master" instructing his disciples), he held readings with adolescents in his library, drawing particularly on Plato or George for inspiration. It suggests that his underlying philosophy, with Eros at the center, had not altered after his breakdown. Nor had he ceased to search for that "son," that charismatic individual, who in October 1928 he had largely described as his successor. What had changed was that, with the youth mission increasingly secure, his quest for a son had a more openly personal motive; on the Greek model of *erastes* and *eromenos*, he required a young man to serve as his close companion. It led him into new sexual territory.

His emotional and physical interaction with many single mature youths accelerated at this time. At work of course was a basic sexual attraction to young men, as exposed in the wartime diary, but just as in 1918 the Wandervogel's homoerotic culture disguised his desires, so in the 1930s the framework of Eros supplied a higher justification for his actions. This is clear from notes he composed in 1931, exploring his search for a special friend. Here he mused "without shame" that, when he had recognized God (Eros) over a decade earlier, he had been ecstatic, realizing that this path combined substance, pleasure and lasting prospects:

It was not at all surprising that amongst many youths and adults . . . I ever more forcefully yearned for the one who not only possessed a beautiful youthful form but would accompany me in the movement and, even more, with the same heart-beat, the same blood and spirit, would become my son and friend for life, more than all others who were loved or desired. Just as a man, after many youth sirens, composes himself for his great love, yearns and fights for her . . . , so I had to grasp all strength and hope of love, all forces, and recast the two beings as one in attitude, spirit and behavior, hoping that precisely this would lead me deeper into the youth, believing that my life through him would continue strong and young, transformed in its course and tone . . . This friendship in my life was the accompaniment to calm and steady work: the two would perform like one being, side by side.[34]

The lines express an elusive quest for a permanent companion who never materialized. Rutha penned them in September 1931 when he was visiting Greece for the first time and was in the company of a singular twenty-one-year-old named Kurt Gansel. Gansel was one of Rutha's first employees in the furniture bureau and one who for years held a special position in the firm.[35] Having arrived in 1926 for a three-year apprenticeship, he worked as a joiner until 1934 when he departed for further training in Germany. According to many witnesses, he was handsome, blond, and athletic—a proficient ski jumper—so he quickly attracted his employer's attention.

Indeed, in the letter to Heinrich of late 1928, when bemoaning female temptations, Rutha had singled out "K. G." as his own "last beloved," someone who "in his boyish glow" was "the nourishment and seal of my own strength," but who unfortunately was being enticed away too early by the female "dark caller." Although Gansel was already known to have an eye for girls in the village, and Rutha gradually doubted his suitability as a "son," the infatuation continued for a long time. Unlike most employees, Gansel lived in the attic of the mill, took meals with the Rutha family, and was seen by fellow workers to be on unusually familiar "Du" terms with his employer. On Gansel's own admission, the initial professional relationship developed into a close friendship. It was cemented through the Oschitz Turn branch, where from 1930 to 1934 Rutha was presiding and pushing through a reform program. After excelling in local Turner skiing competitions, Gansel in 1931 was made responsible for the Turn training of local schoolboys and dispatched by Rutha on a two-week Turn course in Asch.[36] When a new school building was opened in Oschitz in 1933, a photograph (fig.16) captured the Turner ceremony: Gansel stands rigidly next to Rutha, their disciplined bearing a model contrast to the relaxed stance of their fellow Turners.

For Rutha there was always a paternal dimension to this relationship, reinforced because Gansel's father had deserted his family. Rutha treated him like a son, ruffling his hair, patting his shoulder, and even lending him his clothes. He also exaggerated his protégé's industriousness (fellow workers were less generous in their comments), seeing in him, apart from an attractive man, someone who could be molded to assume part of his furniture business. Gansel was duly lent a range of literary works, invited to readings on Greek culture in the library, and even accompanied Rutha on a visit to Heinrich in Vienna sometime in 1930.

Most significant in indicating the patronage was the journey to Greece in September 1931, something Rutha had always desired. Whether or not Gansel pressed to be taken on a largely subsidized trip, Rutha later explained that he had wanted "to show him, an intelligent man of humble origins, a bit of the world and its culture; as he was clever, I hoped he could sometime become a manager in my business."[37] Over a fortnight, starting in Salonika, they sailed around the peninsula, visiting Patras and ending in Athens. There they parted, Gansel traveling home while his patron stayed on for a time to explore the Greek interior. Rutha was greatly enthused. On his return, at a Jungenschaft gathering, he waxed lyrical about the classical Greek model for youth education and singled out ancient Sparta as a disciplined society that the distressed and disunited Sudeten Germans would do well to emulate.[38]

Yet not all was well. Rutha's notes penned in Greece and Gansel's early departure hint at some tension between them, which probably proved a watershed. From this point Rutha seemed to direct his desires elsewhere, although remaining protective of Gansel, whom he still viewed as a protégé deserving of advancement. The moody young man exploited this favoritism, often adopting a superior air with fellow workers at the mill and even dallying with Gretel Rutha. When in April 1934 he finally left Kunnersdorf for a year's training at the Weimar Handwerkschule in Germany, Rutha repeatedly tried to control him from afar. He was sent a monthly allowance of 80 Reichsmark, nagged to keep within the budget, and expected to match his mentor's disciplined lifestyle, training assiduously, educating himself for the future, and confessing all his activities. Well might Rutha be accustomed to the young man's female dalliances, but he took umbrage when in Weimar he was unfaithful to Gretel (only a temporary object of his attention). Most strikingly, he still hoped that, despite the girlfriends, Gansel would eventually want to select a male companion "for a beautiful friendship."[39]

Rutha's professional objective here was clear. When in July 1934 Gansel wrote with suggestions for the bureau, a sign itself of their special relationship, Rutha warmly replied: "You too will have an opportunity with Sp[udich] to discuss and carry out the complete re-organization of the business." By 1935 he was pressing him to study diligently, for then "you can definitely relieve me here."[40] But it was not to be, for Gansel continually veered from the designated course. Although Rutha paid for Gansel's examinations in Weimar in March, he failed to take them; when on a visit to Kunnersdorf he was angrily reprimanded, he resolved never to return there to work. Something of the friendship did remain, for Rutha typically relented and in 1936 directed Gansel, now unemployed, toward new work opportunities. But the dream of training a partner for the business was shattered. While the young man had finally rebelled against such a controlling figure, Rutha's long sexual obsession had blinded him to his companion's actual deficiencies.

This relationship had never become physical, whatever Rutha's own early desires. Arguably it was exploitative on both sides, but usually certain limits were understood, which explain the longevity of the friendship. With another of his employees Rutha was less circumspect, and there were to be fatal consequences. Franz Veitenhansl, a fifteen-year-old who had met Rutha at the Turnverband youth camp of July 1932, joined the firm as a three-year apprentice that autumn. He was an introverted boy, a slow learner, who arrived with his mother and was given an attic room. According to Veitenhansl's account (and it is the only one), just before Christmas when he was about to leave for the vacation, Rutha encouraged him to sleep in his bedroom so they could rise early together and walk to the local train station at Kriesdorf. That night, allegedly, Rutha initiated sex with his employee, and possibly for both of them it was a loss of virginity. Over the following months such incidents seem to have multiplied, Rutha often starting by reading from George or Hölderlin and then drawing his pupil toward "mutual gratification." In Veitenhansl's words, "he played with my genitals until I ejaculated, or took my penis in his mouth and sucked until the semen came, which, as far as I could tell, he swallowed."[41]

Although Rutha would later deny this as "complete fabrication," there seems little doubt that some sexual act occurred in view of Veitenhansl's later state of mind. When from the summer of 1933 he resisted his employer's warm advances, he found that the atmosphere soured. From a committed joiner and enthusiastic local Turner, he turned into a solitary figure, apathetic and depressed. Finally, toward the end of his apprenticeship in 1935, he poured out his tale of "abuse" to several individuals, vowing that he could not stay at the mill. One of the confidants, as we will see, was Rudi Hein, a youth leader who was hoping for revenge against Rutha. Another was the local veterinary surgeon, Rudolf Wolff, who had known Rutha at school in Böhmisch Leipa and then for years on the Oschitz Turn council. Whether or not Wolff had developed a grudge, as family sources claim, is not clear. Possibly he was irritated by Rutha's dominance in the local community. Possibly relations between them were strained because when Wolff had a "disreputable affair" with a local teacher, Rutha forbade Gretel to associate with him. When on 29 September 1935 Veitenhansl visited the veterinarian, he burst into tears and easily convinced Wolff that something "homosexual" had occurred—not just a kiss but oral sex. Wolff encouraged Veitenhansl for protection to write down a statement about Rutha's "homosexual behavior," assuring him that it was confidential and would be kept in a safe place.[42]

A third confidant was Hans Heinl, a former mill employee and head of the regional young Turners, who by chance observed Veitenhansl's melancholy, asked him about it, and was shocked to learn the details. Heinl first proceeded directly to confront Rutha, who was his Turn superior in the Jeschken-Iser Gau. Rutha reacted very angrily and defensively, but Heinl was unconvinced and confided in a friend, who happened to be Rudolf Wolff.[43] In this way, from late 1935, a number of clocks had started ticking for Rutha. Veitenhansl left the mill in October, returning to his parents and swearing to their surprise that he "wanted nothing more to do with that swine [Rutha]."[44] However, his written statements remained in safekeeping, his enemies ready to produce them at an opportune moment.

In the case of some young men, like his employees Veitenhansl and Gansel, Rutha's attention was unevenly reciprocated and crossed a critical professional borderline. But within the homosocial world of the youth movement or the PG, such a border between mentor and pupil was blurred; indeed, a homoerotic spark was often accepted or expected (fig.17). Thus it was far easier for Rutha to satisfy his desires safely among that youth cohort, who clustered around him as devoted followers and who moved steadily in and out of his orbit. A typical case was Willi Hoffmann, a member of the

Reichenberg Jungenschaft who from 1932 sometimes visited Rutha alone, corresponded with him, and received customary presents on his birthday or at Christmas. Soon he was active in the regional Turn youth movement and increasingly someone whom Rutha courted, noting the "clarity and firmness" of their long friendship.[45]

Another even more devoted disciple was Wolfgang Heinz from Silesia, who as a law student in Prague first met Rutha at a PG gathering in late 1933. Immediately the nineteen-year-old was captivated, not least by a common interest in antiquity, and began regularly to visit Kunnersdorf. As early as January 1934, he composed for Rutha a "classical" poem, eulogizing a naked young warrior with shining eyes whose army stands arrayed on the seashore, their weapons glittering in the sun, as he sacrifices a bull to his deity.[46] The attraction was mutual: Rutha observed that "Wolf" was "the most wonderful man I have ever seen, always in control of himself, always receptive to everything beautiful."[47] When he organized a second "study trip" to Greece in September 1934, it was Wolfgang Heinz whom he invited together with Walter Heinrich and two other youths. This time the visit was more ambitious, encompassing the islands of Crete and Delos as well as Athens, Sparta (where they slept in the open air), Delphi, and Olympia.[48] Later Rutha educated his disciple with books about Plato or George, and Heinz fully reciprocated, remaining fiercely loyal and in regular correspondence. By 1935, he was drawn toward Spannist teachings and proceeded to attend lectures in Vienna as an "external student."[49]

To youths like Wolfgang Heinz or Walter Rohn, Rutha was a passionate teacher who gave them a life ideal, whose friendship was homoerotically charged on the purest Platonic model. Rutha in turn preserved this "spiritual dimension" with most disciples, but in some cases where the attraction was strong he could not resist initiating some physical sex. While this was an extra outlet for his "urges," he was undoubtedly in denial that it was "homosexual" activity. The most notable instances were with Jungenschaft members Werner Weiss and Adolf Wagner, both of whom were having minor sexual liaisons anyway with other youths (including Hoffman and Rohn). Perhaps half a dozen times, Werner Weiss, when staying overnight at the mill in 1933–1934, was called from the library to Rutha's bedroom and they mutually masturbated. Since Weiss had similar urges he found it initially satisfying and was in awe of his mentor.[50]

The same pattern occurred between Rutha and Wagner over the same time period. To Rutha, Wagner, who was now a young–Turner leader in the local Gau, seemed an ideal *eromenos* or "son." In January 1934, shortly after the death of Stefan George, his own "spiritual mentor," Rutha sent as a late Christmas present one of his favorite poetry collections by George; it was George, he explained, who "for many years sang to me of beautiful youths when I was alone." He hoped that Wagner too might find in the poems a new means of connecting with Turner youth, but also stressed, "In recent months I have felt very close to you—perhaps as you have matured, you have become more of a brother to me and less of a boy."[51]

The words amply testify to the quest for a companion. Wagner, a few years later, would admit that Rutha had indeed been his idol, and therefore, supposedly, he had automatically consented to sex as something "correct." Like Veitenhansl, however, he grew uncomfortable with Rutha's advances and managed to extract himself by visiting the mill less often. In this case they stayed friends, Rutha finding Wagner a post in Henlein's office in Asch and then being typically solicitous of his welfare.[52]

This particular sexual liaison had been facilitated by the homoerotic youth culture, but it was short-lived. In Rutha's world, it overlapped with many other friendships on different levels of intimacy, the young men often moving out of his orbit yet retaining a permanent bond from their years of close mentoring. Rutha replaced one prospective "son" with another in this elusive quest, where he blurred the emotional and didactic purposes together and justified them via a Platonic model.

SEVEN

A Leap into Ice-Cold Water

The year 1933 was a revolutionary one in Czechoslovakia as a more vibrant strain of Sudeten German nationalism emerged. One impetus was the Nazi revolution in neighboring Germany. In January, Adolf Hitler's inauguration as chancellor alerted many Germans in Czechoslovakia, whether Nazis or Sudeten German conservatives, to a potential dynamic ally in central Europe. The Czechoslovak authorities duly became more vigilant against National Socialism, adopting preemptive security measures in the Sudeten border regions. Yet the catalyst for change did not just emanate from the Third Reich. It was homegrown, long nurtured on Bohemian soil, and 1933 witnessed a significant stage in the maturation of Konrad Henlein's rejuvenated Turn movement. In July, in the small town of Saaz on the Czech-German language border, Henlein staged a meticulously planned Turn festival for seventy thousand people, the first under his new regime. A milestone in Sudeten German consciousness and confidence, it quickly acquired a mythical reputation as the turning point that created a new dynamic political force in Czechoslovakia.

This sudden development complicated the direction of Heinz Rutha's idealistic mission. While it offered a wider playing field for influence, it meant directly confronting Czechoslovak political realities and stepping outside the previous bounds of national segregation. From 1933 the Henleinists would feel pressure to adapt to the Czechoslovak political system, while always trying to retain their radical nationalist vigor. Rutha's youth program could be pushed forward, but the utopian objective of the Comrades' Union (KB)—to construct a Sudeten Spannist state—was gradually eclipsed by new political struggles that had to be won before that could be implemented.

EMERGENCY MEASURES

From the Saaz festival of July 1933 two dramatic rituals stood out, ceremonies that "arose from the spirit of the male union" on display.[1] One evening, fifteen thousand Turners with burning torches processed silently into the town square to honor Sudeten German war dead. As they assembled in a huge semicircle and extinguished their torches, they were illuminated only by the flickering flames from sacrificial bowls hung high up on a tower. Out of the darkness, loudspeakers sounded a stark lament from the mouths of the dead: we are a greater army than those on earth and still expect sacrifice from the living for a glorious ideal. Early the next morning, Henlein assembled the movement's two thousand *Vorturners*—those responsible for training young Turners according to Rutha's precepts. After expressing joy at this "concentrated body of men," Henlein told them the Turn movement had become the "educational body of the Sudeten Germans," for no one else was giving clear direction. Their prime task was to supervise youth recruitment since, he explained, the best adolescents of today would be the pioneering elite of tomorrow. He again urged all Sudeten youths to join the Turner ranks.[2]

If Saaz was a watershed, its significance varied for observers. On one level it was a brilliant propaganda coup, publicizing the Turnverband across German communities as a highly organized, united, and "nonpolitical" force, poised to educate and lead a revitalized nation within Czechoslovakia. Since the whole event passed off peacefully with no demonstrable anti-Czech disturbances (not least as two hundred extra Czech police were present), even the Czechoslovak ministry of health congratulated Henlein on his Turners' physical prowess and discipline.[3] Indeed, the festival was the first public display of his two-year Turn revolution. A strict hierarchical framework had been imposed on the whole network, emphasizing leadership and obedience. The correct mentality was inculcated from late 1930 when a special training school was established at Asch for all officials, and by the time of Saaz the uniformity (including a standard grey uniform) was evident. In place of old-style gymnastics on equipment or in the open air, group athletics and physical endurance were to the fore, befitting what Henlein lauded as the "heroic spirit of the German front-line soldier."[4]

Rutha himself embraced the Saaz phenomenon. For two years he had urged teenagers from his own Jungenschaft to join the Turnverband, secure key positions, and participate in the Asch training courses. But only after Saaz was he resolved to merge his small youth group fully with the Turner youth organization. An announcement in August 1933 recorded that its union with the Scouts had been dissolved; the Jungenschaft, a pioneer of disciplined youth education and leadership, was transposing the ideas and terminology associated with its very name into the Turnverband.[5] Simultaneously, a one-week course took place in Saaz for two hundred new Vorturners, and Rutha was one of the main instructors.

Yet despite all this, the Saaz festival was just one staging post toward Rutha's end goal of galvanizing the Sudeten German tribe *[Stamm]*. Writing on its eve, he felt bound to repeat his vision of a "holistic youth education," graded in three age-stages in order to convert adolescents into a national Männerbund; that framework was still absent though Henlein had publicly backed it a year earlier.[6] At Saaz, therefore, Henlein was simply echoing Rutha in claiming that the Turnverband was the Sudeten educational body, that systematic education was the main tool for fostering Sudeten unity.

Creating the structure for a corporate Sudeten German state on the Spannist model—the grand aim of the elite KB—would naturally take much longer.[7] The KB had been diffusing ideas through its journal *Die junge Front,* and from 1931 when Walter Heinrich returned from Austria, it hosted occasional conferences to educate its small membership. In October 1931, three hundred members attended a KB conference in Leitmeritz to hear lectures by Heinrich and Othmar Spann himself. At a large gathering a year later, Rutha and Henlein were key speakers on the pedagogic mission of the Turnverband.[8] One witness described it as a meeting of idealists drawn together by a secret doctrine of salvation with overwhelmingly Sudeten German dimensions. Konrad Henlein ("a large lean scraggy man") was characterized as apparently suspicious of German National Socialism as well as of the small Sudeten Nazi party. Instead, his priority was an effective Sudeten organization to challenge Czech dominance and demand at least substantial self-government.[9]

Alongside KB idealism there was always this practical application at work. Just as the leaders in October 1928 had urged the creation of "germ cells" as core units for a structure of "estates," so the loose KB membership now constituted such cells. Gradually a Männerbund seemed to be evolving, fostered often through enduring ties from the youth movements or the Turnverband. KB men had managed to join strategically important Sudeten social and political organizations, their diversity testament to the actual disunity in the German nationalist camp. Thus, Willi Sebekowsky entered the German National Socialist Party (DNSAP), while Hugo Liehm played a similar role in the German National Party (DNP) and was influential in one defense society, the *Bund der Deutschen*. In Prague, Ernst Kundt was leader of the *Deutschpolitisches Arbeitsamt* (DPA), since 1919 a coordinating center for the nonsocialist German political parties. In Bratislava in Slovakia, Franz Karmasin, who in the late 1920s had even briefly worked at the Rutha mill, was head of a new German political party as well as the regional *Deutscher Kulturverband*.[10] How far this activity was systematically planned in these years is unclear: probably it depended a great deal on personal initiatives. The original KB core or think-tank of Rutha and Heinrich was undoubtedly most committed to Spannism. But all KB adherents in the organization's outer circles were expected to be diligent, working toward the long-term goal of a Sudeten German corporate state.[11]

From early 1931, it was Henlein's Turnverband that the KB leadership had identified as the prime vehicle, a Spannist vanguard for uniting the Sudeten tribe. It seems clear that Henlein himself, an early KB adherent, was mainly enthused not by Spannism but by Rutha's precepts of leadership and "masculine renewal" on behalf of the nation, ideals that chimed with his own dedication to original Turn principles and the spirit of wartime sacrifice. Nevertheless, since many KB members belonged to the reorganized Turn hierarchy, the broader Spannist vision for restructuring society had a firm base and was regularly articulated in the *Turnzeitung*. Most significant was the refashioning in October 1932 of the role of Dietwart. Formerly, as practiced by Rutha in the 1920s, the Dietwart had managed *völkisch* education. Since that was now systematically integrated into youth education, "Diet work" was revised to include training mature Turners, disseminating Turn pedagogy in the wider national community, and specifically liaising with Sudeten social groups to install the best Turner adults as "germ cells."

To oversee this crucial activity, Henlein chose a fanatical twenty-five-year-old, Walter Brand. A fervent Spannist scholar who had studied in Vienna, Brand had been dispatched by Heinrich in August 1931 to attend an early Vorturner course in Asch. The following January, he proceeded to Prague to inaugurate a permanent Spannist seminar for students of the Pedagogical Community (PG) and other *völkisch* groups; thence he wrote prodigiously in the newspapers and toured the Sudeten region, lecturing to young Turners and defense societies.[12] When appointed as Diet head in early 1933, he was thrust into Henlein's inner circle and secured major influence. While his Diet advisory committee was composed of regional Dietwarts, all from the KB network, it also included Rutha as a senior mentor.

The first task was to help organize the Saaz festival, but Brand's long-term objective, as set out in September 1933, was to propagate and advance the structure of a Sudeten corporate state.

Everyone committed to this vision acknowledged it was embryonic and would take a generation to implement: Heinrich at one KB conference predicted thirty years.[13] Rutha too envisaged slowly educating a tribal elite of young men. However, in the summer of 1933 this methodical program was swiftly overtaken by other events, the pace of Sudeten national consolidation dramatically accelerated and diverted in an unforeseen direction. As the Czechoslovak liberal-nationalist regime grew anxious about Nazi or pan-German support among its German population, it started preemptive emergency measures.[14] In the 1920s, the native DNSAP under leaders like Hans Krebs had been a small, "negativist" parliamentary-political force, retaining links with its cousins in Germany while maneuvering with protestations of state loyalty in Czechoslovakia. In the summer of 1932, however, in the wake of rising support for the party that matched developments in Germany, the Czech authorities pounced on the DNSAP's youth organization, the *Volkssport*, launching a trial of its leaders on charges of subverting the republic. (One of those charged was Rudolf Haider, who in the future would continue to be a radical protagonist in Rutha's eyes.) By 1933, with the defendants pronounced guilty, and Hitler in power, it seemed only a matter of time before negativist parties like the DNSAP and the DNP would be targeted for dissolution.

Indeed, over six months in 1933 Prague passed a series of security measures that, though quite understandable in attempting to protect the fledgling Czechoslovak system, veered the state in an authoritarian direction. Press censorship was tightened, public meetings (like Saaz) far more scrupulously supervised, and Czech state police were now installed in many German-language areas including Oschitz-Kunnersdorf.[15] Under vague criteria it was far easier to arrest individuals or ban organizations that threatened the security or democratic character of the republic. At a time, ironically, when Nazi Germany was introducing its own "enabling measures," Czechoslovakia felt pressured to be vigilant, moving toward what one Czech historian has termed an "authoritative democracy."[16] For some it brought back memories of legislation under the Habsburg Empire. For others, like the German ambassador and most nationalist Germans, it simply unmasked the "true oligarchic character" of the Czechoslovak regime.[17] In this atmosphere the KB-Turnverband mission could not remain unaffected.

What Rutha thought of National Socialism at this time, and what local Nazis thought of him, can only be surmised. Historians have periodically, often polemically, examined the relationship between the KB and National Socialism, some arguing for a tight ideological affinity between the two, others suggesting their inherent distinctiveness. Should the KB-Nazi battles of the mid-1930s be characterized as genuine conflicts of interest or merely as "fraternal strife" between German nationalists? One danger is to evaluate the relationship teleologically through the prism of Sudeten German enthusiasm for Nazi Germany in 1938, thereby diluting any real differences in earlier years.[18] Admittedly, the KB mirrored Nazism in its scorn of liberal democracy, its diminution of the individual, and its authoritarian-fascist character, notably its plans to carve out an authoritarian Sudeten German state in the Bohemian lands. The KB and later Henleinists were also pan-Germanist in anticipating the return of German dominance to central Europe. As a result, there was much potential for ideological blurring, and all the more so because in the Sudeten nationalist camp a long-term goal was to achieve German regional unity, to play down national differences, in the face of a supposed Czechoslovak united front. Some KB men, including Brand and Sebekowsky, had even dabbled with Nazi membership.

Nevertheless, the KB vision still diverged in fundamental ways from both Nazi beliefs and priorities, with distinctive features (including a homegrown leadership principle) that had been honed for decades in the Czech-German crucible. Although KB members, through Spann's universalist creed, envisaged German spiritual dominance across central Europe, their foremost mission as Sudeten German loyalists was to serve the Sudeten tribe, prioritizing that over any Reich expansionist agenda. Their ideal corporate state for the Bohemian lands was also at odds with National Socialism in terms of organization and elite selection. As we have seen, Spannism in contrast to Nazi ideology was not obsessed with the Jews and with Aryan selection; and despite increasing Nazification, an Aryan paragraph was not introduced into the Henlein movement until 1938.[19] The selection that the KB espoused centered rather on a spiritual hierarchy, where those heading society emerged through their inherent charismatic leadership qualities, not—as in the Social Darwinist world—through force or through sheer lust for power.

Rutha's outlook usefully illustrates this idealistic mindset. Possibly, like Walter Heinrich, Rutha initially welcomed Hitler's accession, for Nazism displayed resurgent German confidence and could be a useful ally for implementing Spannism in central Europe.[20] More likely, he was equivocal, viewing National Socialism as something vulgar, plebeian, and violent. Its racist power struggle always sat uneasily next to his own priority of slowly educating an elite charismatic Männerbund. Its aggressive pan-Germanism was equally alarming for someone dreaming of a peaceful revolution in the Bohemian lands; and in contrast to those radicals fixated by the Third Reich, Rutha's interpretation of German spiritual unity always encompassed old Austria as much as the new Germany. In short, his was an elitist German universalism with values quite similar to those espoused in interwar Czecho-slovakia by the old German Bohemian nobility; not surprisingly as we will see, he could always mix comfortably with such aristocrats.[21]

In contrast, from 1933 if not earlier, Rutha was a natural enemy of regional Nazis because of the primacy he accorded the Sudeten mission and his implicit wariness over radical pan-Germanism. In the 1920s too he had made enemies by disrupting the Wandervogel, politicizing the youth move-ment, and by his "unnatural obsession" with systematic youth education. Most notable was Preparedness *[Bereitschaft]*, the society of youth elders founded by Rudolf Staffen specifically against Rutha and the KB. It sought to promote Sudeten patriotism via traditional cultural and economic orga-nizations, in the manner of the Bohemian Lands Movement.[22] From 1930 it had expanded its horizons, allying with *Volkssport* and other *völkisch* splinter groups who were irredentist, seeking Sudeten German unity with Germany. In this spirit, Staffen in late 1931 openly criticized the Spannist or Austrian influence that allegedly permeated the Turnverband, but was quickly confronted by Henlein and expelled from the movement.[23] It was just one incident that revealed the many divisions within the Sudeten German nationalist camp, and it embittered those who already had a grudge against Rutha. As we will see, their ties to National Socialism, including *Volkssport*, made them all the more dangerous from 1933.

The new Czech emergency measures, coupled with the Third Reich's dynamism, crystallized the thinking of the KB as much as the Sudeten Nazis. It seemed vital to act to shore up the "endangered" Sudeten German position in Czechoslovakia. This idea was evident in March 1933 when Ernst Kundt's DPA, whose overall mission was Sudeten political unity, held its annual conference in Reichenberg and discussed finally creating an above-party *Volksrat* or national council in the tradition of that organized by Wenzel Titta before 1914. The lead speaker, Walter Brand, proposed the Volksrat as an embryonic leadership for the emerging corporate state; at first the existing Sudeten bourgeois political parties might merge into it, but he also mentioned Henlein as a leader who could be above party politics. The meeting agreed to create such a Volksrat and began discussions with politicians.[24]

For the DNSAP, such unity seemed all the more crucial to protect their position. Thus when Hans Krebs and other Sudeten Nazi leaders attended the Saaz festival as guests in July and witnessed the impressive display of unity, Krebs was minded to ask Henlein himself to found a common organization *[Volksfront]* encompassing all bourgeois political parties. Henlein seems immediately to have declined this jump into party politics, but Krebs's approach and the Saaz triumph adjusted his thinking about what was possible. On 20 August, when the Oschitz Turnverein hosted a district Turn event, Henlein and Brand attended and used the opportunity to consult with Rutha (fig.18). On a walk by a lake south of Niemes, the three pondered the state of the KB mission and the Sudeten predicament. They resolved not to enter politics prematurely through any Volksfront: as Rutha concluded, with an eye on Sudeten German youth training, "for any political engagement we need at least five more years."[25]

Rutha on this point was consistent over the next weeks, but he and other colleagues were to be surprised at Henlein's own volte-face. What cannot be denied is that Henlein in September 1933 was suddenly under renewed pressure from the DNP and DNSAP (Krebs in particular) to launch and head a Volksfront that their members could enter for protection. But equally clear—though dismissed by historians who approach Henlein simply as a closet Nazi[26]—is Henlein's own repeated vacillation. In a string of intense negotiations with the DNSAP and other parties, he apparently feared that party politicians might too easily secure control of any new body, and he rightly noted that Krebs envisaged any Volksfront largely as a replacement DNSAP. This Henlein would not tolerate, and his wariness shows a certain loyalty to KB ideals (non-Nazi but also non-party political).

This caution seemed clear when Henlein met Rutha again in mid-September. The location, typically inaccessible and panoramic, was the highest point of the Erzgebirge, the Keilberg, at a mountain hut owned by Rutha's professional acquaintance, the Saxon architect Friedrich Wagner-Poltrock. In recent years Rutha had often come here for solitude.[27] Henlein, accompanied by Brand, ascended on foot and found Rutha there together with Artur Vogt and a few other KB assistants. The discussions lasted long into the night, with Rutha vigorously arguing against any premature action. Finally Henlein declared with apparent conviction that, since on the basis of his talks most bourgeois parties were against entering a Volksfront, and since the Czechs would see unity with the DNSAP/DNP alone as a Nazi masquerade, he had resolved to relinquish any political involvement. He would retire and devote himself totally to the Turnverband's national mission. Rutha returned to Kunnersdorf under this impression.[28]

Henlein with this statement was not being candid, for notwithstanding his vacillation, he had not divulged to Rutha or even Brand the extent of his talks with the DNSAP/DNP leaders. In the days after Keilberg these continued, and as it became clearer that Prague was about to dissolve the two parties, so Henlein reverted to the idea of launching a Volksfront. Abruptly summoning Brand to Asch, Henlein told him that, since the parties' dissolution was imminent, he had decided "on his own initiative" to create a new political movement. To the extent that the DSNAP in particular was constantly pressing him in this direction, Henlein's claim of unilateralism was dubious. But he might justify to himself that he had made the final "fatal" decision and that a Volksfront matched the KB's long-term inclusive mission.

Even so, Henlein's friends were shocked at the about-turn. Significantly, Rutha seems only to have been consulted on the 30th, when Henlein together with Brand and leaders of the DNP/DNSAP had moved to a hotel in Eger to finalize details of the new movement for publicity, including its name: the Sudeten German Home Front [*Sudetendeutsche Heimatfront*] (SHF). Rutha on arrival had strong words with Henlein, and then an even sharper confrontation with Brand, whom he met together with Sebekowsky in the Star Hotel. He was apoplectic. He accused Henlein and Brand of violating the Keilberg agreement, damaging collective responsibility and presenting a fait accompli. For Rutha his pride was chiefly wounded on these grounds, not because he wanted the new leadership for himself (except possibly in some spiritual sense). He felt Henlein was acting irresponsibly, launching the mission prematurely into the political field. As Sebekowsky remarked, it was a "leap into ice-cold water," dangerous in view of the Czech reaction, and they could not know where it would end. They could only reluctantly back it since the die was cast: the SHF was already due to be publicized on 1 October.[29]

In view of how tensions between the KB Spannists and the Nazi radicals disfigured the Henlein movement over the next four years, it is important to acknowledge that these divisions were there at its inception. The SHF was not a direct continuation of the DNSAP or the DNP, but Henlein certainly moved when he did because these *völkisch* parties, and therefore the Sudeten nationalist cause, seemed threatened. Indecisive but also stubborn, he felt a personal vocation at that moment. He also, unbeknown to Rutha, Brand,

and other KB colleagues, had indeed made vague promises to the Sudeten Nazis, possibly even before Saaz, through discussions with their youth leaders Rudolf Haider and Ferdinand Fischer. Henlein therefore was already playing a double game in 1933, at least in not being frank with Rutha and his former confidants. And this attempt to be all things to all men—a trait he would demonstrate well later—directly sowed the seeds of the future KB-Nazi clash within the SHF.[30] Although Henlein always swore that no promises had been given to the Nazis, Rutha himself on 30 September was alarmed about potential DNSAP influence. He already despised Hans Krebs as a "coward and a braggart," confirmed when Krebs in October fled across the border to Germany.[31] And his suspicions were naturally aroused because, apparently, it was Ferdinand Fischer who first told him with schadenfreude about Henlein's new idea. Particularly, he feared that Nazi elements around Fischer and Haider might now infiltrate his sacred Turner youth movement.[32]

Despite this, Rutha submitted to the SHF leader in tune with his firm maxim about obedience to a leader. Probably Henlein calmed his fears about unruly Nazi influence, for at the first press conference on 8 October in Prague, his statement was wholly in tune with the KB mission and presented the SHF as a new movement, not a camouflage for the dissolved parties. Its agenda was Sudeten German unity and negotiation with the Czechs from a position of strict equality (*Volk* to *Volk*); it aimed to construct a corporate order for the Sudeten *Volk* in Czechoslovakia while remaining a "living member of the wider German cultural community."[33]

Rutha could not disagree with any of this and found, when the SHF official membership was drawn up, that he was designated member number two (followed by Brand and Sebekowsky). His first task in late 1933, thanks to his wide-ranging grassroots connections in both the Turnverband and the business community, was to create a basic organizational network for the SHF. For three weeks, he was driven in a "rattling Tatra" by a young Turner, Karl Hanke, across the northern Sudetenland on a mission of recruitment. The result was a first network of agents. If a few were contacts from business interests, some were KB links, but most stemmed from the existing Turner network, that homosocial world that proved a crucial foundation for the new movement. By the end of the year five hundred local SHF groups existed.[34]

This was no easy achievement. It was carried out in a tense atmosphere in the wake of the self-dissolution (and then official banning) of the DNP and DNSAP. The Czech authorities, under the emergency legislation targeted at

Nazis, now replaced all members of the banned parties on local councils with reliable "activists," and forced almost a hundred local Turn branches to dissolve because of their Nazi links. Since Prague also, unsurprisingly, viewed the SHF from the start as a substitute Nazi party, its leaders and embryonic framework were immediately suspect. While Henlein might accurately deny irredentism (in the strictest sense of the word) and claim to lead a movement "on the basis of the [Czechoslovak] state," his statement of 8 October showed he wanted a corporate state within a state. When he mouthed loyalty to "democracy" he meant not the parliamentary national democracy of Czechoslovakia, but a new Sudeten German "organic national democracy" organized hierarchically through a corporate structure. Thus on 12 November in an overflowing Reichenberg Turn hall, he told an initial SHF gathering of seven thousand that he was no "party man" and would never become a member of the Czechoslovak parliament.[35]

For the Czech authorities, therefore, these were mixed messages; they rightly interpreted Henlein as disingenuous and were appropriately vigilant. While Rutha was busy recruiting, Brand was arrested and briefly imprisoned, soon to be followed by Sebekowsky and Kundt. On 2 December the Czech police also seem to have searched Rutha's house but found—a sign perhaps of his total lack of contact to nationalist politicians—no incriminating material.[36]

For Rutha, Henlein's launch of the SHF was a watershed, comparable perhaps only to his personal 1918 apocalypse. It set the Sudeten nationalist mission on an unusual course, for the new movement could not just stay isolated in the realm of youth education or Spannist theory. It was forced to engage directly with the reality of the Czech "antagonist," the Czechoslovak state, and in turn confronted the wider power structure of the region with Nazi Germany at the center. As Christmas 1933 approached, news reached Rutha of the death of his own "spiritual mentor," Stefan George, and he surely felt even more on the cusp of something new. He might take heart that George's vision of national renewal would endure—not least via his own pedagogic program for the Sudeten younger generation.[37]

THE EXPERIMENT IN MICROCOSM

At Sudeten German nationalist rallies over the next few years, Henlein's Saaz proclamation acquired mythical status as the spur for "spiritual renewal" across the German communities of Czechoslovakia. Equally legendary was the "struggle for survival" that allegedly took place in late 1933 as the nationalist parties were banned and the SHF launched. As Rutha noted in one speech, a "dark thunderstorm" had gathered over the Sudeten Germans and many had turned for guidance to the grey-uniformed columns of the Turnverband, those at Saaz who were allotted a sacred educational role.[38] While this remained Rutha's focus, Henlein and Brand had resigned from the Turnverband. For them, the SHF was the motor for tribal leadership or, in Spannist terms, the new "political estate," the highest body in the embryonic Sudeten corporate state. Over the next eighteen months, always treading gingerly because of Czech surveillance, they sought above all to strengthen the SHF, liaising with German bourgeois parties in order to win them over.

Rutha, however, besides his initial organizational tour, balked at any further role in the SHF. Only later would he realize that this lost him crucial personal influence with Konrad Henlein.[39] Besides always scorning the conventional political world that the SHF was entering, he judged that Sudeten Germans still required five years of training before they could really challenge the Czechoslovak state. Walter Heinrich felt the same and was even angrier at Henlein's unilateral political move as well as Brand's "disloyalty" to Spannism; relations between them quickly cooled.[40] Indeed, the KB's loose organization, if not its ideology, was now naturally disintegrating; it held its final conference in late 1934.[41]

For Rutha too, the KB had mainly served either as an intellectual forum for Spannist discussions or as a framework for that Männerbund increasingly accommodated by the Turn movement. Nevertheless, while the KB splintered, he maintained his friendship with Heinrich (visiting him in Austria in June 1934, then accompanying him to Greece), and his own thinking was still attuned to the Spannist "nonpolitical" vision. Understandably then, from 1933 for two years, he concentrated on the didactic grass roots, on perfecting those male youths destined to lead the Sudeten tribe. There he could best supply "spiritual guidance" and also felt most at ease; as he told his sister-in-law, "I am happier among the simple, nonpolitical, working men than on the political asphalt."[42]

For some time anyway he had been garnering extra Turn experience at the grassroots level. From March 1930 he had headed the Turnverein at Oschitz, reluctantly accepting annual reelection by peers who saw him as "reliable and very experienced."[43] While tightly integrating the branch into regional structures in line with Henlein's hierarchy, his most notable innovation was to inculcate Turn activity into the local school curriculum. When he surrendered his office on 11 January 1934, he told the annual general meeting with a flourish that the revitalized Turn ideal had now become common property of all Turners; the best proof was the Saaz festival that twenty-one members from Oschitz had attended.[44]

The sparse number of Oschitz Turnrat meetings in 1933, however, indicates Rutha's more substantial commitments that year. At Saaz, he had volunteered to lead a new Turn building office *[Turnbauamt]* (TBA) so as to control the design of Turn infrastructure servicing the national community. On 1 September the appointment was made public, flattering his self-perception as an aesthete and architect, and meshing with his vision of the Turnverband as a tightly structured organism at the heart of all local communities. He called on Turner architects to send him designs, announced a committee of advisers, and in his first TBA guidelines stressed that every construction, whether a training field, hall, or swimming pool, must be a "site of the community," in fullest harmony with the local landscape. As designs trickled in to Kunnersdorf for approval, he issued extra rules, chastising Turn branches who deviated from a simple, vigorous style or those who ignored his TBA altogether.[45]

Yet this public role was trivial when compared to his main Turn activity during the period of Henlein's SHF. That began in February 1934 with his election as head of the Jeschken-Iser Gau. As Henlein's homeland, as seat of the *Turnzeitung* from 1934, this Gau always had a reputation for innovation, and was one of the strongest with 140 local branches and eighteen thousand members. Rutha became *Obmann* or Gau leader at a critical time. In November 1933, the Turnverband leadership had instructed all officials who belonged to the dissolved nationalist parties to resign their posts, to prove to the Czech authorities the movement's nonpolitical affiliation; the Jeschken Obmann, Gustav Thomas, had been a casualty and was left to lick his wounds.[46] To some members, especially those caught up in the purge, Rutha was an outsider, too much the innovator, and someone moving too fast into high office (despite his Oschitz record).[47] Rutha, however, saw his new post as a major opportunity: a chance to implement Saaz principles across a sector of the nation and make his Gau a model for training the Männerbund.

The annual assembly, or *Gauturntag*, where he was elected on 18 February 1934 illustrates well the challenge that the Gau leadership faced in order to sustain the Saaz vision, and seems typical of the missionary zeal stirring Turn leaders in the wake of Czech "oppression."[48] Dramatically staged in the Turn hall in Gablonz, it began with a procession with flags and a rousing address by the regional *Turnwart*, Richard Bernhard, who was a full Henleinist convert with an enviable Turn record.[49] Urging his comrades not to be despondent, he pressed them to embrace the "leadership principle" across the whole Gau and deflect the recent Czech onslaught ("the greatest disgrace in Sudeten German history") by fully abstaining from party politics. As key pedagogic targets for 1934, he identified the Vorturners (the youth leadership) and women, who would receive training for their roles as mothers and wives. Bernhard was Rutha's ideal apostle. In his own address as new Obmann, he characteristically preached discipline, trust, and unity; a new sense of community was spreading everywhere, for as he noted, "we are in a transitional stage toward thinking like members of the whole."

It was lofty Spannist terminology, but it contained a practical agenda that he meant to implement. Crucial was to educate male Turners systematically to serve as leader-personalities in the Sudeten German communities. Most of the hierarchical infrastructure for organizing this already existed through Gau leaders, district leaders, and the 140 grassroots branches, each level run by a triumvirate of Obmann, Turnwart, and Dietwart. But after Saaz, Rutha particularly planned to enhance the role of the Vorturners. Similarly, while the annual Turn calendar continued in time-honored tradition, peppered with administrative meetings and festivals at each level, it required tightening and some imaginative enhancement among Turner youth. One of his new Gau initiatives in October 1934 was "comradeship days," bringing together branch leaders and Vorturners in order to advance uniformity.[50] By the same token, the wider Turn or Sudeten community was never forgotten; members of the Turnverband leadership often visited the Gau festivals, Gau officials were expected to attend training courses in Asch, and from mid-1934 all Turners had to subscribe to the *Turnzeitung*.

Under Rutha's leadership in 1934–1935, the Jeschken Gau measured its success in a number of ways, some of which were purely subjective. Membership statistics from early 1935 showed an increase of almost 10 percent to reach twenty thousand. The Gau program of public outreach also seemed effective, if gauged by its increasing cooperation with the largest Sudeten defense society, the *Bund der Deutschen* (BdD).[51] Yet the best proof that the Jeschken Turners were united with their community, their pedagogic mission "fast advancing," was assumed to be the two major Turngau festivals during the hot summers of 1934–1935. These had long been planned as celebrations, respectively, of the movement's newly disciplined men and women.

Rutha anticipated the first, in July 1934 at Ruppersdorf (a suburb of Reichenberg) as a model for tribal unity and a milestone toward building a solid organization of men.[52] Meticulously planned by Bernhard together with the local Turnverein, the event was a pageant quite familiar to participants and akin to a religious ritual. It consciously imitated the Saaz festival a year earlier, so that alongside the usual competitions and war-dead commemoration, a "splendid Vorturner march-past" took place on the market square in front of their "leader." This time, however, it was Heinz Rutha who spoke to them, reminding them of the Saaz principles. The Gau leadership duly praised the festival as an efficient display on the Saaz model, even describing it as an amazing military review. Rutha only quibbled that next time it needed to be even more "masculine"—presumably disciplined—in character.[53]

Exactly a year later, at Raspenau, the Gau organized an equivalent women's festival. It highlighted the role of women in binding the community together and carefully delineated female duties. In competitive singing, dancing, and free exercises, the hundreds of blue costumes contrasted vividly with the green backdrop of meadows and woods (fig.19). Rutha, in a "profound speech" from the podium, explained that while the men's task was to advance the national struggle, women as wives and mothers had "to keep pure the national soul and create a youth cohort that was strong and high-minded." Finally, he blessed the assembled faithful, praising them as "living witnesses" of a homeland that was German and would remain so for ever.[54]

Rutha's Turn speeches over two years illuminate his underlying Spannist philosophy: the Sudeten tribe, part of the broader German spiritual nation, was itself composed of regional communities whose strength arose from their unity under firm leadership. At one Gautag for winter exercises, he advised a hundred delegates that "common expeditions are entirely suitable for creating small solid communities, without whose existence today a Turnverband is impossible."[55] In this holistic Sudeten mission, he undoubtedly saw himself as near-messianic and irreplaceable—hence his own perpetual search for a "son." Identifying with his spiritual mentor, Stefan George, he probably anticipated his position in the corporate state as akin to the Spannist "wise man" or the Platonic "Philosopher Ruler": someone at the pinnacle of the spiritual hierarchy, and senior to those like Henlein who had moved into the political estate. Thus we might interpret Rutha's words to one of his acolytes: "In this mass movement forwards, I am maintaining the spiritual standpoint which nobody coming after me could uphold and complete."[56]

From the vantage point of the Jeschken Gau, this goal could be industriously pursued, for there he had his work commitments in Kunnersdorf, and there as Obmann he posed as the modest father figure, holding a consultation day each month at the Reichenberg Turn hall when any ordinary Turner could visit for advice.[57] Most strikingly, he resisted any further promotion in the Turn hierarchy. When in June 1934 he attended its annual assembly in Bodenbach and witnessed Richard Bernhard's election as its new head, officials pressed him to become Bernhard's deputy. He declined, for he wanted to keep his hands free for "spiritual leadership," meaning his primary vocation of directing the Sudeten youth mission.[58]

The auspices were good, for in the wake of Henlein's Saaz appeal for youth groups to join the Turnverband, several Wandervogel branches did so as well as the large youth body of the BdD (late 1934). The number of young Turners aged fourteen to seventeen would triple over the next four years, and with Catholic and Agrarian youth bodies increasingly recognizing the Turnverband's primacy, only socialist youth remained fully divorced.[59] From late 1933 Rutha's program for creating a *Jungmannschaft* in three distinct age groups had also begun to be implemented systematically across the Turnverband; in each local branch the age groups were being shaped as squadrons and a network of Vorturners trained up as future stars of the Männerbund.

In this process the Jeschken Gau led by example, with Rutha surrounding himself with a cohort of enthusiasts. His Gau youth leader was Hans Heinl, who, if not a friend, had demonstrated efficiency in the Oschitz branch. Those on Heinl's youth committee were invariably Rutha disciples and often homoerotically linked with each other, Adolf Wagner running the youth office in Reichenberg, Willi Hoffmann responsible for boys' education, and Werner Weiss directing publicity work (succeeding Walter Rohn, who departed to study at Prague University).[60] The calendar of Turner youth events was expanded and prioritized, Rutha waxing lyrical about an annual spring youth camp near Oschitz, which, with 1,300 boys attending, supposedly "caused a sensation across the nation."[61]

Indeed, by early 1935, the Gau leadership was quite satisfied with both youth recruitment and the training of Vorturners, whose number had reached almost a thousand. At the annual Gautag on 13 January, Rutha duly pressed for ever more systematic youth training, stressing that youth unity was the real model for achieving a united nation; indeed, compared to that elusive goal of Sudeten German unity, the Jeschken Gau was proclaimed to be "in the fullest unanimity."[62] It was a questionable judgment in view of what was to come, for the national unity that Rutha both coveted and proclaimed always concealed many cracks.

THE YOUTH LEADERSHIP SCHOOL

While the SHF by this time was contemplating its first party-political elections in Czechoslovakia, and Henlein had sounded Rutha out on the subject, Rutha himself took no part in the electoral campaign, for his focus was elsewhere, on a new initiative.[63] He was now determined to create a youth leader school for the whole Turn movement. It was an enterprise he had long cherished to sustain his mission and the highpoint of his spiritual leadership. By June 1934, as TBA director, he had secured the Turnverband's consent and was seeking a site near Kunnersdorf on which to build.[64] But only at the end of the year did the idea crystallize, when it became entwined with another large-scale Turnverband enterprise, namely the organization of Voluntary Labor Service [Freiwillige Arbeitsdienst] (FAD) across the Sudetenland. Since the first FAD camp was to be opened in March 1935 at Wartenberg, a few miles west of Kunnersdorf, the prime aim of that camp became the construction of Rutha's youth leader school.

From 1935, Rutha was to expend much energy on Wartenberg. One admirer recalled that he "created Wartenberg and was the first to implant his spirit in the camp."[65] Certainly, the experiment neatly combined two facets of his mission of shaping a Männerbund out of the young generation. While adult young men (the Mannschaft) would undergo training in disciplined labor service, youth leaders (from the Jungmannschaft) would be educated there when the youth school was finally built.

By the mid-1930s, voluntary labor service was already a broad European phenomenon.[66] In April 1934 a first "international student labor service conference" had convened in northern Germany with delegates from England, Belgium, Austria, and also Czechoslovakia.[67] The origins of the phenomenon lay in Bulgaria, where in the early 1920s the Stamboliiski regime had introduced compulsory labor service. The concept then spread into central Europe via youth leaders from Silesia in Germany who established a voluntary camp to bond their regional community closer together in practical tasks; training encompassed hard manual work in the mornings and cerebral discussions in the afternoons.[68] In 1928, a few students from Prague, including Sebekowsky from the PG, participated in the Silesian experiment and then organized a series of Sudeten German work camps, gathering together several youth groups including Rutha's Jungenschaft in an early public display of youth cooperation.

With this local example of practical bonding between youth and community, the KB took the idea further in early 1933, precisely when the Sudeten German *Volksgemeinschaft* seemed threatened in Czechoslovakia. On 4 March at Teplitz, the KB had discussed labor service at a large gathering of Sudeten defense societies and political parties. Rutha was present, and together with Werner Pohl (a BdD employee and PG veteran), he called for a Sudeten work camp movement. If this appeal was made against a backdrop of FAD institutionalization in Germany at the height of the Depression, it particularly resonated because of the rising calamity of Sudeten German unemployment. Between 1930 and 1933, unemployment had risen sevenfold across Czechoslovakia, hitting hardest the German borderlands, where so much industry was dependent on a declining export trade. It was easy for Sudeten leaders to stress, when describing the Sudetenland as "one big industrial cemetery," that German unemployment was twice the Czech average and to target their criticism, largely unrealistically, on the economic policy of the Czechoslovak government.[69]

In the wake of the Teplitz meeting, some, like the BdD leader, Gottfried Wehrenfennig, were enthusiastic about labor service, but there followed only fragmented initiatives by local Turn or BdD groups.[70] Overall coordination stagnated until late 1934, hindered undoubtedly—in contrast to many European countries—by the lack of any state subsidy. The Prague government, vigilant against hints of German irredentism, was wary of the pedagogic dimension of the work camp and hesitated to embrace it for welfare purposes in Czech districts either.[71] Sudeten enthusiasts therefore had to rely on their own resources. A crucial galvanizer was the "Sudeten German National Relief" organization *[Sudetendeutsche Volkshilfe]* (SVH), created by the BdD in late 1933 as an umbrella group for targeting charity at needy Sudeten families. In December 1934, the SVH leadership (including Pohl and Wehrenfennig) agreed that early in 1935 a training camp for work camp leaders would be opened as a launchpad for a Sudeten FAD. Although financed by the BdD, its organization and curriculum would be fully in the hands of the Turnverband.[72]

It was due to Rutha's intervention at this juncture that the Wartenberg camp quickly materialized.[73] As TBA director, he proposed that the first work camp should construct a Vorturner school. As head of the Jeschken

Gau, he found Wartenberg's mayor and Turnverein willing to put an ideal location at the FAD's disposal. The spot, isolated in the landscape near a lake, was dominated by the Roll, that ancient mountain covered in beech trees, a promontory, as Rutha noted, that stood erect "like a free warrior over his loyal people." From Wartenberg the young men would gaze at the Roll, its summit topped with a simple monument to the fallen of the Great War, as a symbol of their own courage, beauty, and freedom.[74]

For those who supported the FAD network that would spring from Wartenberg, it had an entwined purpose, social and educational. On the one hand, there was a fresh socioeconomic agenda, to relieve Sudeten unemployment by providing short-term work opportunities for young men aged eighteen to thirty. Rutha himself, not least through his own business, fully empathized; commenting in 1935 on the twelve thousand unemployed Turners, he noted how he "first gained an insight into real poverty" via Wartenberg.[75] Yet welfare was only one dimension. Even more important was the FAD's role in galvanizing the national community; here the leaders repeatedly spoke about "practical" or "real socialism" (in contrast to socialist or Marxist theorizing). Rutha later explained, typically, that FAD had emerged "because young men wished to overcome the common emergency through common action in working for the community."[76] In fact, the work camps were an integral part of his didactic mission whereby young men were being systematically trained and disciplined to lead the corporate state. Thus, as Werner Pohl suggested, FAD was "inserted into the holistic education as the missing link, between the character-building of youth and the adult-male outlook of the Turner."[77]

On 25 March 1935, the camp at Wartenberg for training FAD leaders was opened after a short vigorous recruitment drive. Only unemployed Turners could volunteer for the first training course since in theory they already had the necessary discipline and leadership skills. When over a hundred volunteered, their number was whittled down to thirty-seven by the regional Dietwärte.[78] Very early on a cold misty morning the first recruits arrived at Wartenberg. Rutha as Gau Obmann enthusiastically welcomed them, announcing portentously that much was anticipated in terms of output and comradeship: "As Turners you will shape the camp whose outcome will be the work-camp movement in our country." The men marched off to the frosty worksite with their shovels and barrows, their first task to dig and construct a Turn training area.[79]

Over the next eight weeks the camp was under the firm leadership of Theo Hauck, who had been a member of Rutha's Jungenschaft, a Turner youth leader and also former officer in the Czechoslovak army. The volunteers spent each morning from five o'clock on manual labor, each afternoon on "spiritual training" (discussing key contemporary issues often with visiting expert lecturers like Rutha and Pohl), and each evening relaxing together as "comrades." It was to be the first of four such courses at Wartenberg in 1935, educating 117 camp leaders, including many non-Turners, and moving masses of earth to level an arena for the school. Hauck in his periodic reports for the BdD praised the progress of it all, the fine male bonding that developed, as well as the camp's regular interaction with the local community, particularly in festivals and Turn competitions of the Jeschken Gau.[80]

Rutha doubtless saw these Wartenberg products as the ideal Sudeten Männerbund, a model of masculinity that had been anticipated at the Saaz festival. Of the work camps one Turn pedagogue observed: "A new type of man is arising, one who is marked and ennobled by work and service."[81] And when Hauck proceeded to extol the special masculine qualities of a camp leader, his prototype conformed to the ideal Rutha had advocated for well over a decade. He was to be a "universal man": a charismatic personality, courageous, reliable, industrious, ever mindful of his duty to the national community, ever aware that he would inspire his subordinates and the next male generation. Pictures that appeared of Wartenberg publicized the disciplined bonding that prevailed there, with its homoerotic undertone: the muscular volunteers either stripped to the waist as they performed manual labor in unison, or standing to attention in a special uniform with boots, a uniform that Rutha himself also liked to wear (fig.23).[82]

Although the FAD rejected Czech claims that the training was militaristic, the daily routine, camp rhetoric, and uniform amply justified such fears. Thus, one volunteer publicly reminisced: "We want to be soldiers of work. Hoe and shovel are our weapons and with them we will fight for the labor service's victory . . . This is our substitute for the front experience of the Great War."[83] It was an outlook fully inculcated by Rutha and Hauck, who had long viewed their adulthood as redeeming the traumatic wartime sacrifice, as a struggle on the Czechoslovak home front where the masculine values glimpsed in wartime must be firmly asserted and passed to the next generation. Adult males who evoked these qualities of the "front-line soldier" were, in Rutha's view, the crucial models for educating male youth, and the signs were that Wartenberg was producing such specimens.[84] They were being dispatched to lead work camps elsewhere in the community—or as Hauck starkly admitted, "sent to the front."[85]

By the end of its first year, the FAD network across German Czechoslovakia encompassed seventeen work camps and housed about seven hundred unemployed young men, increasing in 1937 to forty-three camps and 1,168 volunteers. This was not quite the mass phenomenon expected, whereby in 1936 alone the organizers had envisioned housing twenty thousand unemployed.[86] One reason was a constant absence of state funding, the work camps relying mainly on the BdD and private fund-raising.[87] The number of unemployed had also dropped by late 1937 to half the figure of early 1933, removing one plank of the FAD rationale. But perhaps most important in interpreting the sluggish growth, we must question Rutha's underlying assumption that most Sudeten German young men could easily be enticed through their innate sense of community spirit—a contrast to supposed Czech "individualism"—to participate in a highly disciplined work camp.[88] As so often, Rutha's nationalist assumptions about unity outstripped the realities.

Nevertheless, the FAD played some role, however intangible, in enhancing homosocial bonding among three thousand male volunteers, reinforcing in these critical years (1935–1938) the illusion that a Männerbund now existed to serve the Sudeten national community. By 1937 the Turnverband itself judged that labor service had proven value for its pedagogic mission. At its annual festival in Aussig in July 1937, the leadership gave its blessing to FAD as a permanent fixture, the endpoint of a young man's education. It was proposed, with Rutha's full support, that every youth who wished to be accepted into the adult community would have to pass through a work camp.[89]

In the last years of his life the project at Wartenberg continued to give Rutha special satisfaction as the climax of his spiritual youth leadership. He continued as special technical adviser even after 1935 when more pressing business intruded, and would regularly discuss the school with young acolytes who visited Kunnersdorf.[90] During 1936 two special fund-raising appeals for Wartenberg were successful enough to allow further planning. Indeed, after attending the Berlin Olympics in August, Rutha seems to have conceived Wartenberg as a kind of Olympic village, equipped with a youth "community home" and Turn hall as well as the training arena.[91]

By 1937, with the arena virtually complete, the TBA announced an architectural prize competition for designing the rest of the youth center. Rutha drew up rules specifying that the buildings must be in "German style," blended into the landscape using local stone, and only German architects who were Turners could apply.[92] Thanks to this competition, planning of the school buildings began that summer. The spiritual leader once again envisaged it as a long-term project that would slowly progress as funding allowed. It would be a "castle of Sudeten youth" to match the ancient fortress on the Roll, a training community for Vorturners that surely would attract the admiration of neighboring Czechs as a major example of German creativity.[93] Its future seemed very promising.

DISSENT AND HOMOSEXUAL RUMOR

Despite these major advances in the youth mission, with Wartenberg as the showcase, by 1937 Rutha had ceased to be a leading figure in the Turnverband. On 4 October 1935 he had publicly resigned as head of the Jeschken-Iser Gau. The official reason given was positive: because he was assuming an important role in the Henlein movement, he needed to work outside northern Bohemia in Prague.[94] Behind the terse statement, however, there swirled a mass of rumors caused by the crisis of insubordination that had actually besmirched the Jeschken Gau for much of the year. The "fullest unanimity," so loftily proclaimed at the Gautag in January 1935, had quickly proved illusory, for the following months witnessed the first installment of a new struggle for influence within the Sudeten German nationalist movement. In short, Sudeten "loyalists" like Rutha were challenged by "radicals" who promoted an openly pan-German agenda and were excited by National Socialism. As the two frameworks for national unity began to clash, the fact that the protagonists had overlapping ideologies would permit the radical strands to infiltrate and undermine key features of Rutha's goal.

Ronald Smelser has clearly shown how these tensions began to shatter the façade of unity in Henlein's political movement by late 1935.[95] Yet the turmoil in the Jeschken Gau much earlier that year reveals how the same process was already disfiguring the Turner youth movement. There, Rutha's reaction was characteristically blunt, moving to eliminate the recalcitrants while appealing for unity, but the dissent threatened to spiral out of control as his judgments were questioned and his personality scrutinized by skeptics seeking weaknesses to exploit. For the first time since the PG crisis of 1928, he faced a public accusation of homosexuality and could not emerge wholly unscathed. It constituted a dress rehearsal for the full drama two years later on the wider political stage.

While Rutha as Obmann had constantly appealed for Turn uniformity in line with Saaz principles, disunity proved impossible to eliminate. First, the influx of disparate youth groups into the Turnverband after Saaz seriously slowed the momentum of training a disciplined youth cohort. Most significant for Rutha's fate was the full incorporation by 1934 of Wandervogel youth groups and elders from northern Bohemia, for vivid memories survived there of how he had "sabotaged" their organization in the 1920s and then, by 1930, caused chaos among the student associations of Prague's German university.[96] Ironically, having been a leading youth provocateur in the 1920s, he was now a key target of youth provocation.

Second, although Turn officials belonging to the banned German nationalist parties had had to resign in late 1933, many remained as malcontents in the Turner ranks. Those who resented an upstart like Rutha becoming regional Obmann might gain solace from the vibrancy of National Socialism across the border or from those ex-Nazis still prepared to raise their heads in Czechoslovakia. Most notable were the Sudeten Nazi youth leaders, Rudolf Haider and Ferdinand Fischer, who in September 1933 on the eve of DNSAP dissolution had founded a journal loyal to Hitler called *Der Aufbruch (Awakening)*. Somehow it dodged the Czech censor, becoming the focal point for ex-Nazis and lending its name to a loose network of sympathizers—an *Aufbruch* circle. *Aufbruch* adherents were soon prominent in many SHF branches; and especially they were active in a new student association in Prague that vigorously attacked PG students while transmitting radical ideas back into the Turnverband. Although *Aufbruch* was never as organized as its critics liked to suggest (mirroring the amorphous KB in that regard), it became more vocal from early 1935. Its key mentor, Haider, who had been imprisoned after the *Volkssport* trial, was again at liberty to lead the attack on the supposed Spannist focus of the Henlein movement.[97]

From late 1933, sensing correctly that *Aufbruch* elements might penetrate the Turn movement, Rutha regularly warned the Turn and SHF leadership to be vigilant. Publicly, he showed his own conservative colors in late 1934 when he secured an apology from a left-wing newspaper that had likened his Gau youth camp to a Nazi paramilitary event.[98] He probably also felt reassured in October after hearing Henlein, at a major rally at Böhmisch Leipa, advocate a conciliatory Czech-Sudeten solution within the Czechoslovak framework.[99] Although parts of Henlein's speech had been deliberately phrased to allay Czech anxieties, much of the language suited Rutha's perspective. In absolutely rejecting war, dismissing radical pan-Germanism (and pan-Slavism), and openly questioning the viability of National Socialism for Sudeten German circumstances, Henlein was pragmatically focusing on Sudeten interests while still demanding a peaceful dismantling of the Czech nationalist state. However, this type of rhetoric could only act as a red rag to *Aufbruch* radicals: they went on the offensive within the Turnverband.

If by 1935 the Turn leadership had begun to notice this unrest, for Rutha the need for immediate action struck home in early March. He received a disturbing report from his follower Karl Hanke (now a student in Prague) about *Aufbruch* machinations in the youth and student bodies of the capital, where Turn authorities had expressly been trying to tighten discipline. Rutha was furious at the Machiavellian tactics of the *Aufbruch* clique, who in their own lust for power were managing to split the movement. While the Turnverband, including Rutha himself, had stood by, *Aufbruch* had cunningly assimilated into the ranks and steadily professed its loyalty to the leadership.

Replying to Hanke in a letter dated 11 March, Rutha took stock and critiqued the national mission. The leadership, he argued, had recently been too quick to forge ahead and, in their quest for unity, had been wrong to conceal that the spiritual origins of the current program lay in the groundwork of the Jungenschaft and the KB. Denying this heritage had allowed *Aufbruch* to spread rumors about the KB as the real "anonymous clique" and was undermining those (like Hanke or Rohn in Prague) who were trying to counter the attacks. How best then to proceed? Perhaps reflecting on his own mistakes in the 1920s, Rutha was against a public showdown, which could openly split the movement, especially with the imminent parliamentary elections. But he insisted that the Turn leadership act immediately to signal its undisputed commitment to youth education and its complete intolerance of saboteurs. If this failed, he was afraid of the consequences for himself and others in the coming months. He concluded prophetically: "A continuation of the present situation endangers everything, finally even Konrad, and wears down those who need an offensive to maintain their faith in the firmness of the leadership. No troops can be left permanently in the line of fire without becoming demoralized. So the watchword is 'Attack!'"[100]

Since compromise was impossible, Rutha immediately pressed the Turn leadership to eliminate *Aufbruch* agitators, for while appearing to conform, they were actually undermining the movement in their single-minded quest for power—using "well-known N[azi] methods."[101] This letter rapidly set things in motion, producing on 1 April an announcement in the *Turnzeitung*. The Turn leadership chastised incoming youth groups for their insubordination, pursuit of "party" interests, and secret sabotage at every turn of the education program. By 20 April those youth leaders *[Jugendwärte]* who were disloyal in this way had to be replaced and their personal youth groups permanently dissolved.[102]

It is clear that Rutha for many months had felt such insubordination in his own Gau. On 6 April, when his Gau leadership convened in the Reichenberg Turn hall, they unanimously approved the motion of Hans Heinl, the Gau youth leader, that three district Jugendwärte should be suspended. The main culprits were Herbert Baierl and Rudi Hein, youth leaders in the Reichenberg and Maffersdorf districts, respectively. Both individuals had experienced the disruption caused by Rutha's Jungenschaft in the 1920s, had stayed loyal to the Wandervogel at that time, and then brought their prejudices, including a grudge against Rutha, into the Turn movement.[103] Baierl, for example, had objected to the new youth education and at some point been given a "friendly warning" by Rutha.[104]

Rudi Hein was a more dangerous opponent, a Nazi since 1931. According to his later statements to the Czech police (which we must treat with caution), Hein considered Rutha to have a "demonic influence" over youths and had always disliked the strict discipline of his Jungenschaft. On joining the Turn movement Hein had seen how Rutha "advanced his favorites"; like Baierl, as a district youth leader Hein had quickly clashed with Heinl (whom he wrongly labeled a Rutha disciple). Hein would later allege—and we only have his evidence—that once in the Maffersdorf Turn hall he had boldly criticized the pedagogic program in Rutha's presence. When Heinl then accused Hein of separatism, Hein publicly proclaimed a lack of confidence in Heinl's ability to continue as Gau youth leader. The accusations bounced to and fro.[105] What is important is that by April 1935, Rutha and Heinl viewed Rudi Hein as a notorious *Aufbruch* troublemaker who was vindictively undermining the regional youth program.

These months, when the Henlein movement was focused on the election campaign with its denouement of late May, were a stressful period for Rutha, alleviated only by the launch of the Wartenberg camp. He felt "very involved and under pressure," engaged in a "hard but optimistic struggle" with agitators who had deeper roots than he had imagined.[106] For in the wake of the suspension of the three Jugendwärte, supposedly agreed to by his district leaders on 6 April, two of the Gau districts, at Maffersdorf and Reichenberg, refused to implement the decision. Worst was Maffersdorf, where the district leader, Ernst Dedek, pandered to his Turn constituency and accepted Hein's arguments about Rutha's partisanship for KB disciples. Dedek organized a district meeting where critics (including former Obmann Thomas) were allowed to lambaste the Gau leadership and the Wartenberg camp in a manner that Rutha labeled "unturnerisch." A week later a further rowdy Maffersdorf Turn meeting caused Rutha to dissolve the district altogether and amalgamate it with loyalist Gablonz.[107]

It could be argued that Rutha on 6 April had behaved in a typically arbitrary fashion, failing adequately to prove his case against Hein and Baierl to the district leaders. They, however, had approved the resolution, then questioned his authority. In trying to resolve this, Rutha contacted the amenable Reichenberg district leader, Karl Wolf, and insisted rather disingenuously that it was not his "personal ruling" but simply a result of the Turnverband demand for discipline; thus Baierl had been suspended for insubordination and his links to Hein (the main agitator). Nevertheless, Rutha was prepared to soften his stance, agreeing with Wolf that a special assembly of the Reichenberg district should be convened so that he could publicly explain his decisions.[108]

The meeting, held on the evening of 30 May at the Stadt Zittau inn in Reichenberg, certainly drew a line under part of the conflict, but it took a personal direction that was deeply unsettling.[109] Two hundred Turners were present, including the Gau leadership and the head of the movement, Richard Bernhard. From the fragmentary evidence it seems clear that Herbert Baierl now accepted Rutha's olive branch, swearing allegiance to the leadership and its youth program; thereupon he was reinstated. Bernhard then took the chair and effusively praised Rutha's tenure as Obmann, appealing for loyalty while detailing the unwarranted criticisms that had recently arisen. Among these, Bernard mentioned how some had even accused Rutha of homosexuality; he called on those present to substantiate such accusations with evidence. Nobody stirred. For Rutha it was a profoundly embarrassing and surely unexpected moment; from his later statements we can infer that it left a lasting impression.[110] He proceeded to justify his recent behavior over the disobedient Jugendwärte, and wholly dismissed the allegations of homosexuality, which, he declared, had shocked him and affected his health. The meeting dispersed after a vote of confidence in the leadership, and Rutha's position as Obmann seemed secure. In fact, ventilating the subject of homosexuality—a theoretical "outing" of Rutha—had left many questions unanswered and only accelerated the rumormongering.

In the locality, rumors about Rutha's sexual orientation had circulated quietly for many years. Later, several police witnesses acknowledged the local gossip and their own suspicions that he was "not normal sexually." One recalled how at the Gautag in January 1935 he had first overheard that Rutha was homosexual or, euphemistically, a "warm brother" *[warmer Bruder].*[111] This gossip had been perpetuated by the frequent visits of blond Turner youths to the Rutha mill. Admittedly, by 1935 some of Rutha's own sexual outlets had diminished: Werner Weiss was off seducing others, Adolf Wagner had disappeared, and relations with Kurt Gansel had dramatically cooled. But the pilgrimage of curious adolescents to Kunnersdorf had continued, and usually at Rutha's personal invitation. While devoted Wolfgang Heinz was a regular guest, in August 1935 a party of six youths descended on the mill to enjoy discussions in the library and a drive with their mentor into the mountains.[112] Nevertheless, in the wake of the "outing" on 30 May, it required the evidence of Franz Veitenhansl for the rumors to gain more substance. Possibly it was the news of Rutha's public denial that finally pushed Veitenhansl in the summer to blurt out his story to the Oschitz veterinary surgeon, Rudolf Wolff, as well as to Heinl. As we have seen, Heinl had then privately confronted Rutha, drawing an angry reaction, and, in disbelief, had himself confided in Wolff. When Wolff advised Heinl to turn for advice to his colleagues in the Gau leadership, he did so.[113]

In September 1935, a series of meetings took place at Wolff's Oschitz home, as senior members of the Gau leadership gathered to hear the veterinarian's vivid account of Veitenhansl's confession.[114] Wolff backed up his evidence by stressing physiognomic peculiarities he had observed; from a "scientific viewpoint," he noted Rutha's high-pitched voice, the position of his eyes, his facial expression, and his high intelligence as proof that he was a homosexual. For the elders all of this appears to have been a shock, but they were still not completely convinced since Wolff declined to produce the protocol and Veitenhansl remained the sole witness.[115] They resolved to observe Rutha further and wait on events, especially as they expected his resignation anyway because of his new duties in the Henlein movement. When this followed a few weeks later, the waves washed back over the stony beach that Wolff had temporarily exposed. Typically, when Richard Bernhard himself learned of Wolff's accusations, he dismissed them out of hand.

Rutha himself remained completely unaware of these discussions. To that extent his reasons for resigning as Obmann on 4 October seem largely to have been those publicized, namely the excessive workload and the new political role in Prague. However, the insubordination he had struggled to control in the Gau had also contributed; sensing a loss of authority, he had to take responsibility for what might be viewed as mismanagement.[116] From May, the height of the crisis, he had sought ways to counter the *Aufbruch* circle, especially those behind the scenes like Haider whose intrigues seemed geared toward seizing power in the youth movement.[117] Yet all efforts were in vain when it came to the disobedient Maffersdorf district. Since, under the influence of Dedek and Hein, it even refused the Gau order to amalgamate with the Gablonz district, Rutha at a leadership meeting on 24 August abruptly secured the expulsion of all Maffersdorf Turners from the movement. It was a radical assertion of control, but was risky in possibly consolidating the opposition.

Calm seemed to be restored only later in the year when, on 3 November, an extraordinary Gau meeting was convened to consider the Maffersdorf case once and for all. In the presence of Bernhard and other leading officials, Rutha duly justified the expulsions and Bernhard pressed for the assembly to support him. To puncture the opposition, it was agreed that the Maffersdorf district could be reconstituted and its members readmitted—bar those like Hein and Dedek who were still deemed unsuitable for any Turn office.[118] Superficially it concluded the unrest. In fact, Rutha knew it was only an armistice. Rumblings of *Aufbruch* machinations in the youth movement continued well into 1936, and he would press intermittently for the Turn leadership to act firmly before the poison spread.[119]

For the most part, however, his own youth mission had now changed tack as he focused on the youth leader school at Wartenberg. If we consider the state of the Sudeten nationalist youth movement as a whole by 1936, its development since Saaz might be described as phenomenal in terms of implementing Rutha's pedagogic vision. Yet his ideal of a fully united youth cohort had proved much less realistic—or at least it required many more years of preparation, as he himself had always envisaged. As usual, as the "spiritual leader" who disliked lengthy meetings, he had shown little patience with those who questioned his particular model for unity; he expected obedience rather than too much grassroots feedback. It was a tactic that naturally worked for those who fell for his charisma or appreciated his regional devotion and single-minded Sudeten German vision. But the dissenters in 1935 had begun to prove a serious threat; they had not been silenced and had discovered his Achilles' heel.

An important postscript to the Gau crisis was the intrigue of Rudi Hein.[120] Perhaps justifiably, Hein from mid-1935 felt that Rutha was conducting a personal vendetta against him; after the full Maffersdorf expulsion in the summer he had even more reason to retaliate. Long suspecting Rutha's propensity for "blond youths," and knowing about the Oberlik incident of 1928 as well as recent rumors, Hein proceeded to publicize Rutha's "sick disposition" and search assiduously for further evidence. Finally he came upon Franz Veitenhansl (independently of Wolff it seems). After several visits to Oschitz, including a clandestine meeting with Veitenhansl at the Devil's Wall, he persuaded the introverted youth to confess. He knew that Veitenhansl was about to leave Oschitz for good, so he persuaded him to meet a Reichenberg lawyer on 10 October 1935 and make a written statement. Like Wolff's protocol this was kept in safekeeping, for Hein needed more evidence to proceed and alert the authorities. Persistent efforts in the following months failed, and he finally gave up his personal crusade.

Even so, by 1936 many ingredients for a major homosexual scandal had been accumulated and left in aspic. The rumormongering in the local community and the Turner ranks had by no means been stilled. It soon led to the expulsion of two of Rutha's acolytes, Weiss and Hoffmann, from their local Reichenberg branch by a homophobic Turn leader, Karl Karwath.[121] More seriously, through Hein's campaign the rumors began to spread further afield, into Nazi Germany. It was a sign of Hein's wider *Aufbruch* machinations and contacts that, already in early September 1935, he had alerted Germany's consul in Reichenberg, Walter von Lierau, to Rutha's character and its potential repercussions. He explained to Lierau, an avid Nazi, that Rutha was anti-Nazi and from a "degenerate" (Czech) family; he had long been associated with homosexual scandal in the youth movement, had "failed disastrously in the education of the Sudeten German younger generation," and—witness Veitenhansl—was determined to silence those who realized his disposition. Lierau duly informed Berlin about this and decided to explore further.[122] As yet it was a minor development that melted away. Two years later, however, when the homosexual scandal finally broke, it would add another twist to suspicions about who exactly had betrayed Rutha to the Czech authorities.

Figure 1. The coffin at the Rutha mill. Willi Sebekowsky as pallbearer on right. (Courtesy Státní okresní archiv, Liberec)

Figure 2. The funeral cortège crosses Oschitz village square. (Courtesy Státní okresní archiv, Liberec)

Figure 3. The Rutha mill in Bad Kunnersdorf. (Photograph by author)

Figure 4. Oschitz, c.1900. (Courtesy Státní okresní archiv, Liberec)

FIGURE 5. The Rutha family, October 1904. Seated in center: Josef Rutha;
standing back row, *l-r:* Friedel Rutha, Franz Polifka, Marie Rutha, Franz Effert,
Adolf Rutha; standing back row, *r-l:* Uncle Franz, Uncle Ferdinand, Richard
Rutha, Emanuel Max; seated, *l-r:* Anastasie Rutha holding Gretel, Heinz
Rutha. (Author's collection)

FIGURE 6. Heinz and Gretel,
c.1909. (Author's collection)

FIGURE 7. Postcard depicting the Realschule, Böhmisch Leipa, 1915. (Author's collection)

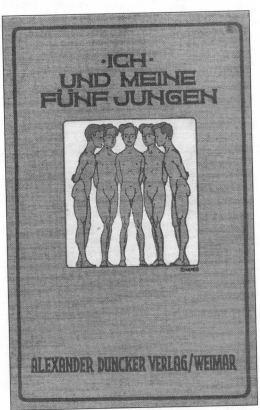

FIGURE 8. *Ich und meine fünf Jungen,* by Ferdinand Büttner (1914).

FIGURE 9. Rutha as Gauwart, c.1917.
(Courtesy Státní okresní archiv, Liberec)

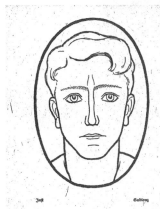

FIGURE 10. Otto Kletzl with
Böhmisch Leipa youths, 1921.
(Courtesy Sudetendeutsche-
Wandervogel Archiv,
Waldkraiburg)

FIGURE 11. The ideal youth, by
Oskar Just. (*Burschen heraus!
Fahrtenblatt der Deutschböhmen*,
October 1918)

Blätter vom frischen Leben

An die, die vom Herzen jung sind!

Keine neue Wandervogelzeitung, kein neues Programm oder Feldgeschrei sollen euch diese Blätter sein. Nichts als eine Lese des Wertvollsten aus dem vielen Wandervogelschriftzeug, dessen Bezug dem Einzelnen zu teuer und nicht einmal lohnenswert wäre, das aber nicht verdient, ungelesen zu verstauben.

Das Gaublattel sollen sie freimachen zur eifrigeren Mitarbeit der Leute.

Eines wollen diese Blätter doch: Frisches Leben bringen. Kämpfen gegen den unaufrichtigen, selbstgefälligen Geist, der sich unter uns so oft breitmacht, gegen die Nörgler und Krittler, die sich nie zu einer Tat aufraffen, obzwar sie alles besser wissen und können. Kämpfen gegen alles Wandervogelpharisäertum.

Ihr sollt freilich auch ehrliche Kritik und Urteil drinnen finden, aber auch Worte und Anregungen, die zur Tat führen. Tat steht über aller Kritik.

Heinz.

Wohin?

Denn wir wissen nicht, wohin und wozu wir wachsen. Wir ahnen nur etwas ganz Großes und ganz Schönes und müssen uns hüten, es zu verraten. Denn das ungläubige Lachen der anderen tut weh.

Ich bin auch überzeugt, daß jenes Unbestimmte, das uns zusammenführt, unsere Stärke ist, und daß jeder Versuch, ein starres Ziel aufzustellen, etwa Schul- und Gesellschaftsreform, Abstinenz, uns schwächt. Das mag den großen Führern vorbehalten bleiben, die wir aus unseren Reihen einstmals für die Zukunft des Volkes erhoffen. Wir wollen nichts weiter sein als stark sein im Wahren und Reinen und nichts weiter tun, als unser Leben und unsere Arbeit wahr und so natürlich zu gestalten, wie einen Tag unter freiem Himmel, wie eine Fahrt über Heimaterde.

Aus der alten sächsischen Landsgemeinde.

Gesinnung und Tat.

Welch großer Lärm auf der öffentlichen Bahn der Reform! Berufene und Unberufene strömen die breite Straße der Neuerungen hinab und rühren gewaltig die Werbetrommel zur Anpreisung ihrer „idealistischen Zwecke".

Der Zulauf ist groß; mancher stolze Werber schmückt reichlich sein Haupt mit unechtem Lorbeer, denn: „Die Zahl der Geworbenen ist so beträchtlich!"

Liebe Wandervögel, laßt Euch nicht betören durch Zahl und Lärm. Das Äußere ist unwichtig und wirkt oft verwirrend; das beste, der dauernde Kristall, wird von innen heraus in der Stille gebildet. Die Tat soll durchgreifend wirken und Gesinnung und Tat müssen verbunden sein, wie Seele und Körper, die auch, von einander getrennt, nichts Fruchtbares vermögen. Gesinnung, durch Trommelwirbel heraufbeschworen, ist Schall und Rauch. Sorgt nicht, ihr wäret „zu wenig bekannt". Eine gute Sache

1

FIGURE 12. *Blätter vom frischen Leben*, 1 May 1919.

Figure 13. Rutha and his youths at the 1919 Gautag. (Courtesy Sudeten-deutsche-Wandervogel Archiv, Waldkraiburg)

Figure 14. Rutha and his family, c.1923. *L-r:* Gretel, Winfried Effert (nephew), Marie Effert, Fritz Polifka, Heinz Rutha, Adolf Rutha, Inge Effert (niece), Friedel Polifka. (Author's collection)

FIGURE 15. "Quality furniture": early advertisement for the Rutha firm, showing the artistic influence of Oskar Just. (Hermann Hrubesch, *Bad Kunnersdorf* (Reichenberg, n.d., ca. 1926))

FIGURE 16. Oschitz Turners at the school opening, 1933. On far left, Heinz
Rutha and Kurt Gansel. (Courtesy Státní okresní archiv, Liberec)

FIGURE 17. Training and relaxing: Turner youth at a Jeschken-Iser Gau
festival. (Courtesy Státní okresní archiv, Liberec)

Figure 18. District Turn event in Oschitz, August 1933. *L-r:* Walter Brand, Konrad Henlein, Heinz Rutha, Ernst Tscherne (member of Turner youth leadership). (Courtesy Státní okresní archiv, Liberec)

Figure 19. Women's training: the festival at Raspenau, July 1935. (Courtesy Sudetendeutsches Archiv, Munich)

FIGURE 20. The Männerbund on skis. (*Turnzeitung des Deutschen Turnver-bandes*, February 1935)

FIGURE 21. "Loyalist" SdP leaders in March 1936. *L-r:* Franz Künzel (organizer of agrarian youth of Moravia-Silesia), Konrad Henlein, Heinz Rutha, Walter Brand, Ernst Tscherne. (Author's collection)

FIGURE 22. "Foreign minister": Rutha in his Prague office in 1937. (Author's collection)

FIGURE 23. The Rutha family and friends at the mill, 20 April 1937. Rutha holds the arm of his aged nanny; either side of him, sisters Marie and Friedel; far right with baby, his niece Inge. (Author's collection)

FIGURE 24. A homosexual scandal: the front page of *Prager Illustrierte Montag*, 11 October 1937.

FIGURE 25. Konrad Henlein and Adolf Hitler after the occupation of the Sudetenland, October 1938. (Courtesy Krajská vědecká knihovna, Liberec)

EIGHT

Sudeten Foreign Minister

On 19 May 1935, Konrad Henlein's movement, campaigning as the Sudeten German Party (SdP), won an astounding victory in the Czechoslovak parliamentary elections. Exceeding even Henlein's predictions, it took two-thirds of the German vote, secured more support than any other party in the republic, and attracted Europe-wide attention. The Czech political landscape seemed to be transformed. Soon afterward, speaking at an SdP festival in a village near Bad Kunnersdorf, Heinz Rutha proclaimed that the *Volk* had swept away the old parties, entrusting Henlein with a crusade for equal rights in Czechoslovakia. Unity must now be the watchword in the face of the "Czech neighbor," as those living on the Czech-German language border were (allegedly) only too aware.[1]

Rutha had taken no part in the vigorous election campaign and refused a parliamentary candidacy. Besides his deep-seated aversion to liberal party politics, he wanted to devote himself to the youth mission and Wartenberg. The mudslinging that characterized the political world had seemed confirmed when, early in 1935, he was slandered in the Czech press, labeled as running the SdP election fund, and wildly accused of acting as a financial courier to the Third Reich; he successfully sued the newspapers. Convinced thus that he was taking the moral high ground by ignoring politics, his career nevertheless was about to shift course in a political direction, and precisely at a time when tensions were culminating in the Jeschken-Iser Turngau.[2]

Since his historic recruitment drive for the Sudeten German Home Front (SHF) in late 1933, Rutha had stood aside from the movement, relinquishing his influence to others around Henlein like Walter Brand or Karl Hermann Frank. But that Henlein acknowledged his special role, and occasionally consulted him, is clear. Minutes of an SHF leadership committee from July 1934 recorded that while "Heinz Rutha is not a member of the main leadership, he remains a personal confidant of Konrad Henlein."[3] Early in 1935 he was the natural consultant when the party considered establishing permanent offices in Prague, visiting the capital regularly in March for talks with Brand and Sebekowsky. It was, however, the election victory that propelled him back into the leadership since Henlein immediately invited him to join the inner "cabinet." The initial justification perhaps was again Rutha's professional expertise, since with the party center moving to Prague a new SdP office infrastructure was required there; when on 29 May Rutha was welcomed to his first weekly leadership meeting, he duly reported on the search for appropriate accommodation.[4] Yet Henlein also now saw Rutha as a crucial aide in managing the radically transformed movement. When on 2 June he assembled all SdP officials and politicians at Eger to swear him a personal oath of loyalty, he entrusted Rutha with a special mission: to explore links with the German diaspora abroad in order to publicize the Sudeten German plight across Europe.

Why was Rutha given this remit? According to family legend he always wanted to be a diplomat and of course knew French and some English. Yet for Henlein, most persuasive was probably Rutha's idealistic Spannist outlook, which set the Sudeten Germans' fate in a European context (as in the Swiss expedition of 1925), as well as his actual disassociation from the SdP political machinery, where he could have no real role. Henlein envisaged his one-time mentor as a roving ambassador who might be allotted "special commissions," someone not just reliable but directly answerable to him alone. Rutha's new position was confirmed at a leadership meeting on 27 June.[5]

In accepting this unusual role, Rutha acknowledged his loyalty to the SdP führer but surely realized that, while pursuing the Wartenberg experiment, he might soon need to disengage from troublesome Turn activities (the embarrassing "outing" had just occurred). About to begin were the two most hectic years of his life, a new expansive mission of traveling to London and Geneva to represent the Sudeten cause. It drew upon him European attention as Henlein's peripatetic diplomat or SdP "foreign minister," a label that by 1936–1937 he was not averse to adopting.[6] His growing reputation abroad was also matched by notoriety within the Czechoslovak establishment. Until this time he had been largely invisible to the Czech leadership; now he suddenly materialized as "an intimate collaborator of Henlein."[7] In time he would appear to President Edvard Beneš as a "rogue," to Jan Masaryk (Czechoslovak minister in London) as a "fanatic," his idealistic Sudeten vision coming up against a sharply critical Czech perspective.[8] Through the publicity that inevitably encircled him he became a Czech household name—and from that dizzy height in 1937 his public fall was abrupt and swift.

THE BASES OF A SUDETEN FOREIGN POLICY

The foreign initiative of the Henlein movement after 1935 has never been analyzed on its own terms. Most historians have viewed it teleologically through the prism of Henlein's pro-Nazi behavior in 1938, deducing that the various moves from 1935 were always mere adjuncts to Germany's foreign policy. In this light the SdP had no foreign policy of its own but was consistently beholden to its masters in the Reich.[9] While we can acknowledge the Reich context as crucial—Ronald Smelser's work guides us well in this direction[10]—a study of SdP initiatives through Rutha's behavior illuminates the predicament that the movement faced after its electoral success, and the ambiguities of its foreign mission. Rutha would never fully represent all strands of SdP "foreign policy" in these years—a direct relationship with the Reich was notably absent from his orbit, perhaps because Germany was never quite seen as foreign. Even so, his tactics significantly colored the movement's foreign perspective until his death. In its own way this was a conservative approach, increasingly at variance with SdP members who were irredentist, who wanted the Reich to overturn the Versailles settlement of 1919 and annex the Sudetenland. Yet it too was radical, seeking pragmatically to exploit the prevailing balance of European forces to reach its own utopian goal: to force the Czechoslovak regime to alter its state structure for the benefit of the Sudeten German "tribe."

The very idea of propagating the Sudeten cause abroad was premised partly on the regime's reaction to the election results. While Henlein had immediately written letters to Prague, proclaiming loyalty to the state and hinting his party was a responsible partner for dialogue, the appeal was ignored. The Czechoslovak coalition government survived by rearranging the governmental seats, retaining two nominal places for small German "activist" parties and cold-shouldering the SdP. Under these circumstances, while ostensibly becoming a constructive opposition in Parliament, the SdP naturally sought other outlets, not least to sustain momentum in the eyes of its electorate.

Foreign publicity for the Sudeten cause was actually something Henlein had mooted for months, particularly through the League of Nations, the upholder of the international order.[11] In this regard, we should emphasize that in June 1935, Henlein and his advisers saw the international framework for any Sudeten foreign policy in conservative, pragmatic terms: the anticipated endpoint at best was a domestic revolution within Czechoslovakia, not an upheaval that would revise the state borders or invite Nazi Germany to intervene. This was simply being realistic. It is true, and has been well documented, that since April 1934 Henlein had actively courted Germany; the Reich had substantially financed the SdP election campaign and continued to pump money into the party thereafter.[12] Rutha also seems to have known about the financial link for the elections although he had nothing to do with it.[13] Yet the agency in Germany with which Henlein principally dealt was Hans Steinacher's *Volksbund für das Deutschtum im Ausland*, a non-Nazi organization whose traditionalist priority was culturally to sustain branches of the German diaspora, not to encourage irredentism on behalf of an expansionist Nazi state.

Moreover, in mid-1935 there seemed little likelihood that the states system would soon be radically revised. Hitler's Germany was only just emerging from international isolation. By reintroducing conscription in March 1935, Hitler had drawn together the "Stresa front" of Great Britain, France, and Italy to oppose him; his speech of 21 May assuring Europe that he would not assimilate any foreign Germans was surely not lost on the SdP either. In short, Henlein could not yet expect much from Germany except increased funding; anything else was fanciful or largely confined to the dreams of committed SdP Nazis (not Henlein or Rutha). Even so, there were two key developments that suggested international flux. One was Czechoslovakia's new alliance with the Soviet Union, a controversial move that highlighted an ideological left-right division on the continent. Another was the signing in June of an Anglo-German naval agreement. Breaking the Stresa front, it showed that London at least was cultivating the new Germany and contemplating moderate revisions to the peace settlement.[14]

For the SdP, a role on the European stage seemed even more enticing because of the immense interest abroad in its victory. Especially jubilant were those organizations that for years had agitated to improve the status of German national minorities across Europe. On 21 May, Ewald Ammende, an Estonian German and leading campaigner for minority rights, sent

Rutha a letter of congratulations. He rejoiced that, after fifteen depressing years, the Sudeten Germans had set an example of national solidarity and overnight made their cause one of European magnitude; they should lose no time in exploiting this.[15] For Ammende, the focus for such propaganda remained the League of Nations, the body that guaranteed minority rights, supervising and upholding the minority treaties that all new nation-states of Eastern Europe including Czechoslovakia had had to sign as an adjunct to their postwar peace treaties.

With the open support of veterans like Ammende, the SdP naturally started its foreign initiative via channels that already existed for promoting national minority rights. There were three of them, each of which Rutha would pursue in the summer of 1935. First was the leading European organization of German minority groups, the *Verband der deutschen Volksgruppen in Europa* (VDV), which since 1922 had agitated for German cultural autonomy on the basis of the European territorial status quo. Long funded by Germany's foreign ministry, its annual conferences from the late 1920s had assumed a *völkisch* character and inclined in a pan-German (and then Nazi) direction under its permanent legal adviser, Werner Hasselblatt.[16]

Second was the European Nationalities Congress (ENC), which since 1925 had held an annual conference, usually in Switzerland. Run by Ammende through a permanent secretariat in Vienna, this organization was an adjunct of the VDV but had a wider remit, to encourage other non-German minorities to lobby for change in the League's minority procedures.[17] Both bodies, the VDV and ENC, offered the Henleinists a European platform. Both had in the early 1930s moved away from considering the German diaspora as national minorities, becoming heavily influenced by a pan-German outlook that threatened to make them willing tools of Nazi foreign policy. However, recent historiography has tended to simplify the Nazi takeover, particularly in assuming that Hasselblatt's own *völkisch* and Berlin-focused mission fully equated with that of the SdP. Rutha's behavior disproves this position and complicates the picture.

A third SdP channel abroad was the *Deutsche Völkerbundliga (Liga),* the German League of Nations Society in Czechoslovakia. This was affiliated to the League of Nations Union, an organization established in 1919 in Brussels, which was a parallel "lay" body to its namesake in Geneva (where the governmental delegates convened).[18] The Union, which also held annual conferences, had rapidly become an international outlet for those peoples like the Sudeten Germans or Transylvanian Magyars who lacked sufficient representation in the existing states system; one of its chief campaigns was for a fully international system of minority rights. For the *Liga* this, and the guarantee of Sudeten German rights, was the major goal. The *Liga*'s dominating personality for over a decade was Wilhelm Medinger, a north Bohemian landowner, who in the 1920s unsuccessfully challenged Czechoslovakia's land reform in many petitions to Geneva.[19] With its small office off Prague's Old Town Square run by a committed secretary, Maria Aull, the *Liga* long managed to retain in its ranks an eclectic, "above party" membership: activist politicians like Franz Spina, academics like Heinrich Rauchberg, or enthusiastic amateurs like the Austrian industrialist Friedrich Nelböck. After 1926, however, when German activist parties entered the Czechoslovak government, *Liga* activity began to dry up as did its petitions to the League. Only Medinger, a strident voice at the ENC, really kept the *Liga* in existence, but when he died suddenly in late 1934 it was left headless and even more devoid of purpose. It was now susceptible to influence from a radical younger generation.[20]

Immediately after the Eger oath on 2 June 1935, Rutha spent a few days in Prague, conferring with Brand and Friedrich Nelböck, the new *Liga* director. Undoubtedly flattered by SdP attention, Nelböck explained that the annual Congress of the League of Nations Union would convene imminently in Brussels; he was seeking a *Liga* member to accompany him there. Since it would offer immediate access to an international forum, Rutha on SdP advice volunteered. But while he had made occasional business trips to southern Germany, the new adventure was still slightly daunting. Apart from being briefed by Maria Aull, he needed to buy a suit, and when Nelböck fell ill at the last minute, he felt bound to persuade Gustav Oberlik (now fully reconciled to him) to be his traveling companion.[21] In fact, Rutha was to find this first visit to western Europe very informative if exhausting. Besides attending conference sessions on minority questions as an observer, the week-long sojourn in Belgium introduced him to a range of European individuals who were committed to the League of Nations or to its radical reform. In mid-June he duly reported back to Nelböck and his SdP colleagues.

These links offer us a window on how Rutha saw his foreign and domestic mission at this critical point. In Brussels he interacted surprisingly well with Czech delegates from the *Liga*'s sister organization in Czechoslovakia, men who were wholly committed to an effective League of Nations and naturally loyal to the Czechoslovak state.[22] But most striking was the impact made on him by Joris van Severen, the charismatic leader of the far-right Flemish nationalist movement, *Verdinaso*. In 1930 Brand had met Van Severen during a study trip to Belgium, and probably now recommended that Rutha seek him out in Bruges.[23]

On 13 June 1935, Van Severen himself recorded that he had dined with an Oschitz architect, someone who was "the right arm of Henlein. Very friendly and interesting man."[24] The feeling was mutual. Rutha in turn described Van Severen as a "new comrade-in-arms of our kind and persuasion," and noted, " I believe that next to us he is leading the only real circle."[25] Rutha was enthralled not only by Van Severen's antiliberal, elitist mindset and his deep nationalist conviction, embedded in the Flemish homeland (he visited some Flemish towns and was "charmed by their architectural richness"). Instructive too was *Verdinaso*'s foreign policy, which was wary of Nazi Germany and inclined to see England as Belgium's natural ally. And particularly enticing was Van Severen's grand scheme for transforming this part of Europe. His "Greater Netherlands," which privileged the Flemings while encompassing both Dutch- and French-speaking peoples in one entity as in the sixteenth-century Burgundian state, equated well with Rutha's own utopian solution for the Sudeten Germans.

That was still an ambitious Spannist vision for central Europe. It envisaged building a corporate state at home in the Sudetenland, while somehow remaining part of the Czechoslovak state structure *and* communing fully, for cultural purposes, with the wider German *Volksgemeinschaft* to the north and south of the Czech people. Such a concept might be fantastic, full of risks, often intangible in its precise outlines. However, for Rutha the encounter with Van Severen, a kindred spirit who offered "deeper comradeship," made such a Sudeten program even more realistic.[26]

Indeed, Rutha could feel satisfied that a Spannist solution was materializing, for the SdP seemed to be following maxims of the Comrades' Union (KB) in formulating a corporate structure for its administration. All SdP districts were due to establish special offices to coordinate labor, agriculture, and business, to be matched by SdP centers in Prague.[27] Rutha hoped that his former mentor, Walter Heinrich (now married and a professor in Vienna), might again advise on this whole process of reorganization and discussed it with him in Vienna in mid-July. In fact, the idea would fizzle out, probably because Heinrich from afar in Austria remained unconvinced that Henlein's movement could be squared with his own precise Spannist model; the friendship that Rutha had always prized so highly would soon weaken, just as the SdP's Spannist principles were slowly diluted.[28] Similarly deceptive, in view of what was to come, was when in mid-1935 the SdP leaders publicly censured dissidents in the ranks and condemned the *Aufbruch* circle.[29] Nevertheless, for the moment Rutha could be optimistic. The firm SdP leadership stance mirrored his own ongoing campaign against Nazis in the local Turnverband, and most significantly, it synchronized with what we can interpret as a Spannist approach to Sudeten foreign policy, on display when Rutha first took to the international stage.

The initial ventures were twofold: hosting the VDV annual conference in Gablonz in late August and, immediately afterward, participating at the ENC in Geneva. A recent history by Sabine Bamberger-Stemmann has portrayed SdP dominance at the latter as tantamount to a takeover of the organizations by Nazi Germany.[30] This might have been the private view of Werner Hasselblatt on reporting back to the foreign ministry in Berlin, and it matched a rising Czech chorus that saw the SdP as Hitler's Trojan horse in Czechoslovakia. But it was not as yet the SdP perspective and certainly not Rutha's. It is true that in the 1930s the VDV and the ENC had shifted away from obsessing about national minority rights within existing states, toward the idea that each European *Volksgruppe* had equal worth. And especially they worked to unite all strands of the German diaspora so as to strengthen their bargaining power at state and international levels. There was a dangerous pan-German dimension to this, the potential for Hitler to exploit the *völkisch* diaspora for his own expansionist interests. However, there was still a gap between that radical development and the arguably more realistic SdP outlook.

When Henlein's movement joined actively in the VDV/ENC publicity work, it expected, as a minimum, firm backing for the basic goal of Sudeten German "tribal" self-government in Czechoslovakia. As a maximum, it pressed via these lobbying bodies for a looser state organization across east-central Europe, so that the German "spiritual" *Volksgemeinschaft* could freely commune regardless of state borders. This itself was a form of pan-Germanism but was focused on Sudeten German interests, with an eye on the past and present Bohemian context, rather than those of Berlin. In short, it was not irredentist, working toward annexation of the Sudetenland by the Reich. Instead, the SdP leaders were behaving pragmatically, even if their vision always contained a large dose of idealism about breaking down state borders. At its most idealistic—and mentioned many times from 1935 onwards—the Spannist-educated figures like Brand and Rutha described the Sudeten Germans as crucial mediators between Czechoslovakia and

Germany, as a bridge across the Czech-German cultural space of central Europe (fig.21).[31]

The VDV descended on Gablonz in late August 1935 not only to emphasize the Sudeten Germans' new European significance, but because the VDV chairman anyway was a north Bohemian industrialist, Max Richter.[32] For Rutha, Richter's presence was reassuring since the textile baron's family was well known to him and trusted both professionally and personally. Hasselblatt may have expected more since Richter was a fellow-traveling Nazi sympathizer. Even so, the Gablonz conference that Rutha helped organize together with these two did not demonstrably push Nazi Germany's agenda. For while Hasselblatt and Ammende were to be found criticizing the system of minority treaties, the focus of attention among the hundred delegates was the Sudeten Germans. Their self-importance as a new vanguard for the VDV was acknowledged, and four of them including Rutha were elected to its executive committee. In turn the SdP foreign program was showcased for all. Brand spoke about the Sudeten Germans as a typical *Volksgruppe* that required its own administration in Czechoslovakia in order to become a bridge between "Germandom" and other peoples.[33]

A week later, this SdP goal was repeated on the shores of Lake Geneva at the eleventh ENC. While Brand, true to Ammende's thinking, stressed that loyalty to one's national community (German) did not contradict loyalty to one's state (Czechoslovakia), Rutha's speech took up the latter sensitive issue. In this first international speech, he promised that Sudeten Germans would "work completely on the soil of the Czechoslovak state and recognize the republican-democratic basis of its state constitution"; but such cooperation could succeed only if Prague guaranteed full national equality, recognizing the equal rights of the Sudeten *Volksgruppe* in this "state of nationalities."[34]

Many Czech commentators naturally saw the words as disingenuous: the SdP did not match these democratic values and its loyalty to the state was clearly conditional. For Rutha, however, it was a principled stance, genuine at least in seeking to carve out a separate Sudeten space and administration (even if he omitted to say what kind of illiberal administration that would be). He subscribed fully to the cross-border German *Volksgemeinschaft* so lauded at the ENC; his *völkisch* values fully chimed with its prevailing mood. But for all the pan-German overtones in the background, his own focus as usual remained solidly Sudeten within the space of the old Bohemian lands and ready to cooperate from a position of strength with the Czech protagonist. Even if Rutha was not a gifted public speaker, Geneva proved to be a competent curtain-raiser both for himself and the SdP in European affairs. Ammende, who was a very sympathetic ear, concluded that the SdP had made an excellent international debut and that only the ENC had made that possible.[35]

RUTHA'S BRITISH COURSE

After the ENC, Rutha began seriously to address his new portfolio. It had been a hectic summer. Alongside continuing Turner commitments he had been shifting his focus toward Prague where the party headquarters was relocating, and demonstrating the acceleration in his lifestyle, he acquired a car for personal use from a flamboyant playboy, Felix Richter (brother of Max).[36] His youthful acolytes could now be taken on trips into the north Bohemian countryside, and there was also time for a vacation with his sister Friedel in the Tyrolian Alps. But otherwise he expended most energy on the new party offices.[37] Once an ideal central location in Prague was discovered, on Hybernská, he set a tight schedule, typically farming out the construction to various German firms but paying precise attention to the office furnishings: his chosen architect had to consult him assiduously about the desks, lamps, clocks, and even types of wood. Here at Hybernská was to be the central "bee hive" of the party.[38] Over the river on Strojnická, in a building housing SdP employees, he rented a small flat for those weekdays when he would work at the Prague office.

The foreign portfolio, which had earlier been publicized simply as supervising minority questions in the SdP's "political office," now started to expand.[39] At Hybernská in September 1935, Rutha established the Office for Nationality and League of Nations Questions [Amt für Nationalitäten- und Völkerbundfragen] (ANV) and for the rest of the year was busy setting its parameters, recruiting an industrious deputy, Artur Vogt, from the Turner youth leadership. The bureau's main remit was to liaise with the German diaspora and League pressure groups to publicize the Sudeten cause; the VDV network was exploited, the Liga's work reactivated, and experts were co-opted to advise on minority questions and international law. More broadly, through Rutha's fastidious nature, the ANV quickly became a center for managing the Sudeten question as a "European business," what Henlein termed "a flywheel in the clockwork of Europe."[40] Since it was vital to know as much as possible about the European context, the ANV recruited empathetic readers of the foreign press, particularly English and French, and petitioned others—like Van Severen or VDV colleagues in Transylvania and the Baltic states—for details about their region.[41] From the myriad channels that converged on the ANV, Rutha was expected to brief Henlein personally on the foreign situation and report regularly at the weekly leadership meetings. Intrinsic to ANV expertise was a desire to control the Sudeten German image abroad and disseminate its message on fertile soil. This facet, though secondary at first, would develop in 1936 as Rutha became the Sudeten German ambassador-at-large.

While the circuit of international lobbying groups would always be central to Rutha's foreign activity, success really depended on the European Great Powers. How he saw the contemporary struggle in the international system is clear from a speech he delivered on 10 November 1935 at a SdP rally in Aussig.[42] His survey is both predictable and revealing. France was naturally disparaged as obstinately trying to uphold the Versailles system while combating leftist instability at home; its ally the Soviet Union, promoter of Bolshevism, was exploiting western weaknesses in order to make advances into Europe (a coded reference to the alliance with Czechoslovakia). More interestingly, Italy could be admired for its ongoing fascist revolution at home, but was reprimanded for attacking Abyssinia in October since that revealed an old imperialist lust for power.

This left Germany and Britain as the two powers that Rutha portrayed positively at Aussig. His assessment of Germany helps us understand the perpetual ambiguities in that SdP relationship. Undeniably, there were hints of admiration when he spoke about National Socialism's *Weltanschauung*, its vision of transforming *völkisch* life and "reorganizing" how peoples and states lived together. Yet this was fully in tune with the VDV mission that the SdP was now championing: namely, moderate revisionism in central Europe in support of a cultural *Volksgemeinschaft*. Rutha did not spell out what role Germany might play in aiding the Sudeten Germans; it seemed to be a sympathetic if uncertain one in the current climate. Besides the VDV, he knew the Reich was continuing to send funds to the party; he surely also knew that Henlein was visiting Germany periodically to secure advice from Hans Steinacher. This all meant a special if fluid relationship with the German "motherland."

Yet there were limits in 1935 to what Germany could achieve for the Sudeten Germans and limits too to Rutha's enthusiasm for Nazi Germany.

Despite what many historians have claimed, Hitler's regime was not yet actively instructing the SdP leadership on how to conduct itself.[43] Nor could many SdP elders see Germany as a credible public partner in their minimum goal of securing territorial autonomy through pressure on Prague. Too close a link with Berlin was always dangerous, for it implied irredentism that the Czechs would pounce upon. Rutha, while assuming that Berlin would aid the Sudeten Germans in some way, did not expect or want Hitler to launch a foreign adventure on the lines of Mussolini; above all he desired peaceful revision of the international order and was therefore cautious about Third Reich intervention. To a degree he could empathize with National Socialism when it conflated with the *völkisch* mission—and this despite his struggle at home with Nazis in the youth movement who threatened Sudeten unity. But a line separated this from backing an expansionist Nazi Germany, one that some of his peers were soon prepared to cross. In 1936, as SdP links to Nazism and Germany increased, the divisions in the Henlein leadership, the ambiguities in its foreign policy, became ever more striking.

While Germany in late 1935 was a dangerous or at least ineffectual partner, calmly biding its time outside the "European system," Great Britain offered Rutha a special key that he would assiduously use.[44] Since the British dimension to the SdP's foreign mission in 1935–1937 was so significant, it is surprising that historians have never satisfactorily explained its emergence. In late 1935 two separate personal channels led Rutha toward Britain, but in the wider international context it was the recent Anglo-German naval agreement combined with British support for the League of Nations that was decisive. The former had confirmed Britain as sympathetic to peaceful treaty revisions that benefited the "German community." The latter seemed clear when on 11 September, with Italy about to attack Abyssinia, Britain publicly proclaimed the League's significance for preserving European peace.[45] While the Czechoslovak government interpreted this as a welcome restatement of European collective security, the SdP read it—in the wake of the ENC—as a sign that petitioning London could be very productive. The British then led the way in pushing for sanctions when Italy attacked Abyssinia in October, confirming that they would seriously uphold League principles, perhaps even over the minority treaties.

Rutha's deductions from this are clear. At Aussig on 10 November he stressed that Britain had become the predominant European power, determined to uphold its own interests and ready to exploit the League of Nations; as the new champion of League policy and international treaties, London deserved special attention. Through the ANV, he therefore investigated English press views of the League, minority protection, and the reorganization of central Europe, and alerted Ammende that the English public might soon need to be told about the Sudeten Germans' legitimate demands.[46]

In late 1935, the direct approach to Britain followed two parallel paths. Only one is usually sketched by historians, namely the mediation between the SdP and London of Group-Captain Graham Christie, former British air attaché in Berlin. It was Christie who arranged for Henlein to speak at Chatham House (the Royal Institute of International Affairs) in December 1935 and thereafter acted as a regular British channel for communication with the party. Rutha was probably little involved in the hazy initial encounters between these two men; if their first meeting was via a Bohemian aristocrat, the tie was solidified in late August when Henlein took a few days' holiday in England. Afterward, on 26 September, Christie wrote enthusiastically to Chatham House, proposing that Henlein, who repudiated war and Nazism, should be invited to lecture since his "constructive peaceful ideas [would] surprise his audience."[47] Rutha then seems to have been instrumental in encouraging a reluctant Henlein to accept the invitation. However, in December he did not accompany Henlein to London but stayed behind in Prague to report about his Brussels trip to the *Liga's* annual general meeting.[48] If this decision underlines ANV priorities and the importance Rutha ascribed to international lobbying groups, it perhaps shows that his status was not yet that of Henlein's foreign minister.

The second parallel avenue toward Britain has not been revealed until now, but there Rutha's role is even clearer. Rather than using links from his business network, the Bohemian nobility, or the youth movement (as some writers have speculated), his main facilitator was Ewald Ammende.[49] In the wake of the Geneva Congress, Ammende was regularly in touch with Rutha and pressed the SdP to make contact with the British historian R. W. Seton-Watson, someone deemed to have great influence with the Czechs. According to Ammende, Seton-Watson would be delighted to meet Henlein and Rutha if they were to visit London, and he had requested an article summarizing the Sudeten problem for *The Slavonic Review*. Rutha pressed both ideas upon Henlein, but at first only the article materialized, dispatched to Seton-Watson for publication in the January edition of the journal.[50] The short piece was a plea by Rutha on the basis of the minority treaty for national equality in Czechoslovakia; setting out the losses the Germans had allegedly suffered over sixteen years, it proclaimed a new Sudeten unity under the

SdP but reassured readers that "national loyalty *[Volkstreue]* in no way conflict[ed] with state loyalty *[Staatstreue]*."[51]

When Henlein visited London in December 1935, Rutha's steady hope for more direct contact with the British was also fulfilled. At Chatham House, Henlein disingenuously denied any links to Nazi Germany (including funding), but much of his lecture was more truthful than historians have usually suggested.[52] Later, the two parallel paths converged when Henlein dined alone with Christie and Seton-Watson. While Christie remained "convinced of the sincerity of the man," Seton-Watson was impressed by Henlein's careful repudiation of both Nazism and pan-Germanism; both agreed that the Czechs needed to put Henlein to the test through negotiations about his minimum demands.[53]

A month later, Seton-Watson visited Prague to probe the SdP further. "I had the same favorable impression of Henlein personally," he wrote, "but found the same reserve as in London, when we got down to the real crux of the whole matter, which is the problem of the Reich." When he met Henlein's colleagues (including Rutha, who did not stand out among them), he found them strangely naïve about Hitler's Germany and surprised at his criticisms. Correctly, he was discovering the basic obstacle to any Czech concessions to the Henleinists: namely, the SdP did believe in an authoritarian regime for the Sudetenland, and while not yet irredentist, it was *völkisch*, increasingly ready to parrot Nazi propaganda in its own organ, *Die Zeit*.[54] Rutha or Henlein might honestly suggest that, in the absence of Czech concessions, their movement was slowly being radicalized. In fact, the content of their own program, their blurring of the line between state and national loyalty, was dangerously opening that door. As Seton-Watson noted with hindsight, "it was playing straight into the hands of pan-Germanism."[55]

Rutha was indeed blinkered to the potential dangers from Hitler's Reich, for while viewing it as a crucial revisionist power, he saw any Nazi menace largely in terms of the *Aufbruch* radicals who were fostering disunity at home. Nor had he sensed any disquiet after meeting Seton-Watson; despite clear differences of opinion, the historian had apparently been "objective and understanding" about the Sudeten cause and even praised its leadership.[56] It was an overly optimistic assessment, and it propelled him forward in a British direction. Over six months he had established a basic foreign network and uncovered useful pressure points, not least in London, where through Christie some soundings had been made at the British Foreign

Office.[57] The reassuring international curiosity could only stir the SdP to intensify its propaganda across Europe.

LOBBYING IN GLASGOW AND LONDON

The year 1936 witnessed growing SdP brinkmanship in the face of the Czechoslovak authorities. The latter in turn were determined to stand firm against what they viewed as a fascist and irredentist movement, fully funded and commanded from Berlin. The usual line expressed by Edvard Beneš (before and after he became president in December 1935) was that the Henleinists would be kept at arms' length, in a "long quarantine," in order to test their loyalty to the state. To Beneš the idea of territorial autonomy was always nonnegotiable, naturally even more so by 1936; at times he hinted that gradually the Sudeten Germans would be assimilated into a Czechoslovak nationality.[58] Others like Milan Hodža, the prime minister, and Kamil Krofta, the foreign minister, were ostensibly more conciliatory toward the German minority, but all agreed that the authoritarian SdP could not be trusted. As Hodža observed, "The government would take care that Henlein achieved no success, and it was confident that the SdP would split up into various factions that could then be more easily handled." Krofta, famously in May 1936, would even describe the Germans as the "second state nation" of Czechoslovakia, but he still insisted they had to demonstrate their loyalty through deeds in what was a "national state of Czechoslovaks."[59] Particularly "disloyal" was Henlein's propaganda abroad, something that Hodža had warned about from the start but that the SdP always claimed as quite justifiable.[60]

If Prague had underestimated the significance of Henlein's lecture at Chatham House, Britain's increasing interest in Czechoslovakia in 1936 started to sound warning bells. The British Foreign Office, long fed hostile reports from its Czechophobe minister in Prague, felt it had enough evidence that the Czech regime was discriminating against the German minority and fueling its grievances. Thereby, Czechoslovakia was giving Nazi Germany an excuse to intervene and endangering the very peace of Europe.[61]

Although the SdP leadership continued to hope that Prague would surrender, the signs were not optimistic. With Beneš as president, Czech obstinacy was fully expected, and most alarming in May 1936 was the new

National Defense Law, which gave the government emergency powers to suppress elements hostile to the state. In view of this, international pressure acquired even more significance. Thoroughly encouraged by the developing British interest, the SdP in 1936 became much bolder due to a radical shift in the international system to Germany's advantage. Most notably, Hitler's daring remilitarization of the Rhineland in March not only dismantled another critical element of the 1919 peace treaty; it shattered Czechoslovakia's defenses, blocking the chance of French military aid. Beneš would be forced later in the year to consider a bilateral treaty with Hitler, much as the SdP desired. Furthermore, when in July Germany signed an agreement with Austria that gave Berlin substantial control over Austrian foreign policy, the shift toward a German-dominated central Europe and a swamping of the Czechs was even clearer.

In this context, it is not surprising that Henlein's speeches became more confident in lauding the cross-border German *Volksgemeinschaft*, in which all SdP leaders believed. On 23 February at the German House (Casino) in Prague, he rejected any common Czechoslovak culture, openly espousing cultural pan-Germanism and the leadership of the Reich in that regard.[62] Four months later at the annual party rally in Eger, he notoriously declared that "we would rather be hated by Germany than derive any advantage from the hate against Germany."[63] Rutha attended both events and would have had no qualms about these sentiments, for they did not contradict his own continued focus of foreign activity. As the international system was demonstrably shifting against Czechoslovakia, it seemed ever more likely that Prague would succumb to international pressure, finally conceding Sudeten German territorial autonomy and a radical reorganization of Bohemian space.

Rutha's main targets in 1936 continued to be London and Geneva, his main instruments the international societies lobbying on behalf of national minorities. If one purpose in spreading the Sudeten message abroad was directly to pressurize Czechoslovakia, another was the optimistic expectation that the principle of minority rights could be strengthened in international law, indirectly forcing a shift in Czech nationalist policy at home. On this basis, as we will see, the SdP would petition the League of Nations.

It was a tactic that also helps explain Rutha's activity in the *Völkerbundliga* in these years. After its election victory the SdP had felt the *Liga* worth patronizing and for that purpose Rutha soon became one of its vice presidents.[64] Yet we might question why he devoted such attention to this small body, amateurishly run, which could surely only have minimal influence. The answer seems to be not just that it offered an extra outlet for propaganda internationally but that Rutha typically empathized with its idealism, its privileging of the Sudeten mission as part of a peaceful international settlement. Appealing was the civilized nature of the *Liga*'s committee meetings; the gentlemen present, like Heinrich Rauchberg or the socialist Emil Franzel, were an eclectic mix from across the Sudeten spectrum, above all sharing a common devotion to the heritage of German Bohemia as well as a German universalist perspective.[65]

Particularly revealing is the unpublished diary of Prince Alfons Clary-Aldringen, a fellow *Liga* vice president. Alongside his fervent anti-Bolshevism, anti-Semitism, and naïve sense that Germany deserved equality in Europe, the aristocrat in 1936 repeatedly longed for a peaceful Czech-German settlement in the Bohemia of Saint Wenceslas. At a meeting with Rutha and Friedrich Nelböck on 27 May, he noted how all of them shared a certain loyalty to Czechoslovakia and berated Prague for stupidly not exploiting it.[66] Indeed, Rutha through his *Liga* commitment roughly fitted into this old German Bohemian outlook and the quest for a regional settlement, while also representing something of the new Sudeten dynamism (Clary called him a "fighter"). It was an interesting balance, but Rutha saw no contradiction. The *Liga* offered opportunities for social work on the home front, while its international agenda meshed with the SdP's other foreign initiatives.

The *Liga*'s overall conservative vision should be kept in mind when assessing Rutha's propaganda exploits in Britain in the summer of 1936. Historians have usually interpreted these as simply dictated by Nazi Germany or, more precisely, as synonymous with the so-called "London Action" that Hasselblatt of the VDV concocted in order to win over British opinion to Berlin's perspective.[67] Although Rutha fully participated in much of Hasselblatt's "Action," he saw it naturally through Sudeten spectacles as a venture to promote the Sudeten cause in the context of advancing European minority rights. Perhaps naïvely and certainly riskily, he did not view it as a Berlin-run operation, let alone a ploy for Nazi Germany's expansion, even though the pan-German contours were fairly clear. Hasselblatt in turn, like Rutha, could naturally see the advantages for the German diaspora of building on the SdP's British links. And from April 1936, a shift occurred to his benefit thanks to the sudden death of Ewald Ammende, someone whom Rutha in a short time had come to esteem. It meant that Hasselblatt could play an ever more prominent role, managing the lobbying bodies in one enormous propaganda venture to the benefit of Germany.[68]

In mid-January 1936 at a VDV committee meeting in Prague attended by Rutha and Henlein, Hasselblatt first set out his scheme for a "London Action" to be coordinated with both the *Liga* and the ENC leadership in Vienna. Two months later the VDV committee was firming up details. It agreed on substantial lobbying of British politicians and journalists and the presentation of a special memorandum at the Foreign Office, the whole enterprise coinciding with the next League of Nations Union Congress to be held in Glasgow in late May.[69] While Hasselblatt juggled all the balls of this diverse operation, including links with a very receptive British League of Nations Union, Rutha was designated as the leading Sudeten German delegate in Glasgow and London. He was after all the Sudeten lynchpin between the VDV, the *Liga,* and the ENC; moreover, the case study of Czechoslovakia was now at the forefront of Hasselblatt's arguments for minority protection.

Rutha's first visit to Britain confirmed for him the correctness of SdP foreign policy in view of British receptiveness. He assured Nelböck that "English opinion and especially that of the authorities is GOOD."[70] Although the major triumph was in London, the League Union Congress in Glasgow was also an initial affirming event; among the delegates gathering at the McLellan galleries on Sauchiehall Street there were many he knew from Brussels. The conference business over four days managed to survive a debate complaining about Germany's treatment of the Jews (something Rutha typically saw as a distraction and wished to sweep under the *völkisch* carpet). More productively, the minority delegates from Czechoslovakia successfully protested against the idea of "state delegations" being represented at future Union congresses and thereby managed to uphold the independence of national minority bodies like the *Liga* within the Union. It was a defeat for those Czech delegates in Glasgow who were lobbying hard for a full merger in a Czechoslovak federation.[71]

For Rutha, captivated always by nature and ethnic cultures, just as uplifting was what he briefly observed of Scotland. From his time in Glasgow he would remember fondly his lodging with a family, the Ures, whom Nelböck had recommended, their warm hospitality (he sent books to their two sons) and also the unusual Scottish handicrafts. In Edinburgh on the weekend after the congress there was time to visit the castle and Holyroodhouse, and explore the Highlands with a car trip to Loch Tay. In its "simple nature," he wrote enthusiastically to the Ures, only Greece could compare; they had a fatherland of which they could be proud.[72]

Traveling third class on a sleeper, Rutha reached London early on 8 June and stayed for four nights at the Alexandra Hotel at Hyde Park Corner. Most of the "London Action" was already under way, fully in Hasselblatt's hands.[73] He had submitted a memorandum at the Foreign Office explaining that Britain was best placed as an objective power (outside the European alliance system) to pursue reform of international minority rights at the League. He also portrayed the Sudeten problem as a key danger to European peace, for it was enflaming the "appendix of Europe," Czechoslovakia. The response in Whitehall was enough to convince him that his visit had been successful.[74]

For Rutha too the London stay was encouraging, for he mixed with many influential politicians and journalists. At an evening reception hosted by Lord Noel-Buxton, he was fêted as a member of an ENC delegation that included Hasselblatt and the (Czechoslovak) Hungarian minority leader, Géza von Szüllő. Szüllő delivered a vivid speech stressing that, although Europe's nationality malady could not be resolved by force, the doctor (the League) summoned to cure it was also rather ill, so everyone was consulting Britain for a remedy based on "common sense."[75] The next day, some of the delegates (not Rutha) met distinguished members of the British League of Nations Union, including Seton-Watson. Again the signs seemed deceptively promising. The British "experts" agreed to set up their own minority commission, to urge upon Whitehall a permanent international body for minority rights, and even to host the ENC in London in 1937.[76]

Before Rutha left London he had met politicians at the House of Commons and prominent journalists from the *Times* and *Daily Telegraph*. He traveled back to central Europe via France. Paris was strike-ridden and alarming, and he only stopped briefly at the Louvre to glimpse the Mona Lisa. In contrast it was London that had been really captivating, the British authorities receptive, the British Museum with its rich classical collections the place he had reluctantly torn himself away from.[77]

The "London Action" could be deemed a success, at least in German eyes.[78] Just as Hasselblatt sent in a rosy report to Berlin, so Rutha immediately briefed Henlein on the triumph and followed up two British leads. He wrote to Seton-Watson, pressing the need for a "far-sighted and large-scale solution" in Czechoslovakia, implementing full federalization of the state on national lines.[79] To Christie, whom he probably met in London, he complained that soothing speeches by Beneš were unfortunately just Czech "window-dressing" that still left the Sudeten population in "hopeless uncertainty." Out of the two it was Christie (who was badgering the Foreign Office anyway) who took up the plea.[80] On 15 July Henlein suddenly received a second invitation to speak at Chatham House, and the next day together with Rutha he boarded a plane for England.

It was Rutha's first experience of air travel, and there was now something symbolic about him accompanying Henlein. As we will see, it steadied his trust at a time when the party at home was in crisis; he needed reassurance that his own international mission was supported and would not be sabotaged by radical elements. Most assessments of the trip have naturally focused on the important encounter that Christie arranged between Henlein and Robert Vansittart, permanent undersecretary at the Foreign Office. At a private lunch, with Rutha and Christie present, Henlein set out the Czechoslovak regime's "oppression," exemplified by the National Defense Law; he explained that, if things continued, radicals would overthrow him and Nazi Germany would invade, bringing ruin to the Sudeten Germans and a European war. Vansittart was duly impressed by the "moderate, honest and clear-sighted" speaker: in the coming months he accelerated the Foreign Office trend toward pressuring Prague for concessions.[81]

Henlein, as historians usually note, had been careful to adapt his arguments to suit the audience, sketching a vague picture of Czech oppression but failing to mention either the SdP's minimum goal of tribal autonomy, its authoritarian character, or the increasing ties to Nazi Germany.[82] Significantly, he passed on to Berlin almost immediately the gist of the lunch conversation. Nevertheless, this diplomatic excursion gains important new facets when viewed through Rutha's eyes. Everything that Henlein told Vansittart was credible to Rutha in the context of the domestic SdP crisis: Rutha approved this "moderate" line, which opposed radical irredentism. And when Henlein left Britain, Rutha continued the diplomacy, arranging separate talks with Lord Cranborne at the Foreign Office and with the Czechoslovak envoy, Jan Masaryk, in both of which he outlined his own vision.

With Cranborne, after complaining about Czech discrimination, he explained his "personal solution" as a federal system like Switzerland with wide autonomy provided for all the nationalities.[83] His conversation with Masaryk on 23 July was even more illuminating for its naïve frankness. Masaryk, already alarmed at the impression Henlein had made on Vansittart, listened with irritation as Rutha demanded full autonomy for the Sudeten Germans to be able to administer their own affairs in the "German spirit"; the Czechs need not fear irredentism but ought to understand that Germans inside and outside the Reich wanted to cooperate together to achieve a "new era" for the *Volk*. According to Masaryk, Rutha described Hitler as a "great statesman" who could not possibly want war as it would destroy everything he was constructing; there was no danger of a war over the Sudetenland if Prague restructured Czechoslovakia and joined with other Great Powers in a front against Bolshevism. In expounding this vision Rutha was consistent and probably hoped to appeal to Masaryk's congenial nature. Masaryk naturally dismissed it as impossible, concluding that he was no longer amused by "Berlin-Henlein propaganda." He reported back to Prague: "Rutha is an absolutely typical 'Messiah' on whom neither logic nor argument has any effect."[84]

A RADICAL THREAT

After suffering a turbulent flight home, Rutha once again gave his colleagues uplifting news about Britain. In *Die Zeit* he noted how British statesmen were very anxious for a "natural solution" of the nationality problem, something only possible via Konrad Henlein who represented the united Sudeten people; but he warned the public against troublemakers who might sabotage this success.[85] For in late July, Rutha was very alarmed at the Sudeten domestic situation, sensing it could endanger his modest international achievements. With his own preoccupations abroad, he had largely escaped the internecine conflict that was slowly engulfing the SdP. Essentially, the crisis of 1936 involved a new challenge by Nazi radicals to the party's Sudeten loyalists and an extension of the battle Rutha had fought with some success in the Turnverband in 1935. As with that, the party turmoil stemmed directly from its holistic claim to represent all Sudeten Germans and its ready incorporation of *Aufbruch* members who actually scorned compromise, pushing for a Reich annexation of the Sudetenland and a violent carve-up of Czechoslovakia.[86]

Faced with this, the leadership demanded party discipline while bringing black sheep back into the fold in a semblance of national unity. In other words, as with Rutha's tactic in the Turn movement, radicals could stay if they tempered their dissent and embraced what was a façade of unity dictated from above. In early 1936, Henlein had invited Rudolf Kasper, a former DNSAP member, into the leadership to manage the SdP laboring class; but at the same time the party moved to subordinate the unruly Nazi student groups at Prague University.

By May, much to Rutha's consternation, this tenuous arrangement had blown up in Henlein's face.[87] Kasper, backed by radical support in regional branches, openly challenged his peers' pressure on the Nazi students. When Henlein dismissed him, he responded by defaming Walter Brand in the radical Sudeten press and, most importantly, appealing to Germany for support. At this point Henlein should have drawn a line in the sand. Instead, swayed by his own need for Berlin's good offices, he agreed to compromise and have the German foreign ministry mediate the dispute. There on 9 June it was proposed that Kasper be recalled to the leadership, a settlement that Henlein saw as attractive, since Brand too might stay.[88] To reassert party confidence in Brand, Henlein unwisely decided that a party "court of honor" should adjudicate Brand's case to confirm that he had behaved honorably.

In fact, this papering over of the cracks quickly backfired again to the radicals' advantage. On returning from his first visit to Britain, Rutha was shocked at what had occurred and scathing about the "ambitious people" endangering the sacred Sudeten mission. On 15 June he told Henlein that he reserved the right to resign from his special post, and confided to Nelböck: "I sincerely take great pleasure from my work looking after the future of the homeland outside the realm of daily politics, but I am not in a position to continue it (sacrificing my business) if I don't again have a guarantee of the most upright leadership and determination necessary to guard against tragic consequences."[89] A week later he seemed to get this assurance. At a rally at Eger, Henlein made a strident speech for unity and was unanimously reelected as party leader. Brand's position also seemed fully secure: Kasper's star had apparently waned, and the party was starting to purge dissident elements. On 7 July Rutha wrote to Christie with satisfaction that "inner party business" was now completely calm.[90]

Yet three days later it was shattered. The honor court, which Henlein expected to clear the air, abruptly declared against Brand and demanded his dismissal; possibly the jury had been swayed by radical elements or even by a letter Othmar Spann had written personally supporting Brand. What matters is that the pendulum abruptly swung back, forcing Brand to resign and wholly compromising Henlein. In the words of one SdP leader, it was a huge blow to the party, bigger than the Kasper case.[91] The two were of course interlinked, for just as Henlein had to respect the court verdict, so Kasper's rehabilitation was now on the cards. Moreover, the radicals had not only claimed Brand's scalp; an indecisive Henlein had become dangerously beholden to Berlin for stabilizing the situation. In retrospect it can be seen as a crucial step toward the radical camp and further interference from Nazi Germany.

Since a major claim by Kasper and other radicals was that the SdP was controlled by a KB faction, a clique committed to Sudeten interests, Rutha was fortunate to have been abroad during much of the Brand crisis. Even so, this detachment limited his influence on Henlein at a crucial time. On 30 July, with Henlein present, he openly told the SdP leadership that it had panicked and caused Brand's downfall. As usual, he was most exasperated by the dissidents' betrayal of Sudeten unity and discipline, for it undermined his whole campaign to impress London and pressurize Prague. (Indeed, President Beneš was gratified that the SdP was falling apart).[92] A secondary consideration was that these troublemakers were "shady characters" and Nazis. Rather naïvely, Rutha was prepared to accept the latter if they adhered to party discipline ; thus on 30 July, while others like Sebekowsky opposed any compromise with Kasper, he was against completely "slamming the door."[93]

We can explain this in terms of Rutha's nationalist mindset, where a common Sudeten German crusade within a pan-German framework blinded him to the real dangers from Germany or the cross-border Nazi links. Yet it would be wrong to suggest that Rutha completely misjudged the radicals. During the summer, after the leadership equivocated over Kasper, he continued to worry about a radical upsurge and Henlein's lack of resolve in that regard. Crucially, he himself considered the "moderate," nonirredentist route via London or Geneva to be the "realistic line" via which the Sudeten cause could triumph by peaceful means.[94]

The Brand disaster of 1936 was a watershed, shifting the SdP focus away from its KB origins in a radical direction and blurring further its objectives with Germany's. At the Eger rally, Henlein, while championing Brand, had felt bound to disown Spannist influence, publicly denying any links with Spann or Heinrich; later in August he would ask Spann to cease all contact with the party in order to preserve stability.[95] These moves did not sever a major connection, for the Spannist link was waning anyway, but they were symbolic in shifting SdP identity in a Nazi direction. Brand now left the leadership, and Rudolf Sandner, another "moderate" who had been leading an anti-Nazi purge, would soon be sidelined. While Rutha in fact had never bonded closely with either Brand or Sandner, their eclipse, like the public Spannist divorce, had to affect his foreign mission in some way.[96] As Henlein's cabinet assumed more radical hues in late 1936, as Kasper was readmitted and Karl Hermann Frank steered in an irredentist direction, Rutha was in danger of losing influence with Henlein, especially because of his own detached method of working, which often caused his absence from key meetings. Once he had described Frank as "a very sincere, serious and decent man."[97] Now perhaps he was less sure and may have sensed Frank's growing radical hold over Henlein.

The danger that Rutha's foreign priorities might diverge from Henlein's in the context of SdP radicalization was evident in August 1936 at the time of the Berlin Olympics, an event that celebrated Germany's international pre-eminence. For Henlein, it was the occasion when he first spoke to Adolf Hitler (having first seen him at the Winter Olympics in February) and also drew closer to the German foreign ministry; both encounters boosted his confidence in future Reich support.[98] In contrast, Rutha only visited the Olympics for a few days. On 12 August, he may have attended with Henlein a gymnastics display by the Asch Turn school in the sports palace, but was probably more interested in trying to meet Robert Vansittart again (present for the games) than in cultivating Reich officials. Pointedly, in an interview with foreign journalists, he even stated that he was not a Nazi, and as a Catholic disagreed with many Reich policies. He proposed that Czechoslovakia should become a "better Switzerland" but warned that if the Czechs remained obstinate the SdP would take a radical direction.[99]

PETITIONING GENEVA

As the SdP relationship with Britain deepened in 1936, an extra means for pressurizing Prague was always the League of Nations. At the start of Rutha's foreign activity, turning to Geneva had been a realistic option; indeed, for international lobbyists like Ammende or Hasselblatt, a perennial debate was how to strengthen the League's protective machinery over Europe's national minorities. In addition, in late 1935 the League's profile was contentiously raised due to the Italian-Abyssinian War and Britain's insistence on economic sanctions against Mussolini. As Rutha learned more about European diplomacy, he increasingly felt that London held the key for enforcing League minority guarantees. Auspiciously, Anthony Eden had been appointed as British foreign secretary (previously he had been minister for the League), and Britain also had extra influence until September 1936 as president of the League Council.

Working via Geneva to browbeat Prague was a conservative tactic since it challenged the Czechoslovak government on its own preferred territory. Edvard Beneš regularly stated that when it came to foreign interference in Czechoslovakia's minority policy, only the League had a legitimate influence due to the state's Minority Treaty of 1919, which was under a League guarantee.[100] Thus when Rutha and Henlein continued to court the League, they were being pragmatic about how best to achieve their goals in the current international system. In this light we should interpret the party's action in Geneva in 1936 as part and parcel of Rutha's strategy for forcing peaceful change upon Prague. Most historians have either paid little attention to this, or viewed it as just a publicity stunt backed by Berlin.[101] Rutha at least took it seriously; by the summer of 1936, with the radical upsurge, he was placing exaggerated hopes on its outcome.

In January 1936, just as the London option was maturing, a new opportunity arose for the SdP to challenge alleged Czech discrimination against the Sudeten Germans. This was the so-called Machník decree, named after the chauvinistic Czechoslovak Minister of Defense. The title in fact was a misnomer since it was neither an official decree nor wholly Machník's work. As part of creeping vigilance about Czechoslovak security, the Ministry of Defense was trying to impose conditions on those businesses allotted state contracts for defense procurements; on 28 January 1936, it sent out letters to a dozen linen factories to this effect. Among the conditions, the number of Czech employees in each business needed to correspond to their national proportion in the locality; and no employee could belong to a political party hostile to the state.[102]

It might be argued that these were legitimate concerns for the state authorities, as they suspected many German firms were already in the Henleinist irredentist camp. Even so, it was a heavy-handed measure, one that questioned German loyalties and seems to have aroused the wrath even of Beneš and Hodža in offering a gift to the SdP.[103] The SdP leaders not only correctly interpreted the decree as discriminating against German employees, who might face redundancy if the Czech quota was imposed.[104] They alleged, in an ironic twist, that it was specifically designed to target them as—despite all their protestations of loyalty—a supposed treacherous element in the state.

Indeed, the SdP leaders pounced on the Machník decree when it was clear in the press that all German parties, even the Social Democrats, condemned it. They immediately directed a parliamentary question at Hodža, who after a month replied that it was simply a measure of national security. Yet for Rutha and Henlein the fuss they were concocting was more than a propaganda coup. It seemed an ideal test case upon which to build a petition to the League of Nations, claiming violation of Czechoslovakia's Minority Treaty. The fact that they turned to this bureaucratic recourse is less surprising if we remember Rutha's cautious strategy alongside the opportunities developing by early 1936. Contrary to J. W. Bruegel's view, there was indeed the chance that Britain might back the petition, thereby forcing the Czechs to treat with the SdP.[105]

With this expectation, Henlein in February dispatched letters to London about a forthcoming petition, pleading for special support but warning that if it failed, the Sudeten Germans' "last shred of faith in the League of Nations would be finally destroyed."[106] This caveat perhaps reflects Henlein's own equivocation or at least uncertainty in the SdP leadership: Rutha later claimed that some radical elements there had opposed him on the grounds that all previous Sudeten petitions (in the 1920s) had failed.[107] For the moment, however, and in line with the "London Action," he seems to have argued a convincing case for submission. On 24 April, after considerable polishing, a lengthy document was sent in to the League's Minorities Section in Geneva.

Although Rutha's ANV had sought expert opinion when composing the petition, the final document was short on analysis and long on bluster. Since it could not yet give proof that the decree was actually harming the German minority, it repeated at length the agitated German press response and exaggerated the number of protests that had taken place in "all German parishes," involving over 150,000 people. As we have seen, it was typical of Rutha, the fervent nationalist, to use colorful rhetoric for effect even if he convinced himself of the core of his arguments. Thus the petition, based on the groundswell of public opinion, insisted that the decree was no Czech error but a calculated "act for deprivation of rights, repression and denationalization"; the League should immediately dispatch a commissioner to Czechoslovakia to examine the question.[108]

For the Minorities Section in Geneva, this type of petulant request regularly accompanied petitions. But it was always rejected since it contradicted the precise procedures that had evolved over fifteen years for handling minority petitions in a detached manner. Instead, if the Minorities Section deemed a petition "receivable," it established a "Committee of Three," composed of three members of the League Council, to decide whether it should be placed on the council agenda for wider discussion. On scrutinizing the SdP petition, the section sensed there was indeed a "certain 'limitative' discrimination" involved, and judged that Hodža's very vague reply had not helped the Czech case. The petition was therefore considered "receivable" and Prague was duly asked to comment.[109]

While profoundly irritated, the Czechoslovak foreign ministry realized that it had to respond very carefully. Not only might the Machník decree open up the whole issue of national discrimination, since "disloyal elements" were indeed likely to be German, but the Czechs had a proud reputation of supporting the League and fulfilling their international obligations. Ironically, once it was clear that the Minorities Section would act, Prague had the same hope as Rutha, namely that Britain as president of the League Council would support its viewpoint. As the Czechoslovak minister in Geneva noted, "If we answer promptly and successfully reject Henlein's case, we can unmask Henlein in the eyes of English public opinion." It was therefore vital to respond before late September, since Britain as president would then be responsible for chairing a Committee of Three.[110]

In its reply, the foreign ministry claimed that the decree was not an official act, only a "condition of form" if any firm desired a state contract. Disingenuously, it stressed that employees' ethnicity was never at issue, only their proven loyalty to the state. By early September these "observations" were finally in the hands of the Minorities Section, Krofta adding as a coda that Geneva should judge the affair as if the Machník "letters" had never existed.[111] Yet this was only partially true. In the preceding months Prague had found a way of implementing the Machník principle by another route. The National Defense Law of May 1936, although it claimed not to discriminate on grounds of nationality, gave the authorities all the powers they needed to act against disloyal elements, whether in the defense industry or elsewhere.[112] Rutha therefore probably came to rue the SdP's premature complaint, for the Defense Law with its far-reaching arbitrary powers would have been a far more effective focus for any petition.

Nevertheless, in the summer of 1936, Rutha set great store by a successful outcome with British support. During their visits to London, Rutha and Henlein championed their petition everywhere and deduced that the Foreign

Office saw that route as ideal for subtly pressurizing the Czechs. Not only was the British envoy in Prague fully convinced about Czech discrimination; so was Vansittart, who, after meeting the Sudeten Germans, felt that the League's September meeting was indeed "of capital performance" for solving a problem that was "the powder magazine of the future."[113]

Thus, the British were determined to act, aware of their own power at Geneva in the council presidency, even praying that the decree still existed so that Czech discrimination could be publicly censured. Rutha would have been gratified if he had known this level of concern in Whitehall, but he could only speculate since silence or rumor emanated from Geneva. By August, in the wake of the radical upsurge in the SdP, he set ever more store by the League and the chance of "the English interest proving its worth." Impatiently, he scribbled to Christie that any postponement over the petition would be "grist to the mill of our local radicals," throwing into question all the success achieved so far; he pressed him to use all his influence with Henlein and Vansittart so that they both followed the "realistic line."[114]

In September at the League, the SdP complaint proceeded apace, yet the bureaucratic procedures there worked against any fast solution. With the Czech "observations" submitted, the Minorities Section resolved under British pressure to set up a Committee of Three to study the case (with the Foreign Office delegate William Malkin as chair).[115] Yet, since the Czech nationalist press clamored that the decree had been withdrawn or never existed, Rutha was justifiably anxious lest the committee close the case at its first meeting. The opportunity for a personal intervention had arrived. In mid-September, he was again one of the delegates to the ENC in Geneva, this time making no speech but conferring with Werner Hasselblatt. They agreed that to forestall closure of the case the SdP should send in a second petition concerning the National Defense Law; Rutha's office had been considering that for some time, experimenting with a number of supplementary petitions.[116] After the ENC this tactic therefore formed a cornerstone of his argument when he proceeded to lobby both Malkin and the head of the Minorities Section, Peter Schou.

In these conversations Rutha was typically both pragmatic and emotional, setting out his "moderate course" but noting what might happen if it were to fail and the "extremists" started dominating the SdP.[117] We should emphasize here that Rutha saw himself as a moderate in the face of both Sudeten irredentists and Czech chauvinists, and could always envisage discussions with Prague if only the government was more accommodating. Yet there was still a dose of wishful and contradictory thinking at work: he claimed that SdP members were not Nazi "and were quite prepared to be loyal citizens if they were decently treated." His grasp of essential detail was also obscured by his broader crusade. Thus, surprisingly, he was unable to tell Malkin if the Machník decree had actually been executed, nor did he think that the Defense Law had superseded it. Overall, his emotional thrust was designed to impress upon his interlocutors the urgency of discussing the petition. At the same time, and probably for effect, he said that another petition was anticipated, a sign that the SdP took the League seriously.[118]

These meetings had a crucial impact on the Committee of Three's judgment, while the anxiety of both the Sudeten and Czech leaders was palpable. With an eye on the petition's fate, Rutha, together with his colleague Hans Neuwirth (the SdP's lawyer), requested an audience with the foreign minister, Kamil Krofta; they were alarmed at mounting Czech press attacks after Neuwirth, in a speech to the ENC, had suggested there was a "new irredenta" in Czechoslovakia.[119] The encounter on 22 September reveals much about the insurmountable suspicions on both sides. Exclaiming that Neuwirth's speech had been "revolutionary," Krofta complained that the SdP's propaganda abroad could only exacerbate Czech-German relations at home. Rutha countered forcefully: "This route will never lead to Germany." He justified the SdP visits to England in terms of the Sudeten Germans' fundamental fear of being denationalized by the Czechs.[120] Since Rutha could not be convinced otherwise, Krofta felt—like Masaryk a few months earlier—that he was faced with a ridiculous fanatic who could not see the logic of his arguments. In short, Rutha seemed a dangerous individual. It was confirmed two days later when the Committee of Three met for the first time. Malkin as chair announced that the petition certainly needed to be thoroughly scrutinized. On behalf of the Minorities Section, Peter Schou agreed, recording from a conversation with Rutha the petitioners' apparent desire "to work and live peaceably with their Czechoslovak co-nationals." The committee therefore agreed to keep the case open and await further information from the petitioners.[121]

In theory this appeared a triumph for Rutha's diplomacy. In fact, it was the start of the slow demise of the case, for the SdP thereafter failed to produce any supplementary petition or evidence for Geneva. Why was this? Possibly by late 1936 the upsurge of radical influence in the SdP leadership was a stumbling block, but more important was probably Rutha's own impatience with and ignorance of the whole byzantine procedure. Immediately after Geneva, he had traveled to Vienna to report to Graham Christie and seemed confident about an imminent committee judgment. A fortnight later he was much less sure. While the trip to Switzerland had indeed boosted his own reputation in the SdP leadership and his argument for moderation, tangible progress was less evident, for the Committee of Three had temporarily dispersed.[122]

Crucially, the League's procedural rules remained obscure to the petitioners. The committee was not allowed directly to request information from them, so they were kept in the dark about their case. Both sides, therefore, were waiting for the other to act. Moreover, if Rutha initially had considered submitting extra evidence (as he had told Christie), he quickly sensed that trumpeting the Machník decree was no longer a viable option. Most sobering was the Czechoslovak government's constant claim that the decree had been withdrawn and no longer existed, thereby eliminating any further evidence for the petitioners. In January 1937 Rutha admitted as much to the British envoy in Prague.[123]

A combination of factors therefore stymied the hopes in 1936 of using Geneva as a vehicle for pressurizing Prague. One clear reason was the League's bureaucracy in slowly handling minority petitions, when Rutha, always intolerant of too much talk, wanted a speedy result. Another was the very basis of the SdP petition, founded as it was on uncertain evidence or at least on shifting sands that the Czech authorities could exploit to prove their argument. Yet despite Czech official claims that the petition's failure proved that it was totally unjustified, this was never the view in London or Geneva.[124] The British Foreign Office in particular still hoped in 1937 that the SdP would supply further documentation so that Prague could be publicly arraigned and forced to talk to Henlein. Only when this was not forthcoming, and rumors suggested that Rutha had lost interest did Malkin reluctantly advise that the case should be terminated.

On 26 May 1937 the SdP petition was finally discussed in full at Geneva, with Malkin and Anthony Eden chairing the Committee of Three.[125] Eden warned that the case must be handled with exceptional care, the committee concurring that the Czech replies had been unsatisfactory. However, they agreed that since the initial Machník decree had lost its force, they could not recommend further action and had to close the case; an official public communiqué to this effect was sent out. While this did not criticize Czechoslovakia, it was not evidence, as some historians maintain, that Geneva rejected the petition or that Britain was satisfied with Prague's minority policy.[126] Rather, Rutha was correct in seeking to portray the League announcement in a positive light. He commented that the muted Czech response after the verdict was evidence that the petition had hit its mark and successfully forced Prague to back down. An additional triumph, he maintained (incorrectly), was that compared to previous Sudeten petitions, a Committee of Three had seriously examined the SdP's case. Less encouraging was its reluctance to push the legal investigation much further.[127]

Indeed, even if Rutha interpreted the Machník case in the long run as a moral victory for the SdP, it had been a very sobering experience, highlighting the real inadequacy of League of Nations procedures. He might hint that the Sudeten Germans could still send a grand petition to the League, but by 1937 that route of redress was moribund.[128] Certainly it was anathema to SdP irredentists like Karl Hermann Frank, perhaps even Henlein, who saw in the Third Reich a much faster "German-international" solution.

Rutha's foreign policy of course also sought its own German-international remedy, yet his German Bohemian focus, coupled with the vague Spannist vision of corporate states straddling central Europe, naturally inclined him toward men who had proven international credentials like German lobbyists or cosmopolitan Bohemian aristocrats. While many of these nationalists, such as Hasselblatt or Clary-Aldringen, could easily be drawn toward Nazi Germany, they also continued with traditional international lobbying that was not wholly Reich-focused and envisaged a nonviolent outcome. Rutha shared this conservative mentality. Therefore in 1937 he maintained his chosen British course, even trying thereby to revise the inadequate international system of minority protection. However, as Hitler's influence mounted across Europe, so Rutha's own foreign strategy was disintegrating, fatally blurring with the agenda of the Sudeten German radicals.

NINE

Premonition of Disaster

In November 1937, Konrad Henlein finally wrote a private letter to Adolf Hitler, surrendering his party and asking the führer to annex all the Bohemian lands to the Third Reich. It was a dramatic, erratic gesture on a par with the launch of the movement four years earlier. Many historians view it as the logical outcome of a steady drift by the Sudeten German Party (SdP) toward Berlin, or even a consciously planned goal. Some have suggested that Heinz Rutha's demise that autumn was a special factor that moved Henlein off a previous "moderate track," forcing him onto a single-minded irredentist course away from Czechoslovakia.[1] An analysis of the last year of Rutha's foreign policy lends some weight to this theory: that Rutha could mentor Henlein and at the same time continue to favor largely traditional avenues of diplomacy to pressurize the Czechoslovak regime.

Against this, one can argue that Rutha's own Sudeten agenda—akin to Henlein's—was hardly harmless to Czechoslovak integrity, for it always envisaged a fundamental restructuring of Bohemian space to reassert German primacy. Indeed, in 1937, as Henlein set out more radical domestic demands that privileged *Volk* over state loyalty, Rutha's own nationalist activity shifted in tandem. He was not quite a treacherous irredentist or "little Ribbentrop" in London as many domestic critics liked to portray him.[2] But his public behavior and speeches certainly intensified the "Sudeten problem," opening the door to pan-German Nazi solutions that far exceeded what he felt desirable for preserving European peace or Sudeten German interests. The paradox of the situation was nicely summed up by one contemporary Sudeten historian who urged a "radicalization of national satisfaction and reconciliation" to achieve a Czech-German settlement.[3]

THE FOREIGN MISSION RELAUNCHED

It might be expected after the SdP domestic turmoil in mid-1936 that Rutha would retire from public gaze, retreating to Kunnersdorf and the business he felt he was neglecting. Certainly, the intense peripatetic activity at home and abroad was affecting his health, which had never been strong. In late October he resolved "to get out of the whole bustle before the winter" and take a rest in Italy for most of November. Where he journeyed is unclear, but according to Artur Vogt, it became a political expedition as much as a holiday, suggesting that he explored once again the German communities of south Tyrol.[4] On his return he was thrown back into administrative work at the ANV and, with Henlein fallen ill, was burdened with a myriad of extra obligations.

One witness in late 1936 felt that although Rutha had successfully won himself the SdP foreign remit he remained very hesitant with it, especially in contrast to Werner Hasselblatt, who in meetings tended to make grand philosophical pronouncements.[5] In fact, while Rutha's reserve in group discussions was typical, his confidence was increasing: after the SdP radicals' success at home and his own industry at Geneva, he moved to extract fresh assurances from Henlein.[6] In early October, the SdP leadership announced a new inner council. Henlein dampened dissent by including Rudolf Kasper, but removed Rutha, who undoubtedly welcomed exclusion from further tedious meetings. Some outside observers were sure that in this reorganization moderates could still outvote radicals, and this may have been the perception too of some insiders.[7] For to offset the radicals, Rutha's own status as the SdP foreign expert was reaffirmed; he wrote to Graham Christie that "Chicken"—their codename for Henlein—had personally guaranteed that the "moderate line" would continue.[8] Henlein thus was relaunching Rutha as a special adviser, particularly responsible for the Sudeten cause abroad and answerable to him alone. Rutha continued to have a peculiar status with both positive and negative implications (special access to Henlein; rather distant from the rest of the leadership) but it was still reassuring. As he told Christie, Henlein had "entrusted him with the leadership of the party's foreign policy relations . . . and the handling of affairs in France, GB, Austria etc." In public meanwhile he continued to be the "special commissioner for League of Nations and nationality questions."[9]

As thus formulated, Rutha's role in Henlein's movement had not changed. There were hints (the reference to Austria, as we will see) that the scope had widened in line with recent developments. But generally, his task was to

promote a radical power shift in the international system, especially lobbying the British, so that Prague would be forced into major concessions in
the Bohemian lands. In late 1936, there were clear signs that the peace settlement of 1919, together with Czechoslovakia's international position, was
crumbling further—to Germany's advantage. In October Belgium declared
neutrality, removing another prop in the system of collective security. Rutha
welcomed the move, noting to Joris van Severen the great excitement it had
aroused in Czechoslovakia, where some (especially in the SdP) hoped it
would be copied; he was intrigued to know whether Belgium was now
inclining more toward England.[10] On 1 November, Mussolini publicly
announced a Rome-Berlin "Axis" running through Europe, reemphasizing
that power had shifted toward the dynamic dictators who were known to be
cooperating in the Spanish Civil War. Ever more fruitful seemed the chances
of reconfiguring the local power relationship between Czechs and Sudeten
Germans.

Indeed, from late 1936 there were more than hints of a Czech willingness
to reach a new settlement with the German minority. Due to the international situation and growing British pressure, Prague was inclining toward
minor concessions to the Germans at home and, separately, some regional
agreement with Germany; in November the president, Edvard Beneš, held
secret talks with two emissaries from Berlin with an eye to achieving a non-
aggression pact. Czech optimism over this continued well into 1937, but the
talks led nowhere. For Hitler, any pact was conditional on the Czechs fully
abandoning their Franco-Soviet alliance, something Beneš would never do,
just as he was adamantly opposed to any discussion with Berlin about the
German minority.[11]

Rutha and the SdP knew nothing about these secret talks, so their continued cry in 1937 for some international agreement is understandable (even
if they too wanted a pact ensuring Czechoslovakia's neutrality and wholly
privileging German influence in the region). What they did notice was
Prague's willingness to discuss the German minority's situation, and how
the conciliatory foreign minister, Kamil Krofta, wished to win over the SdP
as the most significant German body in the republic.[12] Beneš himself, in
response to British pressure, even seemed ready to meet Henlein if the SdP
would put forward precise demands.[13] But most productive was the initiative of Milan Hodža, the prime minister, in negotiating with the three small
German activist parties. By late January 1937, they had produced a memorandum vaguely espousing the principle of national equality, and on 18 Feb-

ruary, an agreement was reached whereby the government guaranteed to enforce existing minority rights, specifically concentrating on areas of economic deprivation and state employment. Even the pro-SdP British envoy in Prague welcomed this "forerunner of a more general reconciliation" while stressing to London that it was largely due to British pressure.[14] Others were quick to note that the agreement was only with the small German governmental parties, it ignored the controversial National Defense Law, and was simply guaranteeing existing rights (so hardly a concession): it was thus "in reality a very modest affair."[15]

For the SdP leaders of course it was completely unsatisfactory, since it was not the radical shift of power they expected. They had deliberately excluded themselves from Hodža's talks after an initial invitation. Possibly we might see these winter months as a final lost opportunity for SdP conciliators to make some breakthrough with the Czechoslovak regime. Germany's envoy in Prague could not quite understand the SdP indecisiveness at this time. If the lull had started when Henlein was temporarily ill (before Christmas), by January 1937 the Czechs were focusing on talks with activist party leaders, whom the SdP always scorned. Hints from Hodža about the modest scale of any concessions also undoubtedly encouraged the Henleinists to sustain their brinkmanship and press forward with a solution on their own terms.[16]

This ratcheted up the confrontation for the future. In the wake of the February agreement, which Rutha earlier predicted as a "few crumbs," the SdP leadership duly set out the radical counterproposals on which it had worked for some months.[17] In a speech at Aussig, Henlein announced for the first time a program for strictly dividing Germans from Czechs in the Bohemian lands. The SdP would bring before Parliament a range of nationality laws to be integrated into the Czechoslovak constitution; these would implement German "self-administration," setting fixed ethnic borders, and permanently registering all citizens' nationality. Although Henlein continued to float the idea that state unity would be preserved, this was still advocating a state within a state. It was entirely consistent with arguments used by the leadership (including Rutha) in the previous two years, but it now became a concrete program for securing the Sudeten *Heimat* in perpetuity.[18]

In 1937 the domestic context for Rutha's diplomacy was framed by these two contrasting initiatives: on the one hand the draft SdP nationality laws, proposing a Sudeten corporate state within a loose Czechoslovakia (something immediately dismissed by Prague); on the other the modest February agreement, which only creepingly produced results.[19] When Rutha himself assessed the Sudeten situation at home, he rightly highlighted widespread economic and social deprivation. Apart from the circumstances of his furniture business, in early 1936 he had spent a week in one of the "distressed areas" of northwest Bohemia, encountering what he described as "really shocking conditions." He noted pointedly: "The people up there are gradually dying of hunger."[20] In 1937, despite a reduction in Sudeten unemployment, the vivid images still permeated his speeches: "In Czech regions plump rosy-cheeked youths, in our areas 25-year old young men, exhausted and looking like pensioners."[21]

Rutha's mindset automatically equated this Sudeten misery with deliberate Czechoslovak economic policy, when it really stemmed from market forces outside state control. Yet complaints about Czech national discrimination always had some underlying substance. By 1936, amid the heightened tensions, the SdP could easily interpret the Czech national strategy as intensified "Czechification" or denationalization of Sudeten territory. Besides the fierce rhetoric of many Czech nationalist societies, there was the evidence of the National Defense Law, under which the Czech authorities were indeed encroaching on the borderlands, moving reliable state police into sensitive areas.[22] It was a crucial development that most historians ignore. Reacting to this "Czech advance," Rutha naturally backed the SdP laws as a basis for defending the "homeland," for they would not only enforce ethnic identities and language borders ("unchanged for the past 500 years"), but would secure self-government especially if, as demanded, new local elections were held that solidified the SdP position.[23] Probably Rutha still envisaged all this as the materialization of a Sudeten "Spannist state," part and parcel of that youth mission whereby a Männerbund would take control of society.

That a universalist solution was Rutha's ideal for restructuring central Europe—though never really enunciated—also helps us understand his attitude to Germany. While some historians have focused single-mindedly on the SdP's "tight relationship" with the Reich, the complex nuances of those links are clear from Rutha's behavior.[24] By 1937 the SdP relationship with Berlin was certainly ever closer. From initial clandestine financial support, Germany in 1936 had helped pacify the party's internecine strife and shown it could influence the SdP radicals. It was partly to control the latter and partly because Berlin was vital for SdP finances (and his own shaky morale), that Henlein was fast "falling into a fateful dependence on the Reich."[25] While his own visits to court Berlin became more frequent and open, others like the ambitious Karl Hermann Frank were already in the radical camp, viewing Reich intervention in Czechoslovakia as the best exit from the Czech-Sudeten impasse. Frank's "conversion" by at least 1937 shows that he understood where the winds were blowing in Germany, how radical groups, including Reinhard Heydrich's intelligence service, were taking over the Reich bodies that handled the German diaspora.[26] Rutha in contrast rarely visited Berlin. A notable exception was early 1937 when alongside Henlein he was present one evening at a Sudeten concert; the pieces largely celebrated German music and the artists were all Sudeten German, raising their special profile in a broad German cultural setting.[27]

In his talks with the British, Rutha regularly complained about the radical upsurge in the SdP and Germany, contrasting it with the peaceful mission of nonradicals on either side of the border. This was sincerely argued, for irredentism or the victory of Reich radicalism (personified for him in Joseph Goebbels or the Nazi youth leader Baldur von Schirach) could produce a European war and the destruction of his Bohemian homeland. A timely, moderate solution was vital before the situation deteriorated. Yet at the same time, while respecting existing state frontiers, Rutha's own vision gave primacy to a broad German *Volksgemeinschaft* and certainly implied an underlying role for Germany in the restructuring of central Europe. This is pictorially clear via the huge map that hung in his Prague office, for it privileged the peoples of east-central Europe with state borders only faintly delineated (fig. 22). Similarly, while he opposed any full *Anschluss,* he favored communality with ideas from the Reich, telling the British in February that there could be "no question of bringing the Sudeten German community into conflict with the German [Reich] renewal."[28] An underlying premise, stressed increasingly in 1937, was that Czechoslovakia must fully reorient its foreign policy away from unnatural allies like France and the Soviet Union toward the friendly German neighbor.

This was therefore a logical, ambitious program that would assure German dominance across central Europe. Indeed, although Rutha always denied it because of his Sudeten and non-Nazi focus, his was a form of pan-Germanism and guaranteed to subordinate the Czechs within German space. The real difficulty was how to implement it peacefully without inviting an even more radical and violent solution. Instinctively Rutha inclined toward exploiting the existing international system, adjusting his horizons to secure minimum goals, but his strategy of pressurizing Prague was still akin to diplomatic bullying. No wonder many contemporaries saw little difference between this and the sinister objectives of the Sudeten irredentists.

While Britain and international lobbying bodies continued to be Rutha's main pressure points, Austria suddenly emerged as a fresh area for flirtation. It is intriguing as an extra touchstone for gauging Rutha's Sudeten-focused yet pan-German perspective in 1936–1937. In March 1934, Austria, with a new constitution, had become an authoritarian corporate state [*Ständestaat*]; thus we might expect Rutha, if he was a fervent Spannist, to have paid special attention there before late 1936.

This did not occur for various reasons that reveal his loose interpretation of Spannism but also the complex spectrum of German-Austrian loyalties in the *Ständestaat*. Firstly, we should not exaggerate Rutha's commitment to intellectual Spannism. Indeed, despite occasional visits to Vienna, his relationship with Walter Heinrich seems to have suffered a "critical schism" when he entered SdP politics and deserted the world of Spannist academia to pursue a foreign mission.[29] Secondly, the *Ständestaat* itself offered the SdP few enticements. Even Othmar Spann himself looked askance at it as an unnatural mixture of ideologies, and he envisaged Austrian Anschluss to Germany as the best solution. Meanwhile, the Austrian chancellor, Kurt Schuschnigg, was publicly hostile to Nazi Germany and wary of pan-German intrigues—whether from the SdP or nearer home—that might threaten Austrian independence.[30] As a result, and as agreed personally with Henlein, Rutha's foreign priorities in 1935–1936 lay elsewhere; only indirectly might we consider his a Spannist foreign policy.

The July 1936 "Gentlemen's Agreement" between Austria and Germany suddenly transformed this impasse. Not only did Austro-German "friendship" offer real potential for a creeping pan-German solution that might include the Sudetenland. Schuschnigg, in appeasing Germany, also slowly incorporated into his regime Austria's so-called "national opposition," men like Edmund von Glaise-Horstenau and Artur Seyss-Inquart who, though not Nazis, were solid Austrian pan-Germans who dreamt of an *Anschluss* where Austria would retain its identity in a greater Reich.[31] By late 1936, therefore, there were several fruitful avenues that Rutha could explore, and as a new vice president of the European Nationalities Congress (ENC) (elected in Geneva in September), he was bound to visit its center in Vienna more often. It was also surely no coincidence that he approached Austria just after experiencing the summer upsurge of SdP radicalism; although Henlein had rejected Spann, the Austrian avenue offered fresh potential for those like Rutha who balked at a blunt and probably violent Reich-led solution.

It was in September 1936 that Rutha, a "very intelligent and serious character," first came to the attention of the Austrian legation in Prague. On first visiting in late October, he stressed his sympathy for Austria—that Sudeten Germans were more Austrian than German—and asked to be received in Vienna. A month later he met Ferdinand Marek, the Austrian envoy to Czechoslovakia. As usual he complained about Czech obstinacy, demanded Sudeten autonomy, and assured a skeptical listener that the party was not directed or funded from the Reich. He then praised the Austro-German agreement, explaining that in the SdP many "old Austrians" like himself wished to heal the wounds and strengthen contacts with Vienna; with a Spannist flourish, he portrayed the Sudeten Germans as the third German tribe who bridged the space between Austria and the Reich. A way forward was for Sudeten Germans to deepen their cultural links to the south, starting in 1937 with a visit to Vienna by the prestigious Turner school from Asch.[32]

It was a propitious overture but immediately dampened by the Austrian chancellery. Vienna was wary of exacerbating Austrian-Czech relations by interfering in the Sudeten dispute and suspicious too about what the SdP really wanted.[33] Rutha in turn conceived rather naïvely that Turn gymnastics could be an effective diplomatic tool. Nevertheless, he managed to secure a private audience in Vienna with Guido Schmidt, the Austrian foreign minister, and adopted the code name "Hauffen" to maintain confidentiality. Schmidt on 10 December 1936 blandly approved further cultural ties but—in line with Schuschnigg's own reserve—was cool about any demonstrative venture that might align Austria politically with the SdP.[34]

Two months later Rutha returned to the Austrian legation, this time accompanied by Frank and by Henlein, who was naturally enthusiastic about the Turner tour. They were shocked to discover that Vienna now wanted postponement, claiming it was internationally problematic and complaining of anti-Austrian Nazi voices in the SdP. In reply, the duo persisted with their pro-Austrian sympathies. Henlein stressed that most Sudeten Germans had fought for Austria in the war, that the Turn movement was wholly nonpolitical; Rutha again requested a resumption of Sudeten-Alpine ties and dismissed any Sudeten Nazi voices as insignificant. These assurances slowly paid off, Vienna relented, and in early April the Turn school performed in the capital. When its propaganda tour of other Austrian centers was blocked, it moved to Germany, where in Leipzig Henlein made a point of being present; to him at least, the Reich seemed far more welcoming.[35]

Yet if this might seem the end of Rutha's brief Austrian foray, there are hints that in 1937 something else was brewing. Particularly, Rutha and other SdP leaders were talking to figures from the Austrian "national opposition," including Glaise-Horstenau and Seyss-Inquart.[36] According to Christie, Rutha in July 1937 also had a secret meeting with Chancellor Schuschnigg, but this is unconfirmed; most likely Christie meant Seyss-Inquart, who certainly cultivated Rutha because, as he told Schuschnigg, "these men, closely connected to me, have a task similar to my own."[37] Like Rutha, Seyss-Inquart hailed from the Czech-German language border, and possibly by mid–1937 their pan-German solutions for central Europe had begun to converge. In short, Rutha too at the end of his life may have felt that the Sudeten Germans and Austrians had reached the same crossroads: their future lay with joining the German Reich, but ensuring that within it their German tribes retained their special identities.

RAISING THE PROFILE

In 1937 Rutha's diplomacy exuded confidence, coupled always with an underlying uncertainty, even nervousness, about the Sudeten Germans' future. The tension seemed to energize him, leading to a rapid rise of his public profile in Czechoslovakia and abroad. At the new year, his increasing grasp of foreign affairs was best expressed in the SdP weekly, *Rundschau*, where he explained the diplomatic revolution that had transformed Europe in 1936.[38] In place of the postwar equilibrium based on the League and European alliances, there now ruled only insecurity and national tensions. Old doctrines had been discredited partly through the League's failure to control the Abyssinian and Spanish wars, partly because Germany (justifiably) had reoccupied the Rhineland and, alongside a "huge peaceful expansion" at home, was calming tensions with Italy and Austria. Crucial too were the national domestic traumas, formerly suppressed, that had surfaced across Europe and cried out for resolution: both the Flemish challenge in Belgium and the resurgent Croatian question in Yugoslavia mirrored the Sudeten struggle in Czechoslovakia.[39] In short, the current restructuring of the "old order" was a European phenomenon.

Rutha identified England as the medium for resolving this change peacefully. While the German *Volksgruppen* might be valuable mediators, England was the great power, uniquely impartial, that understood the urgency of European reform, the redress of national injustice, by peaceful pressure. Only by achieving stability in domestic affairs would states then be strong enough to meet the wider European challenge that was Bolshevism. For the continent this was the real ideological menace, meddling in Spain (no mention of the fascist states), threatening France, and only stoppable if Europe harmonized its domestic and foreign policies.

To resolve the Czech-German antagonism, Rutha therefore still saw Britain as the key and urged the ENC organizers to stand by their decision of hosting the next congress in London.[40] Meanwhile, the direct link via Christie into the Whitehall labyrinth was always alluring; he even hoped that a lecture might be arranged for him at Chatham House.[41] When it failed to materialize, he met Christie in Vienna in late January and pressed for another invitation from London so that Sudeten moderates could put their case to Robert Vansittart and others. Here, far more than previously, he dwelt on the danger of SdP radicalization if "Czechification" continued; it was a calculated argument, sensitive to British concerns about any Nazi German involvement, but also reflecting his own anxieties. Christie scribbled down that "Henlein & Co" were still against border revisions or even pan-Germanism: "Henlein feels British influence stands high in Prag [sic]: only hope for Moderates lies in British action."[42]

Rapidly an invitation arrived to make a third journey to Britain, something Rutha would explain disingenuously as "impolite to refuse."[43] While it proved to be his most controversial visit, arousing a tirade in the Czech press, its course was predictable. In London on 10 February he called on Jan Masaryk to complain about Czech treatment of Henlein, once again irritating Masaryk through his bumptiousness.[44] The next day he was received at the Foreign Office by a congenial Lord Cranborne. All augured well, for the latter had just told Parliament that Britain wanted good relations between Germany and Czechoslovakia; Rutha was well informed and thanked Cranborne at the outset.[45] He proceeded to dismiss current Czech talks with the German activist parties and then, reflecting his recent obsession with Czech infiltration of German areas, produced a large ethnic map to illustrate his arguments. Claiming that Prague's real objective was divide and rule, to break up the Sudetenland and obliterate its individuality, he stressed that "the German minority were fully aware of this process and it kept them in a state of constant and increasing exasperation." The result, he concluded, was a radicalization of the population that was hard to control.[46]

While Cranborne made sympathetic noises, Rutha interpreted even more optimistically the circumspect language of Vansittart, whom he met over a long lunch arranged by Christie. Vansittart made it clear that he opposed any frontier changes, any involvement by the Reich, and only believed in a settlement on a Czechoslovak basis. But his comments otherwise chimed harmoniously in emphasizing Czechoslovakia as Europe's real danger point; he accepted completely that there was regional Sudeten socioeconomic distress and that the Czechs, especially Beneš ("an old fox"), were the main obstacle to rapprochement. From this, rightly or wrongly, Rutha deduced there was British support for the Sudeten cause, albeit within a clear Czechoslovak framework. He duly warned that in the face of Czechification, revulsion might reach such a level that "nobody would any longer have the right or the power to refuse the Sudeten Germans their right of self-determination."[47]

This brief sojourn was therefore very satisfactory. It confirmed British anxieties and their tendency to weigh the Sudeten and Czech cases equitably; indeed, in the coming months it led to increased British pressure on Prague to find a solution.[48] Rutha's own confidence may be deduced from the fact that, traveling home, he made a detour to Brussels to try to visit Van Severen so he could compare notes with the charismatic Flemish fascist.[49] However, waiting in Czechoslovakia in mid-February was a veritable storm of press abuse that pushed him into the limelight. Called into question particularly was his "treacherous" propaganda abroad, precisely at a time when Prague was cementing its agreement with the German activist parties.[50]

Rutha's vigorous riposte raised the temperature and drew Czech politicians into the controversy. Over the next three months, he embarked on a series of major public speeches, which, while allowing him to justify his behavior, equally enabled the SdP leadership to exploit his newfound notoriety in order to gain extra publicity. In *Rundschau* on 20 February, he upheld his London visit on the grounds that the British wanted reliable information and were trying to remove European sources of friction; naturally they focused on Czechoslovakia, pressing Prague to negotiate with Henlein. In a crucial passage that was officially censored from the article, Rutha maintained that twenty years of pauperizing the Sudeten Germans had created a "psychological crisis of confidence" in Czechoslovakia, one that needed a Czech solution on a grand scale if it was to avoid a European crisis.[51] A few days later at a rally in the Turn hall in Teplitz, the audience having swelled to six thousand by press coverage, he openly condemned the censorship of his article and countered press claims about mendacious propaganda; rather, he had spoken truthfully in response to eager foreign interest.[52]

The controversy might now have died down, overshadowed by Henlein's speech in late February announcing the SdP nationality laws. Instead, the question of how Rutha had behaved abroad persisted because Krofta resurrected it when defending his own foreign policy before Parliament. According to Czech information sent through from London, Rutha was exaggerating the level of British support that could have been suggested by Vansittart; his interpretation in *Rundschau* was "a gross and dangerous perversion of the facts" that would simply hinder further Czech-German talks.[53] While believing this, and putting his own overly positive slant on British interest in central Europe, Krofta was fully inclined to mistrust Rutha anyway after their angry exchange in Geneva the previous September.[54] This all informed his stance when the parliamentary debates turned to SdP foreign activity. Krofta relayed a skewed assessment of Rutha's words, relying partly on his memory of the outburst in Geneva, partly on his own interpretation of the censored section of the *Rundschau* article: Rutha had been spreading lies abroad by suggesting that Prague had deliberately tried to starve out the German minority. When this provoked a public denial by Rutha as well as uproar among SdP politicians, Krofta quoted the censored passage as proof of Rutha's mendacity.[55]

If we analyze this intense polemic, the unbridgeable gap between the two sides is clear. Both had a specific national view of the international system, both tended to interpret any British interest in the region in a positive light, and both supported their case with some firm moral substance. Neither would accept the other's viewpoint. Krofta saw the SdP as duplicitous, preaching radicalism at home but moderation abroad. It was, he alleged, a contradiction clear to "objective English observers" who would (here the moral slant) compare unsympathetically any undemocratic party with the democratic state of Czechoslovakia. He also, by arguing a narrow legal interpretation of international minority protection (as the League's sole prerogative), used his exposé to refute the SdP's right to any protest abroad; the German minority should not solicit foreign intervention in what was essentially a domestic Czechoslovak business.[56]

Like Krofta, Rutha's arguments had their own moral thread, since he fervently believed in Sudeten hardship and felt he had told London the truth. To large rallies at Komotau and Carlsbad he constantly returned to this theme of his own honesty, firmly denying any lies or treachery. And in explaining international minority protection he was naturally far more flexible than the Czechs, for the League machinery had been found wanting;

not only did Britain and other powers have an international duty to champion cases of minority protection, but the SdP had simply fulfilled their desire for information.[57]

The aftermath of the polemic brought Rutha a novel notoriety, pushing him center stage for the Czech authorities and public to examine.[58] While his speeches were scrutinized, it meant that the press often pounced on trivial incidents, as when he mistakenly traveled first class on a third-class train ticket.[59] As we will see, it also meant regular court summonses in 1937. The new exposure was unwelcome, for he viewed himself chiefly as a facilitator behind the scenes, telling one SdP colleague that he had no political ambition and preferred not to be in the foreground.[60] Even so, the spring of 1937 led in this direction, and probably as much due to SdP calculations as to Rutha's need to satisfy his personal honor. In the course of three months he gave a dozen public speeches, appearing far more frequently to explain the party's foreign perspective. If some were personal performances, at many, such as that before twenty-five thousand people in Carlsbad on 11 April, he marched alongside Henlein and other SdP leaders.[61] He might never quite secure the press coverage of his comrades, but the recent baptism of fire had won him fresh admiration in the party, and it was duly exploited.

While Rutha was usually preaching a party line, he also modified the message based on his own expertise, for the SdP leaders were expected to exercise considerable autonomy over their portfolios. One of the most striking themes in his speeches was that Prague needed to mend its relations with Berlin, something often stressed by the British. It was a logical conclusion in view of Czechoslovakia's deteriorating international position by mid-1937, and the benefits that the Sudetenland might secure if the Czechs (like Austria) submitted to the Third Reich's sphere of influence. In late May, at rallies in north Bohemia, Rutha boldly tied Czech foreign and domestic policies together—exactly the link to Germany that Krofta rejected. Czechoslovakia, he explained, must now draw the realistic conclusion from the collapse of collective security. Instead of hanging on to alliances with outlying states like Yugoslavia or the USSR, Prague should step out of isolation and conclude a neighborly pact with Germany; this could only occur if Sudeten grievances were solved once and for all on the basis of the SdP's nationality laws.[62]

In pushing this theme so forcefully, Rutha played with fire as never before, for he was asking the Czechs to recognize their weak position and succumb to German dominance. His rhetoric at rallies also acquired a tone that could only sound irresponsible and threatening to Czech police observers. Many times he stressed that Germany—the "German motherland"—could not remain indifferent to the Sudeten plight, and advised one audience of SdP faithful to wait loyally "at least until December 1937" to have their problems solved. These pronouncements could easily play into irredentist hands. Even if Rutha often spoke passionately and for dramatic effect to force his own nonviolent Sudeten solution, he increasingly adopted language that came naturally to SdP radicals and was being echoed by the press in Nazi Germany.[63]

THE LIMITS OF INTERNATIONAL LOBBYING

Rutha's new celebrity status coincided with his final diplomatic forays, in Bratislava and London, alongside other international minority lobbyists. Since June 1935 the Henlein movement had exploited the latter assiduously, for they supplied an immediate European platform and cushioned approaches to London with extra respectability. Crucially they had a continental network of enthusiasts who were trying to transform the treatment of minorities in international law, focusing partly on reforming the League of Nations machinery. By 1937 the SdP leadership viewed the League as a spent force, but there still remained hope that European lobbying with British backing might adjust international law, either by strengthening Europe's national minorities or—the more radical course—by enhancing the legal status of Europe's *Volksgruppen* in their struggle against "dominant state nationalities" like the Czechoslovaks.

The three vehicles for lobbying remained the same: the *Verband der deutschen Volksgruppen in Europa* (VDV), the *Deutsche Völkerbundliga (Liga)*, and the ENC (due to meet in London in July). In 1936 Rutha was the Sudeten lynchpin of these three bodies with their overlapping agendas. Since they enhanced his status as a nationality expert to SdP colleagues and to prominent lobbyists like Hasselblatt, he naturally remained in their networks. Nevertheless, the European framework of these organizations was in flux, the League's image rapidly diminishing while the star of Germany rose to lend ever greater significance to pan-German voices. Thus Rutha's final international conferences sounded not just new nationalist undertones but heralded the actual failure of international lobbying in tandem with the slow collapse of the League.

Among the many strands of Rutha's international work, the *Liga* was a smaller iron he kept in the fire. Intermittently, he attended its executive meetings in Prague, securing respect while in turn sensing that, with an eclectic membership committed to helping impoverished Sudeten communities, it still had a moral purpose. Even so, he was a semidetached vice president and usually had other priorities. In February 1937 when Friderich Nelböck resigned as president, pleading ill health and fatigue, Rutha was dismayed but did not take up the mantle as the "tactful and courageous" Nelböck suggested.[64] The choice therefore fell upon a reluctant Alfons Clary-Aldringen, someone whose colorful diary reveals an aristocrat nostalgic for German Bohemia; he was also a biting judge of character, himself scorning Nelböck as "basically erudite but absolutely lacking in tact and flair!"[65]

Probably Rutha envisaged the League of Nations Union as no more than a propaganda and networking tool, and in this spirit he attended its annual June congress in Bratislava. For the *Liga* leadership there were obvious dangers from participating in such a gathering on Czechoslovak soil, one officially sanctioned by the Czechoslovak government and coordinated by the *Liga*'s Czech sister organization (the *Československé sdružení pro Společnost národů*). It might in Czech hands serve as an embarrassing showcase for lauding the state's nationality policy. Here the *Liga*'s dilemma was compounded by its paranoid relationship with the sister–group. The previous winter, tense talks had taken place between the two societies to try to achieve coordination of their strategies, as advised in the statutes of the League of Nations Union. The Czechs had pushed for a close federation, the Germans for a very loose *"groupement national."*[66] In the end the latter prevailed, upholding their respective autonomies while agreeing they would coordinate business on the European stage. Yet the *Liga* remained suspicious of Czech intentions at the congress and refused to co-organize it. On 25 June, on the eve of the congress, when Clary presided over a meeting of the small "groupement" executive in the center of Prague, he noted that while all seemed amicable, "underneath the velvet paws one senses the [Czech] claws." He was sure the relationship would end very badly, perhaps even in Bratislava.[67]

In retrospect when writing publicly about the four-day congress at the Comenius University, Clary glossed over disharmony and noted the zeal of the conference's "minority committee" where Rutha had been the main Sudeten delegate. It had demanded, as usual, a permanent minority commission with teeth at Geneva, and optimistically pressed the League to launch a special inquiry into how minorities were treated across Europe.[68] Yet amid the superficial goodwill in Bratislava, Rutha and other *Liga* delegates were left with a very sour aftertaste. Justifiably they could accuse the Czech organizers of hijacking the event for propaganda purposes. In a speech wholly anathema to Rutha, the head of the *Československé sdružení* not only lauded European collective security but stressed the humanitarian ideals of Czechoslovak foreign policy as espoused by President Beneš.[69]

Worse was to come on 1 July. On behalf of the *Liga*, Rutha made a speech that clearly referenced Czechoslovakia, challenging any state's claim to take the moral high ground and reject international scrutiny if it could not provide security for its own peoples.[70] Simultaneously a storm blew up in the Czech-German relationship. Although the "groupement" had carefully agreed to a public text summarizing the disparate views of the congress's minority committee, the Czech *sdružení* had managed to slip in an extra phrase: "Many delegates stressed that the protection of minorities in Czechoslovakia is of an ideal standard."[71] Rutha and others exploded—but the text had already been dispatched to Czech press and radio. Although it was a minor incident, it reveals well the skin-deep trust within the infant "groupement." Clary was convinced that the Czech "pigs," buoyed up by the Bratislava atmosphere, had acted unscrupulously. He confided to his diary, "I see at last that we can't count at all on their loyalty, let alone their honesty. This definitely changes my theory that we can work with them as friends. It is all very sad and disheartening."[72]

Rutha too concluded that the *Liga* had to preserve its independence to avoid the "spiritual paralysis" so evident in Bratislava under the shadow of Czech propaganda.[73] But there were more profound lessons for his foreign strategy. Clearly the League of Nations was unreformable, and the League of Nations Union as a pressure group was unlikely ever to agree on a concrete agenda for change to the benefit of all *Volksgruppen*. As the SdP press bureau commented acerbically—undoubtedly inspired by Rutha—Bratislava had shown how many League societies were simply "foreign tools" blinkered by national interests; the Union had lost its significance in tandem with the League of Nations it so revered.[74] Needless to say, the SdP (and Rutha) was being thoroughly disingenuous, suggesting that it had a lofty international ideal to set against narrow Czech nationalism. But it was an argument that meshed easily with the vision of restructuring central Europe, just as "international" could be equated with Spannist pan-Germanism.[75] The reality too was that Rutha had worked to secure the Sudeten German nationalist ideal through Europe's international machinery, but to little effect. The major alternative, as always, was to win Great Power support from either Britain or Germany. With this in mind, the ENC in London seemed to promise far more than Bratislava.

This congress not only offered another opportunity for swaying British opinion. It was, unlike the League Union, a small assembly where the German minorities could easily dominate the discussion. Historians have rightly noted that from the mid-1930s the ENC and VDV had become tightly intermeshed and, under Hasselblatt's influence, permeated with a spirit that served Reich interests.[76] Even so, it would be reductionist to suggest that all these enthusiasts were simply following Nazi Germany's agenda. Most were using the international forum to benefit their particular *Volksgruppe*, albeit realizing the advantages of both German solidarity and Reich backing. In retrospect we might view the ENC or VDV as increasingly malleable Nazi tools, but many involved had their own conservative interpretation of the "pax germanica."

This is clear in 1937 from the behavior respectively of the "Henleinist" Rutha and the "semi-Nazi" Hasselblatt.[77] Rutha was the lynchpin not just because he served as a vice president of the ENC, but because in Hasselblatt's eyes the Sudeten problem was the minority issue where London was proving most responsive. Thus through Hasselblatt's influence, the VDV annual conference in Carlsbad in November 1936 had elected Henlein as its new president.[78] While Rutha was absent from Carlsbad, he was keen to exploit this new Sudeten leadership to coordinate more effectively the German *Volksgruppen* and urged Henlein to take up the baton. Here, however, the growing restrictions on SdP behavior became clearer. The German foreign ministry, desiring to keep the VDV on a leash, forbade the independent direction, and Hasselblatt dutifully obeyed.[79] Indeed, Hasselblatt as "Hitler's man" probably scuppered several initiatives that Rutha contemplated for linking together the German national diaspora.[80] Behind the SdP scenes his role is shadowy, akin to an eminence grise with his own agenda. In early 1937 he was an unofficial adviser on the SdP nationality laws, consistently promoting the SdP cause in his journal, *Nation und Staat*. Later he focused on the ENC, where he hoped to repeat the success of the "London Action" and took care to ensure that the German delegation would be entirely *völkisch* and sing from the same radical hymn sheet.[81]

As the congress loomed, the Czechoslovak foreign ministry became nervous about further Sudeten propaganda abroad. Just when Czechoslovakia's alliance system was visibly weakening and Reich press attacks were mounting, Krofta knew well that the British wanted Prague to talk to Henlein to prevent Germany meddling and exacerbating international tensions. The Foreign Office even warned Prague about the mistakes the British themselves had made in ignoring Irish nationalists.[82] Probably it was this combination of external pressures that led Krofta in mid-June to make conciliatory noises to Rutha. In view of their recent polemic the contact is surprising, but it suggests a lingering mutual perception that neither was quite a radical and that compromise was possible. Rutha on this occasion apparently suggested the SdP could cooperate with the government, perhaps even enter it, if the state guaranteed national equality. For Krofta the sticking point was the SdP nationality laws, now Henlein's new baseline and wholly unacceptable as they would split the state along national lines.[83] On both sides, nevertheless, the conversation offered a glimmer and was duly noticed in London. For the SdP it coincided with draft plans, opportunistically formulated, whereby it might even join a Czechoslovak coalition government with Rutha as a state secretary at the foreign ministry.[84] For the Czechs too the loose Krofta-Rutha liaison had repercussions. Even if Krofta was still irritated at SdP propaganda, the ground was being smoothed for a first meeting between Henlein and Hodža a few months later.

Meanwhile in London, the ENC was being organized as a grand publicity exercise. The aim was to stir up British public opinion and encourage official sympathy for changing international law to the benefit of the German diaspora.[85] Tapping into British anxieties, Hasselblatt gave the Sudeten question special attention; on 26 June in Vienna the ENC executive agreed that Rutha would deliver "the Sudeten German speech" at the conference. Since the content was left vague, Rutha first formulated it in general terms, as a broad appeal for England to protect the rights of European *Volksgruppen*.[86] The final version, however, was much tighter, effectively displaying the SdP nationality laws as a model for European implementation. This reflected an aggressively confident SdP agenda at home and Rutha's own willingness to proclaim it abroad. Equally it showed how the Henlein movement, buoyed up by Germany's ascendency and frustrated at Czech opposition, was dangerously intertwined with a potentially open-ended pan-German program.

How far Rutha's performance in London was schooled by Hasselblatt or coordinated with Henlein is unknown, but building on his frustration in Bratislava there was a discernable radical shift. When the ENC met on 14–15 July, drawing thirty official delegates to Westminster, many speeches pandered to the British by advocating reform of the League of Nations.[87] However, the main tone in discussions was to acknowledge the League's failure over minority rights, proposing instead that all states submit to a special international law to reinforce the legal position of nationalities as collective groups.

This was the thrust of Rutha's speech, which he summarized later at a reception at the House of Commons. Arguing for national self-administration across Europe, he set out the SdP laws for creating national registers and called for understanding in view of Britain's notable record on state devolution. Claiming that "self-administration means peace," he ended with a veiled warning: "Europe's fate depends to a large degree on whether, after the shock to the minorities' faith in an international order, . . . a legal protection of their rights in the majority-national states is successful." He urged the responsible statesmen of Europe to act.[88]

It was a sign of Rutha's reputation that the Czech press singled out this speech as a "new provocation" and distorted it to a degree that the courts even considered prosecuting him for treason.[89] Allegedly he had warned Europe of a catastrophe and the intervention of the German motherland if the minority problem was not settled. It was ostentatious language that has been repeated since by Czech historians, implying that the speech was "menacing" and Rutha a covert irredentist in cahoots with Berlin.[90]

Where Prague's anxieties had more solid foundation was over the further triumph of Sudeten propaganda in London. In contrast to Bratislava, Rutha felt very satisfied at the congress, especially the interest shown by the British press; he had conversed with journalists and his speech had appeared in the *Times*.[91] He had also—uniquely among the conference participants— secured another interview with Lord Cranborne at the Foreign Office. There on 16 July he dwelled particularly on the SdP nationality laws and mentioned his recent conciliatory conversation with Krofta. One might read this simply as a cunning move to entice the British unwittingly to back a radical solution in the Bohemian lands. Yet we can also suggest plausibly that Rutha was sincere when hinting that a Czech-SdP domestic settlement—moderate in his own eyes—might be salvaged if only a little more pressure was exercised from London. The words had their effect, for thereafter the Foreign Office continued to press Prague to be more "cooperative" with the SdP.[92]

And there was a key postscript that indicates Rutha's own direction. A month later he was taking part with the rest of the SdP leadership in a mass celebration for Sudeten war veterans in Carlsbad.[93] By chance he met there a German Bohemian aristocrat who offered to be a liaison between the SdP and the Czechoslovak government in order to facilitate a meeting between Henlein and Hodža. Rutha welcomed it and clearly encouraged Henlein on that course. The upshot on 16 September was a first encounter of the two protagonists. Although it was friendly, the divergent viewpoints remained, for while Hodža spoke about the February agreement and his opposition to international interference, Henlein dwelt on the SdP laws and "a fundamental legal solution of Sudeten German-Czech relations." Learning quickly the substance of the talks, Rutha was convinced that, despite Hodža's objections, the pressure on Prague from London and Berlin must continue.[94]

While the London ENC was Rutha's last appearance on the international stage, the steady evidence of British support offered an illuminated path forward for the SdP. Thus Rutha arranged through Christie that in early October together with Henlein he would pay another visit to London, this time to meet Vansittart; his own diplomatic role, personally responsible to Henlein, was also confirmed on 24 September.[95] Yet from the summer a strong shift in the parameters of that mission could be anticipated. Most notably, while the influence of Britain and Germany was ever more dominant, Rutha realized that the role of the international lobbyists was dwindling. Although he did not sever links with the *Liga* or the ENC, the former had shown its limitations while the latter's potential to effect change would soon be found wanting. Hasselblatt might rightly proclaim the ENC's short-term impact in London, but the British Foreign Office was largely indifferent to congress resolutions while Berlin was starting to withdraw its support.[96]

In other words, for the Henlein movement the real potential for an international breakthrough seemed to lie solely in London or Berlin, not in Geneva or in incestuous discussions among the German diaspora (except perhaps in Austria). Rutha himself had slowly moved in this direction in tandem with the international power shift of 1936–1937, but until the end he maintained several irons in the fire while giving precedence to Britain. How then he would have viewed Henlein's letter to Hitler in November 1937 is hypothetical. Notwithstanding his own drift in a more radical direction, he might still have balked at such a dangerous leap.

RESULTS: A SUDETEN FOREIGN POLICY

Analyzing the SdP's foreign mission, as carried out by its leading exponent, reveals how far it had to be steadily adapted to the peculiar international circumstances of 1935–1937. Rutha's long-term goal was not irredentist, for he did not wish the Third Reich to annex "German Bohemia." But he and others like Walter Brand certainly envisaged an idealistic confluence of loyalty to nation and state, a "big solution" for central Europe, which at its heart would usher in a Spannist experiment for the Bohemian lands.[97] Sudeten German dominance would be reasserted over what they saw as their own space, whether just the borderlands or deeper into Czech territory. As an anticipated minimum, this meant the radical reconstruction of Czechoslovakia into a "state of nationalities," one permitting an authoritarian solution for the Sudetenland. Czech commentators at the time, and many historians since, have correctly portrayed the SdP as wholly at odds with the Czech nationalist democracy of the interwar period. Nevertheless, Rutha's foreign policy was pragmatic, perceiving from 1935 that traditional international routes should be exploited in order to pressurize Prague while preserving European peace. One was the League of Nations—the SdP trumpeting its reform in unison with a range of existing German lobbying bodies. Another was Great Britain, the most influential European power, since London was consistently sympathetic to Sudeten grievances about Czech domination.

If in 1935–1936 the Czechoslovak government had called the Henleinists' bluff, they might have been forced awkwardly to scale back their demands. Instead, after their electoral victory they lacked any real success at home, and gained solace in 1936 from the diplomatic revolution occurring abroad. It was entirely understandable that, as the Versailles system crumbled, as Czechoslovakia's European position disintegrated, they felt a fresh confidence and shifted their program in an openly more radical direction. Rutha himself understood well the international upheaval that was occurring but continued to follow familiar diplomatic paths. Probably he equivocated over Nazi Germany's increasing interference, for Reich radicals, together with the SdP Nazi faction, threatened German Bohemia with a perilous solution. Yet as R. W. Seton-Watson perceptively observed, the notion that Nazi Germany posed a threat often seems to have been sublimated; in Rutha's loose Spannist vision, the "German motherland" was a natural source of support for the German diaspora. His dilemma in 1937 was that an "irresponsible" violent solution loomed much larger. In the face of that he maintained his Cassandra role abroad. But his links in Austria hint too at a possible shift in outlook by the summer, a practical realization that the pan-German framework for the Sudeten Germans might also have to be a Third Reich framework.

At the end, Rutha's foreign mission might be judged successful. Even if reforming the League of Nations was a dead end, the commotion stirred abroad was bearing fruit at home as Prague at last started direct high-level talks with the SdP. Most productive had been Rutha's visits to London—his special diplomatic option—for there, through Christie, he had constructed many relationships. This was not simply "mendacious SdP propaganda" as some historians continue to insist.[98] On the contrary, he was sincere over the righteousness of the Sudeten cause, opportunistically finding the best arguments to convince London. Certainly like Henlein he minimized the SdP's ties to the Reich, but it was a tactical move in order to win over the British for a peaceful Sudeten solution, not part of a duplicitous strategy that craftily concealed an irredentist program.

The very nature of Rutha's diplomacy, moderate and radical in its various hues, explains why British officialdom responded so positively to the Sudeten German cause. His impact resonated in London well into 1938, as the Czechoslovak crisis escalated and the British continued to sympathize. By that time, however, the international framework had shifted once again; Henlein and his peers were contemplating the Reich-centered form of pan-Germanism as the only salvation for the Sudeten nationalist mission.

TEN

The Cell

On 20 April 1937 Heinz Rutha celebrated his fortieth birthday and met up at a north Bohemian mountain retreat with former youth disciples. One of them, Walter Rohn, had just published a long eulogy in the journal he edited, *Volk und Führung*, highlighting his hero's didactic and international missions, his "chivalry, generosity and love of truth."[1] From all corners of Rutha's career the congratulations flowed in (fig.23). Cousins wished him good health, local Sudeten German Party (SdP) leaders thanked him for his vision, and from Prague, Maria Aull praised his role in the *Deutsche Völker-bundliga (Liga)*. Most striking were the sentiments of his youth acolytes, past and present. According to one: "Lucky are the youths you have inspired and assembled in the magic of our native landscape, giving meaning to their confused existence." Another, Werner Weiss, assured Rutha that "while previously we stood unconsciously under the compelling force of a person-ality who far outstripped all contemporaries, recently we realized how you clearly foresaw and showed the way we had to take to escape our spiritual misery." Serving this great task, Rutha had been steadfast and his enemies unable to touch him.[2]

Six months later, Rutha was languishing in a prison cell. On the after-noon of 6 October, just as he had been preparing to accompany Konrad Henlein by train to England, he was arrested in Prague by two Czech policemen. Wearing a sharp grey suit and a coffee-brown hat, he was escorted from Hybernská to the main police station, and that evening trans-ported north to Reichenberg into the hands of the local police who had requested his detention. At 11:40 p.m. they noted down his basic personal details and charged him under §129b of the Czech criminal code.[3] It was a law inherited from the Austrian Empire that criminalized homosexuality as a "sexual offence against nature," proscribing "any act where sexual gratification is sought or found on the body of a person of the same sex."[4]

HOMOSEXUALITY AND ARREST

Events quickly unfolded in what became the most prominent homosexual scandal of interwar Czechoslovakia.[5] Yet despite the flurry of press coverage in late 1937, the circumstances surrounding the arrest were swathed in mystery and have remained so ever since. Most commentators, often presuming innocence, have suggested that Rutha's enemies somehow connived to bring about his demise. Some have merely hinted at antagonists behind the scenes, echoing Henlein himself who in his first comments in Rutha's defense spoke about the "dark powers" at work.[6]

According to Rutha's sister, Gretel, the use of §129b was always only an excuse, an example of the base methods used by political and personal foes to eliminate him from public life: "My brother's enemies had achieved their goal, discrediting him as a man, neutralizing him politically and destroying him physically."[7] The "enemies" might be construed as either the Czech authorities, who self-evidently took the prosecution forward, or some hidden parties who deliberately allowed incriminating evidence to fall into Czech hands. Some newspapers even speculated that London's Scotland Yard had tipped off the Czech police about Rutha frequenting homosexual clubs in England.[8] More realistically, the finger immediately pointed at a malevolent intrigue by the Nazi *Aufbruch* circle within the SdP, the climax of a struggle that had been rumbling on for years. This has become the most common speculation, although denied by some closest to events, like Walter Rohn.[9] From this theory of Nazi conspiracy it was then only a short step to suggest that Rutha's removal was in fact a preemptive strike from the Third Reich, the work of Germany's intelligence service in league with Sudeten Nazi operators.[10] A reexamination of the evidence suggests some truth in this conjecture. Two groups in particular, the Czech police in Reichenberg and some malcontents linked to *Aufbruch,* were crucial in setting the case in motion. But a third element was fundamental, though often dismissed by Sudeten apologists: this was Rutha's sexuality and the suspicion from diverse sources that he had committed "homosexual acts."

Much of the police documentation referred to events in 1935 or earlier. In that year Rutha had been shaken by the public accusations of homosexuality and, probably to escape embarrassment, had agreed to Henlein's foreign commission in return for surrendering his Turn office. Though unsubstantiated, there are hints that Henlein at that time learned about Rutha's "disposition" but resolved to stand by him.[11] Thereafter, the foreign envoy was intensely busy and often absent from north Bohemia. His attendance at youth gatherings became sporadic, usually confined to vacations; his youth mission was concentrated almost exclusively on the leadership school at Wartenberg, which he could easily visit when at home in Kunnersdorf.

Despite this and the extreme schedule Rutha set for himself over the next two years, his life remained peppered with chance or deliberate encounters with young men. After the whiff of scandal in 1935, the intricate network of youth friendships had not disappeared, as most disciples stayed loyal; nor had his own sexual inclinations, for although sublimated they regularly surfaced. His surviving extensive correspondence with mature youths confirms this. When abroad in Glasgow and London in 1936 he encountered several attractive young men whom he hoped to meet again, and his brief liaison with the Flemish leader Joris van Severen also held some erotic spark.[12] Nearer home, even if the homosocial world was diminished, he actively galvanized his youth network by encouraging visits to Kunnersdorf. In September 1937, an eighteen-year-old art student, Fritz Gelinek, who the previous summer had masturbated with Werner Weiss while staying at the Rutha mill, was again invited and asked to bring some drawings of youths' heads.[13] Many young men arrived by invitation, but others made spontaneous pilgrimages to seek advice from their mentor. As one youth leader observed, "I turned to Rutha because I trusted him completely to advise me correctly. He won my trust through his whole bearing and the way he devoted himself to every task including the youth movement."[14]

Rutha now had less time to read poetry to acolytes in his private library in imitation of his own spiritual leader, Stefan George. However, the material the police confiscated in October 1937 included many books he had presented to friends and inscribed with quotations from George's poetry. To Wolfgang Heinz on his twenty-first birthday he sent a study of Plato by Robert Boehringer (a George disciple) and added a stanza from George's mystical *Star of the Covenant*. A few months later, after Heinz in February 1936 had spent some days with Rutha in the Salzburg Alps, he received a book on German art prefaced with lines from the apocalyptic *Seventh Ring*.[15] The idea that a new era was dawning for a Sudeten male elite seemed entirely appropriate at that time. Rutha inscribed another visionary stanza from the *Seventh Ring* when he sent Boehringer's Plato to Werner Weiss "with true affection" on his birthday:

> I saw from afar the tumult of a battle
> And how it came to crash upon our plain.
> I saw the small crowd standing round the banner.
> But all the rest would never see the same.[16]

Enthused by his loose network of disciples, Rutha always cherished a few who were not just loyal but charismatic and enticing company. Such for instance was the blond-haired twenty-year-old, Willi Hoffmann, whom he described modestly to the Czech police as a "decent man."[17] Hoffmann had long flourished in the Reichenberg youth movement, and his firm stance in late 1935 backing Rutha's treatment of Turner malcontents probably brought them closer together.[18] Well into 1936, Hoffmann regularly cycled over Mount Jeschken to the Rutha mill, the trips only interrupted when that autumn he secured a post as a chemist in Freiwaldau in distant Silesia; there he also became district Turn youth leader. From this point Rutha's attitude became quite obsessive, revealing in persistent letters the value he set on their friendship but also a loneliness that accompanied his intensive work schedule. Although he hoped Hoffmann would visit Kunnersdorf on New Year's Eve 1936, he found himself sitting alone in the mill, and abruptly, his first resolution on 1 January was to make a surprise visit by car to Frei-waldau. When this proved abortive because of the snow he returned home irritated, deciding instead to arrange a meeting in Prague where they might attend a classical concert. Typically, he instructed Hoffmann on how to appear, dressed in a dark suit; typically, he was affronted at the young man's cursory negative reply.[19]

Rutha's full diary as well as Hoffmann's evasion conspired to scupper any encounter for months. But as Rutha confided, "I think about you daily and really want to know what you are doing and whether you are with the [Turner] youths."[20] The feelings were not one-sided, but they were certainly unequal; Hoffmann, as a man half Rutha's age, was less solicitous, his time taken up with other preoccupations and friendships. Only at Easter 1937 did he briefly visit Kunnersdorf with his parents, perhaps thereby atoning for what Rutha had termed the "long-missed hours." Rutha reciprocated with a visit to Silesia in late April; on the SdP lecture circuit he was scheduled to make a Mayday speech at Freiwaldau, so could spend an evening with Hoffmann at a youth festival.[21] This finally seemed to puncture an obsession ratcheted up by distance, for thereafter his correspondence was less frenetic: there was no recrimination on either side when they spent their summer holidays separately with other friends.

When the Reichenberg police arrested Hoffmann in October 1937, they were sure that the copious correspondence pointed to "unnatural links," with Hoffmann trying "to conceal everything that might reinforce a suspicion of his homosexual relations with Rutha."[22] Even if the evidence failed to suggest any physical sexual intimacy (which Hoffmann only confessed to with Weiss), it seemed to speak volumes about Rutha's own emotions. When it came to sexual acts, however, as proscribed under §129b, it was the alleged incidents in 1932–1934 with Weiss, Adolf Wagner, and Franz Veitenhansl that would be most damning. The police also closely scrutinized his behavior in August 1937.

There were increasing signs in the last year of his life that Rutha's health was suffering because of intense public activity. In June he felt ill, possibly due to osteoporosis or a recurrent heart problem, and was uncertain about attending the European Nationalities Congress in London; afterward he resolved to take an "urgently necessary" vacation in the mountains to recover.[23] The events that followed would form a key part of the Czech prosecution case. In early August, he arranged a traditional expedition to explore the eastern Alps and invited four young men to accompany him. They included the faithful Wolfgang Heinz and Karl Hanke, but also a nineteen-year-old, Kurt Franzke, who as a Turner had attended the Wartenberg camp and several times enjoyed hospitality at Kunnersdorf. The week-long trip to Tyrol was designed to take in the landscape around Innsbruck and Bolzano, dramatic terrain that Rutha since 1918 had found so awesome. Driving to the Brenner pass, they crossed the Italian border and from accommodation in farmhouses made daily hikes into the mountains.[24]

When the police interrogated Franzke two months later, the blond youth described the "homosexual intercourse" that allegedly had taken place. Twice when staying in the same room in a guest house, he had been summoned to Rutha's bed and obeyed without resistance: "As I lay down in his bed, Rutha put his arm around me, kissed me, then took my genitals in his hand and stimulated them until ejaculation while I held his genitals in my hand. When I came, Rutha dried the semen with a handkerchief and after I had lain in bed with him a while I went back to my bed. In Rutha's bed I lay in my pajamas and he also had his pajamas on."[25] The intimacy between the *erastes* and his *eromenos* was welcome to both parties and had a sequel later in the summer. In early September, Rutha together with his elder sisters made an outing to Franzke's home town in Silesia, met the youth's family, and invited him again to visit Kunnersdorf. Franzke arrived a few days later, stayed for over a week, and again it came to "intercourse" in Rutha's private quarters. In the police protocol the language set down was formulaic and matched almost precisely the earlier sexual description. Nevertheless, there seems little doubt that, even if prompted by detectives, Franzke was telling the truth. He explained to the Czech investigating magistrate that he had acted voluntarily, understanding the intimacy with Rutha as a "sign of friendship," an extra closeness to someone he venerated for his great pedagogic influence. It was a statement he stood by. Rutha in contrast rejected it, denying there had been any sexual liaison or that he had "abused the young lad."[26]

The way that Rutha interpreted this is telling. However modest his experience of physical sex, he continued to interpret such intimacy as fine and didactic, an integral part of a noble youth mission that permitted a platonic outlet for his sexual urges. The "world force" of Eros continued to cast its spell. Even so, it seems highly probable that his old anxieties about homosexuality persisted, resurfacing in the wake of the 1935 "outing." Possibly it was in May 1937, when visiting Silesia, that he finally sought out a doctor to gain some reassurance about his sexuality. According to skimpy secondhand evidence, the doctor, a nephew of the old Wandervogel leader Karl Metzner, examined Rutha and confirmed that he had not committed homosexual "offences" (which presumably excluded acts of mutual masturbation).[27]

Rutha was surely relieved and acted upon it. It explains one of his most cryptic statements to the Czech authorities in October. While fervently denying he was "homosexually inclined," he said he intended soon to marry: "I wish for private reasons not to divulge the name of the lady as she is a lady of society."[28] This might be construed as disingenuous, to reassert his normality under interrogation. However, it can be verified from several sources, not least from a myth that was repeated later in the Rutha family. According to Gretel Rutha, her brother in his last year was planning to marry Maria Habrmann, a vivacious thirty-year-old from Bodenbach who regularly visited the mill and herself expected a good marriage.[29] This is substantiated by

a rare letter that Rutha wrote to his "fiancée" from prison, in which he anticipated their future life together.[30] Possibly in 1937 he realized at last the
social necessity of such a liaison and, after the medical verdict, felt more
confident about such a relationship that he could link to a classical Greek
model. The *erastes* would finally marry but, as in the past, might continue to
embrace the spiritual and even physical Eros of young men.

It seems unlikely, if Rutha moved in this conventional direction, that he
acted through any knowledge or fear of the Czech law on homosexuality.
Rather, any personal dangers he felt as foreign minister stemmed not from
his private life but from the political world where he periodically warned the
SdP and Turn leaderships to curb disloyalty and disruptive criticism. While
certainly sensing an underlying threat to his own position from *Aufbruch*
agitators who were publicly assaulting the so-called "KB clique," he expected
obstinately that Henlein and other comrades would successfully impose
national unity and drown out the dissidents. After all, his SdP foreign policy
in the summer of 1937 still appeared quite fruitful. And in late July at a
major Turn rally at Aussig that he attended, his three-stage youth education
was prominently on display, demonstrating well the advance of the youth
mission in the face of skeptics.[31]

Indeed, probably what Rutha found more irksome and dangerous in 1935–
1937 was the behavior of the Czech authorities. Not only was he slowly
becoming a target of the tabloid press, but the Czech state police in the
border areas were increasingly vigilant over German miscreants who were
endangering state security. Consequently, Rutha's arrest in October 1937
was not sui generis but followed a series of incidents. In May 1935 he had
been apprehended in Reichenberg on a minor excuse and taken to the local
police station.[32] In 1937, as his public profile rose, so did the attention he
received from the police. On 13 January he was summoned to court in Leitmeritz for suggesting at an SdP meeting that Czechoslovakia's alliance with
the USSR might lead to the Sudetenland being bombed; he was acquitted
when his defense lawyer argued that critical discussion was surely vital in a
democracy. On 19 June he was again in court in Niemes to defend a speech
he had made in Komotau. He tried to maintain he had always spoken in
"absolutely moderate" language; in the end, however, the police officer's para-
phrase of the speech seemed unreliable, so the prosecution case was dropped.
Both of these court appearances show his infamy by 1937 in the eyes of the
border police: similar prosecutions were pending at the time of his arrest.[33]

It was this local police vigilance coupled with some elements of chance that produced the personal disaster in October. Although many Reichenberg police documents have been destroyed, enough have survived to show how the investigation began and how far any *Aufbruch* enemies were involved.[34] On 25 August, Reichenberg detectives had apprehended one individual, Wilhelm Purm, on suspicion of involvement in military espionage that threatened national security; it was probably routine and paralleled hundreds of comparable arrests at this time.[35] Before his release Purm denied that he had ever done anything criminal, and then stressed that he had never been a homosexual, as sometimes rumored, nor did he know any homosexuals. He noted, however, that at a Turn event in Reichenberg in 1935 he had first heard that Gau leader Rutha was a "warm brother" *[warmer Bruder]*. Why Purm made this link for the police is unclear; it may have been a casual remark, or perhaps deliberate, since it seems clear from a later SdP inquiry that he was an *Aufbruch* supporter.[36]

Yet from this point it required the Czech authorities to take the case further. A month intervened before more arrests, suggesting that some detectives deliberately pursued threads that would lead to Rutha. This might be interpreted as logical police procedure, on a par with increased Czech vigilance against any "outsiders" to national society including homosexuals, for other prosecutions under §129b were public knowledge at the time.[37] Indeed, there are interesting parallels here between the Czech police behavior and that of their more notorious counterparts in Nazi Germany. It seems quite likely that what historians have suggested for the Reich by 1936–1937 is equally applicable in "liberal" Czechoslovakia: namely that there was a heightened vigilance against sexual deviants but that arrests usually resulted not from any active police surveillance but from private denunciations, naturally more serious if connected to other political or social crimes.[38]

In the Rutha case, the suspicion must linger that after the first hint of sexual deviance, the Reichenberg police targeted Rutha because of his notoriety as a national threat. Most significantly, it was viewed as no common criminal case and therefore was handled not by the ordinary crime office, let alone the vice squad, but by a special department or political division that investigated cases of national security. Two senior Czech officers took charge, Superintendent Jaroš and Inspector Vilém Klement; the latter, on his own admission, was well-versed in handling "homosexual cases."[39]

Their investigation slowly led from Purm to one of Purm's acquaintances,

Rudi Hein, who was only too ready to make a statement incriminating Rutha. Hein's involvement was the happy continuation of his personal vendetta rather than any wider conspiracy by either *Aufbruch* or Nazi Germany. It is true that *Aufbruch* in 1937 was slowly flexing its muscles again and openly spreading propaganda.[40] In July, Walter von Lierau, the Nazi consul in Reichenberg, noted rising tensions in the SdP: the "opposition" was more coordinated and had been appealing to the Reich for support. If in the SdP leadership recalcitrants like Rudolf Kasper were again vocal, in the regional Turn movement there was dissent from individuals whom Rutha had formerly trusted.[41]

Nevertheless, the radicals were as surprised as anyone else at Hein's denunciation of Rutha, and the Prague police found no incriminating evidence when in early October they searched the offices of the *Aufbruch* newspaper.[42] Nor has any evidence emerged that proves either a Reich conspiracy to topple Rutha for his sexual or political deviance or that Hein had backing from radicals in Germany for his private plot—notwithstanding Hein's own attempts to muster support in the Reich. After his initial approach to Lierau in September 1935, Hein had tried to plead his case with the Hitler Youth leadership in Germany, hoping they would intervene, but he failed to make an impact either there or with Lierau.[43] It was in the face of this rebuff, and aware of the rising confidence of local radical forces, that he must have welcomed the sudden approach from the Czech police.

When Inspector Klement questioned him on 1 October, Hein readily explained his personal battle of 1935, how he had realized Rutha's "sick disposition" and persuaded Franz Veitenhansl to deposit a statement with a Reichenberg lawyer. He now agreed to fetch this for the police.[44] It was crucial evidence, for Veitenhansl had not only described Rutha's "seduction" but listed other young men who had stayed overnight at the mill, such as Werner Weiss, Adolf Wagner, and Walter Rohn; both Wagner and Kurt Gansel were alleged to have shared a bed with their host.

The detectives of the political division brought the first three in for questioning and searched their homes. At this stage they still also flirted with their original line of inquiry into military espionage, but rapidly they were drowned in a flood of evidence tied to §129b. While little was secured from Rohn, both Weiss and Wagner when subject to tough interrogation broke down and made statements that incriminated Rutha and others. Weiss became the key axis around which the forthcoming case would revolve, for apart from the alleged sexual acts with Rutha, he detailed his encounters with a dozen other youths over a number of years.[45] The "homosexual inter-course" he described amounted at most to mutual masturbation, often during youth expeditions at home or abroad but sometimes pursued at Kunnersdorf. The police, therefore, sensing that Rutha had perpetrated and facilitated homosexual acts among vulnerable young men (aged under twenty-one), issued a warrant for his arrest as well.

From this point the rumors mounted that Rutha was the victim of a complex political intrigue. In fact the circumstances appear to be more mundane if no less explosive in their political outcome. Since 1935, there was much material accumulated about Rutha's sexuality for his enemies to exploit at an opportune moment. For disgruntled individuals like Hein that opportunity arrived in late 1937 through sheer chance. Yet it was the initiative of the Czech political police in Reichenberg—state police in the borderland—that was decisive. In the summer they secured enticing leads that senior officers doggedly pursued because of Rutha's national status. There was undoubtedly much truth in Lierau's first comment (before he even learned of Rutha's arrest): "All appearances indicate that the local police intend to make an affair out of this for the party [SdP] in order to damage it publicly."[46]

This is not to suggest that the machinations were part of a wider Czech political conspiracy to topple Rutha, for there is no evidence of direct involvement by Prague. Some months before the case broke, rumors about Rutha's sexuality seem to have reached both Edvard Beneš and Jan Masaryk, but what they were is unknown.[47] Beneš would also be sent documents from the police investigation, showing that his aides realized the case's political import. But in October neither the president nor other Czech leaders saw fit to intervene in a scandal that was bound to embarrass the SdP; from afar, Masaryk saw the arrest as "an absolutely German affair, neither provoked nor encouraged by the government."[48] It was consistently portrayed by the authorities simply as a criminal investigation under §129b, although in fact the context was firmly political, something suspected by many observers of the Czech political scene. In short, at a time of heightened national tensions the state police were naturally vigilant, focusing on any individuals who seemed to be straying from safe national, political, or sexual norms. In 1937 this was as much the case in the tense nationalist environment of Czechoslovakia as in totalitarian Nazi Germany. Rutha under several criteria appeared to be a man who was defying the forces of order, so the local police in Reichenberg acted unilaterally and investigated.

THE SCANDAL

When Rutha was questioned in Reichenberg by Superintendent Jaroš, he vehemently denied that he was homosexual or had any experience of "homosexual intercourse." He challenged the statements by Weiss, Wagner, and Veitenhansl as "malicious inventions," questioning why they should suddenly besmirch what had been hearty friendships. He was also quite prepared to outline his youth mission, the "spiritual education" that had drawn youths to Kunnersdorf, even confirming the Turner unrest of 1935 and how he had settled the libel about his sexual abnormality at a public meeting. For the detectives, this picture of a fervent teacher meshed well with statements from others. Walter Rohn waxed lyrical about his mentor's pedagogic passion, comparing him to Plato and Shakespeare: "[Rutha is] one of the most productive and expressive personalities I have ever met. He is of an intuitive nature with a decidedly cultural disposition and a highly creative urge."[49]

The police largely ignored these sentiments, focusing on anything in the homosocial evidence that corresponded to their interpretation of homosexuality, whether it was excessive male bonding, closet readings in Rutha's library, or his simple generosity with gifts to young men. The ringleader might well deny all sexual contacts, but the corroborating statements of Weiss and Wagner—who had little reason to lie—seemed to prove otherwise. Extra confirmation was Rutha's "generally suspicious behavior toward adolescents as it emerges from the witness protocols, from confiscated correspondence [Hoffmann's], and also from the words of the accused himself."[50] On 9 October, as the detectives broadened the scope of their arrests and interrogations, Rutha was transferred to the courthouse in Böhmisch Leipa, to a cell where he would be confined for the next month.

In the outside world, the scandal had now exploded in the Czech and German press, confronting an embarrassed SdP leadership. Their opponents claimed that Henlein had long known about Rutha's sexuality but concealed it: "the sparrows in the party" had long been twittering about what really went on at Rutha's *"moulin rouge."*[51] This, however, only rings true if Rutha's homosocial world had been perceived as homosexual and immoral; in fact it required a lively press campaign coupled with the Czech prosecution to suggest such a clear interpretation. On learning of Rutha's arrest, the SdP leaders had convened, immediately assuming that political machinations were at work; two of them, including Hans Neuwirth, visited Reichenberg and returned convinced that alongside §129b there was indeed some covert political dimension.[52] Henlein suggested as much in a bold speech at a harvest festival in Leitmeritz. Lauding Rutha as "one of my most exposed and most successful protagonists" who was now fighting for his honor, he attacked those left-wing newspapers who were already indulging in a "perverse love of sensation and an inner relish" at SdP discomfort.[53] In the following weeks the SdP press maintained a reserved, almost silent stance, much to the scorn of its opponents. Henlein in fact was unnerved and kept his distance (termed "ostrich behavior" by the Czech press), just as he would eventually stay well away from Rutha's funeral.[54]

The affair was immediately pounced on by Czech and German left-wing and tabloid journalists. Their behavior serves as a classic example of how a modern homosexual scandal was manufactured and exploited unscrupulously. The arguments suggest their distaste for "abnormal sexual practices" in liberal Czechoslovakia, or at least what they felt would resonate with the public. An immediate reference point was to equate the affair with that of Ernst Röhm in 1934 in Nazi Germany, when, in the "Night of the Long Knives," Hitler had "personally" eliminated his homosexual rival. Like Röhm, the papers revealed, Rutha's abnormality was betrayed by his Nazi enemies; the only difference was the outcome, for Henlein under the rules of Czechoslovak democracy could not just shoot the deviant.[55]

This sexual-ideological parallel was then pushed further. The Czechoslovak left-wing press, both socialist and communist, repeatedly suggested a proven link between homosexuality and fascism, an ideology allegedly tied to perverted practices and now effectively on trial (here the SdP was fully equated with Nazism). It was a stereotype long constructed by the left, in Germany as in Czechoslovakia, but one now reinvigorated through the Rutha scandal.[56] Although the Czechoslovak Social Democrats had usually opposed punishing homosexuals, the socialist press seized upon sexual deviance as a political weapon with which to attack the right.[57] It was, ironically, a tactic quite akin to that of the Nazi Gestapo, who only a few years later would be wielding the same weapon against the same Sudeten target.

For Czechoslovakia's tabloid press, whether Czech or German, it was gossip about Rutha's own behavior that was naturally the focus in order to illustrate the "homosexual pestilence" infecting the SdP. Most vivid were homophobic pieces in the *Prager Illustrierte Montag* of Walter Tschuppik (fig.24). Tschuppik was a German Jew who had suffered Nazism at first hand, but his own victimhood did not prevent him repeating scurrilous rumors or probing the sexual pathology of German nationalism. Under one headline, "Orgies in Kunnersdorf," he imagined a symposium with Rutha's Männerbund enjoying "bacchant pleasures," drinking wine until dawn from ancient Greek bowls. Elsewhere he portrayed homosexuality as "a typical new-German vice, an abnormal product of the Männerbünde . . . whose exaggerated claims to power stem from inferiority." Rutha's own "unsavory Männerbund," moreover, was nowhere near the classical Greek ideal: "For here young lads were systematically trained by homosexual experts, and no insolent reference to Greece and Goethe, no dabbling in the poetry of Hölderlin or Stefan George can excuse that." Rutha in short was a "pederast" and should be prosecuted with all severity.[58]

The accusation that Rutha had inveigled adolescents or minors formed a core element in much of the press onslaught. It allowed for some flippant Czech wordplay since the esteemed mentor had proved to be not a *vůdce* (leader) but a *svůdce* (seducer).[59] Some commentators labored the point that a crime under §129b was not the real issue, nor (supposedly) was Rutha's notoriety as Henlein's diplomat. The matter of public concern was Rutha using his pedagogic authority as a cover for sexually abusing innocent youths. Although a comparison was made to the Eulenburg sex scandal of late imperial Germany, the Rutha case was deemed far worse precisely because it affected young people under twenty-one. Thus the anti-SdP media dramatized how this "disgusting news" was affecting the German electorate. Supposedly, members were hemorrhaging away from a party that had proved hypocritical over moral values; parents in turn were outraged, having entrusted their sons to perverts in the youth movement.[60]

Whether this reaction really occurred is difficult to gauge. Some mothers perhaps had qualms, some SdP cardholders may have temporarily swayed in their allegiance; one (Nazi) SdP member of Parliament did resign in protest, in keeping with the stance of the extreme right who sought to make political capital out of youth corruption.[61] Certainly, then, the involvement of adolescents made Rutha's supposed crimes seem far more heinous. Here the press was mirroring, if not widespread social mores, the view of the Czech legal establishment, which in turn differed little from the contemporary stance in Nazi Germany. Namely, homosexuals were usually divided into "real homosexuals" and "pseudo-homosexuals" (often adolescents) who had been "temporarily derailed." In the Reich in the mid-1930s the stereotype of the homosexual as a seducer of youth had gained ground and found legal expression in 1935, when §175a of the criminal code introduced a harsher sentence of up to ten years for men who preyed on "youths" (where the sexual offence could include mutual masturbation).[62] In Czechoslovakia in 1937 the punishments were less severe, the definition of homosexual sex less strict, but the legal-medical approach to homosexuality was comparable; this was clear in December when those associated with Rutha were finally put on trial.

Even so, in the case of Rutha himself there is strong evidence to suggest that many people, especially Germans across north Bohemia, did not believe the gossip about homosexual seduction. For them, Rutha's discourse about a spiritual education of youth proved stronger than press insinuations about pathological behavior. This was evinced by the mass grief and reverence on display at his funeral, the fact that even relatives of his coaccused attended it, and the copious donations from all sections of society that were made in his memory to the labor camp at Wartenberg.[63] Many of course reacted instinctively against the lurid press coverage and thought Rutha a political victim of *Aufbruch* or the Czech establishment (perhaps even murdered in his cell). But many also believed that his national youth mission had been pure and moral: thousands had shared in it and they made a distinction between homosocial and homosexual activity.

VIEW FROM THE CELL

One of the largest buildings in Böhmisch Leipa is the regional courthouse. An imposing ochre-colored neo-Gothic construction that bears witness to German civic pride from 1900, it lies only five minutes' walk from the Realschule that Rutha attended. By 1937, the old German bastion of Leipa was crumbling; an influx of Czech migrants had shifted the demographic balance, and in 1935 a (Czech) police force had been imposed on the town for security purposes. Rutha thus in his last weeks encountered something of "Česká Lípa." Since bail was refused, he returned there as a prisoner to be confined in one of the courthouse cells. His case was transferred to a young Czech investigating magistrate, Dr. Blažek, whose role was to substantiate the indictment, while the Reichenberg detectives sought out more incriminating evidence, eventually uncovering witnesses like the veterinary surgeon Rudolf Wolff.

Only a week after Rutha's arrest the police had submitted to the Leipa court a lengthy document summarizing their findings against him and thirteen young men. Incorporated were statements from suspects like Kurt Gansel and Kurt Franzke, depositions from workers at the mill, and material seized during raids on the homes of the accused. In this indictment Rutha was made the focal point and lavished with the most accusations.[64]

He was portrayed as a typical pederast who had organized his life in order to prey upon male adolescents, whose "working methods" included luring his victims with decadent poetry and pictures of the classical naked body: "Obviously," noted the detectives, "this had to have an impact on maturing youths, developing in them a psychological disposition toward unnatural methods of love." That Rutha cleverly achieved his aim was clear from his sexual seduction of certain youths who in "mental confusion" then proceeded to have sex with each other.[65]

If the youth movement was the main arena that Rutha exploited to find his victims, the indictment suggested that more would be uncovered from his friendship with Gansel and his enthusiasm for the Wartenberg work camp. In addition, there was the largely circumstantial evidence from his library and letters. Reading his correspondence, the detectives noted a very warm tone that "was not usual between men," and interpreted many of his books and photographs as "pornography for the sexually deviant." Diligent homework by Inspector Klement, including perusal of some rare Czech work on homosexuality, had even identified one of Rutha's favorite Renaissance artists as sexually perverted.[66] The accused of course had denied everything, but his answers had been consistently evasive and were contradicted by many witnesses. The indictment therefore had no hesitation (ignoring Rutha's hints of marriage) in declaring him a proven homosexual and clearly guilty. A doctor's report, using exactly the same evidence, made the same conclusion.[67]

With this as their blueprint, Blažek and the legal system fashioned Rutha as a pedagogic pervert, something wholly at variance with his elevated youth mission. Here we might question whether the detectives had secured some confessions through coercion or other dubious means: during the trial of the thirteen young men in December 1937, that issue would be raised by the defense lawyers. Since both Adolf Wagner and Willi Hoffmann complained of making statements under police pressure, Klement was asked whether he had promised leniency if the accused confessed or whether his line of questioning had been overly suggestive, encouraging the youths to view themselves as "homosexual" and deliberately leading the inquiry toward §129b.[68]

While the police denied the insinuations, the trial statements hint that Klement was indeed determined to construct a homosexual case around Rutha and had, to some degree, steered the youths by showing them other confessions. On the other hand, most of the sexual incidents uncovered do not seem to have been fabricated or embellished (including those few linked to Rutha). Here the youths' own interpretation of "homosexual" suggests why they might open up under police interrogation. At the trial, most of them said they had not viewed same-sex sexual acts as a crime. Most also (like Rutha himself) were not interpreting their acts of mutual masturbation as homosexual; as Hoffmann stated, he had learned about homosexuality at school but understood it to be all about "inserting the penis in the anus." The young men's behavior, their lawyers argued, was at best "pseudo-homosexuality" but really a case of "youthful stupidity" as was so common when adolescents gathered together.[69] And by this point, of course, the case had lost much of its import since the main offender or "real homosexual" was no longer alive.

During Rutha's weeks in the Leipa jail under Blažek's interrogation, the indictment against him crystallized further. Rutha never wavered from his denials, dismissing Veitenhansl's protocol as "filth" [Schweinerei] and rejecting Franzke's confession: "I have nothing more to say, I have not abused the young lads." But in line with legal practice, he was then confronted personally with his fellow-accused to see how they interacted. When this occurred with Wagner and Franzke, all of them stood by their statements. In the case of Werner Weiss, confronted with Rutha at midnight on 13 October, their behavior spoke volumes. While a despondent Weiss stood firm, Rutha became very agitated, pacing the room and exclaiming, "This is dreadful." Weiss was then taken back to his cell, but as he left he turned and said: "Heinz, I can only tell the truth."[70]

Even more incriminating was the fresh evidence that the Reichenberg police supplied after they opened Rutha's fireproof safe at the mill. Three documents discovered there were portentous: his wartime diary, his letter of 1928 to Walter Heinrich, and a short piece entitled "last wishes." After having them deciphered, Klement thought them so damning that he asked Blažek for permission to visit on 20 October for a joint interrogation of Rutha; it was an illegal police move and was picked up at the trial. But Rutha in any case was very evasive in the face of the new onslaught, failing to identify names in the "Walter" letter (including "K. G.") and explaining its contents as simply a romantic project for youth education. In contrast, the police continued to link sexual deviance with national deviance or treason: to Klement the letter hinted at a secret homosexual plot with political ramifications.[71]

Similarly, the statement of Rutha's "last wishes" was "momentous proof" of his disposition. Written in December 1930 after his personal crisis, it ordained how at his death the body should be washed and laid in a coffin made of spruce before being cremated. The funeral was to have a homosocial streak: "My coffin should be borne by six of our best and most handsome youths. Leave me alone with them for an hour, or a night, before I must go. If still among them, then I know I am alive even if my body is dead." In June 1935 he had added a coda, some poetry from Stefan George that he hoped Walter Heinrich might read at the ceremony, as a farewell to those young friends who had been his real kindred spirits: now he was assuming a new form, but as he did so he breathed into them courage and strength, leaving them with a kiss burning deep in their youthful souls.[72] It was mystical language from the past, uplifting but innocuous. The Czech police set it alongside their accumulated evidence of Rutha's pederasty and his serial seduction of teenagers.

During almost thirty days in the Leipa cell the prisoner had ample time to dwell on his past and future. Apart from the Czech interrogations, there was a steady trickle of visitors from the outside world, family and friends who all had to conform to the brief visiting hours. On the way to jail, he had been able to stop at the mill and collect reading matter, chiefly some favorite historical and classical works. He was also allowed to write a precise number of short letters every day that were censored by the jailors. Otherwise it was a life of claustrophobic solitude, a bleak contrast to the bright autumn weather outside.

If we probe Rutha's mental state in the weeks before his suicide, much of the evidence suggests somebody trying to appear calm about the future, matching his usual optimism. Thus his former deputy in Prague, Artur Vogt, fended off anxious inquiries, commenting that Rutha was in a "good state."[73] And when his younger sister, Gretel, visited the prison briefly in mid-October, she found him "composed, peaceful and full of confidence" that the accusations would soon be resolved. It was his natural response when talking to a sibling toward whom he always felt protective yet never confided in personally or politically; in fact, according to her memoirs, she departed uncertain whether he could weather the storm.[74] A few weeks later, on 2 November, another female visitor gained a similar mixed impression. The wife of Otto Franke, Rutha's interior designer, was delighted to find that although paler and thinner he continued to take a lively interest in his furniture business, and also asked her for Shakespeare's comedies as a relief from history reading. Even so, he pressed her for more visitors, causing her to reflect that "the uncertainty and compulsory inactivity weighs heavily upon him as he longs for any break in the depressing monotony."[75]

Indeed, several times his correspondence expressed frustration at the "artificial leisure," since for one so industrious it was as if his very breath and movement had been lost.[76] In a positive vein, the half dozen letters that survive focused especially on imaginative plans for the Kunnersdorf business as well as deeper reflections upon his didactic mission. (There was no political talk, probably due to the censor.) Through Franke, he was kept fully abreast of the firm's contracts, the economic upswing of 1937 inclining him to organize a special exhibition that winter, and in the same light we can view his meticulous instructions for the mill's renovation. Alongside modernizing with new windows and glass doors, he typically specified that the mill's color should remain "old-fashioned"; in place of his father's initials, his own and the date "1925"—the launch of the firm—should now appear in Gothic script above the front door.[77]

Just as this musing combined past achievements with future prospects, so Rutha contemplated the character of his Sudeten youth mission. On 24 October he fervently challenged the foul speculation about his own motives, and insisted characteristically to his defense lawyer, "With youths, I have struggled for unity, discipline and a noble dimension, always referring them to what is grand and emboldening. I have never dishonored them. They were too sacred to me: for where is the divine in man more visible than in a bighearted, handsome youth."[78] Through his classical reading he could ponder once again Plato's ideal of beauty, and noted in several letters how he had always pursued the beauty in humanity, that his own life was unsoiled for it belonged "so much to beauty."[79]

Concretely, he expected to build on his precepts for youth education, as described in a recent *Turnzeitung* article where he had noted remarkable progress but also the continued fragility of youth coordination and discipline.[80] On release, he envisaged publicizing in detail his whole pedagogic system, and seemed confident that young men "awakening everywhere" would be enthusiastic about this type of Sudeten education.[81] Fundamental, however, for perpetuating the mission, and a fillip to his own spirit in captivity, was the youth leadership school at Wartenberg. He saw it as both a personal triumph and the real climax of that twenty-year crusade that had set young men on a new national course. It was thus with a messianic flourish that one of his last letters spoke directly to all comrades in the labor service. They were reminded that, despite his current isolation, he was with them as never before as they toiled with their spades by day or sat together reading in the evenings. Their labors were critical and would remain so whatever happened, for under their exemplary auspices, Sudeten youths were to be molded and the vision passed on to another generation.[82]

It was a letter of fervent encouragement but can equally be interpreted as a melodramatic part of Rutha's testament, dispatched from the prison cell to the outside world. For alongside that external calmness or the frequent claims that he was the victim of "character assassination," his fears persisted that the "stupid nightmare" might never end. Those welcome visitors who broke the monotony of the cell were also the chief source of news about how his name and mission were daily defiled in the popular press, placing a question mark over any future respectability or public work.

A vivid glimpse of his alarm had surfaced when confronted with Weiss and the "evidence" of homosexual behavior. Even if he resisted any such interpretation, he could not avoid dwelling on the growing implications of public disgrace. As he wrote to his niece Inge on 2 November, he had been looking forward to his "most personal plans," adding, "It pains me that I am the cause not only of uncertainty but also disgrace, where I wanted to bring only joy."[83] The reference undoubtedly was to his prospective marriage to Maria Habrmann. In one brief letter from the last days he assured his respectable fiancée of how much he had contemplated their life together. But he ended pessimistically: perhaps it was best under the circumstances to forget about their dream of a common house, children, and tranquility, for "between yearning and fulfillment there lies the chasm of the prison."[84]

In modern research, our understanding of what causes prison suicides is still weak, perhaps not surprising in view of the difficulties of performing a psychological autopsy. There is, however, agreement that many prison suicides result from a combination of three main factors: the individual's pre-prison "vulnerability," the impact of outside pressures when in captivity, and the "ecological context" (the actual experience of the prison environment).[85] In Rutha's case, as we have seen, his vulnerability was secretly apparent through his previous thoughts about committing suicide, notably in 1918 and 1928 during the crises over his sexual orientation. He had managed to sublimate those anxieties and give them a positive interpretation through the male bonding of the youth mission. In autumn 1937 this careful personal construction was being publicly unraveled, and unlike the "outing" of 1935, he was helpless to control its direction. From outside the cell, he could feel the pressure of public disgrace and humiliation, knew that his sexuality was openly scrutinized and discussed, the youth mission distorted and soiled by faceless enemies. Since many colleagues in the SdP leadership—including

Henlein—were also keeping their distance, the prospect of any postprison political rehabilitation must have seemed bleak.

In addition, the "ecological context" of the prison was undoubtedly decisive. Although Blažek and the prison authorities seem to have been fair in their treatment, even indulging the whims of some visitors, the confinement was intolerable for an energetic man who worshipped the open landscape. From 23 October there were no further interrogations and he was left in psychological limbo, uncertain about the precise indictment or when the case would come to trial as several appeals were pending at the Prague Supreme Court. It stimulated typical anxiety during the early phase of custody when so many prison suicides occur.[86] His depression, which Franke's wife seemed to observe, was equally apparent to his defense lawyer, who termed it "prison psychosis" and demanded his client's release.[87]

After Rutha's suicide in the early hours of 5 November, many in the popular press interpreted the act with schadenfreude as simple proof of his guilt.[88] Kamil Krofta for example summed up for Czech journalists: "It was probably mental depression in recognition of his guilt and moral debasement. It was the end of his career and perhaps he had a masculine pride which oppressed him so much that he took his own life." The last sentence at least rings true, but so does the concept (pushed by the SdP but denied by Krofta) that Rutha had been "maltreated" in a general sense: both the press harassment and his solitary confinement had had a cumulative impact.[89]

Why Rutha reached the "critical threshold," where he could not cope, on 4 November is impossible to say. If we are to believe one questionable source, he had asked Blažek that evening about the outcome of the case and was told that it looked hopeless.[90] It seems to have been a sudden but calculated decision. The notes that he had scribbled in various books, the precise instructions he sent out in the final days—all suggest someone who had long been pondering his legacy, who then deliberately chose suicide as an honorable exit. The SdP newspaper *Die Zeit* typically interpreted the death in this noble fashion, suggesting that near the end Rutha had been reading Plato's *Phaedo*, where Socrates muses confidently on the immortality of the soul before taking his own life: "I should only make myself ridiculous in my own eyes if I clung to life and hugged it when it has no more to offer." Like Socrates, Rutha had been falsely accused of corrupting youth, and for him a similar type of martyrdom must have seemed appropriate.[91]

Among the various jottings that effectively made up a suicide note there was one letter found only thirty years later, written in shorthand and concealed in a book. It once again asserted his personal integrity, then idealistically foresaw the continuation of that noble youth mission that might still produce national reconciliation in the Bohemian lands:

> To my friends! Be undaunted and believe in the future! . . . Be in your time leaders of youth! And be fathers of sons who will surpass you . . . Believe in the German people, but fight so that it believes in God and not just in the masses. Work for the coexistence of peoples in our land! A difficult but worthy task for a generation that with devotion and sobriety sees the path of history before it.

There, wherever youth flourished, Rutha hoped that his name would be remembered.[92]

Epilogue

Rutha's Ghost

Several death masks of Heinz Rutha survived the war. One of them hung for decades in Gretel Rutha's sitting room, peering out over the Mosel River in western Germany.[1] It was the younger sister who long after the suicide sought to rescue her brother's reputation, threatening first to sue detractors, then in 1938–1939 petitioning the authorities to have his private documents returned to the family. Hers was a vain quest since the case material remained live and was being passed to and from various courthouses.[2] A small consolation was that until 1945 she could preserve the Rutha library under lock and key.

As the Bohemian lands fell under Nazi occupation and the European war began in September 1939, the Rutha sisters struggled to cope with one legacy, the furniture business in Bad Kunnersdorf.[3] The war years saw an accelerated migration in and out of the village. While enemy prisoners of war were housed at the neighboring spa, the mill's workforce was dissipated, its employees conscripted into the Wehrmacht and sent to the eastern front. Even if the military handed the business some extra contracts, and the loyal Otto Franke was able to keep it afloat, the mill was an increasingly ghostly place. In March 1941, the housekeeper, Friedel Polifka (née Rutha), died of cancer and was buried in the local cemetery. Rutha's vivacious fiancée Maria Habrmann was no longer around, for she had briefly married Wolfgang Heinz, one of Rutha's "acolytes"; after a further secret liaison, with a French prisoner at the spa, she emigrated at the end of the war. At that time, one day in May 1945, armed Czech "partisans" suddenly appeared at the mill and ordered its remaining occupants to leave immediately and take only 250 grams of possessions. For months in the rubble of Dresden in postwar Germany, Gretel Rutha had to survive as a wet nurse. Only much later would she find some peace on the banks of the Mosel, a long way from home with few mementos of her brother. Meanwhile a new Czech-speaking population had migrated into Kunnersdorf-Oschitz to replace the Sudeten German expellees. Of the Rutha family there were few traces left except the red mill and their gravestones fixed in the landscape. Rutha's most cherished project, the youth school at Wartenberg, had been completely abandoned in 1938, its meaning lost, its site restored to nature.

AFTERMATH

Besides this personal disaster, the Rutha homosexual scandal cast a shadow over the lives of many young men in the period 1937–1940. Some were directly implicated in the police investigation that went to trial. Others were caught in a net that was cast wide after October 1937, firstly by the Czech authorities in an action that casually snowballed, and then deliberately by the Gestapo after Germany occupied the Sudetenland a year later. Rutha's name became a byword for the crime of male homosexuality (the Czech §129b or Germany's §175), for he was the most celebrated offender, a pederast who could not answer back. His political or social networks were suspect by association and could easily be smeared for political advantage. In this way the manipulation of homosexuality for national or political ends, so evident in Rutha's last weeks, continued long after his death. Often in the individual cases of denunciation, the sexual or political threads making up the fabric are hard to disentangle. And indeed, few historians have tried to do so, focusing instead on the "obvious" political repercussions of Rutha's removal.

In this interpretation, Rutha's death coincided precisely with a Sudeten German nationalist watershed as Konrad Henlein prostrated himself dramatically before Hitler.[4] Yet how far Henlein in November 1937 really crossed the Rubicon—and did not look back—is questionable. Firstly, his own radical direction had strengthened over the previous year, as Germany began to dominate internationally, as Czech concessions seemed minimal, and Karl Hermann Frank increased his control of the SdP inner circle. (Rutha, moreover, with little power base of his own, had had decreasing influence over Henlein, but he too, as we have seen, had been caught in the radical drift as he found various diplomatic options closed off.) Secondly, and attuned to the dead Rutha's strategy, Henlein's behavior remained opportunistic, keeping several irons in the fire and still anxious about Hitler's true objectives. His letter to the führer in fact decided very little in the short term, for Hitler ignored it, leaving him to kick his heels in familiar traces over the next few months. Not until 28 March 1938 was he granted an audience with Hitler in Berlin and given instructions on duplicitous tactics for the future (fig.25).

More accurately, it was the Rutha scandal per se that caused a sharpening of political tensions in Czechoslovakia, exacerbating the Czech-German nationalist struggle while also reopening the festering wounds in the SdP. In both cases, the substance was not just national-political as in the past, for homosexuality added a vibrant moral dimension that many wished to exploit. While many Czech journalists delighted in lampooning Rutha as a German pederast, some Czech politicians proceeded to equate (im)morality with the nation. Soon after Rutha's funeral, one nationalist deputy, Jaroslav Stránský, warned Parliament that the case had frightening parallels "with that mysticism and romanticism which in pre-war and post-war Berlin degenerated from an eccentric notion of friendship and comradeship into the form that destroyed architect Rutha." Stránský, known to be close to President Beneš, then assumed the moral high ground and called on SdP politicians: "Separate yourselves, gentlemen, from this tendency while there is still time, and be grateful to us [Czechs] for protecting our German fellow citizens from its contamination."[5]

Under this moral onslaught, the normally confident SdP leadership was thrown onto the defensive and erratically tried to deflect attention from homosexual slurs. Most notably, Henlein in mid-October dispatched a blunt letter to Beneš, openly demanding Sudeten territorial autonomy while reemphasizing British support. If it was meant to assert his authority, it had the unfortunate outcome of simply intensifying the Sudeten-Czech standoff; Prague resolved to ban all public meetings and postpone the imminent local elections, which might have favored the SdP.[6]

Thus a way forward on the basis of negotiation, which even in September had glimmered for Rutha, looked ever bleaker. Against this background we can understand Henlein's desperate missive to Hitler. At the same time, the British Foreign Office was continuing to press Prague to make concessions. In early October Henlein had again visited London, a path that Rutha had smoothed for him. There were signs now that the British suspected Henlein's "moderation" and viewed Rutha as the more reliable Sudeten envoy; yet it was still Beneš who was labeled the chief obstacle to a settlement that could prevent Germany's intervention and a European war.[7] Late 1937 therefore witnessed renewed British pressure on Prague, as well as a dangerous overture that bypassed the Czechs altogether. For in November, Britain directly assured Hitler that it would not oppose peaceful territorial revision in central Europe. A new phase was beginning in Great Power politics, one that led directly to the Munich agreement of September 1938, the Reich annexation of the Sudetenland, and the full destruction of Czechoslovakia.

If Henlein in the throes of the Rutha scandal was lurching in a radical direction, in other ways he seemed to do the exact opposite. In late 1937 he moved against SdP dissidents who were fomenting discord and undermining unity. To most observers this power struggle had an ideological dimension, since a burgeoning Nazi cohort seemed again to be provocatively challenging those whose Third Reich credentials were suspect, who preferred to privilege the "Sudeten tribe." Rutha's eclipse in shady circumstances had the effect of bringing this simmering struggle to the boil, and on both sides accusations about national betrayal and male honor were made that could not be left unanswered.

As we have seen, many in the party with some justification had accused the *Aufbruch* circle of betraying Rutha to the Czech authorities, supplying incriminating evidence in order to topple a leading non-Nazi, a supposed devotee of the old KB. In this vein, in November, tiny leaflets started to circulate across north Bohemia. They accused *Aufbruch* and its "tool," Rudi Hein, of carrying out a character assassination of Rutha, driving him to suicide. In short, the radicals/dissenters had Sudeten blood on their hands, all the more shocking since their machinations had benefited the Czech enemy.[8] Overt radicals in the SdP leadership like Rudolf Kasper and Gustav Jonak felt bound to take up this challenge to their integrity, realizing too that it might be a springboard for radical advancement at the expense of the "KB clique."

Kasper therefore began boycotting leadership meetings and announced various conditions before he would submit to Henlein. If it all seemed a rerun of the 1936 squabbling that had eliminated Walter Brand, this time Kasper had a joker in his pack that he knew could embarrass the leadership. He demanded that before he would be disciplined, Henlein must chastise all those who in any way had "extolled Heinrich Rutha," branded him a martyr, or unjustifiably accused "respectable men" of his murder.[9] It was a challenge too far, for Henlein himself had at least eulogized Rutha on his death, and some of his closest associates had publicly suggested that *Aufbruch* was responsible. Kasper was insinuating what the far right press was stating openly, that the SdP was run by perverts.[10]

When Henlein acted in December 1937, he perhaps harbored some residual sympathy for Rutha's reputation but chiefly was determined to assert SdP unity, to confront habitual troublemakers, and to protect his own position. Kasper and Jonak were ejected from the party, and there was additional cleansing in the Turn movement where six *Aufbruch* youth leaders were expelled for their recalcitrance. It was the sort of disciplining that Rutha himself would have approved, but it was a mirage. In reality (even more than in 1936), asserting party unity now required compromise with Nazis, who had an ever stronger grassroots base. Additionally, it was a compromise that Berlin recommended and Henlein, encouraged by Frank, accepted. So it was that Henlein finally retained a few obvious irredentists in the leadership, while disciplinary procedures were even started against comrades who had accused Kasper of denouncing Rutha.[11] If this gave the impression by 1938 of party unity, in fact the Nazis had been appeased, just as in tandem Henlein and Frank were taking their movement further into the orbit of the Third Reich. It was uneasy and unfinished business that would return to haunt Henlein in 1939–1940: for homosexuality was now his Achilles' heel too.

Parallel to this tense political fallout with its homosexual subtext, the Rutha case had a serious social legacy. It left a long trail of smaller scandals, exposing briefly for Czech-German society a subject that was normally kept under wraps. While the press avidly uncovered numerous "homosexual offenses" from all corners of Czechoslovakia, the local police forces were all the more vigilant about an extensive "Rutha network" of homosexuals. As at the start of the Rutha investigation, some arrests occurred on the basis of links between sexual abnormality and military espionage, the notion that Czechoslovakia was assaulted by an alien national-sexual hydra. The main focus, however, was those pederasts who were corrupting male youths. Apart from picking up individuals suspected of "seduction," their names then plastered across the local papers, the police naturally targeted the network of labor camps so associated with Rutha. Wartenberg was investigated early on, to no effect, but elsewhere young homosexuals were discovered and at least one work camp closed down.[12]

Yet the most interesting minor scandal was that of Oskar Just. As an artist and former youth leader in Gablonz, Just had often crossed paths with

Rutha, first ideologically in the Wandervogel and then in connection with interior designing. Probably from some hints of this link, but also because Just had many Reich commissions for his art work, the police investigated him under §129b. Their inquiry in November 1937 uncovered a man whose sexual inclinations had continued to focus on older blond adolescents. Like Rutha he had allegedly written homoerotic letters and invited young men to his Gablonz apartment to discuss the Greek model of Eros; he was also given to photographing them naked in the mountains for "professional reasons." As arrests were made and a scandal akin to Rutha's threatened to escalate, Just escaped to Berlin.[13] Although the Czech authorities then abandoned the investigation, the case reveals well the ripple effect of the Rutha scandal. And it has intriguing parallels in terms of the main protagonists, their common background and their sexual idealization of youth.

The "Just affair" and all others were, in any case, always sideshows to the main event. In early December 1937, twelve young men from the Rutha scandal went on trial at the Leipa courthouse. Although the defense lawyers argued successfully that the core proceedings should be held in camera to protect "public morality," the first and last sessions were open, ensuring that the main details slipped easily into the public domain. Rutha was effectively on trial: he was the touchstone for many arguments of both the prosecution and the defense. At the start of proceedings, the police indictment against him was read out to the court, and the claims of both Rudi Hein and Franz Veitenhansl made public. At the end, in his summing up on 7 December, the Czech prosecutor stated bluntly that although Rutha was dead, it had to be said that he and Walter Rohn were homosexuals, and that Rutha had seduced Werner Weiss and other young men: "Weiss had then passed on the filth to other uncorrupted youths" who were no less guilty for being "normal." The danger came not just from teenagers falling into the hands of "sexually abnormal seducers," but from behavior such as mutual masturbation that simply led to more serious unnatural sexual practices damaging to one's health.[14]

A focus on youth, and by inference a condemnation of Rutha's "pederasty," was also a core argument for the defense lawyers. Some of them hinted at Rutha's innocence, arguing that an affair artificially manufactured by police and press had already cost one life. But their natural tendency was to contrast their defendants with the man absent from the dock. As Rohn's lawyer explained with a flourish, it was to have been a stunning criminal drama where "the shadow of a titanic character" would have fallen across the stage; instead, Rutha was being judged in another land, while the titanic trial had become a torso, one of children.[15] For the twelve defendants it was simply a case of "youthful stupidity" or "pseudo-homosexuality," of mutual masturbation that was perfectly common when male teenagers gathered together; none of them were homosexuals but simply naïve youngsters, led astray and then entrapped by the police. As a postscript, the lawyers noted that a new Czechoslovak criminal code was anyway expected soon, which would decriminalize homosexuality or at least soften the impact of §129b on those of the defendants' age group (under twenty-one).[16]

Despite these pleas, when the verdict was announced to a packed court room on 9 December, the judge suggested no respite from the existing law, nor admitted any police intimidation as the defense had argued. Seven of the twelve were found guilty (as they knew what they were doing), and although the sentences were suspended, their crime was publicized. Once again, the chief concern of the law was to protect innocent youth. The twenty-six-year-old Rohn was identified as a seducer and given eight months; Weiss's obsessive behavior earned him four; and Franzke, benefiting from his confession and the idea that Rutha had bewitched him, received only two. Overall, the presiding Czech judge concluded that most of the young men had been "victims of seduction"—hence the sentences, which were conditional for three years.[17] Who precisely had been responsible was often unspoken, but was obvious from reading between the lines.

The SdP leadership could now long for the scandal to evaporate. Weiss and Rohn, the only SdP members found guilty, were summarily expelled from the party. The name of Rutha, condemned in spirit, not only ceased to be mentioned in party circles but quickly became a pariah for the Turn movement. This was perhaps the greatest blow to Rutha's life mission. In December, the Turn leadership under Richard Bernhard took a firm stance against *Aufbruch* miscreants, calling everyone to order, but also noted defensively that any homosexuals would "naturally" be expelled from the movement. Having backed Rutha in 1935, Bernard after the Leipa court decision publicly drew a line in the sand, announcing that, as Rutha had been found "guilty," so his spirit was anathema to the Turn movement.[18] In 1938, in the Reich context, the Turn movement like the SdP would increasingly shift in a radical direction, with many *Aufbruch* troublemakers reintegrated into the common national cause. In contrast, the precepts for male youth associated with Rutha became both sexually and nationally suspect; the "age-stages" for youth education for example were slowly diluted.[19] His enemies had managed to neutralize his lofty pedagogic and political vision for Sudeten Germans.

A year passed before Rutha's ghost was again evoked in order to cleanse the Sudetenland of those too loyal to German Bohemian traditions. By April 1939, Germany had annexed the whole Czech territory, Henlein was put in charge of a new "Reichsgau Sudetenland," and the Nazi security service under Reinhard Heydrich began to purge Sudeten loyalists and assert SS dominance. Since 1935 Sudeten irredentists had been feeding Heydrich reports and insisting that Nazi ambitions were threatened by the insidious KB, including the deviant Rutha; even so, the SS had no direct hand in destroying Rutha. Its turn came in 1939 when it explicitly wielded §175 in order to eradicate political foes, especially those with any history of obstructing "radicalism" in the Sudetenland. Although it was not a new tactic in the Reich, in the Sudetengau Heydrich exploited §175 because his purge started first in the new Sudeten Hitler Youth; his attention was naturally drawn to evidence of the youth movement's old program as advanced by Rutha. When in late June, after a wave of arrests, Heydrich briefed Hitler on the crusade against Sudeten "homosexual circles," he singled out deviant youth education and the legacy of Rutha, who supposedly had copied Hans Blüher and made homosexual acts a precondition for youth group membership. Hitler gave the witch hunt his full blessing.[20]

Many of those initially arrested may have been youth leaders. But the Gestapo spread its net widely to ensnare over two hundred in total, some of whom had KB-Spannist links or a tangential association with Rutha's sexual or national "deviance." They included Walter Brand and Walter Heinrich (whom the SS had fingered in 1938 for their Spannism), and figures from Rutha's early career like Ernst Leibl, Gustav Oberlik, and the architect Wagner-Poltrock. Some, like Walter Rohn, had been tried once and were now rearrested; others tainted by the Rutha trial found their copybook blotted for the rest of the war. The new trials in late 1939, held in Leipa and Dresden, revolved ostensibly around §175, yet as the Dresden prosecutor confessed after the war, it was largely a front for a purge of Sudeten German nationalists. In the words of Oberlik, "Nobody can tell me that it was about weeding out homosexuals."[21]

In January 1940, twenty "homosexuals" were found guilty and given prison sentences. In the absence of the trial papers, we rely mainly on the Nazi press to give a hint of the prosecution case. The Sudeten public learned suddenly about a huge web of "homosexual youth seduction" by criminals who had tried "to veil their own abnormal inclinations under the cloak of muddled ideologies." The link to Rutha was clearly set out in the official SS journal, which, parroting Heydrich's previous report about Blüher's influence, outlined the Spannist context and made Rutha the real ringleader: "He would have been the main defendant in the trials, for his crime reached ever wider circles, spreading out from him as the central point of crystallization. His 'idea' was to create a homoerotic Männerbund as a state-like organization."[22]

For Heydrich, this onslaught was a base from which finally to cripple Henlein and purge his entourage. When the two met in Berlin that spring, Heydrich accused the Gauleiter of complicity in criminal perversion, not least in failing to act fast against Rutha, and demanded full subordination if he was to survive. The bullying had its effect. Henlein resolved to abandon many old comrades (Sebekowsky was sent to the eastern front); and not for the first time he toed an obedient and distasteful line, hinting in the press that while one former colleague (Rutha) had deceived him, others since had soiled the Sudeten German image.[23] On 3 March 1940 at an official rally, there followed his public renunciation of Rutha, a man who had "severely abused his trust." As he behaved on many occasions, Henlein wriggled and fabricated his own version of history, this time severing the link with his old mentor and with all elements of the so-called "Rutha circle." As Oberlik noted acerbically to Frank, "there was a time when K. H. was spiritually subject to Rutha and almost submissive—today he plays the poor victim who knew nothing about it."[24]

*   *   *

One of Rutha's most fervent disciples, Walter Rohn, survived the war and in late 1947 was to be found in a British POW camp in Egypt. A few years after the Dresden court case, he had been called up, dispatched to the Balkans, and saw the acropolis in Athens for the first time: there, he felt, he was "finally in the homeland of the German soul, which [he] always wanted to visit with Heinz." From his prison camp he later reflected on the devastation the war had wrought upon his Sudeten German generation. Heinz Rutha had been first in the "dance of death," but many had followed him; now it was a godsend if the name of a Rutha disciple surfaced as a survivor.[25]

Rutha's grand youth enterprise for Sudeten Germans had been born in the First World War in the framework of the Habsburg Empire and destroyed in the Second World War under Nazi Germany. Its conception originally owed much to the idealistic vision of the Bohemian Wandervogel, the notion that German Bohemian youth had a special creative purpose of steering bourgeois society back to "true German values." In the context of the Great War slaughter, that regenerative message sounded loudly. Rutha, unable to enlist, was one Wandervogel leader who pursued the mission on the home front and steered it in a more nationalist direction, befitting the equivalent sacrifice of youth in the trenches. It meant alerting Wandervögel to the solemnity of the hour, but also led him toward racial purity and by implication to a crusade with a greater anti-Czech focus than before the war.

Rutha's very late enlistment in 1918 ensured that he retained a militant drive when hostilities ended, refusing to retire gracefully like so many veterans in rural communities. Although mentally scarred by the war and always repelled by such violence, his brief experience in the front line had honed one personal theory: that German Bohemia to survive needed "leader-personalities," charismatic individuals who would train the postwar generation with a fresh purpose. In the context of a Czechoslovak nationalizing state after 1918, the regional German nationalists had to reexamine their own identity, jettisoning Austrian traits in favor of forging a new Sudeten German national community. But Rutha, after taking an oath to German renewal alongside other veterans, focused not simply on promoting *Heimat* education but on training a solid youth cohort that eventually would challenge the Czech "usurpation" of Bohemian space.

Accounts of the post-1918 *bündisch* youth movement in Czechoslovakia often note that Rutha was unusual in wanting to politicize adolescents. While presenting himself as a spiritual leader attuned to their youthful desires, he specifically wished to make them responsible for the nationalist mission, turning them into a "secular army" without weapons: a Sudeten Männerbund. It was a phenomenon immensely attractive to scores of postwar youths who had missed out on the wartime adventure and who found him a sympathetic and charismatic teacher.

Yet Rutha's private correspondence reveals that his obsession was not just fueled by nationalist conviction or his self-assurance as a youth leader. Fundamental too were his own sexual desires and insecurities. In the 1920s, through reading Plato and Stefan George, through theories that meshed well with Hans Blüher's, he constructed a pedagogic mission with Eros as its "procreative vitality." While he was not alone in championing pedagogic Eros (as the case of Gustav Wyneken in Germany shows), he was a pioneer in the early twentieth century in integrating it into a nationalist program. Like others around him, he would vehemently deny that he was building a homosexual Männerbund.[26] But certainly he envisaged an elite cohort linked together by erotic sparks and embodying masculine virtues. Just as the classical Greek model gave pedagogic Eros a moral framework, so his chosen life task calmed personal same-sex anxieties that he never really surmounted.

His nationalist youth mission therefore was underpinned by homoeroticism. How his contemporaries viewed this depended very much on their own focus or blind spots. To the fore, for most adolescents and parents, was an enticing homosocial "reform pedagogy" that after 1918, echoing the comradeship of the trenches, privileged male bonding and discipline as a solution to Sudeten German national insecurity. In contrast, the mission's homoerotic traits were only occasionally glimpsed. Homosexuality, criminalized in §129b, was still tolerated or ignored in many Czech-German communities, but when it combined with "youth" it was as combustible as in Nazi Germany.[27] Rutha secretly lived on this edge between homosocial and homosexual, understandably never publicly linking his youth mission to pedagogic Eros. And it was the youth-sex dimension that made the furor so hysterical in 1937.

If Eros was a key pillar of his youth mission, a second was Spannism. As interpreted by Walter Heinrich, Spannist theory provided Rutha's enterprise with an all-embracing sociopolitical future where the Männerbund would lead the Sudeten corporate state. By 1925 he was a convert, helping to found a KB think tank that met occasionally to discuss Spannist ideas and the experiment of nurturing local "germ cells." However, he was not quite the Spannist ideological fanatic that some imagined, for he concentrated on shaping the human material, those young minds and bodies who would constitute the state Männerbund. Having secured a home for his program in the Turn movement, he invested huge energy in its regional implementation after 1933. The youth leadership school at Wartenberg took this a step further, molding "new men" both to lead the community and train the succeeding male generations. In this last period, Rutha still believed that Sudeten youth was autonomous, in control of its own education and destiny. It was a stance fully at odds with developments in Nazi Germany where, with all youth "nationalized" in the Hitler Youth, the old theory of a special age group was fast disappearing.[28]

Spannist theory, moreover, helps explain Sudeten foreign policy and Rutha's precise goals for rearranging the central European map. Growing up as a German Bohemian in the Habsburg monarchy, he personified a fluidity of allegiances, where firm regional loyalty overlapped with an Austrian patriotism as well as the reassurance of belonging to a broader German cultural community; in interwar Czechoslovakia a combination of those allegiances never quite left him. Spannism offered a way, both practical and idealistic, to return to the fluidity of the Habsburg era and a time of supposed German cultural dominance. Central Europe would be restructured as a national federation, the Sudeten Germans achieving their own state, the Czechs knowing their place and accepting minority status in a vast *Volksgemeinschaft* stretching from the Baltic to the Adriatic.

Spannist "universalism" therefore supplied a rough model for implementing a national revolution across Bohemian space. Its spiritual theory matched Rutha's old Wandervogel idealism, and seemed nicely applicable too in other contested national environments like Belgium. Yet as foreign minister, Rutha was pragmatic when faced with the European realities, realizing that the end goal for his Sudeten tribe could only come through a combination of negotiation and steady international pressure.

That final objective, at least for Rutha and many SdP members, was not to manipulate the annexation of Czechoslovakia by an expansionist Third Reich. But nor was it, as apologists imply, simple German autonomy within a Czechoslovak state structure.[29] The Spannist solution was nuanced. It cautions us against labeling Rutha either a Sudeten autonomist or a German irredentist, for while the aim was a Sudeten corporate state (even within some loose Czechoslovak federation), it always had strong pan-German traits. Walter Brand could with reason complain later that the SdP had been caught in a Czech-Nazi crossfire, yet that too borders on the disingenuous, obscuring the fact that Sudeten *völkisch* loyalists always believed in a radical national solution for the Bohemian lands.[30]

All this helps explain why, when Rutha visited London in 1936, the British Foreign Office picked up very mixed messages and could easily be sympathetic to the Sudeten German cause. The confusion was compounded because the Henleinists were opportunistic; after finding their feet in the international system of 1935, by 1936–1937 the chance to achieve a major revolution in central Europe was increasingly on offer. Even Rutha began to flirt more recklessly with a pan-Germanism that was becoming synonymous with Nazi imperialism. Like Henlein he sincerely wanted a peaceful outcome, but his was still a radical objective that played directly into the hands of Nazi German belligerence.

Heinz Rutha's short life illuminates a Bohemian/Sudeten nationalist mindset of the early twentieth century, and explains why the Czech-German relationship ended in disaster. As a personal quest, to combat national and sexual insecurities, it is bound to arouse in us a mixture of emotions, for it unsettles many preconceptions about central European history, and confronts head-on taboos about adolescent homosexuality or same-sex generational relationships. In the end, for all his fanaticism, Rutha was the tragic double victim of an abortive mission. With some success, he challenged the short-lived status quo of Czechoslovakia, consistently taking risks in the national and sexual spheres. But in 1937 both Czech and German enemies surfaced against him. He was sacrificed on the twin altars of Sudeten German patriotism and homosexuality.

Place Names in German and Czech

German	Czech
Alt-Kalken	Stará Skalka
Asch	Aš
Aussig	Ústí nad Labem
Bad Kunnersdorf	Lázně Kundratice
Bodenbach	Podmokly
Böhmisch Aicha	Český Dub
Böhmisch Leipa	Česká Lípa
Brünn	Brno
Brüx	Most
Budweis	České Budějovice
Carlsbad	Karlový Vary
Deutsch Gabel	Jablonné v Podještědí
Devin	Děvín
Duppau	Doupov
Elbe	Labe
Eger	Cheb
Erzgebirge	Krušné hory
Freiwaldau	Jeseník
Friedland	Frýdlant
Gablonz	Jabolonec nad Nisou
Graslitz	Kraslice
Hammer am See	Hamr na Jezeře
Hirschberg	Doksy
Iglau	Jihlava
Isergebirge	Jizerské hory
Jeschken	Ještěd

Johannesthal	Janův Důl
Kaaden	Kadaň
Kamnitzleiten	Kamenická Stráň
Keilberg	Klínovec
Kessel	Kotel
Komotau	Chomutov
Königliche Weinberge	Královské Vinohrady
Kriesdorf	Křižany
Krummau	Český Krumlov
Leitmeritz	Litoměřice
Lobositz	Lovosice
Maffersdorf	Vratislavice nad Nisou
Marienbad	Mariánske Lázně
Merzdorf	Břevniště
Mies	Stříbro
Mukarow	Mukařov
Münchengrätz	Mnichovo Hradiště
Neweklovitz	Neveklovice
Nieder-Gruppai	Dolní Krupa
Niemes	Mimoň
Oschitz	Osečná
Pilsen	Plzeň
Polzen	Ploučnice
Prachatitz	Prachatice
Raspenau	Raspenava
Reichenau	Rychnov
Reichenberg	Liberec
Riesengebirge	Krkonoše
Roll	Ralsko
Ruppersdorf	Ruprechtice
Saaz	Žatec
Schreckenstein	Střekov
Smichow	Smíchov
Tannwald	Tanvald
Tepl	Teplá
Teplitz	Teplice
Teschen	Těšnov
Tetschen	Děčín
Trschiblitz	Třeblivice
Wartenberg	Stráž pod Ralskem
Wrchhaben	Vrchovany
Zetten	Cetenov

Notes

NOTES ABBREVIATIONS

BH   *Burschen heraus! Fahrtenblatt der Deutschböhmen*
Blätter   *Blätter vom frischen Leben*
CLS   Česká Lípa: Krajský soud (trestní spisy)
DGFP   *Documents on German Foreign Policy, 1918–1945*
DjD   *Der junge Deutsche*
FO   Foreign Office
JCH   *Journal of Contemporary History*
MJT   *Mitteilungen des Jeschken-Iser-Turngau*
NPA   Neue Politisches Akten
SEER   *The Slavonic and East European Review*
TZ   *Turnzeitung des Deutschen Turnverbandes*
VdTO   *Verhandlungsschrift deutscher Turnverein für Oschitz*
VuF   *Volk und Führung*
WÖF   *Wandervogel. Österreichisches Fahrtenblatt*

INTRODUCTION

1. "Arch. Heinrich Rutha – tot," *Die Zeit*, 6 November 1937, 2.
2. Since most of this book is set in predominantly German-speaking Bohemia, I have usually used the German version for place-names; a parallel list gives the Czech version.
3. "Die Einäscherung Ruthas," *Deutsche Leipaer Zeitung*, 9 November 1937, 5.
4. "Die letzte Fahrt Heinrich Ruthas," *Die Zeit*, 11 November 1937, 3; and "Die Ueberführung Heinz Ruthas," *Reichenberger Tagesbote*, 10 November 1937 (evening edition), 1.

5. For the following, see "Die letzte Fahrt Heinrich Ruthas," *Die Zeit,* 11 November, 3; and "Heinrich Ruthas letzter Weg," *Rundschau,* 13 November 1937, 1–2.

6. "Die Trauerfeier für Heinrich Rutha," *Reichenberger Tagesbote,* 11 November 1937 (morning edition), 3.

7. "'Unser Anteil ist seine Leistung'," *Die Zeit,* 11 November 1937, 3; and "Totenrede auf Heinz Rutha," *Rundschau,* 13 November 1937, 3–4.

8. Josef Fischer, Václav Patzak, and Vincenc Perth, *Jejich boj: Co chce a čemu slouží Sudetendeutsche Partei* (Prague, 1937), 73.

9. A useful if tendentious summary of this nationalist struggle for Sudeten German unity is Josef Pfitzner, *Sudetendeutsche Einheitsbewegung: Werden und Erfüllung,* 2nd ed. (Carlsbad, 1937).

10. "Le fameux depute des Sudètes," as the French ambassador to Germany described him: Ministères des Affaires Étrangères, *Documents diplomatiques français 1932–1939,* 2nd série (Paris, 1972), 7:324.

11. "Die Toten des Jahres," *Sudeten-Deutsches Jahrbuch 1938,* ed. Wilfried Brosche and Fritz Nagl (Böhmisch Leipa-Zwickau, 1938), 417.

12. Quoted in Ralf Gebel, *"Heim ins Reich!" Konrad Henlein und der Reichsgau Sudetenland 1938–1945* (Munich, 2000), 174.

13. Interviews with Marie Isaides at Lázně Kundratice, 24 August 1999 and 25 March 2000. Isaides avoided expulsion in 1945 because she had helped French POWs employed in the neighbouring spa and then married a Czech national.

14. Since the Rutha relative wishes anonymity, references from this source are given below as "Rutha relative interview."

15. The best include Ronald M. Smelser, *The Sudeten Problem, 1933–1938: Volkstumspolitik and the Formulation of Nazi Foreign Policy* (Folkestone, 1975); Václav Kural, *Konflikt místo společenství? Češi a Němci v československém státě 1918–1938* (Prague, 1993); and the eye-witness account by Elizabeth Wiskemann, *Czechs and Germans: A Study of the Struggle in the Historic Provinces of Bohemia and Moravia* (London, 1938). Other standard but polemical works are Radomír Luža, *The Transfer of the Sudeten Germans: A Study of Czech-German Relations, 1933–1962* (New York, 1962); and J. W. Bruegel, *Tschechen und Deutsche 1918–1938* (Munich, 1967).

16. See the interpretation published under the auspices of the Czech ministry of education: Zdeněk Beneš and Václav Kural, eds., *Facing History: The Evolution of Czech-German Relations in the Czech Provinces, 1848–1948* (Prague, 2002), 66–113. Significantly, it was translated into English and German to present an official Czech history of the relationship.

17. See Christoph Boyer, *Nationale Kontrahenten oder Partner? Studien zu den Beziehungen zwischen Tschechen und Deutschen in der Wirtschaft der ČSR*

(1918–1938) (Munich, 1999); Nancy M. Wingfield, *Flag Wars and Stone Saints: How the Bohemian Lands Became Czech* (Cambridge, MA, 2007); and Tara Zahra, *Kidnapped Souls: National Indifference and the Battle for Children in the Bohemian Lands, 1900–1948* (Ithaca, NY, 2008). For the 1940s especially, see Volker Zimmermann, *Die Sudetendeutschen im NS-Staat: Politik und Stimmung der Bevölkerung im Reichsgau Sudetenland (1938–1945)* (Essen, 1999); and Benjamin Frommer, *National Cleansing: Retribution against Nazi Collaborators in Postwar Czechoslovakia* (Cambridge, 2005).

18. See the incisive discussion in Eva Hahnová, *Sudetoněmecký problém: Obtížné loučení s minulosti* (Ústí nad Labem, 1999), 25, 29.

19. In the Sudeten German case it has mainly been used for Konrad Henlein. See Gebel, *"Heim ins Reich!"*; the unannotated study by Stanislav Biman and Jaroslav Malíř, *Kariéra učitele tělocviku* (Liberec, 1983); and an apologetic work, Franz Katzer, *Das große Ringen: Der Kampf der Sudetendeutschen unter Konrad Henlein* (Tübingen, 2003). Other biographies include Ludwig Weichselbaumer, *Walter Brand (1907–1980): Ein sudetendeutscher Politiker im Spannungsfeld zwischen Autonomie und Anschluss* (Munich, 2008); and René Küpper, *Karl Hermann Frank (1898–1946): Politische Biographie eines sudetendeutschen Nationalsozialisten* (Munich, 2010).

20. For recent scholarship about "national indifference," see Pieter M. Judson, *Guardians of the Nation: Activists on the Language Frontiers of Imperial Austria* (Cambridge, MA, 2006); and Zahra, *Kidnapped Souls*.

21. Smelser in *The Sudeten Problem* suggests Rutha's influence, but the works of Luža and Bruegel reference him only briefly.

22. Walter Brand, *Die sudetendeutsche Tragödie* (Wunsiedel, 1949), 30, 43, 54.

23. For instance, Peter Nasarski, ed., *Deutsche Jugendbewegung in Europa* (Cologne, 1967); Johannes Stauda, *Der Wandervogel in Böhmen, 1911–1920*, ed. Kurt Oberdorffer, 2 vols. (Reutlingen, 1975–1978); Peter Becher, ed., *Deutsche Jugend in Böhmen 1918–1938* (Munich, 1993); and Andreas Luh, *Der Deutsche Turnverband in der Ersten Tchechoslowakischen Republik: Vom völkischen Vereinsbetrieb zur volkspolitischen Bewegung* (Munich, 1988). See also one impressive *Magisterarbeit*, Dunja Berthold, *Die sudetendeutsche Jugendbewegung und die Turnerjugend des Deutschen Turnverbandes in der Erste Tschoslowakischen Republik von 1919 bis 1938* (Bochum, 1985).

24. Walter Becher to author, 28 June 2001. Compare Walter Becher, *Zeitzeuge: Ein Lebensbericht* (Munich, 1990), 53, 84; and his denial of Rutha's homosexuality: BHA, Becher papers, 84, talk to "Historiker Arbeitskreis des Witiko-Bundes" [undated], 3.

25. See Václav Král, ed., *Die Deutschen in der Tschechoslowakei 1933–1947: Dokumentensammlung* (Prague, 1964); and Otto Novák, *Henleinovci proti*

Československu: Z historie sudetoněmeckého fašismu v letech 1933–1938 (Prague, 1987), 150. See also Jaroslav César and Bohumil Černý, *Politika německých buržoazních stran v Československu v letech 1918–1938* (Prague, 1962), 2:388; and Zdeněk Kárník, *České země v éře první republiky (1918–1938),* vol.3, *O přežití a o život (1936–1938)* (Prague, 2003), 88.

26. Biman and Malíř, *Kariéra,* 182.

27. See Tomáš Kasper, *Výchova či politika? Úskalí německého pedagogického hnutí v Československu v letech 1918–1933* (Prague, 2007).

28. See now Pavel Himl, Jan Seidl, and Franz Schindler, eds., *Homosexualita v českých dějinách a společnosti* (Prague, 2012). Previously, a lone popular work was Jiří Fanel, *Gay historie* (Prague, 2000).

29. See Harry Oosterhuis, "Medicine, Male Bonding, and Homosexuality in Nazi Germany," *JCH* 32, no. 2 (1997): 187–205; George Mosse, *Nationalism and Sexuality: Middle-Class Morality and Sexual Norms in Modern Europe* (Madison, WI, 1985), 159–169; and Dagmar Herzog, *Sex after Fascism: Memory and Morality in Twentieth-Century Germany* (Princeton, NJ, 2005), 12, 33–36.

30. See Christoph Boyer and Jaroslav Kučera, "Die Deutschen in Böhmen, die Sudetendeutsche Partei und der Nationalsozialismus," in *Nationalsozialismus in der Region: Beiträge zur regionale und lokalen Forschung und zum internationalen Vergleich,* ed. Horst Möller, Andreas Wirsching, and Walter Ziegler (Munich, 1996), 273–285. See also Zimmermann, *Die Sudetendeutschen im NS-Staat,* 56, 69. In English, J. W. Bruegel's most cited work is *Czechoslovakia before Munich: The German Minority Problem and British Appeasement Policy* (Cambridge, 1973).

31. Walter Heinrich, review of Smelser, *Sudeten Problem,* reprinted in J. Hans Pichler, ed., *Im Prism des Geistes* (Graz, 1982), 299–303.

32. See the incisive essays in *Bohemia* 38/39 (1997–1998) by Václav Kural and others in response to the arguments of Boyer and Kučera.

33. See Bruegel, *Czechoslovakia;* Jindřich Dejmek, *Nenaplněné naděje: Politické a diplomatické vztahy Československa a Velké Británie 1918–1938* (Prague, 2003); and Paul Vyšný, *The Runciman Mission to Czechoslovakia, 1938: Prelude to Munich* (Basingstoke, 2003).

34. For the benefits of this approach, see Jeremy King, *Budweisers into Czechs and Germans: A Local History of Bohemian Politics, 1848–1948* (Princeton, NJ, 2002).

I. THE DEVIL'S WALL

1. Franz Wurm, *Die Teufelsmauer zwischen Oschitz und Böhm.-Aicha* (Böhmisch-Aicha, 1884), 19–20. For other devil legends see Josef Alfred

Taubmann, *Märchen und Sagen aus Nordböhmen: Aus dem Volksmunde gesammelt* (Reichenberg, 1887), 78–83.

2. See Anna Sluknová-Caforčice, *Vyprávěnky z Podještědí* (Liberec, 1981), 17.

3. Karl Freiherr von Czoernig, *Ethnographische Karte der österreichischen Monarchie* (Vienna, 1855).

4. Joseph Hain, *Handbuch der Statistik des österreichischen Kaiserstaates* (Vienna, 1852), 1:227.

5. For the authorities' dilemmas on this point, see Emil Brix, *Die Umgangssprachen in Altösterreich zwischen Agitation und Assimilation: Die Sprachenstatistik in den zisleithanischen Volkszählungen* (Vienna, 1982). See also Mark Cornwall, "The Struggle on the Czech-German Language Border, 1880–1940," *English Historical Review* 109, no. 433 (1994): 914–951.

6. For context on themes in this chapter, see especially Pieter M. Judson, *Guardians of the Nation: Activists on the Language Frontiers of Imperial Austria* (Cambridge, MA, 2006). While Judson stresses the politicization of an artificial language border in the late nineteenth century, those like Czoernig had "revealed" the existence of such a concept many decades before.

7. Johannes Zemmrich, *Sprachgrenze und Deutschtum in Böhmen* (Brunswick, 1902), 1–3, 47.

8. This was the case in the parish of Zetten (which included Teschen on the other side of the language border). In the 1900 census, compared to 1890, the proportion of those identifying as Germans had dropped from 29 to 24 percent.

9. *Večerník práva lidu,* 15 October 1937, 1.

10. See the impressive study by Miroslav Hroch, *Na prahu národní existence* (Prague, 1999).

11. For clear discussions of the late nineteenth-century relationship, see Jan Křen, *Die Konfliktgemeinschaft: Tschechen und Deutsche, 1780–1918* (Munich, 1996); and Elizabeth Wiskemann, *Czechs and Germans: A Study of the Struggle in the Historic Provinces of Bohemia and Moravia* (London, 1938), 19–69.

12. Mark Cornwall, "The Construction of National Identities in the Northern Bohemian Borderland, 1848–1871," in *Different Paths to the Nation: Regional and National Identities in Central Europe and Italy, 1830–70*, ed. Laurence Cole (Basingstoke, 2007), 150–154.

13. František L. Rieger, *Čechy, země i narod: Obraz statisticko-historický* (Prague, 1863), 1.

14. See the hostile response in Reichenberg, where all public correspondence had always been handled in German: *Reichenberger Zeitung,* 6 May 1880, 1.

15. Andrew Whiteside, *Austrian National Socialism before 1918* (The Hague, 1962), 37–50.

16. Schmeykal quotation from: Lothar Höbelt, *Kornblume und Kaiseradler: Die deutschfreiheitlichen Parteien Altösterreichs 1882–1918* (Vienna, 1993), 56. See also for the challenge of *völkisch* nationalism, Pieter M. Judson, *Exclusive Revolutionaries: Liberal Politics, Social Experience and National Identity in the Austrian Empire, 1848–1914* (Ann Arbor, MI, 1996), chapters 7–8; and Uwe Puschner, Walter Schmitz, and Justus Ulbricht, eds., *Handbuch zur "völkischen Bewegung" 1871–1918* (Munich, 1996).

17. Roman Karpaš, ed., *Kniha o Liberci* (Liberec, 1996), 154–155.

18. Judson, *Guardians of the Nation,* 42–63, 77–84.

19. Gary Cohen, *The Politics of Ethnic Survival: Germans in Prague, 1861–1914* (Princeton, NJ, 1981), 208.

20. *Die Hochwasser-Katastrophe vom 30 und 31 Juli 1897 im Gebiete des Iser- und Riesengebirges etc* (Reichenberg, 1897).

21. Nancy M. Wingfield, *Flag Wars and Stone Saints: How the Bohemian Lands Became Czech* (Cambridge, MA, 2007), 48–78.

22. Berthold Sutter, *Die Badenischen Sprachenverordnungen von 1897* (Graz, 1960), 2:104–129; here 128n91.

23. See Whiteside, *Austrian National Socialism;* and Cornwall, "Struggle," 928, 945.

24. SOkAL, MAO, Obecní výbor [parish council], book 1, "Protocoll–Buch. Gemeinde Ausschuss Oschitz" (council minutes), 162, 173, 197.

25. Alena Wagnerová, *Neodsunuté vzpomínky: Česká zkušenost pohraničí* (Prague, 2000), 68.

26. Franz Köhler, ed., *Heimat zwischen Jeschken, Roll and Bösig im Heimatkreis Niemes, Sudetenland* (Ludwigsburg, 1984), 123–124. On Světlá see for example Josef Špičák, *Ještěd Karoliny Světlé* (Liberec, 1958).

27. Hermann Hrubesch, *Bad Kunnersdorf: Moorbad und Sommerfrische* (Reichenberg, n.d., ca. 1926), 5; and the pamphlet, *Moorbad und Sommerfrische Bad Kunnersdorf bei Oschitz in Böhmen* (Gablonz, n.d., ca. 1920), 10–11.

28. See the local histories in F. Hantschel, *Heimatkunde der politischen Bezirkes B.-Leipa* (Böhmisch Leipa, 1911), 1088–1093; and Rudolf Jäschke, *Geschichte der Stadt Oschitz* (Arnsdorf-Haida, 1915), 70–71.

29. [Walter Rohn],"Heinz Rutha: Ein Leben für Volk und Heimat," *VuF* 4 (1937): 153–154.

30. The Merzdorf parish records show that Josef's father was Ferdinand Rutha (b. 1796) and his mother Helena Hönig (1800–1852), daughter of a "master baker" from Oschitz. Ferdinand's parents were Ferdinand Rutha, a miller,

and Apollonia Weigelt, a peasant farmer's daughter from Kunnersdorf: SOAL, Matriky, Merzdorf, L111/6 and L111/13. The lintel with its date of 1844 survives to this day.

31. Karolina's father, Wenzel, was a "master tanner" in Oschitz; her mother, Klara Wander (1801–1883), hailed from a weaver's family in Gablonz: SOAL, Matriky, Oschitz, L111/12.

32. Adolf Gustav (1851), Ferdinand (1856), Marie (1859), and Franz Josef (1861). The latter's name is undoubtedly testament to the Rutha family's imperial allegiance (to Emperor Franz Joseph).

33. Miloslav Sovadina, *Správní vývoj českolipska* (Česká Lípa, 1998), 66–67.

34. Köhler, *Heimat zwischen Jeschken,* 155–159.

35. Ladislav Holy, *The Little Czech and the Great Czech Nation* (Cambridge, 1996), 34–37.

36. [Rohn],"Heinz Rutha: Ein Leben für Volk und Heimat," *VuF* 4 (1937): 153.

37. According to the Alt-Kalken parish records, Johann Wenzel Storch was born in July 1809, the son of Franz Storch, a (peasant) farmer, and Barbara Puntzman, a miller's daughter: SOAL, Matriky, Alt-Kalken, L27/4. On the feudal ties in Alt-Kalken, see Friedrich Bernau, *Der politische Bezirke Dauba: Eine Heimatskunde für Haus und Schule* (Dauba, 1888), 327; some labor obligations continued until 1848.

38. For the following detail about the Storch family I am indebted to the late Josef Štorch and his sister Marie Bařinová: interview at Dolní Krupa, 7 April 2002.

39. See Stanislav Biman and Jaroslav Malíř, *Kariéra učitele tělocviku* (Liberec, 1983), 13–15.

40. For example, Wenzel and Barbara Storch's son Josef (1865–1935) married, in the 1890s, Emilie Jihlavcová from Neveklovice (and the census of 1921 shows that in their inn at Nieder-Gruppai the servants were both German and Czech). Josef and Emilie's own son Josef (1895–1969) married, after the First World War, Marie Flanderková, who was from Mukařov, a Czech village next to Neveklovice; they seem to have made their home in Czech-speaking Neveklovice before moving to Nieder-Gruppai in the 1930s.

41. Rutha relative interview, 8 July 2000.

42. See *Österreichischer Zentralkataster sämtlicher Handels-, Industrie- und Gewerbebetriebe,* vol. 8 no.1, *Die Betriebe von Böhmen: Handelskammer-bezirken Eger, Reichenberg* (Vienna, 1903), 412.

43. Rutha relative interview, 5 August 2001. During the Ruthas' tenure as directors of the spa, capital of 200,000 crowns was invested and the cure houses substantially renovated: Hrubesch, *Bad Kunnersdorf,* 5.

44. Franz Rutha was a miller, baker, and parish head in Kunnersdorf before the First World War: *Adressbuch der politischen Bezirk B.-Leipa* (Böhmisch Leipa, 1913), 53. Ferdinand Rutha appears in Ferdinand Sagasser, ed., *Adress-Buch und Wohnungs-Anzeiger der Stadt Reichenberg* (Reichenberg, 1887), 69. Emanuel Max's father, Ignaz Max, was a prominent local figure, regularly mentioned in Oschitz council minutes from 1889 and serving as the local school inspector in the 1890s: Jäschke, *Geschichte der Stadt Oschitz,* 84. Emanuel was already dead in November 1907.

45. On reform pedagogy see Tara Zahra, *Kidnapped Souls: National Indifference and the Battle for Children in the Bohemian Lands, 1900–1948* (Ithaca, NY, 2008), 54–57; and for the potential influence from Germany see Andrew Donson, *Youth in the Fatherless Land: War Pedagogy, Nationalism, and Authority in Germany, 1914–1918* (Cambridge, MA, 2010), 22–29.

46. Karl Seibt, *Ehrentafel für die im Weltkriege gefallenen deutschen Lehrer Böhmens* (Reichenberg, n.d., ca. 1920), 118.

47. SOkAL, MAO, Oschitz school, book 3, "Protokolle" of teaching corps meetings (1903–1909), 4 February 1905.

48. Zahra, *Kidnapped Souls,* 52ff; and Judson, *Guardians of the Nation,* 82. One historian has defined the *Heimat* movements that emerged across German space from the 1890s as "popular engagement with and interest in the characteristics and traditions of a particular locality, state or region, as a unique expression of the wider national culture": Abigail Green, *Fatherlands: State-Building and Nationhood in Nineteenth-Century Germany* (Cambridge, 2001), 330.

49. Such societies flourished in German Bohemian towns from the 1870s as civic pride boomed; for example, one was founded in Böhmisch Leipa in 1875: Jaroslav Panáček, Marie Vojtišková, and Ladislav Smejkal, *Z dějin České Lípy* (Česká Lípa, 1999), 121.

50. SOkAL, MAO, karton 11 (Spolky), documents concerning the Schiller memorial; and "Protokollbuch des Gesang- und Musikvereines in Oschitz."

51. SOkAL, MAO, book 3, "Protokolle" of teaching corps meetings (1903–1909), 9 March 1908; and Seibt, *Ehrentafel,* 62.

52. Heinz Rutha, "Teufelsmauer," *Wandervogel: Monatschrift für deutsches Jugendwandern. Heft der Österreicher* 5/6 (1918): 121–122.

53. Compare Judson, *Guardians of the Nation,* 3; and Zahra, *Kidnapped Souls.* A key distinction might be made here between the nationalist activism of a minority and the national consciousness of a majority.

54. Zemmrich, *Sprachgrenze,* 47.

55. Heinz Rutha diary, 99, entry for 22 August 1918, SOAL, Krajský soud Česká Lípa, trestní spisy [Regional Court at Česká Lípa, criminal records, hereafter CLS], karton 242, Tk 665/37/147.

56. Margarete Ikrath-Rutha, "Heinrich Rutha: Seine Lebensarbeit und seine Ziele für das Sudetendeutschtum" (typed memoir, in Sudetendeutsches Haus library, Munich, 1986), 1; and Rutha relative interview, 8 July 2000.

57. Rutha diary, 84, entry for 22 July 1918.

58. Jan A. Herold, *Mnichovohradišťsko: Přírodou a památkami* (Mnichovo Hradiště, 1914), 12–13.

59. Compare Zahra, *Kidnapped Souls*, 1.

2. A GERMAN BOHEMIAN EDUCATION

1. Václav Ledvinka and Jiří Pešek, *Praha* (Prague, 2000), 496.

2. Franz Kafka, *The Diaries of Franz Kafka, 1910–1923,* ed. Max Brod (London, 1972), 20.

3. Gary Cohen, *The Politics of Ethnic Survival: Germans in Prague, 1861–1914* (Princeton, NJ, 1981), 91, 100.

4. Ibid., 140–235, for a thorough analysis of the rise of liberal-*völkisch* tensions.

5. Ibid., 123–124.

6. Ledvinka and Pešek, *Praha*, 541–543.

7. Although the 1910 census returns for Vinohrady have not survived, this is clear from Heinz's school record: AHMP, III. něm. realka Jindřišská, Haupt-katalog der 1-VII Klasse 1910–1911. Richard's address is given as Kanalgasse.

8. Cohen, *Politics of Ethnic Survival*, 114.

9. *Zwölfter Jahresbericht der k.k. III Deutschen Staatsrealschule in Prag-Neustadt, Heinrichsgasse* (Prague, 1910), 41, 64. For Czech-German anti-Semitism around 1900, see Michal Frankl, *"Emancipace od židů": Český antisemitismus na konci 19. století* (Prague, 2007); and Hillel J. Kieval, *Languages of Community: The Jewish Experience in the Czech Lands* (Berkeley, CA, 2000).

10. Gary Cohen, *Education and Middle-Class Society in Imperial Austria, 1848–1918* (West Lafayette, IN, 1996), 72, 212.

11. See the Realschule annual reports for 1910–1911: *Dreizehnter Jahresbericht der k.k. Deutschen Staatsrealschule* (Prague, 1911).

12. Anton Gindely, *Lehrbuch der allgemeinen Geschichte für die unteren Classen der Mittelschulen,* vol. 2, *Die Mittelalter,* 7th ed. (Prague, 1884), 47, 60–66. For context on this typical attempt to fuse a national-dynastic patriotic education across Austria, see Ernst Bruckmüller, "Patriotic and National Myths," in *The Limits of Loyalty: Imperial Symbolism, Popular Allegiances, and State Patriotism in the Late Habsburg Monarchy,* ed. Laurence Cole and Daniel L. Unowsky (New York, 2007), 23–30.

13. See *Dreizehnter Jahresbericht*, 7–8, for recommended reading for the lower classes. The list also included translated escapist novels such as *Robinson Crusoe* and *Uncle Tom's Cabin*.

14. Ibid., 45–46.

15. This had nullified the Bohemian Diet's 1863 law requiring all pupils in Bohemia's secondary schools to study a second provincial language.

16. AHMP, III. něm. realka Jindřišská, Haupt-katalog 1910–1911.

17. He briefly mentioned it to the Czech police in October 1937: SOAL, CLS, karton 360, Tk 665/37/27, 1.

18. Realschule annual reports; and AHMP, Haupt-katalog 1910–1911. There were four end-of-year grades: distinction; pass; fail and re-sit the year; complete fail.

19. *Zwölfter Jahresbericht*, 50.

20. Jaroslav Panáček, Marie Vojtíšková, and Ladislav Smejkal, *Z dějin České Lípy* (Česká Lípa, 1999), 132.

21. See Nancy M. Wingfield, *Flag Wars and Stone Saints: How the Bohemian Lands Became Czech* (Cambridge, MA, 2007), 17–47.

22. Panáček, Vojtíšková, and Smejkal, *Z dějin České Lípy*, 126.

23. SOkAČL, Státní reálka Česká Lípa, karton 1, L. *Jahresbericht der Staats-Realschule in Böhm.-Leipa für das Schuljahr 1912–13* (Böhm.-Leipa, 1913), 1–52.

24. SOkAČL, LI. *Jahresbericht der Staats-Realschule in Böhm.Leipa für das Schuljahr 1913–14* (Böhm.-Leipa, 1914), 1–2.

25. Ibid., 13–16.

26. Ibid., 10, 17. Pechmann noted that new governmental guidelines of September 1912 were a precursor to making Czech a compulsory subject in the Realschulen of Bohemia.

27. Helmut Engelbracht, *Geschichte des österreichischen Bildungswesens: Erziehung und Unterricht auf dem Boden Österreichs* (Vienna, 1986), 4:35–36.

28. The school had about ten Jewish pupils, and there were usually a couple in Rutha's class; few Czech boys attended the school.

29. SOkAČL, XLIX. *Jahresbericht der Staats-Realschule in Böhm.-Leipa für das Schuljahr 1911–12* (Böhm.-Leipa, 1912), 46.

30. Rutha relative interview, 6 August 2001.

31. Schooling across Germany witnessed the same limitations: Andrew Donson, *Youth in the Fatherless Land: War Pedagogy, Nationalism, and Authority in Germany, 1914–1918* (Cambridge, MA, 2010), 129–130.

32. Marie Vojtíšková, "Českolipské náměty v díle Karla Poláčka," *Českolipsko Literární* (1978): 26–37. See Karel Poláček's novel, *Hrdinové táhnou do boje* (Prague, 1936).

33. SOkAČL, *LI. Jahresbericht*, 55.

34. SOkAČL, *LIII. Jahresbericht der Staats-Realschule in Böhm.-Leipa für das Schuljahr 1915–16* (Böhm.-Leipa, 1916), 2, 29. In December 1915 a requiem mass was held for Johann Malle; as Rutha's fourth-form teacher, he had taken pupils on several excursions, most notably to Tetschen in northwestern Bohemia.

35. Ibid., 27.

36. Ibid., 24–25; and *LII. Jahresbericht der Staats-Realschule in Böhm.-Leipa für das Schuljahr 1914–15* (Böhm.-Leipa, 1915), 16. A shift in patriotic themes is clear when compared with those prescribed at Rutha's Prague Realschule in 1910; there, exam questions included, "Wherein lies the greatness of Maria Theresa?" and "What examples do we find in Austrian history of heroism and love of the fatherland?" (AHMP, files of III. něm. realka Jindřišská, oral examination topics). For comparable war pedagogy in Germany, including the increased use of "free compositions," see Donson, *Youth*, 59–90.

37. Tomáš Kasper, *Výchova či politika? Úskalí německého pedagogického hnutí v Československu v letech 1918–1933* (Prague, 2007); and Johannes Stauda, *Der Wandervogel in Böhmen, 1911–1920*, ed. Kurt Oberdorffer, 2 vols. (Reutlingen, 1975–1978). See also the following essay collections: Peter Nasarski, ed., *Deutsche Jugendbewegung in Europa* (Cologne, 1967); Peter Becher, ed., *Deutsche Jugend in Böhmen 1918–1938* (Munich, 1993); and Marek Waic, ed., *Německé tělovýchovné a sportovní spolky v českých zemích a Československu* (Prague, 2008).

38. Peter Stachura, *The German Youth Movement, 1900–1945* (London, 1981), 17. Among many studies on the Wandervogel in Germany, see Ulrich Hermann, ed., *"Mit uns zieht die neue Zeit . . . " Der Wandervogel in der deutschen Jugendbewegung* (Weinheim, 2006).

39. A classic book of such "spiritual" maxims was Georg Stammler, *Worte an eine Schar* (Heidelberg, 1914).

40. Kasper, *Výchova*, 35–36.

41. For the following the most reliable account remains Stauda, *Wandervogel*. See also Helmut Richter, *Geschichte des Reichenberger Wandervogels* (Waldkraiburg, 1984).

42. SOkALov, Karl Metzner papers, "Gedenkschrift" by Metzner, January 1939.

43. Stauda, *Wandervogel*, II:13.

44. Karl Metzner, "Burschen heraus!," *Burschen heraus! Fahrtenblatt der Leitmeritzer Ruderriegen und des Wandervolgels,* March 1913, 1.

45. Karl Metzner, "Der Wandervögel Deutschtum," *BH*, April–May 1914, 111.

46. Karl Metzner, "Zum inneren Ausbau des österreichischen Wandervogels," *BH*, June 1913, 11–13.

47. Stauda, *Wandervogel*, 1:31; and Cohen, *Education and Middle-Class Society*, 219.

48. Ernst Keil, quoted in Werner Kindt, ed., *Die Wandervogelzeit: Quellenschriften zur deutschen Jugendbewegung 1896–1919* (Düsseldorf, 1968), 333.

49. For variations on this theory (focusing mainly on primary schools) see Pieter M. Judson, *Guardians of the Nation: Activists on the Language Frontiers of Imperial Austria* (Cambridge, MA, 2006), 72–84; and Tara Zahra, *Kidnapped Souls: National Indifference and the Battle for Children in the Bohemian Lands, 1900–1948* (Ithaca, NY, 2008), 52–56. Neither work mentions youth movements.

50. Karel Kazbunda, *Otázka česko-německá v předvečer Velké Války* (Prague, 1995), 18–21; Erich Schmied, "J. W. Titta und der Deutsche Volksrat für Böhmen," *Bohemia* 26 (1985): 309–330; and Josef Pfitzner, *Sudetendeutsche Einheitsbewegung: Werden und Erfüllung* (Carlsbad, 1937), 29–30.

51. Stauda, *Wandervogel*, 1:14, 2:9.

52. Karl Metzner, "Der Wandervogel Deutschtum," *BH*, April–May 1914, 111.

53. K. Hacker, "Die vor 100 Jahren und wir," *BH*, January–February 1914, 65–66.

54. Stauda, *Wandervogel*, 1:20, 2:57, 73.

55. Ibid., 1:31–33.

56. See Günther's comments: ibid., 2:48. Thus, naturally, the Bohemian Wandervogel had participated in the gathering in Germany at Hoher Meissner (October 1913).

57. Ibid., 1:41–42, 2:58–59.

58. Ibid., 2:34–35.

59. Ibid., 1:33. Compare Kasper, who suggests that in the Bohemian Wandervogel parents and headmasters had little involvement: *Výchova*, 32.

60. Karl Günther, "Vom Wandervogel. Rundschau," *BH*, October 1913, 10. Günther specifically warned the Leipa, Prague, Leitmeritz, and Eger groups.

61. Erich Pelikan, "Nach Johnsdorf," *BH*, June 1913, 5–6; and "Wandervogel Böhmisch Leipa," *BH*, November 1913, 35.

62. Otto Kletzl, "Wandervogel Böhmisch Leipa," *BH*, December 1913, 55; and Stauda, *Wandervogel*, 2:114.

63. Willi Riewald, "Wandervogel Böhmisch Leipa," *BH*, January–February 1914, 81.

64. Rudolf Siegl, "Winterlager 1913," *BH*, January–February 1914, 74–76. For typical maxims on how to appreciate the mountains, see Stammler, *Worte an eine Schar*, 23–24.

65. There is no thorough study of socialist youth in Bohemia, but see Wolfgang Neugebauer, *Bauvolk der kommenden Welt: Geschichte der sozialistischen Jugendbewegung in Österreich* (Vienna, 1975), 48–71.

66. See Daniel Langhans, *Der Reichsbund der deutschen katholischen Jugend in der Tschechoslowakei 1918–1938* (Bonn, 1990), 17–25. The mission of Catholic youth organizers like Anton Orel has interesting parallels to nationalist pedagogues like Metzner.

67. Rudolf Feldberger, "Wandervögel," *BH,* July 1914, 156.

68. Heinz Rutha, "Wandervogel Böhmisch-Leipa," *BH,* July 1914, 171.

69. Otto Kletzl, "Im Höllengebirge," *BH,* October–November 1914, 5–6; and Heinz Rutha, "Die Geschichte einer Fiedel," *BH,* May 1915, 101. The group of five had walked through south Bohemia and visited the city of Linz.

70. [Johannes Stauda], "Wandervogel Deutschböhmens," *BH,* July 1914, 155.

3. THE SACRIFICE

1. Marriage date given in the Czechoslovak census of 1930: NA, SO 1930, "Sčítání obyvatelstva ČSR v roce 1930, Praha," karton 3705, 259/202 Lázně Kundratice, č.p. 45 rod.

2. For context see Ivan Šedivý, *Češi, české země a Velká válka 1914–1918* (Prague, 2001), 74–89. Polifka was at first in Infantry Regiment 94, Effert in Feldjäger Battalion 12.

3. For the experience of captivity, see Alon Rachamimov, *POWs and the Great War: Captivity on the Eastern Front* (Oxford, 2002), chapters 1 and 3.

4. Karl Seibt, *Ehrentafel für den im Weltkriege gefallenen deutschen Lehrer Böhmens* (Reichenberg, n.d., ca. 1920), 62, 118; and Rutha relative interview, 5 August 2001.

5. Heinz Rutha, "Die Geschichte einer Fiedel," *BH,* May 1915, 101.

6. Hew Strachan, *The First World War,* vol. 1, *To Arms* (Oxford, 2001), 162.

7. Johannes Stauda, *Der Wandervogel in Böhmen, 1911–1920,* ed. Kurt Oberdorffer (Reutlingen, 1975–1978), 2:64.

8. Ibid, 64–65.

9. Otto Kletzl, "Vom Leipschen Wandervogel," *BH,* January 1915, 45; and Heinz Rutha, "Vom Leipschen Wandervogel," *BH,* April 1915, 94.

10. Catholic and socialist youth activity diminished markedly during the war, but these subjects require more research. See Daniel Langhans, *Der Reichsbund der deutschen katholischen Jugend in der Tschechoslowakei 1918–1938* (Bonn, 1990), 23–27; and Wolfgang Neugebauer, *Bauvolk der kommenden Welt: Geschichte der sozialistischen Jugendbewegung in Österreich* (Vienna, 1975), 103–104: across Bohemia, socialist youth membership dropped from over seven thousand (1913) to just over two thousand (1917).

11. Heinz Rutha, "Vom Leipschen Wandervogel," *BH,* June 1915, 127.

12. Otto Kletzl, "Vom Leipschen Wandervogel," *BH,* February 1915, 60.

13. See the exemplary case study of sacrifice on the home front, Maureen Healy, *Vienna and the Fall of the Habsburg Empire: Total War and Everyday Life in World War I* (Cambridge, 2004).

14. Heinz Rutha, "Unsere Wandervogelsoldaten und wir," *BH*, April 1916, 86.

15. Stauda, *Wandervogel*, 1:8, 2:31–32, 71; and Šedivý, *Češi*, 37.

16. See Hans Jürgen Ostler, "'Soldatenspielerei?' Vormilitärische Ausbildung bei Jugendlichen in der österreichischen Reichshälfte der Donaumonarchie, 1914–1918" (master's thesis, Hamburg University, 1990), 87–90; for the limited success of official pre-military training in Bohemia, see 109–110, 152–157, 169, 171, 239. See also Manfried Rauchensteiner, *Der Tod des Doppeladlers: Österreich-Ungarn und der Erste Weltkrieg* (Graz, 1993), 274–275.

17. Stauda, *Wandervogel*, 1:46, 2:66–69; and Stauda, "Die militärische Vorbereitung der Jugend," *BH*, December 1915, 35–36. For the comparable debate in Germany, see Andrew Donson, *Youth in the Fatherless Land: War Pedagogy, Nationalism, and Authority in Germany, 1914–1918* (Cambridge, MA, 2010), 116–123, 218–219.

18. Stauda, *Wandervogel*, 1:47.

19. Stauda, "Gauspiegel," *BH*, December 1915, 35. Significantly, at the 1916 Gautag one Wandervogel guest from Germany caused some offense when he made an overtly pan-German speech: Stauda, *Wandervogel*, 1:51.

20. Even here we should not exaggerate the national antagonism, for Stauda notes that Wandervögel visiting pure Czech areas could be welcomed by Czech Scouts: ibid., 49.

21. Stauda, "Unser Gautag," *BH*, June 1915, 115.

22. George L. Mosse, *Fallen Soldiers: Reshaping the Memory of the World Wars* (New York, 1990), 74.

23. Rudolf Feldberger, "Sterben," *BH*, April 1916, 80.

24. [Wilhelm Flatz], "Worte am Totenfeuer," *WÖF*, October 1916, 9.

25. Stauda, *Wandervogel*, 2:70, 72.

26. For a new analysis of Czech military behavior and how the myth of mass desertion was exploited by German nationalists, see Richard Lein, *Pflichterfüllung oder Hochverrat? Die tschechischen Soldaten Österreich-Ungarns im Ersten Weltkrieg* (Vienna, 2010).

27. See Jörg Osterloh, *Nationalsozialistische Judenverfolgung im Reichsgau Sudetenland 1938–1945* (Munich, 2006), 37–45; and for a stimulating overview, Peter Pulzer, "The Return of Old Hatreds," in *German-Jewish History in Modern Times*, ed. Michael A. Meyer, vol. 3, *Integration in Dispute, 1871–1918* (New York, 1997), 196–251.

28. Gerhard Seewann, *Österreichische Jugendbewegung 1900 bis 1938* (Frankfurt am Main, 1971), 1:92–93.

29. Stauda, *Wandervogel,* 2:81; and Harry Pross, *Jugend, Eros, Politik: Die Geschichte der deutschen Jugendverbände* (Bern, 1964), 169, 173. For the clash in Germany see Andreas Winnecken, *Ein Fall von Antisemitismus: Zur Geschichte und Pathogenese der deutschen Jugendbewegung vor dem Ersten Weltkrieg* (Cologne, 1991).

30. See Rutha's comments in "Leipa," *BH,* December 1915, 37; and for Leipa Jews, see Marie Vojtíšková, *Židé v České Lípě* (Libice, 1999).

31. Quoted in Seewann, *Österreichische Jugendbewegung,* 1:92. On refugees see David Rechter, *The Jews of Vienna and the First World War* (London, 2001), 78–79; and Marsha Rozenblit, *Reconstructing a National Identity: The Jews of Habsburg Austria during World War I* (Oxford, 2001), 66, 192n57.

32. Stauda, *Wandervogel,* 2:41.

33. Erich Frühauf, "Von den Führern," appendix to *Gablonzer Wandervogel: Geschichtlicher Abriss von 1913–1938,* ed. Walter Jantsch (Schwäbisch Gmünd: self-publication, 1974), 9.

34. Ferdinand Büttner, *Ich und meine fünf Jungen* (Weimar, 1914), vii, 21–22, 51–52. In the boys' bedroom Büttner placed portraits of German heroes to inspire them and prevent masturbation. See also Stauda, *Wandervogel,* 1:50.

35. Frühauf, "Von den Führern," 9–10.

36. Stauda, *Wandervogel,* 2:104. See also Ernst Frank, ed., *Ernst Leibl: Einführung in Leben und Werk* (Dettingen am Main, 1965); and Leibl's own short memoir, "Zur Person und Sache, ein Selbstporträt" (1976), in SWA, R036. The memoir hints at Leibl's anti-Semitism and explains his view of the wartime sacrifice, as he lost two brothers on the eastern front and was himself severely wounded on the Italian front.

37. *BH,* December 1915, 35, 37: Rutha's report.

38. Stauda, *Wandervogel,* 2:81. Perhaps unsurprisingly, it has been impossible to track down the exact wording of the cryptic "Tetschen declaration."

39. Ibid., 1:50, 2:82.

40. Ibid., 1:51–52, 2:83–86; Rudolf Feldberger, "Unser Gautag," *BH,* July 1916, 113–116; and for Feldberger on Büttner: "Aus Feldbergers Briefen," *BH,* October 1918, 8.

41. Heinz Rutha, "Leipa," *BH,* April 1916, 88.

42. See Kurt Ferster, "Unsere Semesterfahrt 1916," *BH,* February–March 1916, 61.

43. SOkAČL, *LIII. Jahresbericht der Staats-Realschule in Böhm.-Leipa für das Schuljahr 1915–16* (Böhm.-Leipa, 1916), 24–25. These examination reports for 1916 are unfortunately missing from the Česká Lípa archives.

44. Stauda, *Wandervogel,* 2:96.

45. Heinz Rutha, "Böhmisch Leipa," *BH*, October–November 1916, 5. In Judenburg he looked up one Wandervogel, Rudolf Fritsch, who a year later would be killed on the Italian front.

46. See Rudolf Oppelt and Camillo Popper, *75 Jahre Prager Handelsakademie 1856–1931* (Prague, 1931), 76. In 1916 the course had been running for twenty-five years.

47. Stauda, *Wandervogel*, 2:96.

48. See the entries of 4 April and 22 August 1918 in Rutha's transcribed diary, 14, 102–103: SOAL, CLS, karton 242, Tk 665/37/147. See also Rutha relative interviews, 8 July 2000 and 29 March 2009.

49. Margarete Ikrath-Rutha, "Heinrich Rutha: Seine Lebensarbeit und seine Ziele für das Sudetendeutschtum" (typed memoir, in Sudetendeutsches Haus library, Munich, 1986), 3.

50. Heinz Rutha, "Gau Deutschböhmen," *WÖF*, March 1917, 120.

51. Ibid., 120–121; and Kurt [Oberdorffer], "Prag-'Wetterhart'," *BH*, February–April 1917, 29.

52. Stauda, *Wandervogel*, 1:54–55, 2:93.

53. Ibid., 1:53–54, 2:88–92. See also the uplifting reports about Linz by Rutha, Just, and Feldberger in *WÖF*, October 1916.

54. Heinz Rutha, "Gau Deutschböhmen," *WÖF*, December 1916, 58.

55. Heinz Rutha, "Noch einmal die Soldaten," *WÖF*, December 1916, 51–52.

56. For the following see Rutha's report, *BH*, February–April 1917, 21–23; and Stauda, *Wandervogel*, 1:54. Rutha had also already formulated some of these ideas in a circular to branch leaders: see NA, SdP, karton 67, "Gauschreiben," 21 January 1917. Misleadingly, the Czech historian Tomáš Kasper implies that Rutha in 1916–1917 was already a visionary with a clear program of "regeneration" (*Výchova*, 44, 74). In fact Rutha's moves were largely pragmatic and a response to existing weaknesses; the vision came later.

57. *WÖF*, May 1917, 157–158; and *BH*, May 1917, 33–37, with subsequent branch reports.

58. Stauda, *Wandervogel*, 2:98–99.

59. *BH*, June–July 1917, 60, 62: branch reports from Prachatitz and Alt-Prag.

60. Heinz Rutha, "Gau Deutschböhmen: Unser Gautag," *WÖF*, July 1917, 206–208.

61. Heinz Rutha, "Unser wehrhaft Gautagfeuer," *Wandervogel: Monatschrift für deutsches Jugendwandern. Heft der Österreicher*, 5/6 (1918), 122.

62. For Kampe's career see Stauda, *Wandervogel*, 2:78–79, 104.

63. [Rudolf Kampe], "Worte am Feuer," *BH*, June–July 1917, 52–53.

64. For the following see Rutha's reports: *WÖF*, July 1917, 209–210; and *BH*, June–July 1917, 49–50.

65. The Leibl-Rutha friction is cryptically referenced in the sources. In Prague, Leibl long had a reputation for flitting between branches and probably felt Rutha's sudden influence in "Prague-Lützow" was at his own expense and hypocritical after Wrchhaben. See Stauda, *Wandervogel,* 1:58.

66. The idea that the Austrian Bund might join Germany's *Freideutsche Jugend* had been rejected anyway at a special Bund meeting in Vienna on 14 January 1917, and Rutha already knew that most Bohemian Wandervögel opposed such a union. See his circular of 21 January: NA, SdP, karton 67.

67. Stauda, *Wandervogel,* 1:60–61, 2:106. Rutha at least could enthuse about the Wandervogel exhibition at Iglau: "Von der Ausstellung und was ich mir dabei dachte," *Wandervogel: Österreichisches Bundesblatt,* September 1917, 17–19.

68. There is no evidence that Rutha cut short his studies. Compare František Kolář, ed., *Politická elita meziválečného Československa 1918–1938: Kdo byl kdo* (Prague, 1998), 216.

69. Heinz Rutha, "Gau Deutschböhmen: Unser Gautag," *WÖF,* July 1917, 206. For the Trschiblitz group photograph with a smiling Rutha, see SWA, R139 (Ortsgruppe Leitmeritz).

70. Otto Kletzl, "Rudolf Feldberger gefallen," *BH,* January–February 1918, 49. Extracts from Feldberger's frontline diary were published in ibid., October 1918, 5–6.

71. See note 48 above.

72. The following draws on the reports in ÖSA, Kriegsarchiv [KA], Militärschulen karton 1691, Rangierungsliste, Reserve Offizierschule der k.k. Artillerie Linz, 30 March 1918. My thanks to Karl Rossa for locating this source for me.

73. Rutha diary, 2–3, entry for 16 February 1918. In August 1917, Rutha had made an expedition to southern Bohemia with another member from Prague-Lützow.

74. Ibid., 8, entry for 28 March 1918. Hänke nevertheless finished thirteenth in the final examinations and was officially judged to be "serious, industrious and hardworking." Only twenty years later would Rutha and Hänke's acquaintance be renewed (AAVČR, Beneš papers, karton 142, pisemnosti opisy, Hänke to Rutha, 19 April 1937).

75. Ibid., 1, entry for 17 February 1918, and Flatz's inscription; and Otto Kletzl, "Über das Tagebuchschreiben," *WÖF,* November 1916, 53–54.

76. Rutha diary, 5–8, entries for 18 February and 28 March 1918.

77. The catalyst for the leadership meeting had been Janiczek trying to sack Stauda as editor of *Burschen heraus.* See Stauda, *Wandervogel,* 1:62–63, 2:110–11; for Janiczek's perspective see "Gauspiegel," *BH,* October–November 1917, 15–17; and "Gauspiegel," *BH,* December 1917, 44–45.

78. See the correspondence in Stauda, *Wandervogel,* 2:114–118.
79. Rutha diary, 9, entry for 1 April 1918.
80. Ibid., 9, 13. See also Stauda, *Wandervogel,* 1:65–66, 2:119–120.
81. For instance, on the launch of a Jewish nationalist youth movement in Vienna in 1917–1918, see Rechter, *Jews of Vienna,* 104–119.
82. Frank later recorded how he had first met Rutha through the movement: Karel Vykusa, ed., *Zpověď K. H. Franka* (Prague, 1946), 19.
83. Stauda, *Wandervogel,* 1:65, 2:118.
84. Rutha diary, 100, entry for 22 August 1918 (anniversary of Polifka's death).
85. Ibid., 12–14, entries for 1–4 April 1918.

4. REBIRTH

1. SOAL, Krajský soud Česká Lípa, trestní spisy [Regional Court at Česká Lípa, criminal records, hereafter CLS], karton 360, Tk 665/37/114, Reichenberg police report, 21 October 1937. The original of the diary has not survived, although Gretel Rutha in 1939 tried repeatedly to recover it: see CLS, karton 242, Tk 665/37, Margarete Rutha to Hans Krebs, 17 April 1939.
2. Hans Blüher, *Die deutsche Wandervogelbewegung als erotische Phänomenon: Ein Beitrag zur Erkenntnis der sexuellen Inversion.* References hereafter are to the second revised edition (Berlin-Tempelhof, 1914).
3. The following draws on the fine analysis by Ulfried Geuter, *Homosexualität in der deutschen Jugendbewegung: Jungenfreundschaft und Sexualität im Diskurs von Jugendbewegung, Psychoanalyse und Jugendpsychologie am Beginn des 20. Jahrhunderts* (Frankfurt am Main, 1994), 14–117. See also Julius Schoeps, "Sexualität, Erotik und Männerbund: Hans Blüher und die deutsche Jugendbewegung," in *Typisch deutsch: Die Jugendbewegung: Beiträge zu einer Phänomengeschichte,* ed. Joachim Knoll and Julius Schoeps (Opladen, 1988), 137–154.
4. As one excellent introduction to the contemporary scientific debates about homosexuality, see Vernon A. Rosario, ed., *Science and Homosexualities* (New York, 1997).
5. See Harry Oosterhuis and Hubert Kennedy, eds., *Homosexuality and Male Bonding in Pre-Nazi Germany* (New York, 1991), 1–19.
6. For a recent controversial study see James Davidson, *The Greeks and Greek Love: A Radical Reappraisal of Homosexuality in Ancient Greece* (London, 2008). Davidson challenges the "sexed-up" interpretation offered by Kenneth Dover in *Greek Homosexuality* (London, 1978) with its emphasis on genital acts, and he reasserts many views that Blüher or Brand would have understood and welcomed.

7. Quoted in Oosterhuis and Kennedy, *Homosexuality and Male Bonding*, 3.

8. Geuter, *Homosexualität*, 87.

9. Blüher, *Die deutsche Wandervogelbewegung*, 35.

10. Ibid., 40, 47.

11. Geuter, *Homosexualität*, 83–84.

12. Ibid., 94–103.

13. Cultivating Eros in the youth community was a maxim taught in key youth manuals or textbooks like Georg Stammler's *Worte an eine Schar* (Heidelberg, 1914), 10; Rutha knew Stammler's works well.

14. Johannes Stauda, *Der Wandervogel in Böhmen, 1911–1920,* ed. Kurt Oberdorffer (Reutlingen, 1975–1978), 2:96 (Oberdorffer had encountered Rutha in the Prague-Lützow Wandervogel); and SOAL, CLS, karton 242, Tk 665/37/24, Rutha protocol, 23 October 1937.

15. Stauda, *Wandervogel,* 2:89, 94.

16. Erich Frühauf, "Von den Führern," appendix to *Gablonzer Wandervogel: Geschichtlicher Abriss von 1913–1938,* ed. Walter Jantsch (Schwäbisch Gmünd: self-publication, 1974), 9–10.

17. Rutha diary, 11, 43, 101: entries for 1 April, 27 May, and 24 August 1918..

18. Ibid., 21, entry for 7 April 1918; see also 14, 100: 4 April and 22 August 1918.

19. Ibid., 22, 57: entries for 7 April and 8 June 1918.

20. Ibid., 5–6, 8: entries for 8 February and 29 March 1918.

21. Ibid., 19–21: entry for 7 April 1918. For a similar example of lust and repression as recorded in a Wandervogel diary, see Geuter, *Homosexualität,* 133–134.

22. Rutha diary, 44, entry for 28 May 1918.

23. Ibid., 2, 9: entries for 16 February and 1 April 1918.

24. Ibid., 2, 23, 38: entries for 16 February, 8 April, and 27 May 1918.

25. Ibid., 96–98: entry for 21 August 1918.

26. Ibid., 8, 40, 52: entries for 28 March, 27 May (long quotation), and 5 June 1918. See also Rutha's comment that to be "a fashionable man" was "un-German" (108, entry for 23 August 1918).

27. Ibid., 5, 21–22: entries for 18 February and 7 April 1918. Typically he felt aggrieved when a potential male intimate went off instead with a "floozy" 28, entry for 8 April 1918.

28. Ibid., 40, entry for 27 May 1918.

29. Ibid., 2, 9, 16: entries for 16 February, 1 April, and 4 April 1918.

30. Rutha diary, 9, entry for 1 April 1918. Just doted on Schöler to the neglect of the Gablonz Wandervogel: Frühauf, "Von den Führern," 9–10.

31. Hermann Hesse, *Demian: The Story of Emil Sinclair's Youth* (New York, 1999), 40.

32. Rutha diary, 104, 125: entries for 23 and 26 August 1918.

33. Ibid., 100–101: entry for 22 August 1918.
34. Mark Cornwall, *The Undermining of Austria-Hungary: The Battle for Hearts and Minds* (New York, 2000), 74–83, 278–282.
35. "Heinz Rutha an die Arbeitsmänner," *Heimatruf,* 17 November 1937. See also [Walter Rohn], "Heinz Rutha: Ein Leben für Volk und Heimat," *VuF* 4 (1937): 3; and Margarete Ikrath-Rutha, "Heinrich Rutha: Seine Lebensarbeit und seine Ziele für das Sudetendeutschtum" (typed memoir, in Sudetendeutsches Haus library, Munich, 1986), 4.
36. Rutha diary, 73, entry for 15 June 1918.
37. Ibid., 23, entry for 8 April 1918.
38. Ibid., 24, 48: entries for 8 April and 31 May 1918.
39. For the following, see ibid., 25–43: entries for 8 April to 27 May 1918.
40. See Constantin Schneider, *Die Kriegserinnerungen 1914–1919* (Vienna, 2003), 497–500.
41. Rutha diary, 38, entry for 14 May 1918.
42. Ibid., 41–42, entry for 27 May 1918.
43. For the following, see ibid., 47–93: entries for 31 May to 4 July 1918.
44. Edmund von Glaise-Horstenau, *Ein General im Zwielicht: Die Erinnerungen Edmund Glaises von Horstenau,* ed. Peter Broucek (Vienna, 1980), 1:471. See also Peter Fiala, *Die letzte Offensive Altösterreichs: Führungsprobleme und Führerverantwortlichkeit bei der öst.-ung. Offensive in Venetien, Juni 1918* (Boppard am Rhein, 1967), 52–59.
45. ÖSA, KA, 11th Army Command Generalstabsabteilung, Operation Akten 1918, 1–17/15–7/3, Op. Nr 2500/13, material reports for 1 June 1918. See also Cornwall, *Undermining,* 289, for the similar experience of a neighboring division.
46. Rutha seems to have been assigned to Heavy Field Artillery Regiment 72. According to his sister, it was a Polish regiment, and Rutha later sometimes threw in Polish expressions when speaking: Ikrath-Rutha, "Heinrich Rutha," 3.
47. Cornwall, *Undermining,* 283; and ÖSA, KA, 11AK Gstbstsabt., Op. Akten 1918, 1–17/15–7/30, GM Julius Vidalé (18ID) to 6KK, 13 June 1918.
48. Ibid., 1–17/15–18/8, 18ID (Vidalé) to 11AK, 20 June 1918.
49. Rutha diary, 80–82: entries for 18–20 June 1918.
50. The Rutha family, rather typical of north Bohemian Catholics, do not seem to have been avid churchgoers anyway. See Daniel Langhans, *Der Reichsbund der deutschen katholischen Jugend* (Bonn, 1990), 38.
51. Rutha diary, 96–97, 121 (the "dogmatic church"): entries for 21 and 25 August 1918.
52. Ibid., 91–92, entry for 3 July 1918..

53. For the rural outlook, see Benjamin Ziemann, *War Experiences in Rural Germany, 1914–1923* (Oxford, 2007). Rutha dutifully informed the Wandervogel of his changing address in the war zone: see the Prague-Lützow branch report in *BH*, June–July 1918, 169.

54. Rutha diary, 82, 84–85, 88: entries for 18, 22, 24 and 30 June 1918.

55. Ivan Šedivý, *Češi, české země a Velká válka 1914–1918* (Prague, 2001), 327–333.

56. Stauda, *Wandervogel,* 1:61.

57. Rutha diary, 17, entry for 7 April 1918.

58. Ibid., 55–56, entry for 7 June 1918. See Hans Watzlik, *O Böhmen* (Leipzig, 1917).

59. Rutha diary, 37, 41, 54: entries for 29 April, 27 May and 6 June 1918. This man, Ewald Heller, was from Prague (the Smichow district) and attended the same Linz artillery course as Rutha.

60. Stauda, *Wandervogel,* 1:61–62, 64, 2:112–113; and the articles in *Soldaten-blatt: Österreichischer Wandervogel,* February 1918, 5–10.

61. H.R. [Rutha], "Sudetendeutschtum auf dem Wege zur Einigung," *VuF* 2 (1935): 51.

62. Stauda, *Wandervogel,* 1:69.

63. The following draws on Rutha diary, 105–127: section recorded later on 21 November 1918.

64. Ibid., 106, entry for 23 August 1918.

65. In fact the Bohemian leadership took some racially based decisions at Krummau, resolving not to approve a Prague girl's group until it accepted Aryan selection: *BH,* October 1918, 26.

66. Rutha diary, 127, entry for 26 August 1918.

67. Heinz Rutha, "Gedanken über die Führerschaft," *BH,* October 1918, 12–13. The theoretical teenage addressee may have been Medikus or Juppe.

68. *BH,* October 1918, 2. Kletzl was more forthright: "The keystone of our movement is as strict a selection as possible of pure German young men" (Kletzl, "Gauspiegel," *BH,* November–December 1918, 53).

69. See his condemnation of "anti-Semitic rabble-rousing": *Der Weg: Blätter für das neue Deutschösterreich,* March 1919, 125.

70. Heinz Rutha, "Teufelsmauer," *Wandervogel: Monatschrift für deutsches Jugendwandern. Heft der Österreicher,* 5/6 (1918): 121–122.

71. *29. Jahrbuch des Deutschen Gebirgs-Vereines für das Jeschken- und Isergebirge in Reichenberg* (Reichenberg, 1919), 49–50. For the Czech takeover, see J. W. Bruegel, *Tschechen und Deutsche 1918–1938* (Munich, 1967), 48–60.

72. See Kletzl's report on Krummau: *BH,* November–December 1918, 45–47.

73. Stauda, *Wandervogel,* 2:137–138.

74. See Johannes Stauda "Das Böhmerland" (1943), *Sudetenland* 4 (1975): 280; and Rutha, "Sudetendeutschtum auf dem Wege zur Einigung," *VuF* 2 (1935): 51.

75. For a critical perspective, see SDA, Walter Hergl papers, karton 1, "Es spricht Walter Hergl zur Böhmerlandbewegung . . . ," 7–12.

76. Stanislav Biman and Jaroslav Malíř, *Kariéra učitele tělocviku* (Liberec, 1983), 28.

77. Rutha diary, 11, entry for 1 April 1918; and Rutha relative interview, 8 July 2000.

78. SOAL, CLS, karton 360, Tk 665/37/27, Rutha police protocol, 7 October 1937, 2.

79. Rutha relative interview, 8 July 2000. It is unknown whether the family recouped anything from their loans.

80. Šedivý, *Češi*, 342

81. Rutha diary, 102, entry for 22 August 1918.

82. SOkAL, MAO, book č.11, "Friedhof Grundbuch über Grabstellen" (1903–1942), 24. The cause of death was "inflammation of the heart muscle."

83. Heinz [Rutha], "Zum Schlusse," *Blätter* 1, no.7, 25 February 1920, 80.

5. THE MILITANT YOUTH MISSION

1. See for instance Zdeněk Kárník, *České země v éře první republiky (1918–1938)*, vol.1, *Vznik, budování a zlatá léta republiky (1918–1929)* (Prague, 2000), on how early crisis gave way to the "golden years" of the late 1920s. For a useful critique, see Peter Bugge, "Czech Democracy, 1918–1938—Paragon or Parody?," *Bohemia* 47, no. 1 (2006–2007): 3–28.

2. See Elizabeth Wiskemann, *Czechs and Germans: A Study of the Struggle in the Historic Provinces of Bohemia and Moravia* (London, 1938), 118–127, 131–134 (quotation at 132).

3. See J. W. Bruegel, *Tschechen und Deutsche 1918–1938* (Munich, 1967), 186.

4. Ronald M. Smelser, "Castles on the Landscape: Czech German Relations," in *Czechoslovakia, 1918–1988: Seventy Years from Independence*, ed. H. Gordon Skilling (Basingstoke, 1991), 98.

5. Tara Zahra, *Kidnapped Souls: National Indifference and the Battle for Children in the Bohemian Lands, 1900–1948* (Ithaca, NY, 2008), 131. Foreign diplomatic reporting in the 1920s—German or British for example—focused overwhelmingly on Prague and on parliamentary politics. For the German grass roots, Andreas Luh's *Der Deutsche Turnverband in der Ersten Tchechoslowakischen Republik: Vom völkischen*

Vereinsbetrieb zur volkspolitischen Bewegung (Munich, 1988) was until recently a lone study.

6. SOAL, CLS, karton 242, Tk 665/37/27, statement to police, 7 October 1937, 7. Compare Tomáš Kasper, *Výchova či politika? Úskalí německého pedagogického hnutí v Československu v letech 1918–1933* (Prague, 2007), 75, 81, which implies that already by 1919 Rutha had a set program.

7. The following discussion on Oschitz draws on the minute book of the Oschitz Turnverein, preserved in SOkAL, MAO, karton 10, "Verhand-lungsschrift deutscher Turnverein für Oschitz und Umgebung, 1897–1937" [hereafter VdTO].

8. Luh, *Deutsche Turnverband*, 19–34.

9. Figures from *TZ*, 1 June 1923, 124–125. The Jeschken-Iser Gau was the second largest Gau, composed of six districts *[Bezirke]*: Friedland, Gablonz, Maffersdorf, Reichenberg, Tannwald, and Deutsch Gabel (to which Oschitz belonged).

10. VdTO, Turnrat meeting of 29 November 1920.

11. VdTO, Turnrat meetings of 25 August and 16 September 1921. See also Benjamin Ziemann, *War Experiences in Rural Germany, 1914–1923* (Oxford, 2007), 212, 248.

12. See Luh's discussion of "Dietwesen" in *Deutsche Turnverband*, 72–79, 52n24.

13. VdTO, Turnrat meeting of 31 May 1922.

14. VdTO, Turnrat meetings of 27 February 1920 and 29 October 1924.

15. Luh, *Deutsche Turnverband*, 146–157.

16. For Henlein's early Turn career, see Rudolf Jahn, *Konrad Henlein: Leben und Werk des Turnführers* (Carlsbad, 1938), 50–59.

17. [Walter Rohn], "Heinz Rutha: Ein Leben für Volk und Heimat," *VuF* 4 (1937): 157.

18. Fritz Hoffmann, "Turnerjugendtreffen Jeschken-Isergau," *DjD*, December 1923, 167; and Jahn, *Konrad Henlein*, 61.

19. BHA, Becher papers, 84, "Zeit-Tafel" by Fritz Köllner, 3.

20. VdTO, Turnrat meetings of 4 January and 6 February 1924.

21. VdTO, Turnrat meeting of 25 March 1924.

22. Stauda died before he could write a history of the movement. See Johannes Stauda, *Der Wandervogel in Böhmen, 1911–1920*, ed. Kurt Oberdorffer (Reutlingen, 1975–1978), 1:80–81. See also Stauda, "Das Böhmerland," *Sudetenland* 4 (1975): 279–283; and Ernst Leibl's comments on it, "Das Wesen, das sich Böhmerland nannte," SWA, R034, "Böhmerland-bewegung." For the phenomenon of *Heimat* education, see Josef Pfitzner, *Sudetendeutsche Einheitsbewegung: Werden und Erfüllung*, 2nd ed. (Carlsbad, 1937), 38–43; Zahra, *Kidnapped Souls*, 155–159; and Kasper, *Výchova*, 68–72.

23. See Kletzl's own upbeat summary of Sudeten *Heimat* education: "Der böhmerländische Gedanke," *Sudetendeutsches Jahrbuch 1929* (Eger, 1929), 5–11.

24. Kasper, *Výchova*, 209–225.

25. H. R. [Heinz Rutha], "Sudetendeutschtum auf dem Wege zur Einigung," *VuF* 2 (1935): 52–53. Quoted also in Josef Fischer, Václav Patzak, and Vincenc Perth, *Jejich boj: Co chce a čemu slouží Sudetendeutsche Partei* (Prague, 1937), 74–75.

26. Heinz Rutha, "Der Wandervogel—eine deutsche Jugendbewegung," *Der Weg: Blätter für das neue Deutschösterreich*, March 1919, 124–125.

27. It is telling that Pfitzner in his Sudeten history, written in 1936 when there was a radical upsurge, only mentioned Rutha once: as a pioneer seeking to bring a "front spirit" into the postwar youth movement (*Sudetendeutsche Einheitsbewegung*, 69–75).

28. For an overview of youth groups see Dunja Berthold, "Die Sudetendeutsche Jugendgemeinschaft (SJG)," in *Deutsche Jugend in Böhmen 1918–1938*, ed. Peter Becher (Munich, 1993), 16–48. For *Staffelstein*, see Hans Schmid-Egger and Ernst Nittner, *Staffelstein: Jugendbewegung und katholische Erneuerung bei den Sudetendeutschen zwischen den Grossen Kriegen* (Munich, 1983).

29. Robert E. Norton, *Secret Germany: Stefan George and His Circle* (Ithaca, NY, 2002), 359–369.

30. Stauda, *Wandervogel*, 1:72.

31. AAVČR, Beneš papers, karton 142, pisemnosti opisy, Rutha to Willi Hoffmann, 28 October 1935.

32. All have been located except Blatt 4 of Series 1 (pages 33–48). No archive or library seems to have a complete run. The best collection exists in the SWA, while the AdJB has several editions.

33. Heinz [Rutha], "An die, die vom Herzen jung sind!," *Blätter* 1, no.1, 1 May 1919, 1.

34. For the Swiss vigor, see Fritz Baumann, *Der Schweizer Wandervogel* (Aarau, 1966).

35. *Blätter* 1, no.1, 1 May 1919, 1; "Zum Schlusse," *Blätter* 1, no.7, 25 February 1920, 80; and "Zum Schlusse," *Blätter* 3, no.5, 1 July 1922, 84.

36. "Betrachtung," *Blätter* 1, no.2, 15 May 1919, 13; and "Der Wandervogel – jung?," *Blätter* 1, no.5, 6 September 1919, 53. Others used the metaphor negatively, describing a huge glittering lake with worthless debris at the bottom: see Stauda, *Wandervogel*, 2:141.

37. "Ein Gespräch," *Blätter*, 1, no.2, 21–24.

38. "Unsere Führer," *Blätter*, 1, no.2, 15 May 1919, 10–13. Rutha dated this 1 November 1918.

39. Stauda, *Wandervogel*, 1:76–77, 2:150.

40. BHA, Becher papers, 84, "Zeit-Tafel" by Fritz Köllner.

41. See Heinz R.[Rutha], "Isergebirge," *BH*, May 1919, 98–99. In this romantic piece Rutha eulogized a local writer (Gustav Leutelt) as fully in harmony with the national landscape.

42. Heinz Rutha, "Deutschböhmens Wandervogel," *Böhmerlandjahrbuch 1920*, 73–74. Stauda also quotes this article but omits the crucial line: *Wandervogel*, 1:75.

43. Jaroslav César and Bohumil Černý, *Politika německých buržoazních stran v Československu v letech 1918–1938* (Prague, 1962), 2:203.

44. "Von Singen und von unseren Liedern," *Blätter* 2, no.3, 13 July 1920, 36.

45. See his later bitter comments: "In eigener Sache," *Blätter* 3, no.1, 20 October 1920, 8.

46. See Ulfried Geuter, *Homosexualität in der deutschen Jugendbewegung: Jungenfreundschaft und Sexualität im Diskurs von Jugendbewegung, Psychoanalyse und Jugendpsychologie am Beginn des 20. Jahrhunderts* (Frankfurt am Main, 1994), 180–185.

47. *Blätter* 1, no.3, 5 June 1919, 26, 29, 31.

48. *Blätter* 1, no.6, 12 November 1919, 66–72 and 75 (where Rutha in "Zum Schlusse" summed up his own views).

49. George Mosse, *Nationalism and Sexuality: Middle-Class Morality and Sexual Norms in Modern Europe* (Madison, WI, 1985), 30, 64–65. For general studies of the phenomenon, see Helmut Blazek, *Männerbünde: Eine Geschichte von Faszination und Macht* (Berlin, 1999); and Gisela Vögler and Karin Welck, eds., *Männerbande, Männerbünde: Zur Rolle des Mannes in Kulturvegleich*, 2 vols. (Cologne, 1990).

50. Jürgen Reulecke, *"Ich möchte einer werden so wie die": Männerbünde im 20. Jahrhundert* (Frankfurt, 2001), 38–40. Reulecke offers the fullest analysis.

51. Hans Blüher, *Die Rolle der Erotik in der männlichen Gesellschaft* (Jena, 1917/1919), 1:7–9, 2:102–103; Reulecke, *"Ich möchte,"* 42–43; and Geuter, *Homosexualität*, 163–174. A useful summary is Claudia Bruns, "Der homosexuelle Staatsfreund: Von der Konstruktion des erotischen Männerbunds bei Hans Blüher," in *Homosexualität und Staatsräson: Männlichkeit, Homophobie und Politik in Deutschland 1900–1945*, ed. Susanne zur Nieden (Frankfurt, 2005), 100–117.

52. "Bücher," *Blätter* 3, no.5, 1 July 1922, 82.

53. See "Den Erkennenden!," *Blätter* 3, no.4, 1 May 1921, 44; and 3, no.5, 1 July 1922, 76–77. Rutha devoted one edition of the *Blätter* to an exemplary leader, Erwin Dressel from Böhmisch Leipa, who had followed his advice but then died young: see 2, no.2, 31 May 1920; and "Erwin Dressel," *BH*, January 1920, 71.

54. "Der Wandervogel – jung?," *Blätter* 1, no.5, 6 September 1919, 52–55; and "Zum Schlusse," *Blätter* 1, no.6, 12 November 1919, 75–76.

55. Stauda, *Wandervogel*, 1:78.

56. For the confusion, see the articles by Rutha and Theo Keil in *Blätter*, Sonderblatt [2, no.4], July 1920, 3–5; "Gewordenes und Werdendes," *Blätter* 2, no.2, 31 May 1920, 27; and "Zum Schlusse," *Blätter* 3, no.3, 10 February 1921, 40.

57. The following framework draws on *Zeittafeln zur Geschichte des sudetendeutschen Wandervogels* (Waldkraiburg, 1992).

58. "Frage" and "Zum Schlusse," *Blätter* 3, no.5, 1 July 1922, 65–68, 84.

59. The Gauwart's cryptic report only hints at these leadership tensions. See Adolf Tosch, "Der Gautag in Mies," *Sudetendeutscher Wandervogel*, November 1923, 18–19.

60. Walter Jantsch, ed., *Gablonzer Wandervogel: Geschichtlicher Abriss von 1913–1938* (Schwäbisch Gmünd: self-publication, 1974), 12, 55. Oskar Just was still influential in Gablonz.

61. BHA, Becher papers, 84, Walter Becher talk to "Historischer Arbeitskreis des Witiko-Bundes" (n.d.), 2.

62. *Blätter* 2, no.2, 31 May 1920, 24–26.

63. VdTO, Turnrat meetings of 8 February and 20 August 1922. For favorable comments on other youth bodies, see *Blätter* 2, no.2, 31 May 1920, 19 [the Zionists]; 3, no.2, 20 December 1920, 12, 27 [the Socialists]; and 3, no.4, 1 May 1921, 55–56 [the Catholics].

64. See his two articles: "Wandern" and "Wellen," *Blätter* 3, no.5, 1 July 1922, 60, 78.

65. On this organization, which had its own journal, *Der junge Deutsche*, see Kasper, *Výchova*, 60–62. It numbered fifty thousand members in 1931.

66. Heinz [Rutha], "Das Kreuz," *Sudetendeutscher Wandervogel. Bundes- und Fahrtenblatt*, 2 (1924/1925): 30.

67. One catalyst was that members of the Tyrol expedition broke the Wandervogel code of abstaining from alcohol. See Walter Becher, *Zeitzeuge: Ein Lebensbericht* (Munich, 1990), 54; and BHA, Becher papers, 84, "Zeit-Tafel," 3.

68. Ibid. The first groups joining the Rutha circle were from Asch, Graslitz, Alt-Carlsbad, Kaaden, Lobositz, Tetschen, Schreckenstein, Niemes, Gablonz, and Tannwald. For the split in Kaaden, see Walter Brand, *Auf verlorenem Posten: Ein sudetendeutscher Politiker zwischen Autonomie und Anschluss* (Munich, 1985), 32–33.

69. See the comments and chronology in "Geschichtstafel," *Sudetendeutscher Wandervogel* 3 (1930–1931): 99–106.

70. Consider for example the comparable organizational struggle among Catholic youth: see Daniel Langhans, *Der Reichsbund der deutschen katholischen Jugend in der Tschechoslowakei 1918–1938* (Bonn, 1990), 60.

71. Hans Riehl, "Walter Heinrich, sein Leben und sein Werk im Dienste seiner Zeit," in *Festschrift Walter Heinrich: Ein Beitrag zur Ganzheitsforschung* (Graz, 1963), 1–3.

72. BHA, Becher papers, 557, taped interview by Becher with Walter Heinrich (1983); and Heinrich, "Gemeinschaft der Jugend," *DjD*, April 1922, 53–55.

73. *Blätter* 3, no.5, 1 July 1922, 77–78. Here were quoted extracts from Plato, *Republic*, 395c–d, 401c–d, 410c–e, 412a–e, 414a, about how best to educate the leaders from childhood onwards.

74. BHA, Becher papers, 84, Becher talk to "Historischer Arbeitskreis," 4–5.

75. For this discussion see Martin Schneller, *Zwischen Romantik und Faschismus: Der Beitrag Othmar Spanns zum Konservatismus der Weimarer Republik* (Stuttgart, 1970); Klaus-Jörg Siegfried, *Universalismus und Faschismus: Das Gesellschaftsbild Othmar Spanns* (Vienna, 1974); Othmar Spann, *Der wahre Staat: Vorlesungen über Abbruch und Neubau der Gesellschaft*, 3rd ed. (Jena, 1931); and for wider context, Paul Nolte, "Ständische Ordnung im Mitteleuropa der Zwischenkriegszeit," in *Utopie und Politische Herrschaft im Europa der Zwischenkriegszeit*, ed. Wolfgang Hardtwig (Munich, 2003), 233–250.

76. For prewar Brno, see Nancy Wingfield, *Flag Wars and Stone Saints: How the Bohemian Lands Became Czech* (Cambridge, MA, 2007), 79–106.

77. Schneller, *Zwischen Romantik*, 51–54, 97, 188; Siegfried, *Universalismus*, 200–210; and Nolte, "Ständische Ordnung," 250–254.

78. [Walter Rohn], "Heinz Rutha: Ein Leben für Volk und Heimat," *VuF* 4 (1937): 156.

79. See Gustav Butschek, *Der "Bund der böhmerlandischen Freischaren," seine Freischaren und die Nachfolgegemeinschaften* (Hamburg, 1984), 55–56, for PG membership and the organization of Prague student societies.

80. The following draws on Robert Großmann's account (1985), "Die Schweizfahrt 1925," in BHA, Becher papers, 84; and 557, Becher interview with Heinrich.

81. For a defense of Beneš, see Bruegel, *Tschechen und Deutsche*, 99–105, who questions whether the Swiss model would have satisfied the Germans anyway.

82. VdTO, Turnrat meeting of 5 November 1925.

83. See the circular sent to parents in mid-1928 by Robert Großmann, then head of the Jungenschaft, about the expedition to Alsace: in this "fateful land of German history . . . the boy will be deeply stirred by the nobleness

of the German spirit, by belief in the future of German culture" (SWA, R031).

84. SDA, Walter Hergl papers, karton 1/1: "Es spricht Dr Walter Hergl" [transcript of an undated talk], 22–23.

85. Luh, *Deutsche Turnverband*, 167–170. In May 1925, they had organized military-style youth training for Turners in the Jeschken-Iser Gau. See Stanislav Biman and Jaroslav Malíř, *Kariéra učitele tělocviku* (Liberec, 1983), 31, 35.

86. SDA, Hergl papers, karton 1/1, "Es spricht," 21–22, 24. Hergl's chronology is askew, but he suggests that Henlein too played a key role.

87. See PAAA, R103654: Walter Hergl, "Die deutsch-tschechische Frage im Rahmen der gesamtdeutschen Politik" (1936–1937), 130–133. This enormous manuscript was sent to Berlin in March 1937, but Hitler, even when faced with a summary, declared that he had no interest: PAAA, R103656.

88. For an introduction to the KB, see John Haag, "'Knights of the Spirit': The Kameradschaftsbund," *JCH* 8, no. 3 (1973); Fischer, Patzak, and Perth, *Jejich boj*, 41–44; and Luh, *Deutsche Turnverband*, 240–261. The works of Schneller and Siegfried are very thin on the Spannist application in Bohemia.

89. *Die erste Position* (1929), copy in SDA. Another speaker was Kurt Hildebrandt, a member of the George circle in Berlin, who stressed that "poet-philosophers" like George and Plato offered exemplary guidance for the national community.

90. Konrad Fest [Walter Heinrich], "Der Neue Staat, sein Bild und seine Verwirklichung," in ibid., 5–11.

91. See Siegfreid, *Universalismus*, 79–100; C. Earl Edmonson, *The Heimwehr and Austrian Politics, 1918–1936* (Athens, GA, 1978), 72–74, 93, 98; and John T. Lauridsen, *Nazism and the Radical Right in Austria, 1918–1934* (Copenhagen, 2007), 189–208. For a sympathetic study, see Walter Wiltschegg, *Die Heimwehr: Eine unwiderstehliche Volksbewegung?* (Munich, 1985), which mentions (151) Rutha's former friend Willi Flatz as being involved with the Heimwehr in Salzburg. For Spannism and Italy (where Heinrich spent four months in 1929), see Siegfried, *Universalismus*, 100–123.

92. Walter Heinrich, ed., *Othmar Spann: Leben und Werk* (Graz, 1979), 21:43–44.

93. For the following, see Richard Lenk [Rutha], "Der sudetendeutsche Stammeskörper," in *Die erste Position*, 12–30; and Heinz Rutha, "Die Erziehung zum sudetendeutschen Stammeskörper," *DjD*, August 1928, 9–11. The latter seems based on a talk to the Prague PG.

94. Lenk [Rutha], "Der sudetendeutsche Stammeskörper," *Die erste Position*, 30.

95. Ibid., 15.

96. Compare Schneller, *Zwischen Romantik*, 114.

97. SWA, R031, "Sudetendeutscher Wandervogel," handwritten "Forderung," signed by Rutha and Oberlik, 1 May 1926. For Staffen's reaction, see "Die Kreisbildung im Jungengau 'Böhmerland'," *Beiblatt der Älteren zum "Sudetendeutschen Wandervogel*," November 1926, 9–11.

98. BHA, Becher papers, 84, Becher talk to "Historicher Arbeitskreis," 11. Becher suggests this also meant communing with the Czechs. For *Staffelstein*'s move in a *bündisch* direction from about 1928, see Schmid-Egger and Nittner, *Staffelstein*, 129–155.

99. "Der Pfadfinder", *DjD*, January 1927, 5–6; and Gustav Butschek, "Erinnerungen" (1983), in Helmut Richter, *Geschichte des Reichenberger Wandervogels* (Waldkraiburg, 1984), 94.

100. See his article "In die Wälder!" and his commentary on the New Scout journal *Der weisse Ritter: Blätter* 3, no.5, 1 July 1922, 69–72, 81–82. For the *Neupfadfinder*, see Werner Kindt, ed., *Die deutsche Jugendbewegung 1920 bus 1933: Die bündische Zeit* (Dusseldorf, 1974), 389–392.

101. "Der sudetendeutscher Pfadfinder," *DjD*, November 1926, 2. And for a history of the Federation, see [Ernst Krause], "Sudetendeutscher Pfadfinder," *DjD*, September 1928, 2–7.

102. In January 1928 the Federation held a five-hour general meeting in Reichenberg. Rutha lectured and a lengthy discussion followed. See *DjD*, March 1928, 5.

103. VdTO, annual report for 1925, noting diminished activity due to a lack of younger members.

104. According to Hergl: SDA, Hergl papers, karton 1/1: "Es spricht," 23–24.

105. Konrad Henlein, "Grundsätze über unsere Erziehung und Führung," *TZ*, 1 May 1928, 117–120.

106. Heinz Rutha, "Lage, Aussichten und Aufgaben der Erziehung in der Turnerschaft," *TZ*, 15 May 1928, 147–148; and "Der sudetendeutsche Stammeskörper," *Die erste Position*, 18–19, 28.

107. See Henlein's two articles in *TZ*, 15 January 1929, 17–19; and 23 November 1929, 355–357.

108. *TZ*, 1 December 1930, 361–363. For a full analysis of the reforms, see Luh, *Deutsche Turnverband*, 172–181.

109. VdTO, annual general meeting, 23 March 1930; and Turnrat meetings of 27 February and 20 November 1931. (The latter planned a walk bearing heavy equipment from Rutha's house to Hammer and back.)

110. *TZ*, 1 March 1931, 74; and 1 April 1931, 103–104.

111. Although Nietzsche was mentioned in Rutha's *Blätter* (2, no.4, July 1920, 5), this was otherwise a rare reference to the fact that Rutha had read the philosopher.

112. Heinz Rutha, "Das Erziehungs- und Bildungs- Ideal des 19. Jahrhunderts und unsere Zeit," *Die junge Front*, April 1932, 111–121. This was a revised version of the lecture.

113. See [Rohn], "Heinz Rutha: Ein Leben für Volk und Heimat," *VuF* 4 (1937): 157. In contrast, note the complete omission in Pfitzner, *Sudetendeutsche Einheitsbewegung*, 79–81; and Jahn, *Konrad Henlein*, 110–111.

114. W. R. [Walter Rohn], "Das Herbstfest der sudetendeutschen Jungenschaft," *Die junge Front*, January 1932, 33.

115. Konrad Henlein, "Die Erziehung unserer Mannesjugend," *TZ*, 1 June 1932, 163–165; and Rutha, "Ziel und Stufenbau der Gesamterziehung," *TZ*, 1 June 1933, 186–188.

116. W. R. [Rohn], "Görkau: Das erste Jungturnerlager des Turnverbandes," *Die junge Front*, November 1932, 327–330.

117. Kasper, *Výchova*, 20, 63–64, 93–97.

118. See *DjD*, August 1928, 11.

119. See Jürgen Reulecke, "Utopische Erwartungen an die Jugendbewegung 1900–1933," in Hardtwig, *Utopie und politische Herrschaft*, 210–213.

120. "Der sudetendeutsche Stammeskörper," *Die erste Position*, 16.

6. EROS

1. SOAL, CLS, karton 360, Tk 665/37/27, police protocol with Hoffmann, 8 October 1937, 20; and Tk 665/37/1, Weiss protocol, 5 October 1937, 5, 9.

2. Ibid., Tk 665/37/27, Rutha police protocol, 7 October 1937, 9.

3. Ibid., Tk 665/37/24, Rutha statement to Czech magistrate Blažek, 23 October 1937.

4. See the career statement Rutha prepared for Henlein in August 1935: SOkAL, Policejní ředitelství Liberec (J. Rutha) [hereafter, Reichenberg police records], [book] I, 200.

5. Otto Kletzl, "Oskar Just," *Sudetendeutscher Wandervogel*, February 1923, 123; and Rutha relative interview, 22 May 2011.

6. Much of the following draws on Rutha relative interviews, 6 August 2001, 10 May 2003, and 11 September 2006.

7. For example, a villa interior was designed for the Nosofski family in Bodenbach.

8. SOAL, CLS, karton 360, Tk 665/37/126, Heinl protocol, 14 October 1937, 2–3. Heinl was first co-opted onto the Turnrat in December 1930 and became the Turnwart in April 1931.

9. See Rutha's own designation in the 1930 Czechoslovak census: NA, SO 1930, "Sčítání obyvatelstva ČSR v roce 1930, Praha," karton 3705, 259/202, Lázně Kundratice, c.p. 45 rod; and his police statement: SOAL, Tk 665/37/27, 7 October 1937, 2. For a Czech view, see Josef Fischer, Václav Patzak, and Vincenc Perth, *Jeijich boj: Co chce a čemu slouží Sudetendeutsche Partei* (Prague, 1937), 71.

10. AAVČR, Beneš papers, karton 142, Spudich protocol, 13 October 1937.

11. SOAL, CLS, karton 242, Tk 665/37/253, Rutha to Kurt Gansel, 12 June 1934.

12. See SOAL, CLS, karton 242, Tk 665/37/147, including correspondence with Rudolf Sandner in the winter of 1930–1931. The incident partly explains Rutha's later coolness toward Sandner, who had supported Langhans.

13. SOAL, CLS, karton 242, Tk 665/37/253, Rutha to Gansel, 12 June 1934; and Rutha relative interview, 11 May 2003. Rutha's library contained a large book on meticulous garden management by Johannes Böttner.

14. SOkAČL, Okresní úřad, karton 55, 9 4R/154, Rutha to regional authorities, 19 April 1933, enclosing building plans.

15. Official figures quoted in Rudolf Kasper, "Sudetendeutscher Wirtschaftverfall und seine sozialen Auswirkungen," *VuF* 3 (1936): 110.

16. SOAL, CLS, karton 242, Tk 665/37/253, Rutha to Gansel, 16 July 1934.

17. SOkAL, Reichenberg police records, I, Rutha letters to Andrée Šámalová, 8 April 1935, and to Otto Kletzl, 26 April 1935; and SOAL, CLS, karton 242, Tk 665/37/253, Rutha to Gansel, 12 May 1936.

18. See the numerous advertisements taken out in *Rundschau*, February–June 1936.

19. SOAL, CLS, karton 360, Tk 665/37/24, Rutha protocol at Leipa courthouse, 9 October 1937. The statements made to the police by Rutha's employees confirm that 1935 and 1936 were the worst years.

20. Ibid., karton 242, Tk 665/37/147, Rutha to "Lieber Walter," 22 October 1928 (copy also in AAVČR, Beneš papers, karton 142).

21. Ibid., karton 360, Tk 665/37/114, Reichenberg police to state authorities, 21 October 1937; and Tk 665/37/24, Rutha protocol, 23 October 1937.

22. SWA, R028, "Freischaren Böhmen," Gustav Butschek, "Erlebnisbericht zur Geschichte des Bundes der böhmerländischen Freischaren," September 1982; and for the context of PG activity, see Gustav Butschek, *Der "Bund der böhmerlandischen Freischaren," seine Freischaren und die Nachfolgegemeinschaften* (Hamburg, 1984).

23. PAAA, R103654, Hergl, "Die deutsch-tschechische Frage im Rahmen der gesamtdeutschen Politik," 191. Butschek (in *"Bund"*) details the complicated splits that continued to beset the student societies after 1930.

24. Here he mentioned two from the PG, Georg [Hois] and Egbert [Sittig], who despite initial hopes had disappointed him. It was Sittig who had first introduced Walter Heinrich to Rutha.

25. "Bücher," *Blätter* 3, no.5, 1 July 1922, 83.

26. See Ulfried Geuter, *Homosexualiät in der deutschen Jugendbewegung: Jungenfeundschaft und Sexualität im Diskurs von Jugendbewegung, Psychoanalyse und Jugendpsychologie am Beginn des 20. Jahrhunderts* (Frankfurt am Main, 1994), 195–210.

27. BHA, Becher papers, 557, Becher interview with Walter Heinrich (1983).

28. Plato, *Symposium*, 210d.

29. "Sonstige gute Bücher," *Blätter* 3, no.2, 20 December 1920, 18.

30. See James Davidson, *The Greeks and Greek Love: A Radical Reappraisal of Homosexuality in Ancient Greece* (London, 2008), 34.

31. Plato, *Republic*, 403c.

32. AAVČR, Beneš papers, karton 142, příloha III, list of books confiscated from Rutha's library. Researching Rutha's relationship with Walter Heinrich is very difficult, since all Heinrich's correspondence was destroyed upon his death in 1984. My thanks to Reinhard Müller (University of Graz) for this information.

33. SOAL, CLS, karton 360, Tk 665/37/27, Rohn protocol, 8 October 1937, 10–11.

34. SOAL, CLS, karton 242, Tk 665/37/147, document 7 of those in Rutha's safe, "The Journey to Greece 1931." Since the Czech police made errors in transcribing Rutha's notes, its translation cannot be precise either, but the general tone is clear.

35. The following draws on SOAL, CLS, karton 360, Tk 665/37/34, police protocols with Gansel, 8–11 October 1937.

36. SOkAL, VdTO, Turnrat meeting of 9 April 1931. Gansel had been on the Turnrat since mid-1929, before Rutha assumed leadership.

37. SOAL, CLS, karton 360, Tk 665/37/27, Rutha police protocol, 7 October 1937, 15.

38. W.R.[Walter Rohn], "Das Herbstfest der sudetendeutschen Jungenschaft," *Die junge Front,* January 1932, 33–34. Rutha delivered a lecture with lantern slides.

39. SOAL, CLS, karton 242, Tk 665/37/253, Rutha to Gansel, 12 June 1934. On his only visit to Gansel in Weimar, Rutha found he had a new girlfriend. Ibid., karton 360, Tk 665/37/36, Gansel statement, 12 October 1937.

40. Ibid., karton 242, Tk 665/37/253, Rutha to Gansel, 16 July 1934 and 12 February 1935.

41. Ibid., karton 360, Tk 665/37/1, Veitenhansl statement, signed 10 October 1935.

42. Ibid., karton 360, Tk 665/37/126, Wolff protocols, 15 and 29 October 1937; also Rutha relative interview, 8 July 2000.

43. Ibid., karton 360, Tk 665/37/126, Heinl protocol, 14 October 1937, 5–6.

44. AAVČR, Beneš papers, karton 142, protocol of Veitenhansl's parents, 11 October 1937.

45. Ibid., Rutha to Hoffmann, 4 January 1937.

46. SOAL, CLS, karton 242, Tk 665/37/147, copy of poem, "Das Opfer," 13 January 1934.

47. Ibid., karton 242, Tk 665/37/253, Rutha to Gansel, 12 June 1934.

48. One of the group, Karl Hanke, told Rutha that the tour had been one of the greatest experiences of his life, convincing him that youth education must be modeled on the classical example: AAVČR, Beneš papers, karton 142, pisemnosti opisy, Hanke to Rutha, 8 October 1934.

49. SOAL, CLS, karton 360, Tk 665/37/34, Wolfgang Heinz protocol, 9–10 October 1937; and Tk 665/37/67, material confiscated from Heinz's apartment, including a leather-bound book of photographs of the Greek trip, sent by Rutha at Christmas 1934. Two years later Heinz sent Rutha a two-volume translation of Plutarch.

50. Ibid., karton 360, Tk 665/37/7, Weiss protocol, 11 October 1937.

51. AAVČR, Beneš papers, karton 142, pisemnosti opisy, Rutha to Wagner, 24 January 1934.

52. SOAL, CLS, karton 360, Tk 665/37/1 and Tk 665/37/6, Wagner protocols, 4 and 8 October 1937.

7. A LEAP INTO ICE-COLD WATER

1. Rudolf Jahn, *Konrad Henlein: Leben und Werk des Turnführers* (Carlsbad, 1938), 114.

2. Andreas Luh, *Der Deutsche Turnverband in der Ersten Tchechoslowakischen Republik: Vom völkischen Vereinsbetrieb zur volkspolitischen Bewegung* (Munich, 1988), 202–203; and Jahn, *Konrad Henlein,* 114–116. See also Walter Brand, "Zwei Jahre Kampf: Geschichte einer Volksbewegung" (unpublished manuscript, copy in the Krajská vědecká knihovna, Liberec, October 1935), 1–2.

3. Luh, *Deutsche Turnverband,* 204. This event publicized Saaz in the 1930s, yet in a recent Czech history it merits only one sentence. See Petr Holodňák and Ivana Ebelová, eds., *Žatec* (Prague, 2004), 357.

4. Jahn, *Konrad Henlein,* 101.

5. See *TZ*, 1 August 1933, 290; and Kurt Hora, "Unsere Jungenschaft im Turnverband," *DjD*, July 1931, 5.

6. Heinz Rutha, "Ziel und Stufenbau der Gesamterziehung," *TZ*, June 1933, 186–188.

7. For the following see Luh, *Deutsche Turnverband*, 243–252.

8. "Das Herbstfest des Kameradschaftsbundes," *Die junge Front*, November 1932, 325.

9. Ernst von Salomon, *Der Fragebogen* (Reinbeck bei Hamburg, 1961), 172–175.

10. Karmasin was briefly Rutha's bookkeeper and married a farmer's daughter from Oschitz: Rutha relative interview, 11 September 2006.

11. See Wilfried Jilge, "Zwischen Autoritarismus und Totalitarismus: Anmerkungen zu einer Kontroverse," *Bohemia* 39 (1998): 102–105.

12. Walter Brand, *Auf verlorenem Posten: Ein sudetendeutscher Politiker zwischen Autonomie und Anschluss* (Munich, 1985), 36–46, 53–57.

13. *DjD*, October–November 1931, 4.

14. For the following see Elizabeth Wiskemann, *Czechs and Germans: A Study of the Struggle in the Historic Provinces of Bohemia and Moravia* (London, 1938), 138–139, 198–200; Ronald M. Smelser, *The Sudeten Problem, 1933–1938: Volkstumspolitik and the Formulation of Nazi Foreign Policy* (Folkestone, 1975), 50–56; and for the Czech emergency measures, see Zdeněk Kárník, *České země v éře první republiky (1918–1938)*, vol.2, *Československo a české země v krizi a v ohrožení (1930–1935)* (Prague, 2002), 136–140. A useful if uncritical discussion is Giovanni Capoccia, "Legislative Responses against Extremism: The 'Protection of Democracy' in the First Czechoslovak Republic (1920–1938)," *East European Politics and Societies* 16 (2002): 691–738.

15. Interview with Marie Isaides, 25 March 2000, Lázně Kundratice.

16. Kárník, *České země*, 2:116–142.

17. Heidrun Dolezal and Stephan Dolezal, eds., *Deutsche Gesandschaftsberichte aus Prag: Innenpolitik und Minderheitenprobleme in der Ersten Tschechoslowakischen Republik* (Munich, 1991), 4:45.

18. See for example Christoph Boyer and Jaroslav Kučera, "Die Deutschen in Böhmen, die Sudetendeutsche Partei und der Nationalsozialismus," in *Nationalsozialismus in der Region: Beiträge zur regionale und lokalen Forschung und zum internationalen Vergleich*, ed. Horst Möller (Munich, 1996), 273–285. But see also the debate in *Bohemia* 38/39 (1997–1998).

19. As Boyer and Kučera acknowledge: "Die Deutschen in Böhmen," 278.

20. Martin Schneller, *Zwischen Romantik und Faschismus: Der Beitrag Othmar Spanns zum Konservatismus der Weimarer Republik* (Stuttgart, 1970), 147.

Heinrich, optimistic that Nazi Germany could introduce a corporate state, was by June 1933 heading an *Institute für Ständewesen* in Dusseldorf.

21. See the example of Karl Anton Prince Rohan, discussed in Eagle Glassheim, *Noble Nationalists: The Transformation of the Bohemian Aristocracy* (Cambridge, MA, 2005), 111–112, 164–166

22. There is little research on *Bereitschaft,* but see Wiskemann, *Czechs and Germans,* 137–138; and Wilhelm Jesser, "'Bereitschaft,' 'Kameradschaft' und 'Aufbruch' in den Sudetenländern," in *Deutsche Jugendbewegung in Europa,* ed. Peter Nasarski (Cologne, 1967), 359–365.

23. NA, SdP 1933–38, karton 4, material about the Staffen case (where Henlein notes Staffen's long-standing hostility to Rutha).

24. Luh, *Deutsche Turnverband,* 206–207; Dolezal and Dolezal, *Deutsche Gesandschaftsberichte,* 34; and Stanislav Biman and Jaroslav Malíř, *Kariéra učitele tělocviku* (Liberec, 1983), 52–54.

25. Brand, *Auf verlorenem Posten,* 64–65. It seems most likely that this meeting coincided with the Oschitz Turn event (see photographs in SOkAL, MAO, karton 10).

26. See Kárník, *České země,* 2:183–187; and a popular account of supposed KB-Nazi conspiracy in 1933, Emil Hruška, *Konrad Henlein: Život a smrt* (Prague, 2010), 68–81. Kárník, by inadequately assessing the KB and the Turnverband, more than implies that Henlein's SHF was just a straight replacement for the DNSAP. He also repeats the error that in late July 1933 Hitler received Henlein in Stuttgart: *České země,* 2:185. Compare Ludwig Weichselbaumer, *Walter Brand (1907–1980): Ein sudetendeutscher Politiker im Spannungsfeld zwischen Autonomie und Anschluss* (Munich 2008), 209–210.

27. Rutha had, for example, visited Keilberg in December 1932. In early 1932 he had taken Gansel there to meet Wagner-Poltrock and discuss architectural plans: SOAL, CLS, karton 360, Tk 665/37/34, Gansel statement, 8 October 1937, 5.

28. Walter Becher, *Zeitzeuge: Ein Lebensbericht* (Munich, 1990), 78; and Brand, *Auf verlorenem Posten,* 67–68.

29. Brand, *Auf verlorenem Posten,* 69–73; Weichselbaumer, *Walter Brand,* 226–228; Luh, *Deutsche Turnverband,* 209–211; and Emil Franzel, *Sudetendeutsche Geschichte: Eine volkstümliche Darstellung* (Mannheim, 1990), 366.

30. Weichselbaumer, *Walter Brand,* 229–232. On Henlein's chameleonic behavior, see Mark Cornwall, "The Czechoslovak Sphinx: 'Moderate and Reasonable' Konrad Henlein," in *In the Shadow of Hitler: Personalities of the Right in Central and Eastern Europe,* ed. Rebecca Haynes and Martyn Rady (London, 2011), 206–226.

31. SOkAL, Reichenberg police records, I, Rutha to Andrée Šámalová, 8 April 1935.
32. Ibid., III, Rutha to Karl Hanke, 11 March 1935. Possibly Rutha had met Haider and Fischer in Prague in May 1933 and they had revealed their antipathy to him: Biman and Malíř, *Kariéra*, 56. Brand later surmised that a significant rivalry developed between Rutha and Haider for control of the Turner youth movement: SDA, Sebekowsky papers, Brand to Sebekowsky, 10 March 1963.
33. Henlein's speech, in Rudolf Jahn, ed., *Konrad Henlein spricht. Reden zur politischen Volksbewegung der Sudetendeutschen* (Carlsbad, 1937), 11–17.
34. Brand, *Auf verlorenem Posten*, 80. Evidence about local SHF branches shows a group founded in Aussig on 15 November, in Schreckenstein on 17 November, in Gablonz on 24 November, and in Tetschen on 6 December. In Schreckenstein and Wartenberg the designated SHF leaders were both architects, while in Oschitz it was Emil Hain, husband of Rutha's niece Inge, who assumed the post: see NA, SdP 1933–38, karton 14. The first SHF branch was founded in Carlsbad by a bankrupt publisher, the notorious Karl Hermann Frank: René Küpper, *Karl Hermann Frank (1898–1946): Politische Biographie eines sudetendeutschen Nationalsozialisten* (Munich, 2010), 60–61.
35. Brand, "Zwei Jahre Kampf," 17, 25; and the German consul's report from Reichenberg: PAAA, R73840, 15 November 1933.
36. Biman and Malíř, *Kariéra*, 82.
37. AAVČR, Beneš papers, karton 142, pisemnosti opisy, Rohn to Rutha, 23 December 1933 (enclosing a poem on George by Friedrich Wolters).
38. *MJT*, August 1934, 1.
39. SOkAL, Reichenberg police records, I, Rutha to Andrée Šámalová, 8 April 1935.
40. Weichselbaumer, *Walter Brand*, 226.
41. BHA, Becher papers, 84, Becher talk to "Historischer Arbeitskreis," 13; and Luh, *Deutsche Turnverband*, 260–261.
42. SOkAL, Reichenberg police records, I, Rutha to Andrée Šámalová, 26 March 1935.
43. VdTO, Turnrat meeting of 21 March 1932.
44. VdTO, Annual general meeting of 11 January 1934.
45. Rutha, "Aufforderung des Turnbauamtes," *TZ*, 1 October 1933, 359; "Verlautbarung des Turnbauamtes," *TZ*, 1 September 1934, 318–319; and "Turnbauamt," *TZ*, 1 August 1935, 283. In February 1936, Henlein himself emphasized that architecture must be in tune with the community: Jahn, *Konrad Henlein spricht*, 143–144.

46. Richard Bernhard, "Wechsel in der Führung," *MJT,* December 1933, 1. Across the Turnverband 1,200 officials had to resign.

47. The view of one local Turner: AAVČR, Beneš papers, karton 142, statement of Artur König, 13 October 1937, 1.

48. For the following, see "Gauturntag," *MJT,* March 1934, 1–3.

49. See the glowing assessment of Bernhard, a "pioneer in creating the Männerbund": *MJT,* February 1935, 2.

50. *MJT,* November 1934, 2, reporting the "Gauturnratsitzung" of 20 October 1934.

51. "Auf zur Sprachengrenzfahrt nach Labau," *MJT,* September 1934, 1.

52. Rutha, "Aufruf des Gauführers zum Männergauturnfest," *MJT,* July 1934, 1.

53. "Unser Männerturnfest," *MJT,* August 1934, 1–2; "Sitzung des Gauturnrates," *MJT,* September 1934, 2; and "61. ordentlicher Gauturntag," February 1935, 1.

54. "Das Fest unserer Frauen und Mädchen," *MJT,* August 1935, 1–2. See also Henlein's view of women: Jahn, *Konrad Henlein spricht,* 94–104.

55. "Gautag für winterliche Uebungen," *MJT,* November 1934, 3.

56. SOkAL, Reichenberg police records, I, Rutha to Wolfgang Heinz, 25 June 1935.

57. "Amtstag," *MJT,* April 1934, 1. Rutha's industry was later publicized in statistics. In his first year he sent precisely 537 letters and had 102 telephone conversations: "Die turnerische Arbeit des Jahres 1934 in Zahlen," *MJT,* March 1935, 1.

58. SOAL, CLS, karton 242, Tk 665/37/253, Rutha to Gansel, 12 June 1934.

59. Luh, *Deutsche Turnverband,* 331, 338–350.

60. "Jungturnerschaft," *MJT,* March 1934, 6. Rohn from 1934 was mainly based in Prague, but became a member of the Turnverband's main "youth committee."

61. SOAL, CLS, karton 242, Tk 665/37/253, Rutha to Gansel, 12 June 1934. See also *MJT,* June 1934: reports by Rutha and Heinl.

62. "61. ordentlicher Gauturntag," *MJT,* February 1935, 1–3.

63. SOkAL, Reichenberg police records, I, Rutha to Brand, 3 November 1934. Rutha probably saw Henlein on 23 November when he spent the night in Asch.

64. SOAL, CLS, karton 242, Tk 665/37/253, Rutha to Gansel, 12 June 1934.

65. NA, SdP, karton 67, Rudi Hejl to Artur Vogt, 16 October 1937.

66. For the following see particularly Luh, *Deutsche Turnverband,* 317–330; and Rudolf Jahn, *Sudetendeutsches Turnertum: Im Auftrag der Arbeitsgemeinschaft sudetendeutscher Turner und Turnerinnen in der sudetendeutschen Landsmannschaft* (Frankfurt am Main, 1957–1958), 1:192–199.

67. See *Die Arbeitsdienst in der Welt und die studentische Jugend,* ed. die Deutsche Studentenschaft (Hamburg, 1935). The reports from England were made by Rolf Gardiner and Richard Crossman. For the English perspective, see Andrew Best, ed., *Water Springing from the Ground: An Anthology of the Writings of Rolf Gardiner* (Springhead, 1972), 109–125. Although Gardiner was enthusiastic about Anglo-German youth links and knew some Sudeten Germans, there is no evidence that he was a key contact for Rutha's links to Britain (compare Becher, *Zeitzeuge,* 81). His papers in Cambridge University library leave this subject untouched.

68. See Peter Dudek, *Erziehung durch Arbeit: Arbeitslagerbewegung und Freiwilliger Arbeitsdienst 1920–1935* (Opladen, 1988), for a case study of labor service in Germany.

69. A useful summary is Rudolf Kasper, "Sudetendeutscher Wirtschaftverfall und seine sozialen Auswirkungen," *VuF* 3 (1936): 109–116

70. See Karl Wild, "Neugestaltung der Sozialfürsorge durch Arbeitslager," *VuF* 3 (1936): 119–123; and Luh, *Deutsche Turnverband,* 323.

71. The situation in 1934 is clear from the "Czech report" to the international student conference, where the degree of Czechoslovak state support was much exaggerated: *Die Arbeitsdienst,* 106–107.

72. NA, SdP files, karton 6 [Henlein office], Albin Friedrich (head of SVH) to BdD, 4 March 1935, Beilage.

73. SOkAL, Reichenberg police records, III, Pohl to Rutha, 11 January 1937.

74. Heinrich Rutha, "Die Jugendturnschule: Plan und Verwirklichung," *TZ,* 1 November 1936, 412.

75. SOkAL, Reichenberg police records, I, Rutha to Andrée Šámalová, 8 April 1935.

76. Rutha, "Die Jugendturnschule," *TZ,* 1 November 1936, 413. Rutha wrote here about "*völkisch* socialism."

77. Werner Pohl, "Arbeitslager—Arbeitsbeschaffung," *TZ,* 15 January 1935, 18.

78. Rutha found it "disgraceful" that only one volunteer came from the Jeschken Gau though it had over two thousand unemployed Turners; he publicly appealed for more. See Heinrich Rutha, "Turnbrüder!," *MJT,* April 1935, 1; and the advertisement in *MJT,* July 1935.

79. "Der erste Spatenstich," *TZ,* 1 April 1935, 121.

80. See NA, SdP, karton 6, Hauck's reports of 25 May and 21 July 1935.

81. Franz Krautzberger, "Pioniere der jungen Mannschaft," *VuF* 3 (1936): 102.

82. Theo Hauck, "Der Lagerführer," *VuF* 3 (1936): 103–106; and photographs between 112–113.

83. Otto Rinn, "Ein Tag im Arbeitsdienst," *TZ*, 15 July 1935, 258. A Wartenberg song ran: "Our rifles are sparkling spades / Our grenades are solid stones."

84. Heinz Rutha, "Jugenderziehungswerk Wartenberg," *TZ*, July 1937, 288–289.

85. Theo Hauck, "Von sudetendeutschen Arbeitsdienst," *TZ*, July 1937, 281.

86. Luh, *Deutsche Turnverband*, 329. See also *TZ*, 1 July 1936, 250; and Jahn, *Sudetendeutsches Turnertum*, 1:194.

87. SOkAL, Reichenberg police records, III, Pohl to Rutha, 11 January 1937.

88. Werner Pohl, "Das Verhältnis des Arbeitsdienstes zu Staat und Demokratie," *VuF* 3 (1936): 106–109. See also *TZ*, 15 May 1936, 184, where Pohl countered criticism of the camps by the Czech journal *Přítomnost*.

89. Werner Pohl, "Aussig und der Arbeitsdienst," *TZ*, 15 October 1937, 327–328.

90. For example at Easter 1936 with Rohn, Becher, and others: SOkAL, Reichenberg police records, I, Rutha to Alfons Wondrak, 15 April 1936.

91. Heinrich Rutha, "Die Jugendturnschule," *TZ*, 1 November 1936, 413.

92. This competition was in the hands of Max Kriegler, an architect who in 1935 had won a TBA prize competition for the design of a Turn hall. Rutha had then placed him in charge of the TBA bureau in Prague and typically delegated there much of the TBA's everyday work in Bohemia (see *TZ*, 15 May 1935). In 1936 he officially succeeded Rutha as TBA director. See Kriegler's memorandum in SOkAL, Reichenberg police records, III, December 1936.

93. Rutha, "Jugenderziehungswerk Wartenberg," *TZ*, July 1937, 290.

94. SOkAL, Reichenberg police records, III, Rutha to Turn leadership etc, 4 October 1935; and Franz Engel, "Turnschwestern, Turnbrüder!," *MJT*, November 1935, 1.

95. Smelser, *Sudeten Problem*, 135–140.

96. For the complex shifts in student loyalty, see Gustav Butschek, *Der "Bund der böhmerlandischen Freischaren," seine Freischaren und die Nachfolgegemeinschaften* (Hamburg, 1984).

97. Luh, *Deutsche Turnverband*, 375–376, 382.

98. "Ungerechtfertigte Angriffe gegen die Turnerschaft," *MJT*, January 1935, 2. The offensive article was in *Vorwärts*, 14 July 1934.

99. For Henlein's speech, see Jahn, *Konrad Henlein spricht*, 22–30; and the critiques of it by Smelser (*Sudeten Problem*, 101), Wiskemann (*Czechs and Germans*, 203), and the German envoy (Dolezal and Dolezal, *Deutsche Gesandschaftsberichte aus Prag*, 155–161).

100. SOkAL, Reichenberg police records, III, Rutha to Karl Hanke, 11 March 1935.

101. Ibid., Rutha to Ernst Kittel, 11 March 1935.

102. Luh, *Deutsche Turnverband,* 352.

103. For this allegiance of Baierl and Hein (against the Reichenberg Jungenschaft run in the late 1920s by Rohn), see Helmut Richter, *Geschichte des Reichenberger Wandervogels* (Waldkraiburg, 1984), 22.

104. A personal element was present here. Rutha accused Baierl of trying to remove an "excellent and incorruptible" Reichenberg youth leader, Ossi Günther (see SOkAL, Reichenberg police records, III, Rutha to Willi Horak, 22 February 1936). Günther had alerted Rutha early in 1935.

105. SOAL, CLS, karton 360, Tk 665/37/1, police protocol with Rudi Hein, 1 October 1937; and AAVČR, Beneš papers, karton 142, Hein protocol, 11 October 1937. See also Hein's file in BA, Berlin Document Center, RS Rudolf Hein.

106. NA, SdP, karton 36, Rutha to Uli Hermann, 27 April 1935; and SOkAL, Reichenberg police records, I, Rutha to Otto Kletzl, 26 April 1935.

107. SOkAL, Reichenberg police records, III, Rutha to Karl Wolf, 16 May 1935. See also Dedek's grievance that Rutha appointed a KB man in Hein's place: AAVČR, Beneš papers, karton 142, Dedek protocol, 13 October 1937.

108. SOkAL, Reichenberg police records, III, Rutha to Karl Wolf, 16 May 1935.

109. For the following see especially SOAL, CLS, karton 360, Tk 665/126, police protocols with Richard Bernhard and Karl Wolf, 18–19 October 1937.

110. AAVČR, Beneš papers, karton 142, Rutha police protocol, 20 October 1937, 4. To the Czech police, he also implied that at the meeting he had taken the lead in discussing the homosexual accusation, which seems unlikely: SOAL, CLS, karton 360, Tk 665/37/27, Rutha protocol, 7 October 1937, 8.

111. SOAL, CLS, karton 360, Tk 665/37/1, Wilhelm Purm police protocol, 25 August 1937. This term had been used since the late eighteenth century: Graham Robb, *Strangers: Homosexual Love in the Nineteenth Century* (London, 2003), 94.

112. SOAL, CLS, karton 360, Tk 665/37/55, Anton Funk protocol, 13 October 1937, 8–9; and Tk 665/37/58, Kurt Franzske protocol, 15 October 1937. (Others on this visit included Hanke, Weiss, and Hoffmann.)

113. Ibid., Tk 665/37/126, Heinl police protocol, 14 October 1937.

114. For the following see ibid., the police protocols of October 1937 with Wolff and Turn leaders, Franz Engel, Anton Ries, Rudolf Lange, and Richard Lammel. (Lange recounted Wolff's physiognomic evidence.)

115. Wolff had agreed with Veitenhansl not to use the protocol without his permission: SOAL, CLS, karton 242, Tk 665/37, Wolff statement, 29 October 1937.

116. SOkAL, Reichenberg police records, III, Rutha to Hans Buschek, 11 October 1935.

117. For Rutha's efforts to gather incriminating evidence against *Aufbruch* for the Turn leadership, see his letters to Ernst Kittel and Tonl Sandner on 31 May 1935: ibid., III.

118. "Ausserordentlicher Gauturntag,", *MJT,* December 1935, 1. See also "Beschluss des erweiterten Gauturnrates," *MJT,* September 1935, 1.

119. See SOkAL, Reichenberg police records, III, Rutha to Willi Horak, 22 February 1936; and to Willi Brandner, 19 February 1936. In these letters Rutha complained that Baierl might be appointed as the new Gau youth leader; Baierl indeed continued publicly to malign him: see SOAL, CLS, karton 360, Tk 665/37/15, Leo Wagner protocol, 7 October 1937, 4.

120. For the following see SOAL, CLS, karton 360, Tk 665/37/1, Hein police protocol, 1 October 1937; and AAVČR, Beneš papers, karton 142, Hein police protocol, 11 October 1937. See also CLS, karton 360, Tk 665/37/1, protocol of the lawyer Ernst Berndt, 2 October 1937.

121. See AAVČR, Beneš papers, karton 142, Karl Karwath police protocol, 12 October 1937.

122. PAAA, R103656, Walter von Lierau to German foreign ministry, Pers.K 95, 15 October 1937, enclosing copy of his report of 8 September 1935.

8. SUDETEN FOREIGN MINISTER

1. SOkAL, Reichenberg police records, I, Rutha speech at Johannesthal, 21 July 1935.

2. Ibid., Rutha to Andrée Šámalová, 26 March 1935 and 8 April 1935. The case (notably against *Lidové noviny*) was settled in the Brünn court in October 1935, the evidence declared false. However, some Czech historians have chosen to believe it: see Stanislav Biman and Jaroslav Malíř, *Kariéra učitele tělocviku* (Liberec, 1983), 128.

3. NA, SdP, karton 6, Hauptleitung minutes, 30 July 1934.

4. Ibid., 29 May 1935.

5. Ibid., 27 June 1935.

6. Josef Fischer, Václav Patzak, and Vincenc Perth, *Jejich boj: Co chce a čemu slouží Sudetendeutsche Partei* (Prague, 1937), 77; and Václav Král, ed., *Die Deutschen in der Tschechoslowakei 1933–1947: Dokumentensammlung* (Prague, 1964), 18.

7. A note about Rutha dated 1 June 1935 reached the president's office: AKPR, T517/35.

8. AKPR, T348/37, memorandum by Přemysl Šámal, 22 February 1937, quoting Beneš; and AMZV, Politické zprávy Londýn, Jan Masaryk to foreign ministry, 24 July 1936.

9. See for example Sabine Bamberger-Stemmann, *Der Europäische National-itätenkongreß 1925 bis 1938: Nationale Minderheiten zwischen Lobbyistentum und Großmachtinteressen* (Marburg, 2000); and Jindřich Dejmek, *Nenaplněné naděje: Politické a diplomatické vztahy Československa a Velké Británie 1918–1938* (Prague, 2003). And for the older standard viewpoint, see J. W. Bruegel, *Tschechen und Deutsche 1918–1938* (Munich, 1967); Radomír Luža, *The Transfer of the Sudeten Germans: A Study of Czech-German Relations, 1933–1962* (New York, 1962); and J. W. Bruegel, *Czechoslovakia before Munich: The German Minority Problem and British Appeasement Policy* (Cambridge, 1973).

10. Ronald M. Smelser, *The Sudeten Problem, 1933–1938: Volkstumspolitik and the Formulation of Nazi Foreign Policy* (Folkestone, 1975). The book's subtitle, however, indicates its focus on Nazi foreign policy.

11. SDA, Gustav Peters papers, "Erinnerungen," 197.

12. Jaroslav Kučera, "Mezi Wilhelmstraße a Thunovskou: Finanční podpora Německé říše Sudenoněmecké straně v letech 1935–8," *Český časopis historický* 95 (1997): 387–405. The implication here (as in Bruegel, *Tschechen und Deutsche*, 259, 282–283) is that financing from Berlin meant the SdP was unconditionally working for the Reich.

13. See SOkAL, Reichenberg police records, I, Rutha to Andrée Šámalová, 8 April 1935.

14. Gerhard L. Weinberg, *The Foreign Policy of Hitler's Germany: Diplomatic Revolution in Europe, 1933–36* (Chicago, 1970), 210–216.

15. SOkAL, MAO, karton 9, file 3, Ewald Ammende (from Vienna) to Rutha, 21 May 1935. See also Ammende's warning of "fatal results" if Prague did not engage with the SdP: *Nation und Staat* 8, no. 9 (June 1935): 556–560; and see more generally Martyn Housden, "Ewald Ammende and the Organization of National Minorities in Inter-war Europe," *German History* 18, no. 4 (2000): 439–460.

16. For a good summary of Hasselblatt's thinking, see Xosé-Manoel Nuñez Seixas, *Entre Ginebra y Berlín: La cuestión de las minorías nacionales y la política internacional en Europa 1914–1939* (Madrid, 2001), 480–485.

17. John Hiden, *Defender of Minorities: Paul Schiemann, 1876–1944* (London, 2004), 114–122.

18. Nuñez Seixas, *Entre Ginebra y Berlín*, 208–224.

19. See Mark Cornwall, "'National Reparation'?: The Czech Land Reform and the Sudeten Germans, 1918–38," *SEER* 75, no. 2 (1997): 259–280; and Eagle Glassheim, *Noble Nationalists: The Transformation of the Bohemian Aristocracy* (Cambridge, MA, 2005), 105–107.

20. See the useful retrospective by Friedrich Nelböock, "Ein Kämpfer für Recht und Wahrheit," *Sudetenland* 3 (1963): 217–221.

21. SOkAL, Reichenberg police records, I, Rutha to Oberlik, 7 June; ibid., note on Rutha's expenses, 28 June 1935. For the Brussels trip see also Nelböck's correspondence in SOkAD, Alfons Clary-Aldringen papers, karton 661.

22. SOkAL, Reichenberg police records, I, Rutha to Jaroslav Kose [Czech delegate], 21 June 1935. Nelböck, while concerned not to leave the Czechs an open field in Brussels, had alerted Rutha to the potential for Czech-German cooperation: AAVČR, Kamil Krofta papers, karton 19, č.584, Nelböck to Krofta, 5 June 1935.

23. Walter Brand, *Auf verlorenem Posten: Ein sudetendeutscher Politiker im Spannungsfeld zwischen Autonomie und Anschluss* (Munich, 1985), 51. More generally on Van Severen, see Wilfried Wagner, *Belgien in der deutschen Politik während des Zweiten Weltkrieges* (Boppard am Rhein, 1974), 22–27.

24. KUL, Van Severen papers, diary, 13 June 1936.

25. SOkAL, Reichenberg police records, I, Rutha to Wolfgang Heinz, 25 June 1935.

26. KUL, Van Severen papers, Rutha to Van Severen, 5 July 1935.

27. NA, SdP, karton 6, SdP Hauptleitung minutes, 17 June 1935 [incorrectly dated 12 June].

28. SOkAL, Reichenberg police records, I, Rutha to Walter Heinrich, 19 June 1935. See also Walter Heinrich, ed., *Othmar Spann—Leben und Werk* (Graz, 1979), 21:44.

29. NA, SdP, karton 6, Hauptleitung minutes, 27 June 1935 and 4 July 1935.

30. Bamberger-Stemmann, *Der Europäische Nationalitätenkongreß*, 267–274.

31. See for example Walter Brand, "Die Idee des 'sudetendeutschen Stammes,'" *VuF* 1 (1935): 9; Henlein quoted in Elizabeth Wiskemann, *Czechs and Germans: A Study of the Struggle in the Historic Provinces of Bohemia and Moravia* (London, 1938), 243; and Frank's more aggressive interpretation: René Küpper, *Karl Hermann Frank (1898–1946)* (Munich, 2010), 75.

32. See Hasselblatt's report on a VDV meeting in Prague: PAAA, R60495, Koch to AA, 20 February 1935. The report shows that Hasselblatt and Henlein were already thinking about cooperating to highlight the Sudeten plight earlier in the year.

33. *Sudetendeutsche Presse-Briefe*, 29 August 1935; and for the view that this was irredentism, see Otto Novák, *Henleinovci proti Československu: Z historie sudetoněmeckého fašismu v letech 1933–1938* (Prague, 1987), 86–87.

34. See the reports, "Der IX Nationalitätenkongress in Genf," *VuF* 7 (1935): 301–307; PAAA, R60532, Krauel to AA, 9 September 1935; and TNA, FO 371/19673, Warner to Hoare, 10 September 1935. See also Nuñez Seixas, *Entre Ginebra y Berlín*, 419.

35. PAAA, R60531, Ammende to Hasselblatt, 12 September 1935. Bamberger-Stemmann, *Der Europäische Nationalitätenkongreß*, 272, concludes that the ENC was now a complete tool of Nazi foreign policy, yet Ammende clearly did not interpret it as such.

36. SOkAL, Reichenberg police records, I, Rutha to Alfons Wondrak, 5 July 1935: Karl Hanke was secured as Rutha's driver. Felix Richter was well known in automobile circles, and later in 1937 offered to stand bail for Rutha when he was in prison.

37. See, ibid., the detailed correspondence with the architect Eduard Bergmann.

38. SDA, Gustav Peters papers, "Erinnerungen," 210.

39. *Sudetendeutsche Presse-Briefe*, 19 July 1935.

40. Rudolf Jahn, ed., *Konrad Henlein spricht: Reden zur politischen Volksbewegung der Sudetendeutschen* (Carlsbad, 1937), 112.

41. Although a detailed ANV program was drawn up on 19 November 1935, only parts have survived (SOkAL, MAO, karton 9, file 2). But see the ANV's 1935 correspondence in NA, SdP files, karton 36 (material seized by the police in October 1937). See also Rutha's notes to Van Severen in October 1935, requesting information about the Belgian press and about Flemings living in Bohemia: KUL, Van Severen papers.

42. Heinz Rutha, "Sechs Mächte," *Die Zeit,* 12 November 1935, 1. This speech can usefully be contrasted with Frank's more radical foreign policy stance in parliament at this time: Küpper, *Karl Hermann Frank*, 74–76.

43. Compare Luža, *Transfer,* 75; and Bruegel, *Czechoslovakia,* 109 (where Henlein is a complete henchman of Hitler).

44. As Walter Heinrich stressed later in his interview with Walter Becher: BHA, Becher papers, 557. See also Walter Brand, *Die sudetendeutsche Tragödie* (Wunsiedel, 1949), 34, 38.

45. Dejmek, *Nenaplněné naděje,* 264–265; and for the British context, R. A. C. Parker, *Chamberlain and Appeasement: British Policy and the Coming of the Second World War* (Basingstoke, 1993), 50.

46. NA, SdP files, karton 36, Rutha to Ammende, 23 October 1935, and ANV to Ernst Mühlbauer [a reader of the English press], 19 November 1935.

47. CCC, Christie papers, CHRS 1/11, Christie to Toynbee, 26 September 1935. Christie was not a member of the British secret service as many have suggested (e.g., Biman and Malíř, *Kariéra*, 126–127) but largely acting on his own initiative and reporting to Robert Vansittart in the Foreign Office. See Laurence Thompson, *The Greatest Treason: The Untold Story of Munich* (New York, 1968), 275.

48. NA, SdP files, karton 67, "Bericht der Deutsche Liga . . . 1935/6."

49. Compare explanations lacking sufficient evidence: Biman and Malíř, *Kariéra*, 127–128; Walter Becher, *Zeitzeuge: Ein Lebensbericht* (Munich, 1990), 81; and Brand, *Auf verlorenem Posten*, 128. See also Glassheim, *Noble Nationalists*, 174.

50. NA, SdP files, karton 36, Ammende to Rutha, 10 October; and ANV to Seton-Watson, 28 November 1935. No letters about this interchange have survived in the Seton-Watson papers.

51. A German Bohemian Deputy, "The German Minority in Czechoslovakia," *SEER* 41 (1936): 295–300. For Rutha's authorship: NA, SdP, karton 6, SdP Hauptleitung minutes, 27 November 1935.

52. Compare Bruegel, *Tschechen und Deutsche*, 285–286.

53. SSEES, Seton-Watson papers, SEW/10/6/4, Christie to Seton-Watson, 12 December; and SEW/10/4/3, confidential memo by Seton-Watson about Henlein's visit, 14 December 1935. Significantly, Henlein confessed to Seton-Watson that if all rebuffed him he could only turn to Germany.

54. CCC, Christie papers, CHRS 1/11, Seton-Watson to Christie, 21 February 1935; and Christie's notes on meeting Seton-Watson, 4 March 1936.

55. R. W. Seton-Watson, *A History of the Czechs and Slovaks* (London, 1943), 393.

56. SOkAL, Reichenberg police records, I, Rutha to Ernst Merker, 3 February 1936.

57. For the start of contacts with the Foreign Office, see TNA, FO 371/19493, R7511/234/12.

58. ÖSA (AdR), NPA, karton 72, Ferdinand Marek to Berger-Waldenegg, 2 May 1935; and TNA, FO 371/20373, Robert Hadow to Eden, 31 January 1936. On Beneš see now the panegyric study by Jindřich Dejmek, *Edvard Beneš: Politická biografie českého demokrata*, 2 vols. (Prague, 2008). Dejmek implies rather uncritically that Beneš had a clear and constructive strategy (2:30–31).

59. TNA, FO 371/20374, Christie to Orme Sargent (private letter), 19 June 1936; and Jindřich Dejmek, *Historik v čele diplomacie Kamil Krofta* (Prague, 1998), 40–41.

60. Heidrun Dolezal and Stephan Dolezal, eds., *Deutsche Gesandschaftsberichte aus Prag: Innenpolitik und Minderheitenprobleme in der Ersten Tschecho-slowakischen Republik* (Munich, 1991), 4:260.

61. On negative reporting from Prague see Mark Cornwall, "A Fluctuating Barometer: British Diplomatic Views of the Czech-German Relationship in Czechoslovakia," in *Great Britain, the United States and the Bohemian Lands, 1848–1938,* ed. Eva Schmidt-Hartmann and Stanley B. Winters (Munich, 1991), 321–333.

62. Jahn, *Konrad Henlein spricht,* 137, 155. Rutha, on hearing this speech, could be satisfied at Henlein's emphasis on youth education (152–153) and also his espousal of communal architecture (143–144).

63. Ibid., 60–67.

64. NA, SdP, karton 6, SdP Hauptleitung minutes, 20 November 1935. Brand and Sebekowsky were also assigned to its ruling council.

65. That Rutha favored contact with Sudeten Germans from outside the SdP is clear in a letter to Ammende of 1 October 1935: NA, SdP files, karton 36. It suited his vision of "national unity."

66. SOkAD, Alfons Clary-Aldringen papers, karton 583, 1936 diary. See also Glassheim, *Noble Nationalists,* 107–108, 173.

67. Bamberger-Stemmann, *Der Europäische Nationalitätenkongreß,* 358–364. This conflation was also made by the Czech communist historian Václav Král. On the basis of a copy in the Czech archives, Král incorrectly ascribed to Rutha the London Action report actually authored by Hasselblatt (Král, *Die Deutschen in der Tschechoslowakei,* 97–101), as did Ronald Smelser, in "Documents on the Sudeten Question: Genuine or Forged?," *Bohemia* 26 (1985): 97–98.

68. Nuñez Seixas, *Entre Ginebra y Berlín,* 423–424; and NA, SdP, karton 36, Uexküll von Guldenbrand to Rutha, 18 April 1936.

69. PAAA, R60496, for Hasselblatt's reports to Berlin.

70. SOkAL, Reichenberg police records, I, Rutha to Nelböck, 16 June 1936. The following draws on Hasselblatt's report on the London Action (as reproduced by Král).

71. SOkAL, Reichenberg police records, I, Rutha to Wondrak, 15 April 1936. For the Glasgow program, see SOkAD, Clary-Aldringen papers, karton 662.

72. SOkAL, Reichenberg police records, II, Rutha to Ure family, 23 June 1936.

73. See Hasselblatt's overview of British minority policy in the special edition of *Nation und Staat* 9, no. 8 (May 1936): 495–513, disseminated in Britain in advance of the London Action; PAAA, R60532, reports to Berlin; and the correspondence in TNA, FO 371/20485. See also the perceptive

analysis in Nuñez Seixas, *Entre Ginebra y Berlín,* 429–431. Compare Novák, *Henleinovci,* 90–91, who misinterprets Rutha's role.

74. TNA, FO 371/20485, Hasselblatt to Cranborne, 28 May 1936, enclosing memorandum; and FO minutes.

75. *Nation und Staat* 9, no.10–11 (July–August 1936): 735–736.

76. Yet the British League of Nations Union was still rather guarded. See their report in TNA, FO 371/20485, Maxwell Garnett to Strang, 30 June 1936.

77. SOkAL, Reichenberg police records, II, Rutha to Ure family, 23 June 1936.

78. Compare Bamberger-Stemmann, *Der Europäische Nationalitätenkongreß,* 362–364.

79. SOkAL, Reichenberg police records, II, Rutha to Seton-Watson, 22 June 1936. His expectations were dampened when Seton-Watson publicly criticized the SdP in "Czechoslovakia in its European Setting," *SEER* 15, no. 43 (1936): 105–120. See Rutha's complaint to Christie: CCC, Christie papers, CHRS 1/11, 1 August 1936.

80. CCC, Christie papers, CHRS 1/11, Rutha to Christie, 7 July 1936; and TNA, FO 371/20374, Christie to Sargent, 19 June 1936, enclosing memorandum.

81. There are two records of the conversation: Vansittart's (TNA, FO 371/20374, Eden to Addison, 27 July 1936); and, indirectly, Henlein's, which was sent to the German legation in Prague (DGFP, Series C, vol.5 [London, 1966], 796–797).

82. Compare the interpretations in Dejmek, *Nenaplněné naděje,* 319; and Bruegel, *Tschechen und Deutsche,* 287.

83. TNA, FO 371/20374, Eden to Addison, 5 August 1936.

84. AMZV, Politické zprávy Londýn (1936), Masaryk to Krofta, 24 July 1936.

85. Heinrich Rutha, "Mahnworte aus London," *Die Zeit,* 26 July 1936, 1.

86. For the following the best detailed discussion remains Biman and Malíř, *Kariéra,* 133–170.

87. See Rutha's desire for clarification in a letter to Gustav Knöchel: SOkAL, Reichenberg police records, I, Rutha to Knöchel, 22 May 1936.

88. DGFP, Series C, vol.5 (London, 1966), 608–609.

89. SOkAL, Reichenberg police records, I, Rutha to Nelböck, 16 June 1936.

90. CCC, Christie papers, CHRS 1/11, Rutha to Christie, 7 July 1936.

91. NA, SdP, karton 6, Hauptleitung minutes, 15 July 1936. For interpreting the honor court's behavior, see Ludwig Weichselbaumer, *Walter Brand (1907–1980): Ein sudetendeutscher Politiker im Spannungsfeld zwischen Autonomie und Anschluss* (Munich 2008), 375–386.

92. ÖSA, NPA, karton 74, Marek to Guido Schmidt, 24 July 1936.

93. NA, SdP, karton 6, Hauptleitung minutes, Eger, 30 July 1936.

94. See CCC, Christie papers, CHRS 1/11, Rutha to Christie, 10 August 1936.

95. Weichselbaumer, *Walter Brand*, 372–373.

96. For Rutha's friendly but formal relationship with Brand, see Weichselbaumer, *Walter Brand*, 402n1672. For his distance with Sandner, see Sandner's postwar interrogation in March 1947: SOAP, Mimořádný lidový soud v Praze, Ls 0749/47, especially 72.

97. SOkAL, Reichenberg police records, I, Rutha to Gustav Flögel, 28 June 1935.

98. DGFP, Series C, vol. 5, (London, 1966), 898–899; and Smelser, *Sudeten Problem*, 158–159.

99. AMZV, Politické zprávy Berlín (1936), Miroslav Schubert [Czech chargé d'affaires] to Krofta, 22 August 1936. Rutha maintained that Henlein only spoke to Hitler for a few minutes at a social evening at the Reich chancellery. For his hopes about Vansittart, see CCC, Christie papers, CHRS 1/11, Rutha to Christie, 10 August 1936; for the Turner display, see "Tausende jubeln der Ascher Turnschule zu," *Die Zeit*, 13 August 1936, 2.

100. See his speech at Reichenberg in August 1936: Edvard Beneš, *Projevy—články—rozhovory 1935–1938* (Prague, 2006), 188.

101. Bruegel, *Tschechen und Deutsche*, 300–301; Novák, *Henleinovci*, 89–90 (for a communist viewpoint); and Smelser, *Sudeten Problem*, 160.

102. Zdeněk Kárník, *České země v éře první republiky (1918–1938)*, vol. 3, *O přežití a o život (1936–1938)* (Prague, 2003), 74–78. See also the explanation in AMZV, Krofta papers, krabice 11, Czechoslovak Ministry of National Defense to Krofta, 24 July 1936.

103. CCC, Christie papers, CHRS 1/11, Christie notes on meeting with Seton-Watson, 6 March 1936.

104. Thus the Czech legal expert in Beneš's office, Emil Sobota, observed privately: "The only point of discrimination is that the Ministry of Defense intended to implement its criteria solely against German suppliers, never against Czech" (AAVČR, Beneš papers, karton 250[2], Sobota notes, 3 June 1936).

105. Bruegel, *Tschechen und Deutsche*, 301.

106. CCC, Christie papers, CHRS 1/11, Henlein to Chistie, 7 February; TNA, FO 371/20373, Harold Nicolson to William Strang, 14 February 1936 (enclosing Henlein letter).

107. ALN, registry files, section 4, box R/3930, 25825/5021, Peter Schou to Joseph Avenol, 21 September 1936.

108. Ibid., 23533/5021, SdP petition sent to the secretary general of the League, 24 April 1936.

109. Ibid., minute by Dalal at the Minorities Section, 4 May 1936. For the petition procedures see C. A. Macartney, *National States and National Minorities* (London, 1934).

110. AMZV, II Sekce 1918–1939, číslo 697/61344, Rudolf Künzl-Jizerský to Krofta, 6 May 1936.

111. ALN, registry files, section 4, box R/3930, 24468/5021, Künzl-Jizerský to Avenol, enclosing Czech observations, 2 September 1936.

112. See AMZV, II Sekce 1918–1939, cislo 697/24237, Heidrich memorandum for Beneš, 31 August 1936, noting that the Defense Law had superseded the Machník decree.

113. TNA, FO 371/20374, Vansittart minute on memorandum by Hadow, 21 July 1936.

114. CCC, Christie papers, CHRS 1/11, Rutha to Christie, 10 August 1936.

115. ALN, registry files, section 4, box R/3930, 25422/5021, minutes by Schou and Avenol, 5 September 1936.

116. PAAA, R60533, Kurt Graebe [ENC chair] to German foreign ministry, 20 September 1936. See also the example of a draft SdP petition complaining about the abolition of Sudeten private schools: AKPR, T56/38.

117. See the reports on Rutha's visits: ALN, registry files, section 4, box R/3930, 25825/5021, Schou to Avenol, 21 September 1936; TNA, FO 371/20375, R5599/32/12, UK delegation at League of Nations to Eden, 21 September 1936.

118. The uncertainty in SdP circles about any new petition is clear from *Die Zeit,* which denied the rumors outright and confirmed only the gathering of "supplementary information" (22 September 1936, 1).

119. In the speech, Neuwirth (who had been responsible for advising the SdP over the Machník decree), argued that Europe needed to be restructured as a mass of "*Volk* personalities"; rather than changing the territorial status quo, this meant the end of nationalist states where denationalization was occurring. See Hans Neuwirth, "Reale Rechtsstaatlichkeit—Rechtpersönlichkeit der Volksgruppen," *Nation und Staat* 10, no.1 (October 1936): 13–22. While this program was "moderate" to Neuwirth or Rutha, it was of course radical and threatening to the Czech authorities. The Czech *Prager Presse,* 24 September 1936, 3, attacked it, belittling the SdP petition and agitation abroad.

120. AMZV, II Sekce 1918–1939, číslo 697/154965, Krofta notes on meeting, 22 September 1936. See also Dejmek, *Historik v čele diplomacie Kamil Krofta,* 77.

121. ALN, registry files, section 4, box R/3930, 25422/5021, first and second meetings of the Committee of Three, 24 September 1936 and 9 October 1936.

122. CCC, Christie papers, CHRS 1/19: Christie notes on meeting with Rutha, 25 September 1936; and Rutha to Christie, 7 October 1936.

123. TNA, FO 371/21125, Charles Bentinck to Eden, 8 January 1937. And see Rutha's later explanation: "Beschwerde 23," *VuF* 7 (1937): 302.

124. See Künzl-Jizerský's irritation in comments to Schou: ALN, registry files, section 4, box R/3930, 25422/5021, Schou minute, 28 January 1937.

125. Ibid., Committee of Three meeting, 26 May 1937.

126. Dejmek, *Nenaplněné naděje*, 326; and Dejmek, *Edvard Beneš*, 2:26.

127. Rutha, "Beschwerde 23," 301–303.

128. See his aside at the Foreign Office: TNA, FO 371/21130, R4896/188/12, minute, 16 July 1937.

9. PREMONITION OF DISASTER

1. Ronald M. Smelser, *The Sudeten Problem, 1933–1938:* Volkstumspolitik *and the Formulation of Nazi Foreign Policy* (Folkestone, 1975), 204.

2. The language of Erwin Zajicek, a German activist minister in the government: Heinrich Rutha, "Mahnworte aus London," *Die Zeit*, 26 July 1936, 1.

3. Josef Pfitzner, *Sudetendeutsche Einheitsbewegung: Werden und Erfüllung* (Carlsbad, 1937), 5, 105.

4. AAVČR, Beneš papers, karton 142, pisemnosti opisy, Rutha to Willi Hoffmann, 24 October 1936; NA, SdP files, karton 37, Vogt to Henlein, 24 November 1936.

5. OSK, Géza Szüllő papers, X/38, Szüllő memorandum on meeting to discuss ENC [Vienna, September 1936?]: "A kisebbségi konferencia . . . "

6. Rutha's speech on foreign policy at a major SdP conference on 1 October was well received: "Klubtagung der SdP in Bad Ullersdorf," *Die Zeit*, 3 October 1936, 2.

7. NAW, central files, 59/860f (Czechoslovakia), Butler Wright (American envoy) to secretary of state, 7 October 1936. See also *Die Zeit*, 7 October 1936, 2.

8. CCC, Christie papers, CHRS 1/19, Rutha to Christie, 7 October 1936.

9. Ibid., CHRS 1/11, Christie notes on talk with Rutha, 22 January 1937; *Die Zeit*, 2 March 1937.

10. KUL, Van Severen papers, Rutha to Van Severen, 14 December 1936. Rutha's query over Belgium's inclinations was rather naïve; see Zara Steiner, *The Triumph of the Dark: European International History, 1933–1939* (Oxford, 2011), 279–280.

11. Jindřich Dejmek, *Historik v čele diplomacie Kamil Krofta* (Prague, 1998), 90–95; Jindřich Dejmek, *Edvard Beneš: Politická biografie českého demokrata*,

(Prague, 2008), 2:46–53; Gerhard L. Weinberg, *The Foreign Policy of Hitler's Germany: Diplomatic Revolution in Europe, 1933–36* (Chicago, 1970), 316–320.

12. See Krofta's views: ÖSA, NPA, karton 74, Marek to Guido Schmidt, 14 October 1936 and 3 December 1936; TNA, FO 371/20375, Bentinck to Eden, 19 December 1936.

13. DGFP, Series C, vol.5 (London, 1966), 142–144.

14. TNA, FO 371/21127, Robert Hadow to Eden, 24 February 1937.

15. Elizabeth Wiskemann, *Czechs and Germans: A Study of the Struggle in the Historic Provinces of Bohemia and Moravia* (London, 1938), 255.

16. For explanations, see Stanislav Biman and Jaroslav Malíř, *Kariéra učitele tělocviku* (Liberec, 1983), 172–173; and DGFP, Series C, vol.6 (London, 1983), 308–310.

17. CCC, Christie papers, CHRS 1/11, 22 January 1937.

18. Konrad Henlein, *Heim ins Reich: Reden aus den Jahren 1937 und 1938*, ed. Ernst Tscherne (Reichenberg, 1939), 7–21. For critical assessments, see Wiskemann, *Czechs and Germans*, 257–259; and Otto Novák, *Henleinovci proti Československu: Z historie sudetoněmeckého fašismu v letech 1933–1938* (Prague, 1987), 124–127, 131–132.

19. Wiskemann, *Czechs and Germans*, 264, 269; and J. W. Bruegel, *Tschechen und Deutsche 1918–1938* (Munich, 1967), 310–313, who suggests the impossibility of securing fast results.

20. AAVČR, Beneš papers, karton 142, pisemnosti opisy, Rutha to Adolf Wagner, 29 February 1936.

21. SOAL, Krajský soud v Mostě, karton 502, Tk 785/37, police report on Rutha speech at Komotau, 24 March 1937.

22. This important subject requires more research, but see the German envoy's report: PAAA, R101346, 16 January 1937. For British concern about Czech police activity, see: TNA, FO 371/21129, Basil Newton to Eden, 21 May 1937; and FO 371/21125, 31 May 1937. See also Rutha's complaints: CCC, Christie papers, CHRS 1/11, Christie notes, 22 January 1937.

23. See Rutha's speech at Komotau. Already in December 1936, local elections had been held in 269 parishes and the SdP vote held up favorably: PAAA, R103649, Eisenlohr to German foreign ministry, 9 December 1936.

24. See the useful discussions in *Bohemia* 38–39 (1997/1998). On the one hand, there are historians who downplay SdP/Nazi differences and view developments largely through the prism of 1938; on the other, there are those who underline the SdP's specific characteristics and the singular impact of the Czech context.

25. Smelser, *Sudeten Problem*, 160.

26. Ibid., 199, and chapter 8. Frank's recent biographer, René Küpper, argues that Frank needed no conversion.

27. "Konzert sudetendeutscher Künstler in Berlin," *Rundschau*, 30 January 1937, 6. Compare Novák's statement: "Rutha was in constant contact with the Reich" (*Henleinovci*, 138).

28. DGFP, Series C, vol.6 (London, 1983), 477; CCC, Christie papers, CHRS 1/19: Christie notes, 25 September 1936. See also OSK, Szüllő papers, X/38: Szüllő recorded Rutha always arguing for the "inviolability of [state] borders."

29. BHA, Becher papers, karton 84, Becher talk to "Historischer Arbeitskreis," 13.

30. See Martin Schneller, *Zwischen Romantik und Fascismus: Der Beitrag Othmar Spanns zum Konservatismus der Weimarer Republik* (Stuttgart, 1970), 110–112; Klaus-Jörg Siegfried, *Universalismus und Fascismus: Das Gesellschaftsbild Othmar Spanns* (Vienna, 1974), 154–156; and for the Austrian climate, see Oswald Dutch, *Thus Died Austria* (London, 1938).

31. See Edmund von Glaise-Horstenau, *Ein General im Zwielicht: Die Erinnerungen Edmund Glaises von Horstenau*, ed. Peter Broucek (Vienna, 1983), 2:122–123, 165. And for a useful critique of Austrian pan-Germanism, see Julie Thorpe, "Austrofascism: Revisiting the 'Authoritarian State' 40 Years On," *JCH* 43, no. 2 (2010): 315–333.

32. ÖSA, NPA, karton 74, Marek's reports of 10 September, 31 October, and 30 November 1936.

33. Ibid., karton 686, Bundeskanzleramt to Marek, 7 December 1936: "We are still studying why this party is currying favor with us."

34. Ibid., karton 752, Marek to Schmidt, 3 December 1936; karton 686, Bundeskanzleramt to Marek, 12 December 1936.

35. Ibid, karton 75, Marek to Schmidt, 5 and 16 February 1937; "Begeisterter Auftakt zur Turnschulereise," *Die Zeit*, 6 April 1937, 3; and *Die Zeit*, 9 April 1937, 1.

36. See Glaise-Horstenau's positive view of Rutha: *Ein General im Zwielicht*, 2:192. The Czech legation in Vienna also later suggested that in 1937 Rutha had, under cover of academic and other cultural links in Vienna, tried to set up a new organization, the "Germany-Austria-Sudetenland Triangle", in order to promote Sudeten goals in a wider German framework; supposedly the Austrian government blocked the initiative, but no more is known about it. See AMZV, II Sekce 1918–39, krabice 278, Künzl-Jizerský to foreign ministry, 26 February 1938.

37. ÖSA, NPA, karton 686, Seyss-Inquart to Schmidt, 24 September 1937; CCC, Christie papers, CHRS 1/21A, Christie report, "Germany, September 1937." In the Austrian archives there is no record of Rutha meeting

Schuschnigg. For Seyss-Inquart's own complicated national loyalties, see Wolfgang Rosar, *Deutsche Gemeinschaft. Seyss-Inquart und der Anschluss* (Vienna, 1971).

38. H.[Heinz] Rutha, "Europa—Vom Gleichgewicht in die Schwebe," *Rundschau,* 1 January 1937, 7.

39. Rutha also used the Flemish example for a historical lecture he delivered in Vienna on 22 January: SOkAL, MAO, karton 9, file 2, "Der Kampf des Sudetendeutschtums um Recht und Frieden in Mitteleuropa."

40. OSK, Szüllő papers, X/38, Szüllő memorandum; NA, SdP files, karton 36, Rutha to Uexküll von Guldenbrand, 20 December 1936.

41. CCC, Christie papers, CHRS 1/19, Rutha to Christie, 7 October 1936.

42. CCC, Christie papers, CHRS 1/11, 22 January notes.

43. "Rutha: Ich bin bei der beweisbaren Wahrheit geblieben," *Die Zeit,* 4 March 1937, 1.

44. Jan Masaryk's report to Prague has not survived, but see PAAA, R103654 for Hodža's comments; and TNA, FO 371/21127, R1086/188/12, Vansittart minutes, 16 February 1937. Masaryk continued to be furious at Rutha: see SOkAD, Clary-Aldringen papers, karton 583, Clary diary, 17 February 1937.

45. *Parliamentary Debates, 5th Series, vol. 319, House of Commons Official Report* (London, 1937), 349.

46. TNA, FO 371/21127, Cranborne memorandum, 11 February 1937 (with nationality map enclosed, the Sudeten region clearly delineated).

47. The only source for this discussion is Rutha's later conversation with Ernst Eisenlohr, Germany's minister in Prague: DGFP, Series C, vol. 6 (London, 1983), 475–478.

48. Jindřich Dejmek, *Nenaplněné naděje: Politické a diplomatické vztahy Československa a Velké Británie 1918–1938* (Prague, 2003), 298.

49. KUL, Van Severen papers, Rutha to Van Severen, 8 February 1937; and ÖSA, NPA, karton 75, Marek to Schmidt, 23 February 1937. It is unclear whether the meeting actually took place.

50. Summary of Czech press attacks: "Trommelfeuer gegen Rutha," *Die Zeit,* 13 February, 1.

51. "England und die Sudetendeutsche Frage," *Rundschau,* 20 February 1937. The full uncensored article is in SOkAL, MAO, karton 9, file 2.

52. "Rutha berichtet über seine Englandreise," *Die Zeit,* 27 February 1937, 3. Such interest was only too apparent, for he had just met three British women politicians who were visiting Prague: PAAA, R103654.

53. AMZV, II Sekce 1918–39, krabice 278, note from a London source [February 1937].

54. Dejmek, *Historik v čele diplomacie Kamil Krofta,* 96, 102–103.

55. See Rutha's denial: "Rutha: Ich bin bei der beweisbaren Wahrheit geblieben," *Die Zeit,* 4 March 1937, 1; and "Die Wahrheit siegt!," *Rundschau,* 6 March 1937, 1. For Krofta's statements and SdP responses, see *Die Zeit,* 4, 10, and 12 March 1937. That Krofta had Rutha's Geneva outburst in mind is clear from his private briefing to Czech journalists: AAVČR, Krofta papers, karton 13, č.522, 12 March 1937.

56. For Krofta's speech, see "Unser Kurs bleibt fest," *Prager Presse,* 12 March 1937.

57. For Rutha's speeches at these two rallies, see "Krofta wollte mit Rutha nicht sprechen," *Die Zeit,* 26 March 1937, 2; and "Das Volk ist gegen einen 'Ausgleich'," 13 April 1937, 2.

58. It was at this time that a Czech analysis of the Henlein movement was published that highlighted Rutha's role. See Josef Fischer, Václav Patzak, and Vincenc Perth, *Jejich boj: Co chce a čemu slouží Sudetendeutsche Partei* (Prague, 1937).

59. The case went to court even though Rutha agreed to pay the difference: "Cestování architekta Ruthy," *Lidové noviny,* 9 April 1937, 11.

60. SOkAL, Reichenberg police records, I, Rutha to Franz May, 25 May 1937.

61. "Das Volk ist gegen einen 'Ausgleich'," *Die Zeit,* 13 April 1937, 1.

62. "Heinz Rutha: 'Unteilbarer Frieden'–in der Innen– und Aussenpolitik," *Rundschau,* 29 May 1937, 1–2; "15,000 bei der SdP-Kundgebung in Gablonz," *Die Zeit,* 23 May 1937, 1–2; and [Rutha],"Friede mit dem Gesamtdeutschtum," *Die Zeit,* 25 May 1937, 2.

63. See Rutha's speech at Marienbad, briefly reported in the Czech journal *Národní politika,* 14 April 1937, 7. The speech was picked up in Richard Freund, *Watch Czechoslovakia!* (London, 1937), 74; and in Fischer, Patzak, and Perth, *Jejich boj,* 135–136. Rutha used similar language at Carlsbad on 13 April, while Karl Hermann Frank's own speech there stressed even more militantly the idea of a "united Germandom" (*Rundschau,* 17 April 1937, 4). For echoes in the Reich press, see Novák, *Henleinovci,* 128.

64. SOkAD, Clary-Aldringen papers, karton 664, Rutha to Clary-Aldringen, 6 February 1937; and Nelböck to Clary, 16 February 1937.

65. Ibid., karton 583, Clary diary, 25 June 1937.

66. Ibid., karton 662, 664, especially summary in karton 664, "Material zur Bildung des 'Groupement' [1937]."

67. Ibid., karton 583, Clary diary, 25 June 1937.

68. Alfons Clary-Aldringen, "Die Verhandlungen über die Minderheiten Frage auf dem Völkerbundligenkongress in Bratislava," *Ženeva: Časopis věnovaný otázkám mezinárodním* 3, no.2 (1937): 21–25.

69. Ibid., 2–5, 13–15.

70. "Erklärung Architekt H. Ruthas in der Völkerbundligen-Union," *Nation und Staat* 10, no.11–12 (August-September 1937): 817–818.

71. *Sudetendeutsche Presse-Briefe*, 8 July 1937, 3.

72. Clary diary, 1 July 1937. See also "Missbrauchtes Kommuniqué der Völkerbundligen in Pressburg," *Die Zeit*, 4 July 1937, 2; and SOkAD, Clary-Aldringen papers, karton 664, Artur Vogt to Maria Aull, 13 July 1937.

73. NA, SdP files, karton 36, Rutha to Aull, 17 July 1937.

74. *Sudetendeutsche Presse-Briefe*, 8 July 1937, 2–3. For context on the League Union's decline see Xosé-Manoel Nuñez Seixas, *Entre Ginebra y Berlín: La cuestión de las minorías nacionales y la política internacional en Europa 1914–1939* (Madrid, 2001), 218–221.

75. The position taken by the SdP can be set alongside Beneš's "world view" as espoused at Bratislava University in April 1937; he explained the international crisis as a struggle of "humanistic universalism" against "national or state exclusivity" (Dejmek, *Edvard Beneš*, 2:58).

76. See the monographs by Nuñez Seixas, *Entre Ginebra y Berlín*; and Sabine Bamberger-Stemmann, *Der Europäische Nationalitätenkongreß 1925 bis 1938: Nationale Minderheiten zwischen Lobbyistentum und Großmachtinteressen* (Marburg, 2000).

77. Szüllő's expression: OSK, Szüllő papers, X/38, memorandum.

78. See some perceptive Czech remarks: AMZV, II Sekce, krabice 296a, ministry of interior to foreign ministry, 29 December 1936, enclosing police report on the Carlsbad conference. See also Nuñez Seixas, *Entre Ginebra y Berlín*, 421.

79. NA, SdP files, karton 37, Vogt to Henlein, 24 November 1936; and PAAA, R60497, minute by Twardowski, 29 January 1937.

80. Exceptions were Henlein's visit to south Tyrol as VDV president, and the Asch Turner school visit to Vienna, both in April 1937.

81. Notably this involved excluding Hungary's moderate German leader Gusztáv Gratz from the ENC, something Rutha fully supported; at the Bratislava conference he spent much of his time negotiating with Szüllő about Gratz's exclusion. See the letters in SOkAL, MAO, karton 9, file 3; NA, SdP files, karton 36; and OSK, Szüllő papers, X/38. In a very conciliatory speech on 12 May 1937 (which Rutha marked "very important") Gratz had warned Hungary about the danger of Germany's expansion.

82. AMZV, Politické zprávy Londýn, Černý to foreign ministry, 21 May 1937. See also Dejmek, *Nenaplněné naděje*, 301.

83. TNA, FO 371/21130, Newton to Cadogan, 12 July 1937; and R4896/188/12, Cranborne minute on talk with Rutha, 16 July 1937.

84. Novák, *Henleinovci,* 132–133.

85. TNA, FO 371/21252, W11580/1042/98, minute by Roger Makins on meeting with Hasselblatt, 14 June 1937; and Nuñez Seixas, *Entre Ginebra y Berlín,* 433–435.

86. See the draft speech in SOkAL, MAO, karton 9, file 3, "1. Fassung des Referats." See also NA, SdP files, karton 36, Rutha to Hasselblatt, 22 June 1937.

87. Congress reports in *Nation und Staat* 10, no.11–12 (August-September 1937): 803–814; and TNA, FO 371/21252.

88. Rutha's annotated speech, "Gemeinschaft und Selbstverwaltung der Volksgruppen," SOkAL, MAO, karton 9, file 3. Reproduced also in *Nation und Staat* 10, no.11–12 (August–September 1937): 710–714

89. See for example "Sjezd evropských menšin a podivné řeči pana Rutha," *Český deník,* 17 July 1937; and *Reichenberger Tagesbote,* 17 July 1937. For potential court action against Rutha, see AMZV, II Sekce 1918–39, krabice 278, č.140440, Krajský soud trestní to foreign ministry, 21 October 1937.

90. Biman and Malíř, *Kariéra,* 181; and Novák, *Henleinovci,* 130. I have found no evidence that Rutha actually used this language. An official police report sent to the Czechoslovak foreign ministry in late July also suggests Rutha's relative moderation: AMZV, II Sekce 1918–39, krabice 278, č.105018.

91. NA, SdP files, karton 36, Rutha to Aull, 17 July 1937; and "Der Londoner Nationalitätenkongress," *Rundschau,* 24 July 1937, 2.

92. TNA, FO 371/21130, R4896/188/12, Cranborne minute, 16 July 1937; AMZV, Politické zprávy Londýn, Masaryk to foreign ministry, 7 August 1937 (reporting talk with Vansittart).

93. "Konrad Henlein ehrt die Kriegstoten," *Die Zeit,* 22 August 1937, 3; and "Konrad Henlein übergibt das Fresko des Egerländer Heldenmals," *Rundschau,* 28 August 1937, 1. A key part of the pageant was Henlein unveiling a fresco in Eger honoring the war dead.

94. Václav Král, ed., *Die Deutschen in der Tschechoslowakei 1933–47: Dokumentensammlung* (Prague, 1964), 125–130; and Novák, *Henleinovci,* 134.

95. SOkAL, Reichenberg police records, I, Rutha to Henlein, 24 September 1937.

96. Nuñez Seixas, *Entre Ginebra y Berlín,* 437–440.

97. Walter Brand, *Die sudetendeutsche Tragödie* (Wunsiedel, 1949), 37, 49.

98. Dejmek, *Edvard Beneš,* 2:26.

10. THE CELL

1. [Walter Rohn], "Heinz Rutha: Ein Leben für Volk und Heimat," *VuF* 4 (1937): 158–159.

2. AAVČR, Beneš papers, karton 142, pisemnosti opisy, Alfons Wondrak to Rutha, 24 April; and ibid., Weiss to Rutha, 21 April 1937.

3. The preliminary documents of arrest are in NA, Policejní ředitelství Praha II (PŘ 1931–1940), karton 10229, sign: R 2304/17; and SOAL, CLS, karton 360, Tk 665/37/21, 6 October 1937.

4. Jaroslav Kallab and Vilém Herrnritt, eds., *Trestní zákony československé platné v Čechách, na Moravě a ve Slezsku* (Prague, 1923), 98. This law applied to men and women.

5. For an initial study, see Mark Cornwall, "Heinrich Rutha and the Unraveling of a Homosexual Scandal in 1930s Czechoslovakia," *GLQ: A Journal of Lesbian and Gay Studies* 8, no. 3 (2002): 319–347.

6. "Politische Intriganten am Werke," *Die Zeit,* 12 October 1937, 2; see also Walter Brand, *Auf verlorenem Posten: Ein sudetendeutscher Politiker zwischen Autonomie und Anschluss* (Munich, 1985), 131.

7. Margarete Ikrath-Rutha, "Heinrich Rutha: Seine Lebensarbeit und seine Ziele für das Sudetendeutschtum" (typed memoir, in Sudetendeutsches Haus library, Munich, 1986), 16–18.

8. *Právo lidu,* 9 October 1937, 2.

9. Andreas Luh, *Der Deutsche Turnverband in der Ersten Tchechoslowakischen Republik: Vom völkischen Vereinsbetrieb zur volkspolitischen Bewegung* (Munich, 1988), 395n95. See also Ronald M. Smelser, *The Sudeten Problem, 1933–1938:* Volkstumspolitik *and the Formulation of Nazi Foreign Policy* (Folkestone, 1975), 203; Otto Novák, *Henleinovci proti Československu: Z historie sudetoněmeckého fašismu v letech 1933–1938* (Prague, 1987), 150; Emil Franzel, *Gegen den Wind der Zeit: Erinnerungen eines Unbequemen* (Munich, 1983), 316; and Franz Katzer, *Das große Ringen: Der Kampf der Sudetendeutschen unter Konrad Henlein* (Tübingen, 2003), 428–429.

10. Walter Becher, *Zeitzeuge: Ein Lebensbericht* (Munich, 1990), 84.

11. AAVČR, Beneš papers, karton 142, "Důverné zprávy," 13 October 1937.

12. For the British flirtations, see SOkAL, Reichenberg police records, II, Rutha's letters to Alastair Heggie [Glasgow], 23 June 1936; and Franz Porsch [London], 27 July 1936.

13. SOAL, CLS, karton 242, Tk 665/37/70, Rutha to Gelinek, 14 September 1937. Rutha told Gelinek that one youth had "a beautiful head, is a blond lad, a Germanic type" (karton 360, Tk 665/37/14, 7 October 1937).

14. Ibid., Tk 665/37/55, police protocol of Fritz Funk, 12 October 1937, 4–5.

15. Ibid., Tk 665/37/67, list of books confiscated from Wolfgang Heinz; and Tk 665/37/114, Rutha to Adolf Wagner, 29 February 1936.

16. Ibid., Tk 665/37/126, book confiscated from Werner Weiss (inscription 23 March 1936); my translation. For interpretation, see Robert E. Norton, *Secret Germany: Stefan George and His Circle* (Ithaca, NY, 2002), 367–368.

17. SOAL, CLS, karton 360, Tk 665/37/27, Rutha protocol, 7 October 1937, 12.

18. See AAVČR, Beneš papers, karton 142, pisemnosti opisy, letters of Rutha to Hoffmann, 28 October 1935 and 9 December 1935.

19. Ibid., Rutha to Hoffmann, 24 October 1936, 22 December 1936, 4 January 1937, and 18 January 1937.

20. Ibid., 29 January 1937.

21. Ibid., 8 March 1937, 10 April 1937, 26 April 1937, and 6 May 1937.

22. SOAL, CLS, karton 360, Reichenberg police report to Leipa court, 13 October 1937, 29–31, summary of case against Hoffmann.

23. NA, SdP files, karton 36, Rutha to Hasselblatt, 22 June; SOkAL, Reichenberg police records, I, Rutha to Ludwig Eichholz, 17 July 1937.

24. SOAL, CLS, karton 360, Tk 665/37/63, Franzke protocol, 12 October 1937.

25. Ibid.

26. SOAL, CLS, karton 360, Tk 665/37/58, Franzke statement, 14–15 October 1937; and ibid., Tk 665/37/24, Rutha on Franzke's statement, 15 October 1937.

27. SOkALov, Karl Metzner papers, karton 3, Wenzel Metzner to Karl Metzner, 29 November 1937.

28. SOAL, CLS, karton 360, Tk 665/37/27, Rutha protocol, 7 October 1937, 17.

29. Rutha relative interviews, 6 August 2001 and 11 September 2006. According to Hans Neuwirth too, Rutha for some months had been engaged: Hans Neuwirth, "Begegnungen im böhmischen Raum," *Bohemia* 1 (1960): 247.

30. SWA, file "Biographisches Dokumentar-Material zu Stauda-Oberdorffer Wandervogel in Böhmen," copy of Rutha to "Maria" [undated].

31. Luh, *Deutsche Turnverband,* 336–337, 392.

32. SOAL, CLS, karton 360, Tk 665/37/1, Weiss protocol, 4 October 1937, 4.

33. *Die Zeit,* 14 January 1937 (Leitmeritz court case); SOAL, Krajský soud v Mostě, karton 502, Tk 785/37/6, Niemes court case. See also SOAL, Krajský soud v Litoměřicích, karton 790, Tk 1479/37, case imminent against Rutha in September 1937 because of his Tetschen speech on 23 May.

34. Compare Stanislav Biman and Jaroslav Malíř, *Kariéra učitele tělocviku* (Liberec, 1983), 177.

35. According to the Czechoslovak minister of justice, on 19 November 1937 there were 926 people being prosecuted for espionage, of whom 423 were Germans: PAAA, R103696.

36. SOAL, CLS, karton 360, Tk 665/37/1, Wilhelm Purm protocol, 25 August 1937; and AAVČR, Beneš papers, karton 142, "Gedächtnisprotokolle" of SdP leadership meeting, 7 October 1937.

37. See the case against three men in Pilsen as reported in "Henleinovce bolí hlava z Ruthovy aféry," *Právo lidu,* 19 October 1937, 7. Research into homosexuality in interwar Czechoslovakia is in its infancy, but the evidence suggests an increased level of prosecutions in the 1930s in tandem with heightened fears for national security. See Jan Seidl, "Úsilí o odtrestnění homosexuality za první republiky" (master's thesis, Brno, 2007).

38. See Stefan Micheler, "Homophobic Propaganda and the Denunciation of Same-Sex-Desiring Men under National Socialism," *Journal of the History of Sexuality* 11 (2002): 109–110, 127.

39. "Sensationelle Folgen des Homosexuellen-Skandals," *Der Prager Illustrierte Montag,* 11 October 1937, 1; and Klement's cryptic comments in December 1937: SOAL, CLS, karton 242, Tk 665/37/216, trial minutes, 64, 68.

40. For *Aufbruch*'s rise in 1937 and renewed attempts at mediation from Berlin, see Smelser, *Sudeten Problem,* 194–198; Novák, *Henleinovci,* 145–148; and Luh, *Deutsche Turnverband,* 388–390. See also *Aufbruch*'s polemical tract, *Was ist der KB: Der Kameradschaftsbund: Die Entlarvung einer Clique* (Prague, 1937), where Rutha was scathingly singled out as the KB's "spiritual father" (9).

41. PAAA, R103655, Lierau to German foreign ministry, 29 July 1937. Lierau here mentioned talking to a local *Aufbruch* ringleader (Kleinert) whom Rutha in early 1936 had trusted to assert discipline in the Jeschken-Iser Turngau: SOkAL, Reichenberg police records, III, Rutha to Kleinert, 3 February 1936.

42. BA, NS/10/34, Hans Krebs to Fritz Wiedmann (Reich Chancellery), 9 October 1937, enclosing report from Prague. For the police raid, see AAVČR, Beneš papers, karton 142, "Důverné zprávy," 13 October 1937.

43. PAAA, R60237, Lierau to German foreign ministry, 22 February 1937, enclosing letter from Hein and Karl Karwath to Reichsjugendführung (19 February 1937) where they stressed their loyalty to Hitler.

44. SOAL, CLS, karton 360, Tk 665/37/1, Hein protocol, 1–2 October 1937.

45. Ibid., Tk 665/37/1, Weiss protocols, 4–6 October 1937.

46. PAAA, R103656, Lierau to German foreign ministry, 7 October 1937. Lierau's report also appears in Václav Král, ed., *Die Deutschen in der Tschechoslowakei: Dokumentensammlung* (Prague, 1964), 124–125.

47. AKPR, T1649/37, memorandum by Přemysl Šámal, 8 October 1937.

48. SSEES, Lisický papers, box 5, 3A/6, aide-mémoire by Masaryk, 4 November 1937.

49. SOAL, CLS, karton 360, Tk 665/37/27, Rutha protocol, 7–8 October 1937, 17–18; Rohn protocol, 8 October 1937, 13.

50. Ibid, Reichenberg police chief to Česka Lípa court, 8 October 1937.

51. K.Z. Klíma, "Oplátka za Ruthu," *České slovo,* 23 October 1937, 1.

52. AAVČR, Beneš papers, karton 142, "Gedächtnisprotokolle" of SdP leadership meetings, 7 October 1937. The leadership divisions were clear here since a radical, Gustav Jonak, refused to accompany Neuwirth to Reichenberg.

53. "Politische Intriganten am Werke," *Die Zeit,* 12 October 1937, 2; and "Konrad Henlein zur Angelegenheit Heinrich Rutha," *Rundschau,* 16 October 1937, 2.

54. See for example *Večerní česke slovo,* 13 October 1937.

55. "Mravnostní aféra henleinovců," *Večerník práva lidu,* 9 October 1937, 1; and *Právo lidu,* 9 October 1937, 2.

56. See Klaus Sator, "Die Sexualdenunziation als Kampfmittel der Propaganda der organisierten Arbeiterbewegung gegen den Nationalsozialismus: Der 'Fall Rutha' in der sudetendeutschen marxistischen Presse," *Internationale wissenschaftliche Korrespondenz zur Geschichte der deutschen Arbeiterbewegung* 3 (1994): 404–413. The communist press publicized homosexuality as a degenerate example of capitalism (410).

57. Franzel, *Gegen den Wind,* 316–317. This and the experience of Rutha's funeral were the triggers that caused Franzel to abandon social democracy.

58. *Der Prager Illustrierte Montag,* 11 October 1937, 1–3; see especially "Achilles und Patroklos," "Orgien in Kunnersdorf," and "Homosexualität und SdP."

59. *Večerník práva lidu,* 16 October 1937, 1.

60. Among many examples, see K.Z. Klíma, "Oplátka za Ruthu," *České slovo,* 23 October 1937, 1; "Zděšení a poprask v SdP," *Večerník práva lidu,* 10 October 1937, 1; and "Rutha—nejbližší Henleinův přítel," *Ještědský obzor,* 14 October 1937, 1. See also (as a respectable paper) *Národní listy,* 15 October 1937, 3; 17 October 1937, 2 ("Aféra Eulenburgova a Ruthova"); and 20 October 1937, 3. No mention was made of the comparable case of Gustav Wyneken in 1921.

61. See "Die sudetendeutsche Frage," *Die junge Front,* December 1936, 381–382; and Novák, *Henleinovci,* 150–151.

62. For context see Harry Oosterhuis, "Medicine, Male Bonding, and Homosexuality in Nazi Germany," *JCH* 32, no. 2 (1997): 187–205; and John C. Fout, "Homosexuelle in der NS-Zeit," in *Nationalsozialistischer Terror gegen*

Homosexuelle, ed. Burkhard Jellonek and Rüdiger Lautmann (Paderborn, 2002), 167–170.

63. See the endless lists of donations in *Die Zeit* in November 1937.

64. SOAL, CLS, karton 360, Pravomil Raček [Reichenberg police chief] to state authority in Česká Lípa, 15320 pres. 37, 15 October 1937, 55–76.

65. Ibid., 59–60.

66. Ibid., 65–66. The artist was Andrea del Sarto, whose picture of a youth's head Rutha had once sent to Hoffmann. Klement's information came from one of the few Czech works on homosexuality: František Jelínek, *Homosexualita ve světle vědy* (Prague, 1924).

67. AAVČR, Beneš papers, karton 142, "Lékařský posudek ve věci Jindřicha Ruthy" [undated]: it was "a clear case of pederasty."

68. SOAL, CLS, karton 242, Tk 665/37/216, minutes of trial, 2–9 December 1937.

69. Ibid., 3, 5, 32.

70. SOAL, CLS, karton 360, Tk 665/37/24, protocols of Rutha's meetings with Blažek, 13 and 15 October 1937; and ibid., karton 242, Tk 665/37/216, minutes of trial, 69, Blažek statement to court, 6 December 1937.

71. SOAL, CLS, box 360, Tk 665/37/114, police headquarters in Reichenberg to state authorities, 21 October 1937; Tk 665/37/24, protocol of interrogation, 23 October 1937; and AAVČR, Beneš papers, karton 142, protocol of interrogation, 20 October 1937 (Klement present).

72. SOAL, CLS, karton 242, Tk 665/37/147. The lines are from the introduction to George's *Star of the Covenant.*

73. NA, SdP files, karton 36, Vogt to Rudi Hejl, 18 October 1937.

74. Ikrath-Rutha, "Heinrich Rutha," 14.

75. Frau E.F. [Lia Franke], "Ein letzter Besuch bei Heinz Rutha," *Rundschau,* 13 November 1937.

76. Rutha to Inge Hain (niece), 2 November 1937 (copy in author's possession).

77. Rutha to Otto Franke, 28 October 1937 (copy in author's possession); and Rutha to Hermann Hönig, editor of *Rundschau,* 28 October 1937 (published in *Rundschau,* 6 November 1937, 1).

78. Rudolf Herzog quoting letter from Rutha: "Prozess überraschend vertagt," *Die Zeit,* 8 December 1937, 5.

79. Rutha to anonymous woman, 24 October 1937, published in *Deutsche Tages-Zeitung* (Carlsbad), 9 November 1937, 2; and extract from letter published in Johannes Stauda, *Der Wandervogel in Böhmen 1911–1920,* ed. Kurt Oberdorffer (Reutlingen, 1975–1978), 2:98.

80. Heinz Rutha, "Jugenderziehungswerk Wartenberg," *TZ,* July 1937, 288–290.

81. Rutha to Hönig, *Rundschau,* 6 November 1937, 1.

82. "Heinz Rutha an die Arbeitsmänner" [31 October], *Heimatruf,* 17 November 1937.
83. Rutha to Inge Hain, 2 November 1937.
84. SWA, file "Biographisches Dokumentar-Material," copy of Rutha to "Maria" [undated].
85. For summaries of recent British research, see Alison Liebling, *Suicides in Prisons* (London, 1992); David Crighton, "Suicide in Prisons: A Critique of UK Research," in *Suicide in Prisons,* ed. Graham Towl, Louisa Snow, and Martin McHugh (Oxford, 2002), 26–47; and Alison Liebling, "The Role of the Prison Environment in Prison Suicide and Prisoner Distress," in *Preventing Suicide and Other Self-Harm in Prison,* ed. Greg E. Dear (Basingstoke, 2006), 16–28.
86. This is widely acknowledged: Crighton, "Suicide," 40; and Liebling, *Suicides,* 42.
87. "Ruthas letzter Abend," *Prager Mittag,* 6 November 1937, 1; and *Večerník práva lidu,* 3 November 1937.
88. "Henleinovec Rutha se sám odsoudil," *Právo lidu,* 6 November 1937, 7; and "Sebevražda potvrdila podezření," *Lidové noviny,* 6 November 1937 2.
89. AAVČR, Krofta papers, karton 13, 5 November 1937. The SdP press office dwelt on the impact of prison and the irresponsible press campaign: "Heinrich Rutha †," *Reichenberger Tagesbote,* 6 November 1937 (evening edition), 2.
90. "Ruthas letzter Abend," *Prager Mittag,* 6 November 1937, 1. Rutha apparently sent letters to both Blažek and the Prague chief of police, but these have not survived.
91. "Heldischer Tod: Die Heimkehr des Sokrates," *Der Sonntag der Zeit,* 14 November 1937, 1. This comparison was scorned by the Nazi organ, *Die junge Front*: see "Wenn zwei dasselbe tun oder zweimal Sokrates, " *Die junge Front,* December 1937, 383.
92. Stauda, *Wandervogel,* 2:98, 164.

EPILOGUE

1. Another found its way to Munich in the possession of one of Rutha's disciples, Walter Becher: Becher to author, 28 June 2001.
2. See SOAL, CLS, karton 242, Margarete Rutha to Landesgericht Leipa, 25 November 1938; and ibid., Margarete Rutha to Hans Krebs, 17 April 1939. See also *Prager Mittag,* 27 November 1937, 2.
3. The following is based on Rutha relative interviews.
4. Volker Zimmermann, *Die Sudetendeutschen im NS-Staat: Politik und Stimmung der Bevölkerung im Reichsgau Sudetenland (1938–1945)* (Essen,

1999), 54–55; Ronald M. Smelser, *The Sudeten Problem, 1933–1938: Volkstumspolitik and the Formulation of Nazi Foreign Policy* (Folkestone, 1975), 202–205; and Otto Novák, *Henleinovci proti Československu: Z historie sudetoněmeckého fašismu v letech 1933–1938* (Prague, 1987), 155.

5. Speech of 16 November 1937, quoted in *Lidové noviny*, 17 November 1937, 2.

6. Novák, *Henleinovci*, 151–154; Smelser, *Sudeten Problem*, 204; and Detlef Brandes, *Die Sudetendeutschen im Krisenjahr 1938* (Munich, 2008), 48–49.

7. See the documents in TNA, FO 371/21131.

8. SOAL, CLS, Tl 48/37, Česká Lípa regional court sitting, 13 November 1937, which assessed the content of one leaflet. A few months later Hein, who was expelled from the SdP, sued unsuccessfully for libel: SOAL, Krajský soud Liberec 1938, karton 480, Tk 296/38.

9. NA, SdP files, karton 28 (dodatky), Kasper to Henlein, 30 November 1937.

10. "Brief an den 'Aufbruch'," *Der Aufbruch*, 18 December 1937, 10; "Die sudetendeutsche Frage," *Die junge Front*, December 1937, 381–382; and Andreas Luh, *Der Deutsche Turnverband in der Ersten Tchechoslowakischen Republik: Vom völkischen Vereinsbetrieb zur volkspolitischen Bewegung* (Munich, 1988), 397.

11. Novák, *Henleinovci*, 157–160; and Luh, *Deutsche Turnverband*, 355–356, 401.

12. Mark Cornwall, "Heinrich Rutha and the Unraveling of a Homosexual Scandal in 1930s Czechoslovakia," *GLQ: A Journal of Lesbian and Gay Studies* 8, no. 3 (2002): 334–335.

13. "Justova aféra na Jablonecku," *Severočeský deník*, 25 November 1937, 3. The Just case documents are in SOAL, Krajský soud Liberec, karton 580, ZO 126/38. See also BA, Berlin Document Center, RK/Oskar Just: with his own studio in Berlin, Just acquired many commissions for Aryan and rural pictures from the Nazi authorities from 1936 into the 1940s.

14. "Prozessbeginn in Böhmisch-Leipa," *Die Zeit*, 3 December 1937, 4; "Prozess überraschend vertagt," *Die Zeit*, 8 December 1937, 5; and *Mährisch-Schlesisches Tagblatt*, 8 December 1937, 4.

15. Dr. Kriegelstein, quoted in *Reichenberger Tagesbote*, 8 December 1937, 3.

16. See SOAL, CLS, karton 242, Tk 665/37/216, stenographic protocol of trial proceedings, 2–3, 5, 61; and "Prozessbeginn in Böhmisch-Leipa," *Die Zeit*, 3 December 1937, 4.

17. SOAL, CLS, karton 242, T665/37/217, court verdict, 9 December 1937. See the different press interpretations of the outcome: "Sieben Schuldsprüche in Böhm.-Leipa," *Reichenberger Zeitung* (evening edition), 9 December 1937, 5; and (more positive), "Fünf Freisprüche in Böhm.-Leipa," *Die Zeit*, 10 December 1937, 5. Compare also Gretel Rutha who

implies that all defendants were found not guilty: Margarete Ikrath-Rutha, "Heinrich Rutha: Seine Lebensarbeit und seine Ziele für das Sudetendeutschtum" (typed memoir, in Sudetendeutsches Haus library, Munich, 1986), 17. Willi Hoffmann and Wolfgang Heinz were acquitted.

18. Luh, *Deutsche Turnverband*, 397–398.

19. Ibid., 401.

20. Zimmermann, *Die Sudetendeutschen im NS-Staat*, 237–239.

21. Ralf Gebel, *"Heim ins Reich!" Konrad Henlein und der Reichsgau Sudetenland 1938–1945* (Munich, 2000), 166, 177. See Ludwig Weichselbaumer, *Walter Brand (1907–1980): Ein sudetendeutscher Politiker im Spannungsfeld zwischen Autonomie und Anschluss* (Munich 2008 (Munich, 2008), 453–461, for the prosecutor's serious reservations about the scope of the Heydrich witch hunt; he persuaded Brand to plead guilty to §175 in order to escape further investigation by the Gestapo.

22. Gebel, *"Heim ins Reich!"* 168–169; and Zimmermann, *Die Sudetendeutschen im NS-Staat*, 243–244. For part of the journal text: Günter Grau, ed., *Hidden Holocaust? Gay and Lesbian Persecution in Germany, 1933–1945* (London, 1995), 223–225.

23. Zimmermann, *Die Sudetendeutschen im NS-Staat*, 244–251. On 18 January 1940 in Berlin, Henlein told a Hitler Youth meeting that Rutha had been the "greatest [Sudeten] criminal of them all" (241).

24. Gebel, *"Heim ins Reich!"* 174–175.

25. Rohn to Raimund Schönlinde, 18 November 1947 (letter in Rutha family possession).

26. As one youth leader also denied: SDA, Eduard Burkert interview (March 1983 with Edgar Pscheidt), Teil 1.

27. Noteworthy are the comments of one Czech policeman in north Bohemia: "The official drew a distinction between homosexuality among adults and corruption of the young. The former is common here and the homosexuals are merely kept under police supervision. Corruption of the young is a different matter and requires different action" (TNA, FO 371/21135, R7836/6805/12, Pares to Newton, 13 November 1937).

28. See Jürgen Reulecke, *"Ich möchte einer werden so wie die." Männerbünde im 20. Jahrhundert* (Frankfurt, 2001), 138–140.

29. See Walter Becher's description in *Österreichisches Biographisches Lexikon 1815–1950* (Vienna, 1988), 9:337.

30. Walter Brand, *Die sudetendeutsche Tragödie* (Wunsiedl, 1949), 49–50.

Select Bibliography

ARCHIVES

Austria

ÖSA (AdR)   Österreichisches Staatsarchiv, Vienna (Archiv der Republik)

Belgium

KUL   Katholieke Universiteit Leuven

Czech Republic

AAVČR   Archiv Akademie věd České republiky, Prague
AHMP   Archiv hlavního města Praha, Prague
AKPR   Archiv Kanceláře prezidenta republiky, Prague
AMZV   Archiv Ministerstva zahraničních věci, Prague
MAO   Mistní archiv Osečná [in SOkAL]
NA   Národní archiv, Prague
SOAL   Státní oblastní archiv, Litoměřice
SOAP   Státní oblastní archiv, Prague
SOkAČL   Státní okresní archiv, Česká Lípa
SOkAD   Státní okresní archiv, Děčín
SOkAL   Státní okresní archiv, Liberec
SOkALov   Státní okresní archiv Litoměřice at Lovosice

Germany

AdJB   Archiv der deutschen Jugendbewegung, Burg Ludwigstein
BA   Bundesarchiv, Berlin
BHA   Bayerisches Hauptstaatsarchiv, Munich
PAAA   Politisches Archiv des Auswärtiges Amt, Berlin
SWA   Sudetendeutsche-Wandervogel Archiv, Waldkraiburg
SDA   Sudetendeutsches Archiv, Munich [in BHA]

Great Britain

CCC   Churchill College Archives, Cambridge
SSEES   School of Slavonic and East European Studies Archive, London
TNA   The National Archives, London

Hungary

OSK   Országos Széchenyi Könyvtár, Budapest

Switzerland

ALN   Archives of the League of Nations, Geneva

United States of America

NAW   National Archives, Washington, DC

NEWSPAPERS AND JOURNALS

Der Aufbruch
Beiblatt der Älteren zum "Sudetendeutschen Wandervogel"
Blätter vom frischen Leben [Blätter]
Böhmerlandjahrbuch 1920
Burschen heraus! Fahrtenblatt der Deutschböhmen [BH]
České slovo
Český deník
Deutsche Leipaer Zeitung
Deutsches Tages-Zeitung
Heimatruf
Ještědský obzor

Der junge Deutsche [DjD]
Die junge Front
Lidové noviny
Mährisch-Schlesisches Tagblatt
Mitteilungen des Jeschken-Iser-Turngau [MJT]
Národní politika
Národní listy
Nation und Staat
Der Prager Illustrierte Montag
Prager Mittag
Prager Presse
Právo lidu
Reichenberger Tagesbote
Reichenberger Zeitung
Rundschau
Severočeský deník
The Slavonic and East European Review [SEER]
Soldatenblatt: Österreichischer Wandervogel
Sudetendeutsche Presse-Briefe
Sudetendeutscher Wandervogel
Sudetenland
Turnzeitung des Deutschen Turnverbandes [TZ]
Večerní česke slovo
Večerník práva lidu
Volk und Führung [VuF]
Wandervogel: Monatschrift für deutsches Jugendwandern. Heft der Österreicher
Wandervogel: Österreichisches Bundesblatt
Wandervogel: Österreichisches Fahrtenblatt [WÖF]
Der Weg: Blätter für das neue Deutschösterreich
Die Zeit
Ženeva: Časopis věnovaný otázkám mezinárodním

DOCUMENT COLLECTIONS

Documents on German Foreign Policy, 1918–1945. Series C, vols. 5–6 (London, 1966/1983) [DGFP].

Dolezal, Heidrun, and Stephan Dolezal, eds. *Deutsche Gesandschaftsberichte aus Prag; Innenpolitik und Minderheitenprobleme in der Ersten Tschechoslowakischen Republik.* Vol. 4 (Munich, 1991).

Král, Václav, ed. *Die Deutschen in der Tschechoslowakei 1933–1947: Dokumentensammlung* (Prague, 1964).

MAIN MEMOIRS AND CONTEMPORARY STUDIES

Becher, Walter. *Zeitzeuge: Ein Lebensbericht* (Munich, 1990).

Blüher, Hans. *Die Rolle der Erotik in der männlichen Gesellschaft.* 2 vols. (Jena, 1919).

Brand, Walter. *Auf verlorenem Posten: Ein sudetendeutscher Politiker zwischen Autonomie und Anschluss* (Munich, 1985).

———. *Die sudetendeutsche Tragödie* (Wunsiedel, 1949).

Butschek, Gustav. *Der "Bund der böhmerlandischen Freischaren," seine Freischaren und die Nachfolgegemeinschaften* (Hamburg, 1984).

Fischer, Josef, Václav Patzak, and Vincenc Perth. *Jejich boj: Co chce a čemu slouží Sudetendeutsche Partei* (Prague, 1937).

Franzel, Emil. *Gegen den Wind der Zeit: Erinnerungen eines Unbequemen* (Munich, 1983).

Henlein, Konrad. *Heim ins Reich: Reden aus den Jahren 1937 und 1938.* Edited by Ernst Tscherne (Reichenberg, 1939).

Ikrath-Rutha, Margarete. "Heinrich Rutha: Seine Lebensarbeit und seine Ziele für das Sudetendeutschtum" (typed memoir, in Sudetendeutsches Haus library, Munich, 1986).

Jahn, Rudolf, ed. *Konrad Henlein spricht: Reden zur politischen Volksbewegung der Sudetendeutschen* (Carlsbad, 1937).

Jahn, Rudolf. *Konrad Henlein: Leben und Werk des Turnführers* (Carlsbad, 1938).

Jantsch, Walter, ed. *Gablonzer Wandervogel: Geschichtlicher Abriss von 1913–1938* (Schwäbisch Gmünd: self-publication, 1974).

Jelínek, František. *Homosexualita ve světle vědy* (Prague, 1924).

Lenk, Richard [Heinrich Rutha]. *Die erste Position* (private publication, 1929: copy in SDA).

Pfitzner, Josef. *Sudetendeutsche Einheitsbewegung: Werden und Erfüllung.* 2nd ed. (Carlsbad, 1937).

Stauda, Johannes. *Der Wandervogel in Böhmen, 1911–1920.* Edited by Kurt Oberdorffer. 2 vols. (Reutlingen, 1975–1978).

Wiskemann, Elizabeth. *Czechs and Germans: A Study of the Struggle in the Historic Provinces of Bohemia and Moravia* (London, 1938).

KEY SECONDARY WORKS

Bamberger-Stemmann, Sabine. *Der Europäische Nationalitätenkongreß 1925 bis 1938: Nationale Minderheiten zwischen Lobbyistentum und Großmachtinteressen* (Marburg, 2000).

Becher, Peter, ed. *Deutsche Jugend in Böhmen 1918–1938* (Munich, 1993).

Biman, Stanislav, and Jaroslav Malíř. *Kariéra učitele tělocviku* (Liberec, 1983).

Bruegel, J. W. *Tschechen und Deutsche 1918–1938* (Munich, 1967).

Dejmek, Jindřich. *Nenaplněné naděje. Politické a diplomatické vztahy Československa a Velké Británie 1918–1938* (Prague, 2003).

Donson, Andrew. *Youth in the Fatherless Land: War Pedagogy, Nationalism, and Authority in Germany, 1914–1918* (Cambridge, MA, 2010).

Gebel, Ralf. *"Heim ins Reich!" Konrad Henlein und der Reichsgau Sudetenland 1938–1945* (Munich, 2000).

Geuter, Ulfried. *Homosexualität in der deutschen Jugendbewegung: Jungenfeundschaft und Sexualität im Diskurs von Jugendbewegung, Psychoanalyse und Jugendpsychologie am Beginn des 20. Jahrhunderts* (Frankfurt am Main, 1994).

Kasper, Tomáš. *Výchova či politika? Úskalí německého pedagogického hnutí v Československu v letech 1918–1933* (Prague, 2007).

Langhans, Daniel. *Der Reichsbund der deutschen katholischen Jugend in der Tschechoslowakei 1918–1938* (Bonn, 1990).

Luh, Andreas. *Der Deutsche Turnverband in der Ersten Tchechoslowakischen Republik: Vom völkischen Vereinsbetrieb zur volkspolitischen Bewegung* (Munich, 1988).

Norton, Robert E. *Secret Germany: Stefan George and His Circle* (Ithaca, NY, 2002).

Novák, Otto. *Henleinovci proti Československu: Z historie sudetoněmeckého fašismu v letech 1933–1938* (Prague, 1987).

Nuñez Seixas, Xosé-Manoel. *Entre Ginebra y Berlín: La cuestión de las minorías nacionales y la política internacional en Europa 1914–1939* (Madrid, 2001).

Reulecke, Jürgen. *"Ich möchte einer werden so wie die." Männerbünde im 20. Jahrhundert* (Frankfurt, 2001).

Smelser, Ronald. *The Sudeten Problem, 1933–1938*. Volkstumspolitik *and the Formulation of Nazi Foreign Policy* (Folkestone, 1975).

Weichselbaumer, Ludwig. *Walter Brand (1907–1980): Ein sudetendeutscher Politiker im Spannungsfeld zwischen Autonomie und Anschluss* (Munich, 2008).

Zahra, Tara. *Kidnapped Souls: National Indifference and the Battle for Children in the Bohemian Lands, 1900–1948* (Ithaca, NY, 2008).

Zimmermann, Volker. *Die Sudetendeutschen im NS-Staat: Politik und Stimmung der Bevölkerung im Reichsgau Sudetenland (1938–1945)* (Essen, 1999).

Acknowledgments

Having lived with Heinz Rutha for a decade, I have many historians and archivists to thank for their advice and guidance. I am particularly indebted to the late Zbyněk Zeman, an inspiring and inquisitive mentor, who from 1986 first steered me on my own kind of Czech-German mission.

In my research in Czech archives and libraries, I have been assiduously aided: in Liberec, by Jiří Bock, Hana Chocholoušková, Václav Kříček, and Markéta Lhotová; in Česká Lípa, by Miloslav Sovadina, Dagmar Šimánková, Ladislav Smejkal, and Magdalena Sobotová; in Lovosice by Jindřich Tomas; and in Prague, by Jan Seidl, Dagmar Hájková, and Ivan Šedivý. In Germany, the town archivist of Waldkraiburg, Konrad Kern, generously immersed me in Wandervogel documentation; at Burg Ludwigstein, as a new generation of "wandering birds" played outside, I enjoyed the solitude of the Youth Movement library. Colleagues at the Collegium Carolinum and the Sudeten German Archive in Munich have tirelessly helped me: Martin Schulze Wessel, Peter Haslinger, Robert Luft, Martin Zückert, Stephanie Weiss, and Edgar Pscheidt. The late Ferdinand Seibt encouraged my "Rutha pursuit," and Peter Becher sent me crucial material. My research in Geneva (the League of Nations) took place in 1988 under the auspices of archivist Sven Welander. In Vienna, Lothar Höbelt and Rudolf Jeřábek as usual gave up their time to pinpoint archival sources. Finally, for assistance in uncovering Rutha correspondence in the papers of Joris van Severen, I am most grateful to Maurits Cailliau, Wannes Dupont, and to Mark Derez of the Leuven University archive.

At the University of Southampton, my faculty deans, Michael Kelly and Anne Curry, allowed me leave to complete sections of the book, while departmental colleagues have discussed chapters and kept my spirits high: Joan Tumblety, Neil Gregor, George Bernard, Julie Gammon, and Sarah Pearce. Others who since 2001 have significantly shaped my thinking include David Halperin, John Horne, Robert Evans, David Rechter, Charles McKean, Hew Strachan, Martyn Housden, Robert Pynsent, Frank Magee, John Paul Newman, David Higgs, Jim Bartley, Brian Pronger—and Lynne Viola who unwittingly spurred me on. In Pieter Judson and another anonymous reader I secured the best possible advice on how to revise the manuscript. And many thanks to my editor, Kathleen McDermott, who has quietly kept faith with the project until fruition; and to Isabelle Lewis for creating the fine maps.

Lastly, I mention two people who have really inspired me to tell this remarkable story. One is an anonymous Rutha relative, a product of 1930s Bad Kunnersdorf, who more than anyone else has generously guided me in the lost world of "German Bohemia." Although the book scrutinizes both the bright and dark sides of Rutha, I hope this relative finds it a product worthy of our rewarding hours of conversation. The other is Dan Healey, who in his support and companionship has never wavered, supplying the real spark I have needed to complete *The Devil's Wall*.

Index